D1169775

ONE
IN A
MILLION

CLAIRE LORDON

CANDLEWICK PRESS

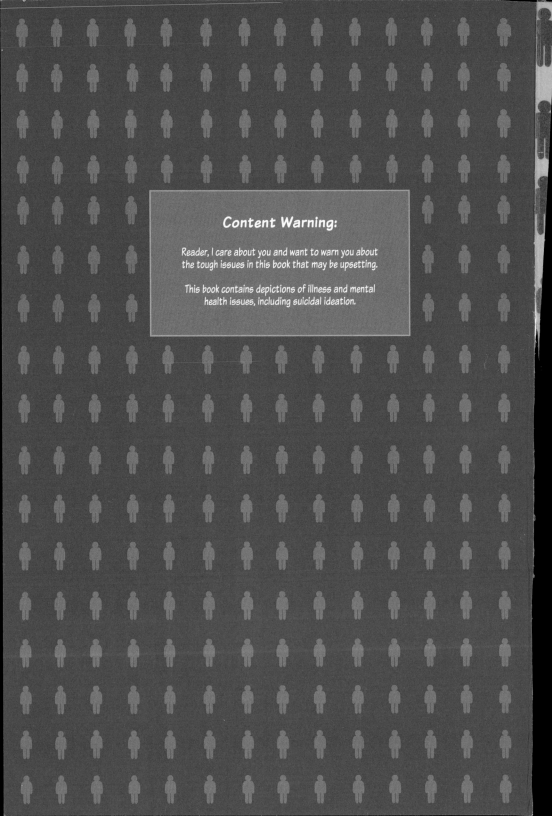

Content Warning:

Reader, I care about you and want to warn you about
the tough issues in this book that may be upsetting.

This book contains depictions of illness and mental
health issues, including suicidal ideation.

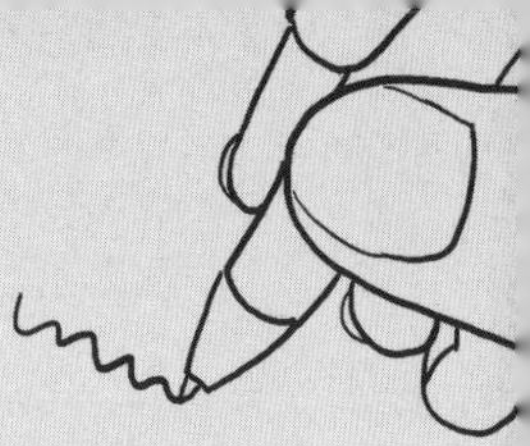

PREFACE

It's funny in hindsight that even while I was experiencing the events in this book, I was thinking, *This could be a book someday.* Maybe that's why I wrote in my diary almost daily.

This book takes place when I was sick in high school, a sequence of events that changed my life and still affects me to this day. After sharing small pieces of my story with people, I realized that my experiences could help others. So I set out to make the book I needed as a teen.

This graphic memoir depicts the chronological time line of events as well as visual representations of what my symptoms felt like. I thought creating it would be easy, but it wasn't. It was supposed to be cathartic, but I stumbled and got stuck along the way, reliving my worst moments. I cried. I sat unable to move, scared to draw what I had experienced.

But I kept pushing, knowing that if my story helps one person, it will have been worth it.

I wrote this book for the ones who are overlooked, misunderstood, a medical mystery, or hurting. You are not alone. I also wrote it for people who've never experienced anything like this in hopes that they gain an understanding of what being unwell as a teen can entail.

Before we start, I want to share some things about this story, reader, because I care about you. This book contains triggers related to suicide ideation, medical trauma, depression, and anxiety. Don't worry: the story has a happy ending (I'm writing this fourteen years after these events took place), and if you need to pause or take a break from reading, that's totally valid.

Please note that I've done my best at telling MY story. During the time of the events I describe, my memory was not always the best, so I relied heavily on my detailed diary. I've also spoken with my parents and friends about parts of the story where my memory is hazy. So the events told here may not be 100 percent accurate, but know that I have done my best and tried to embody what seventeen-year-old me thought and felt at the time.

Although I have changed the names and appearances of the people featured in the book (unless I got written permission from them), I have done my best to depict their character and dialogue accurately.

Thanks for reading. Now on to the story.

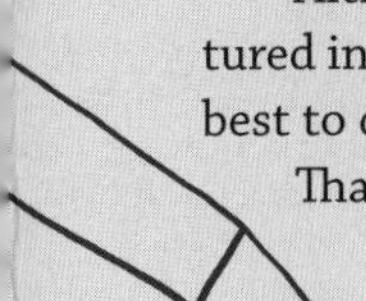

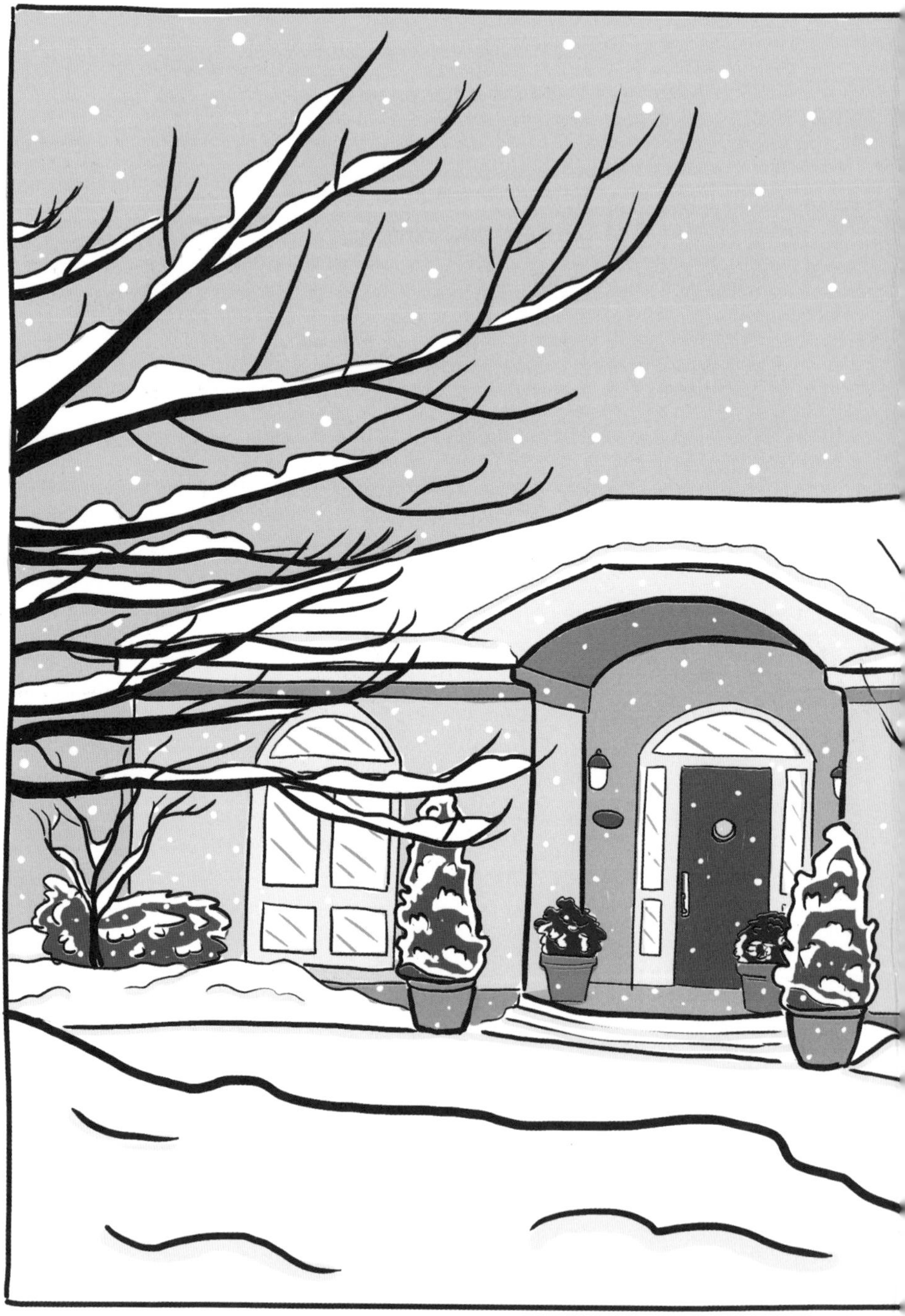

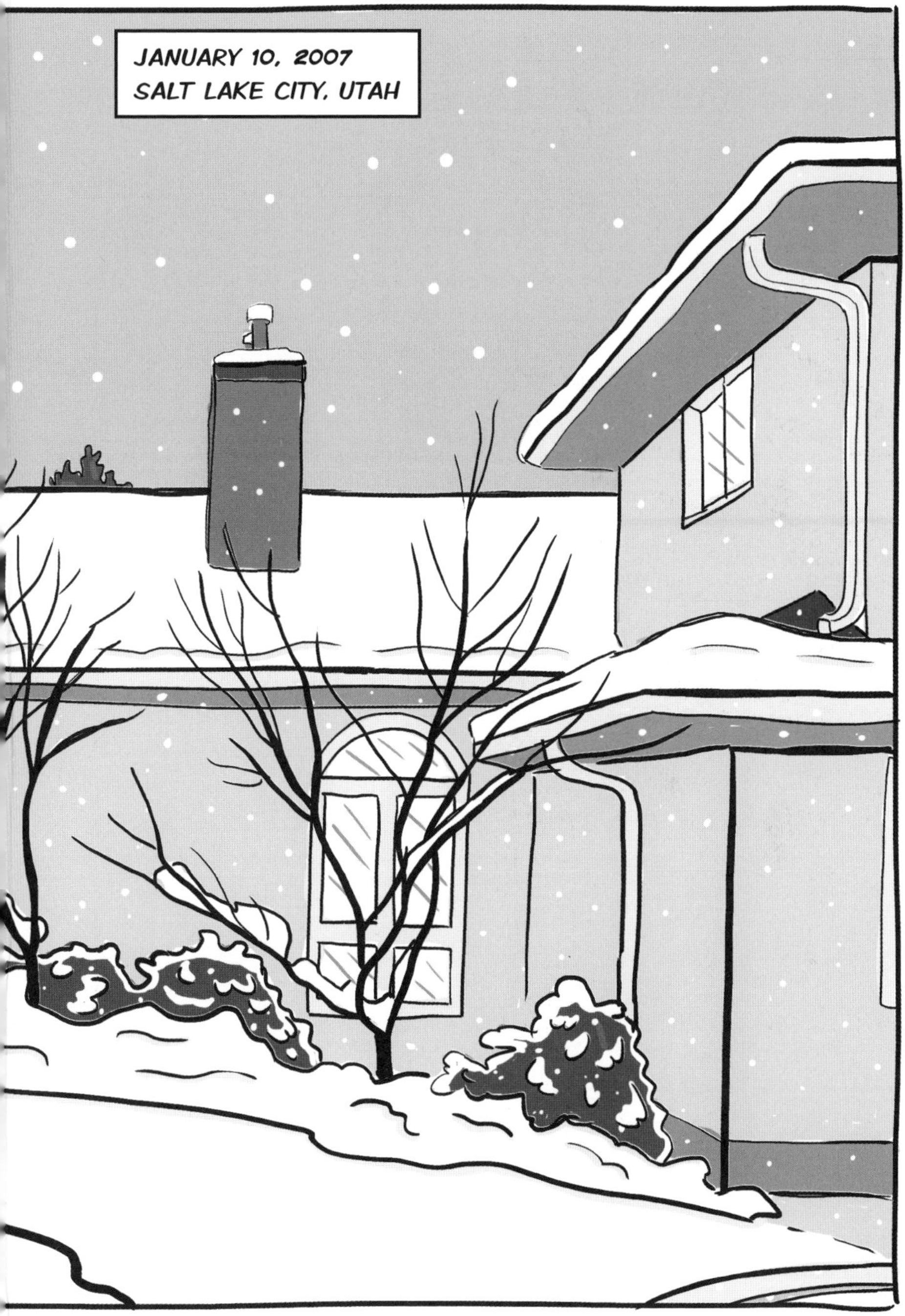
JANUARY 10, 2007
SALT LAKE CITY, UTAH

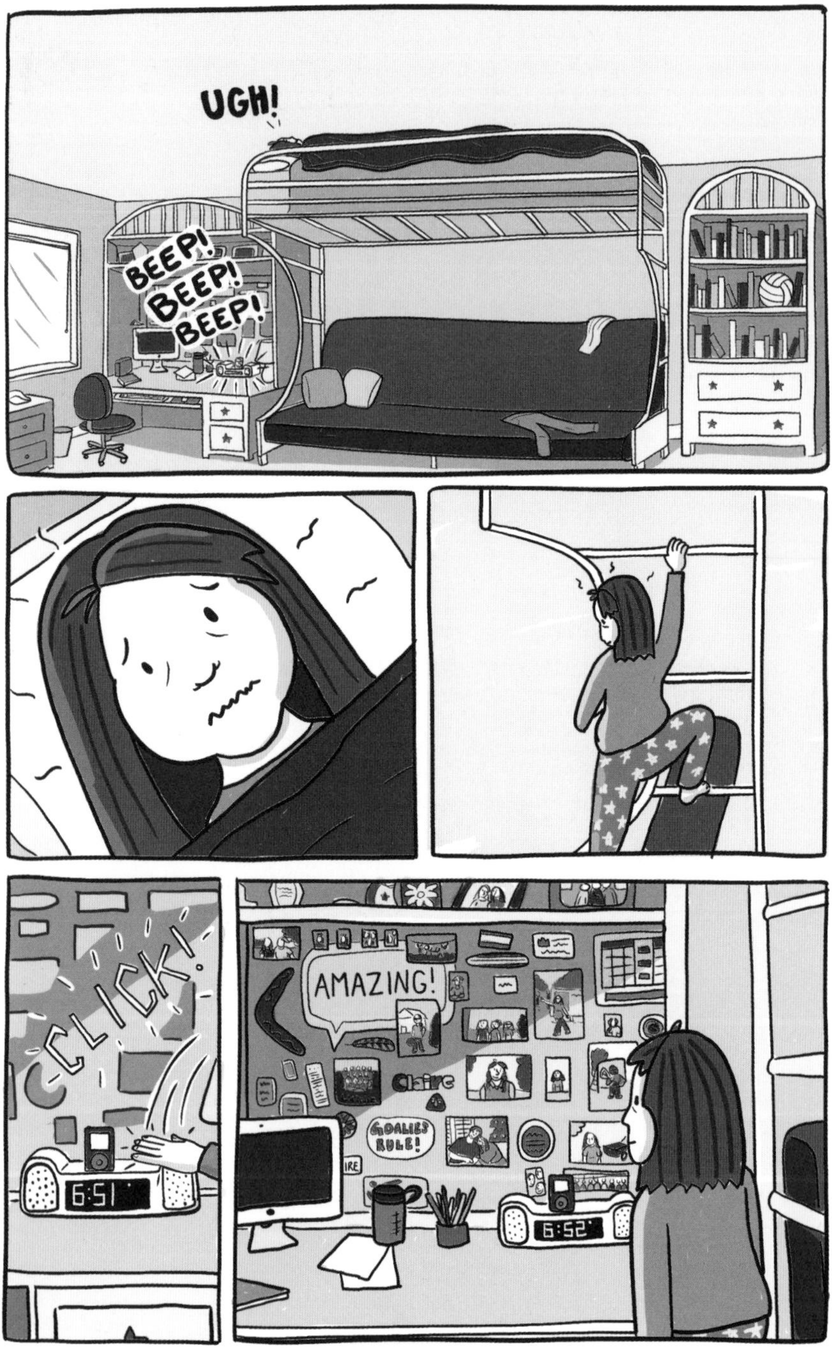
UGH!
BEEP! BEEP! BEEP!
CLICK!
6:51
AMAZING!
Claire
GOALIES RULE!
6:52

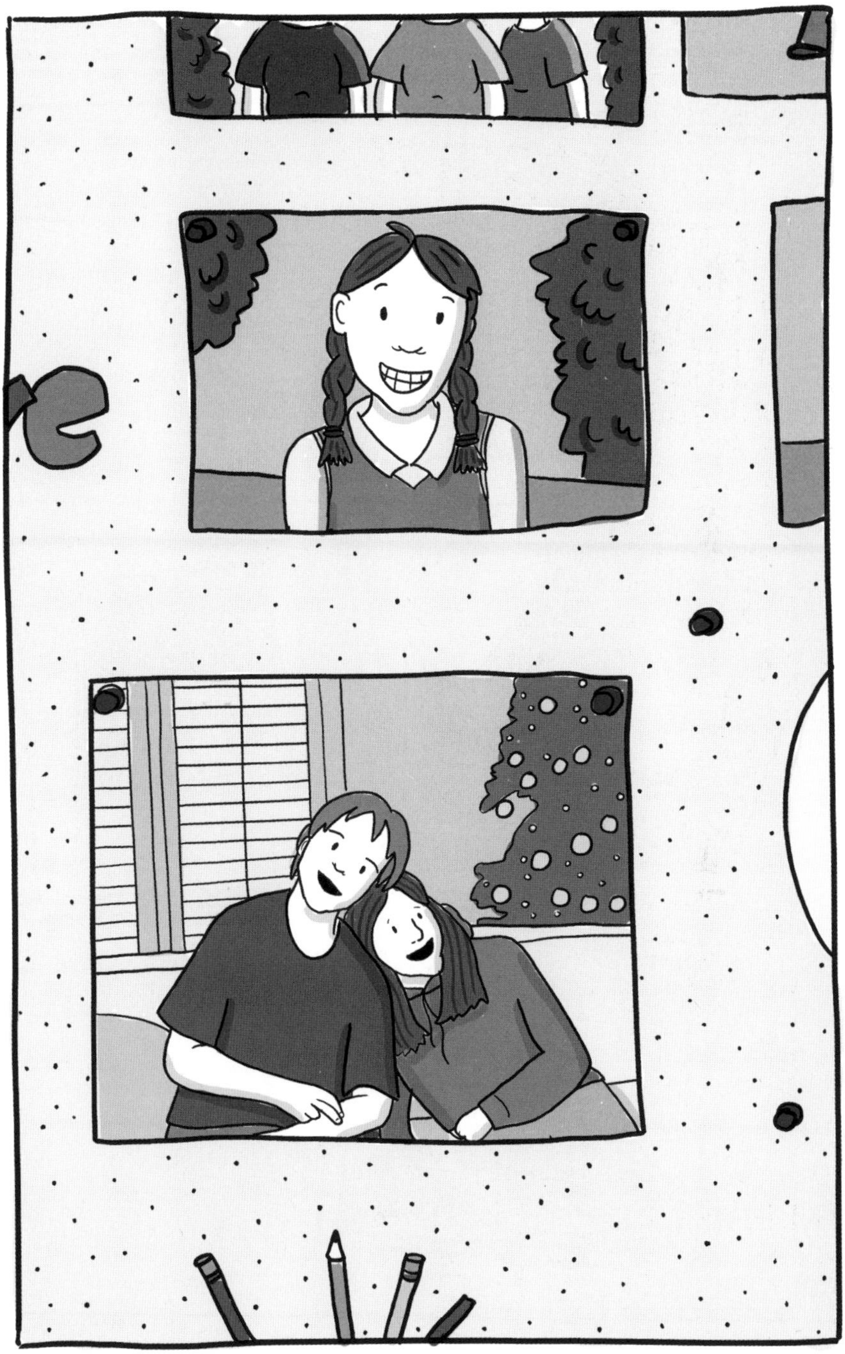

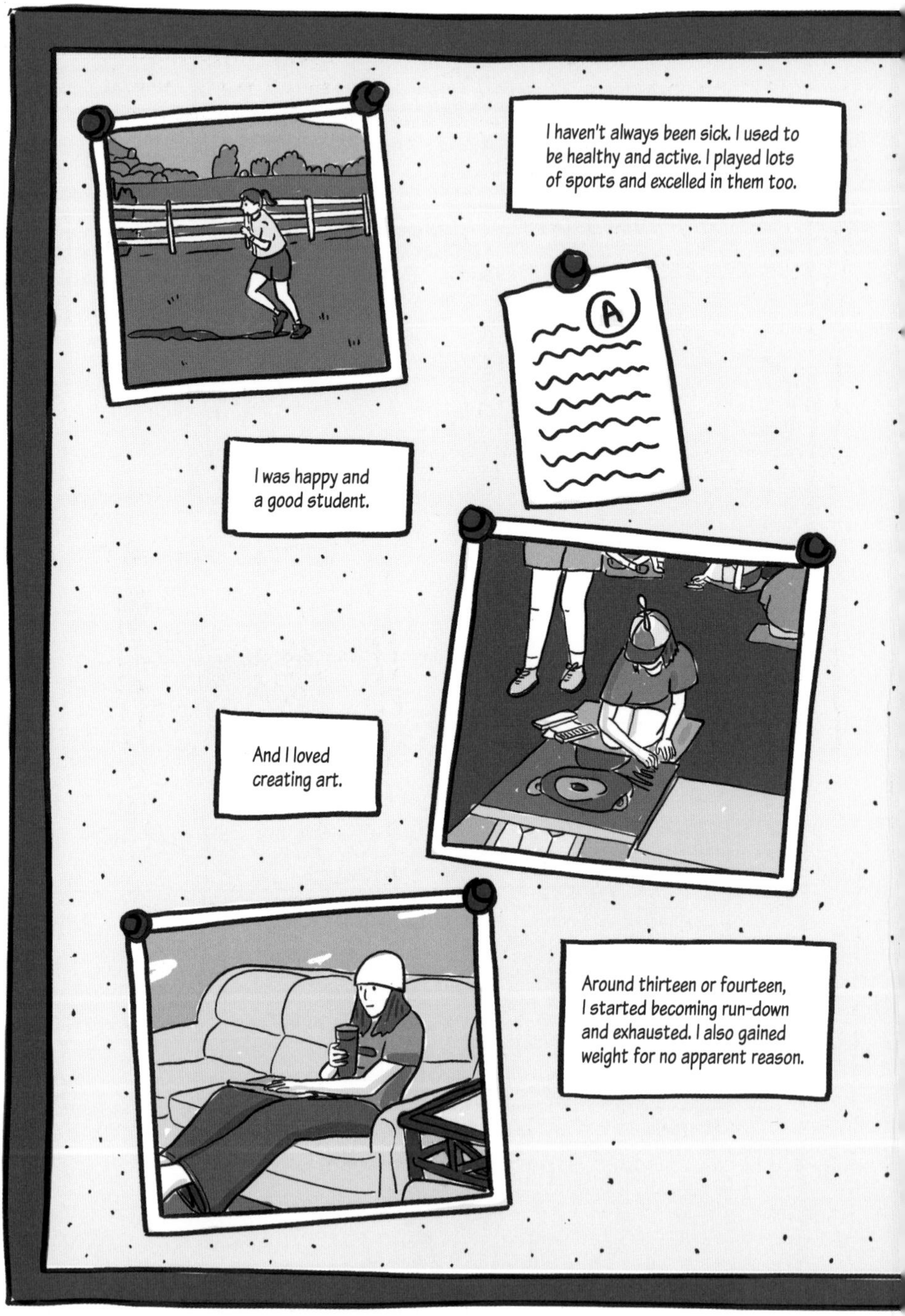
I haven't always been sick. I used to be healthy and active. I played lots of sports and excelled in them too.
A
I was happy and a good student.
And I loved creating art.
Around thirteen or fourteen, I started becoming run-down and exhausted. I also gained weight for no apparent reason.

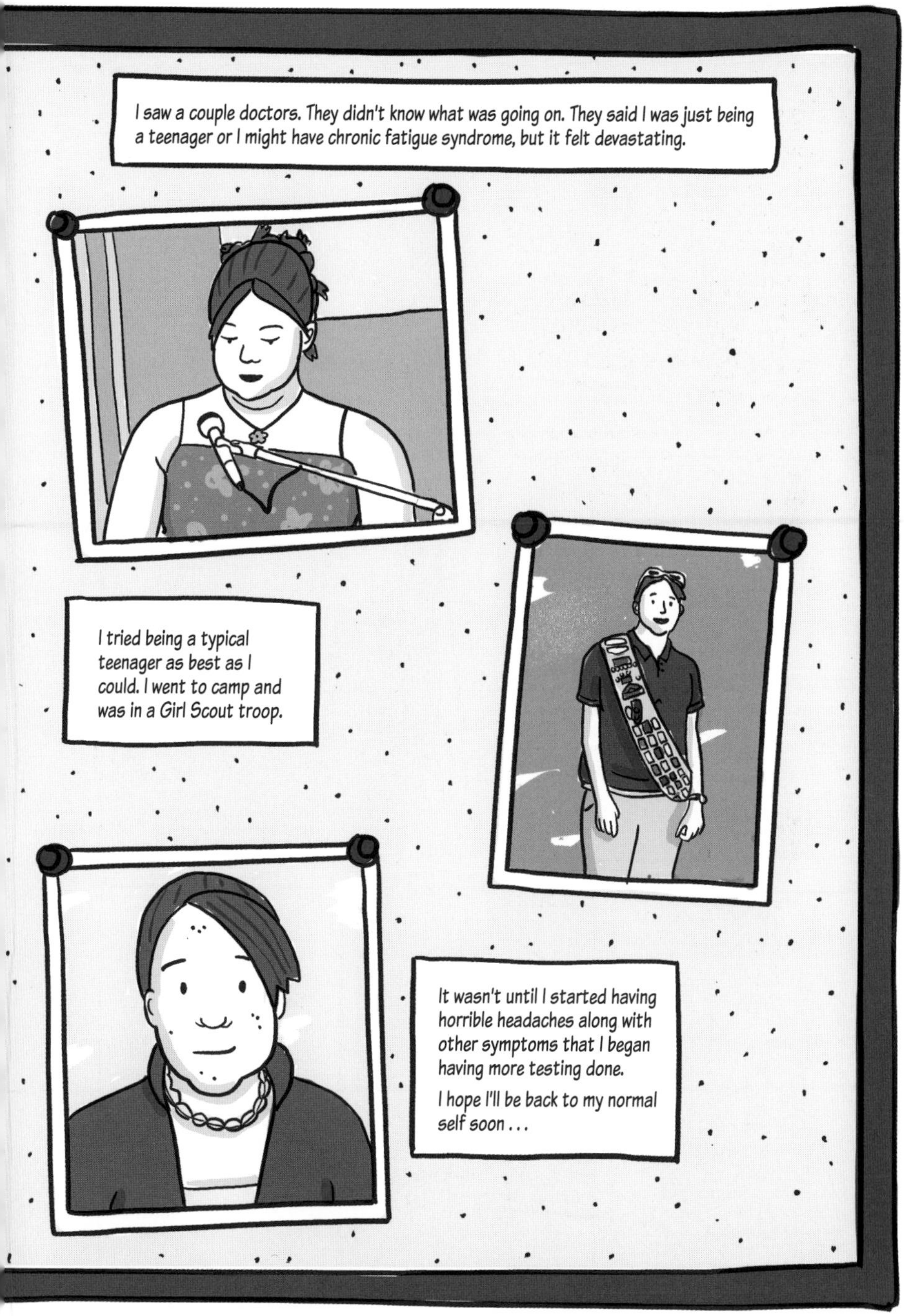
I saw a couple doctors. They didn't know what was going on. They said I was just being a teenager or I might have chronic fatigue syndrome, but it felt devastating.
I tried being a typical teenager as best as I could. I went to camp and was in a Girl Scout troop.
It wasn't until I started having horrible headaches along with other symptoms that I began having more testing done.
I hope I'll be back to my normal self soon . . .

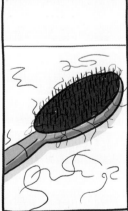

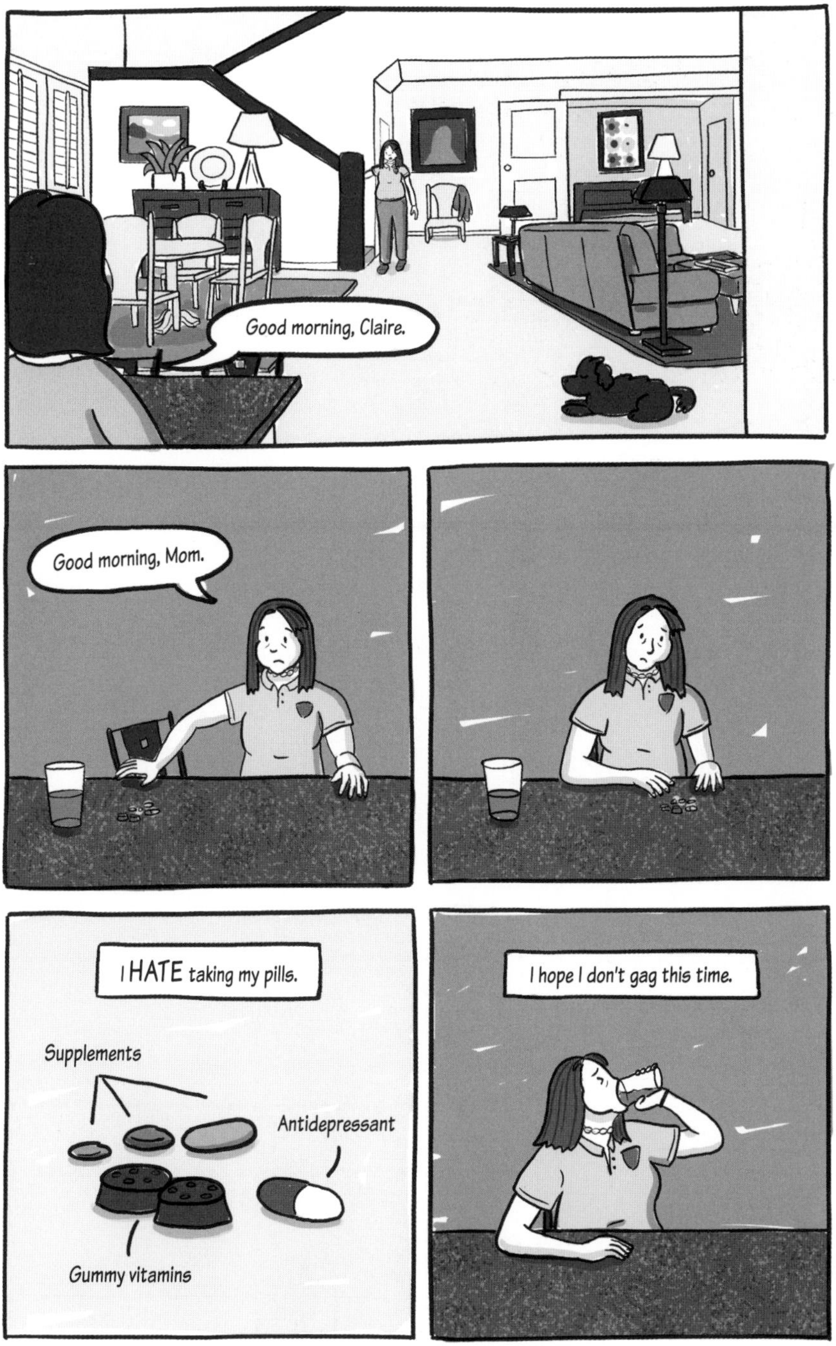
Good morning, Claire.
Good morning, Mom.
I HATE taking my pills.
Supplements
Antidepressant
Gummy vitamins
I hope I don't gag this time.

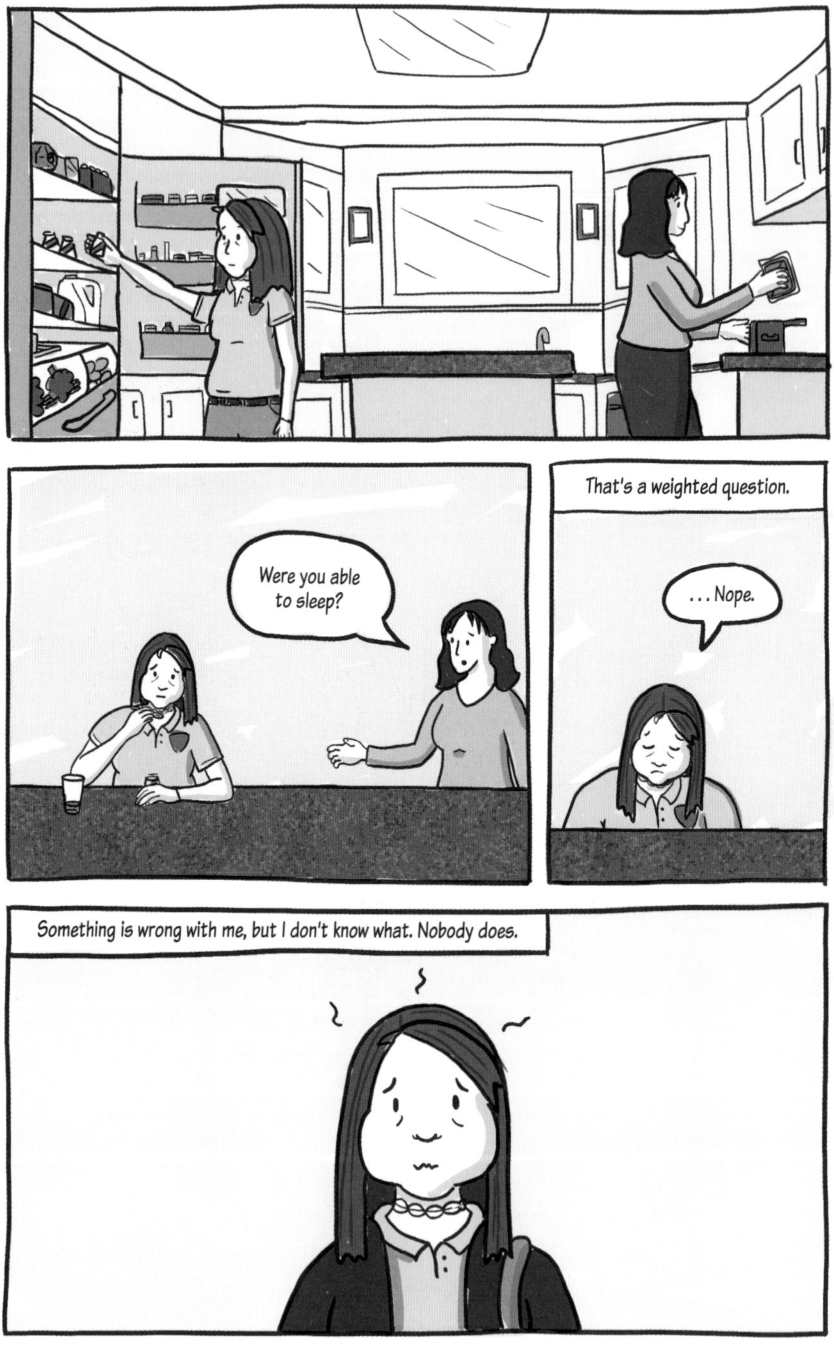
Were you able to sleep?
That's a weighted question.
. . . Nope.
Something is wrong with me, but I don't know what. Nobody does.

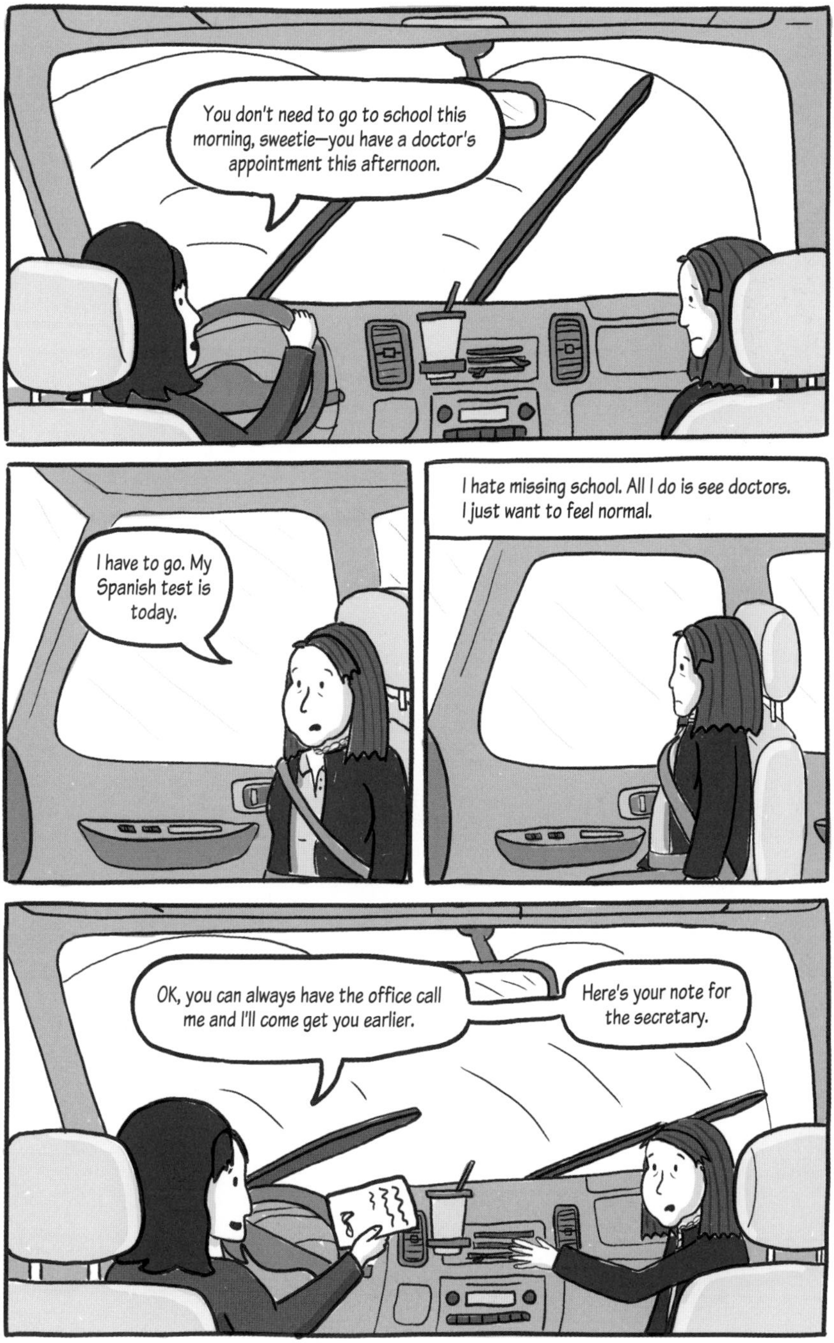
You don't need to go to school this morning, sweetie—you have a doctor's appointment this afternoon.
I have to go. My Spanish test is today.
I hate missing school. All I do is see doctors. I just want to feel normal.
OK, you can always have the office call me and I'll come get you earlier.
Here's your note for the secretary.

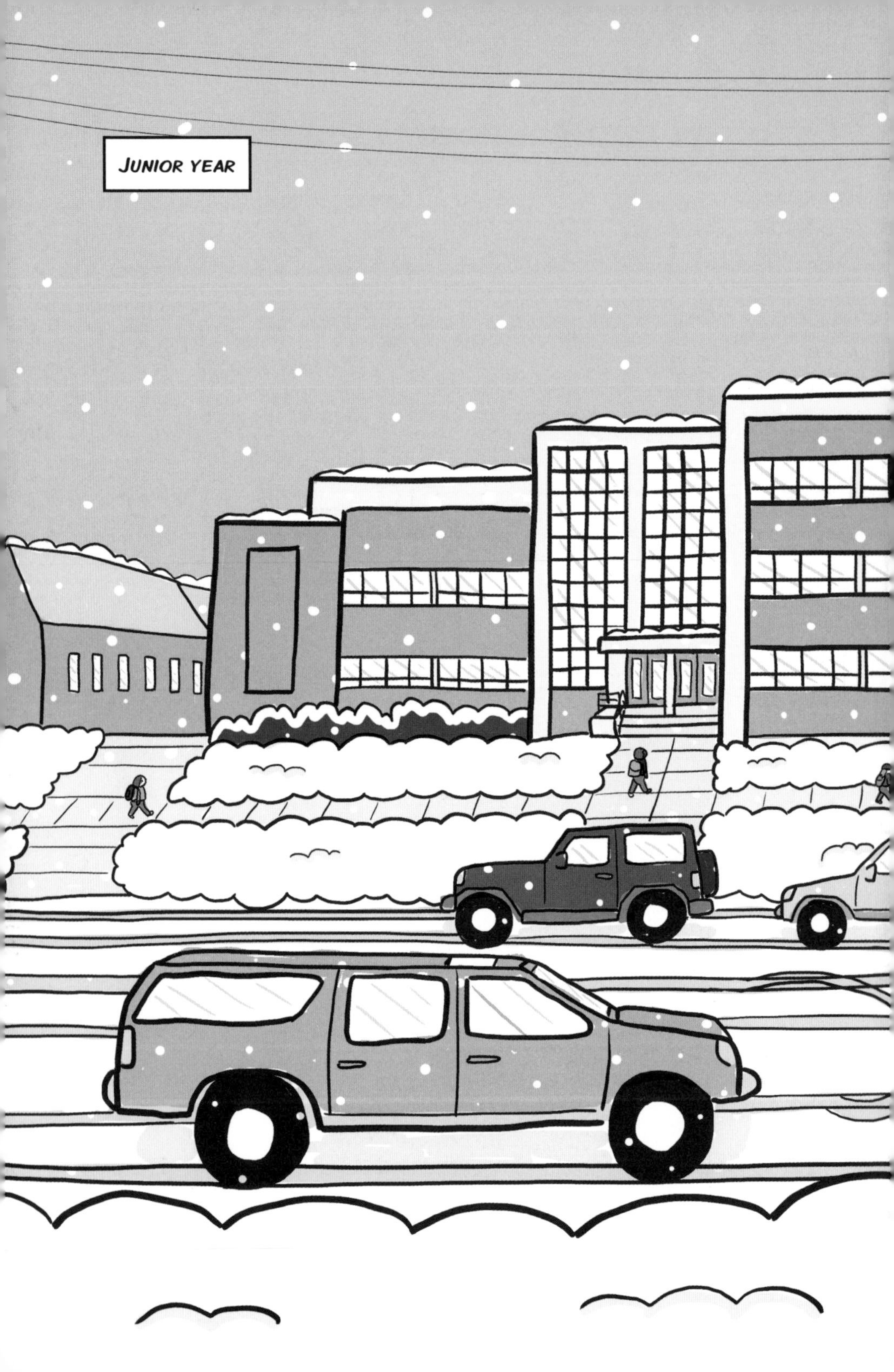
JUNIOR YEAR

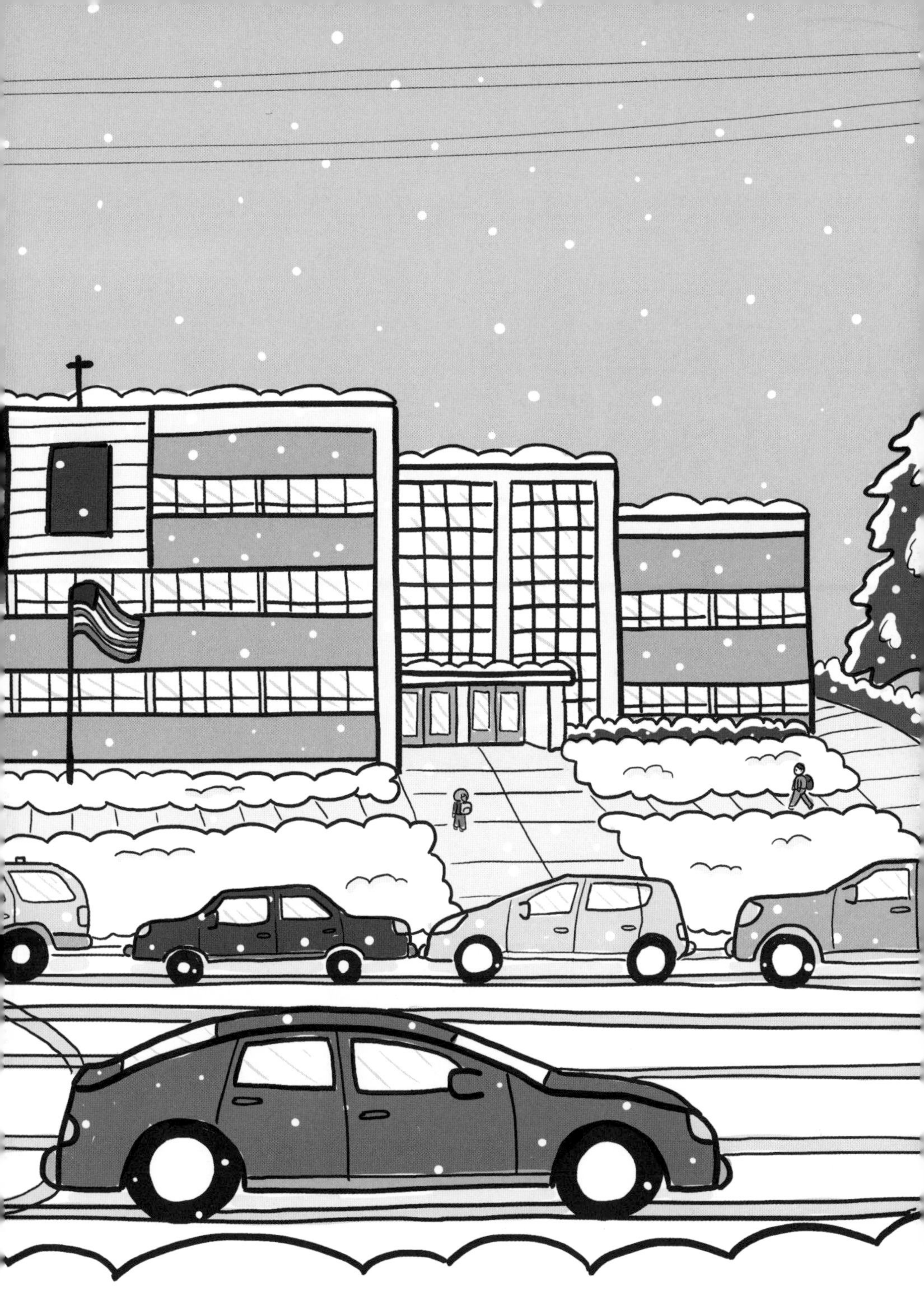

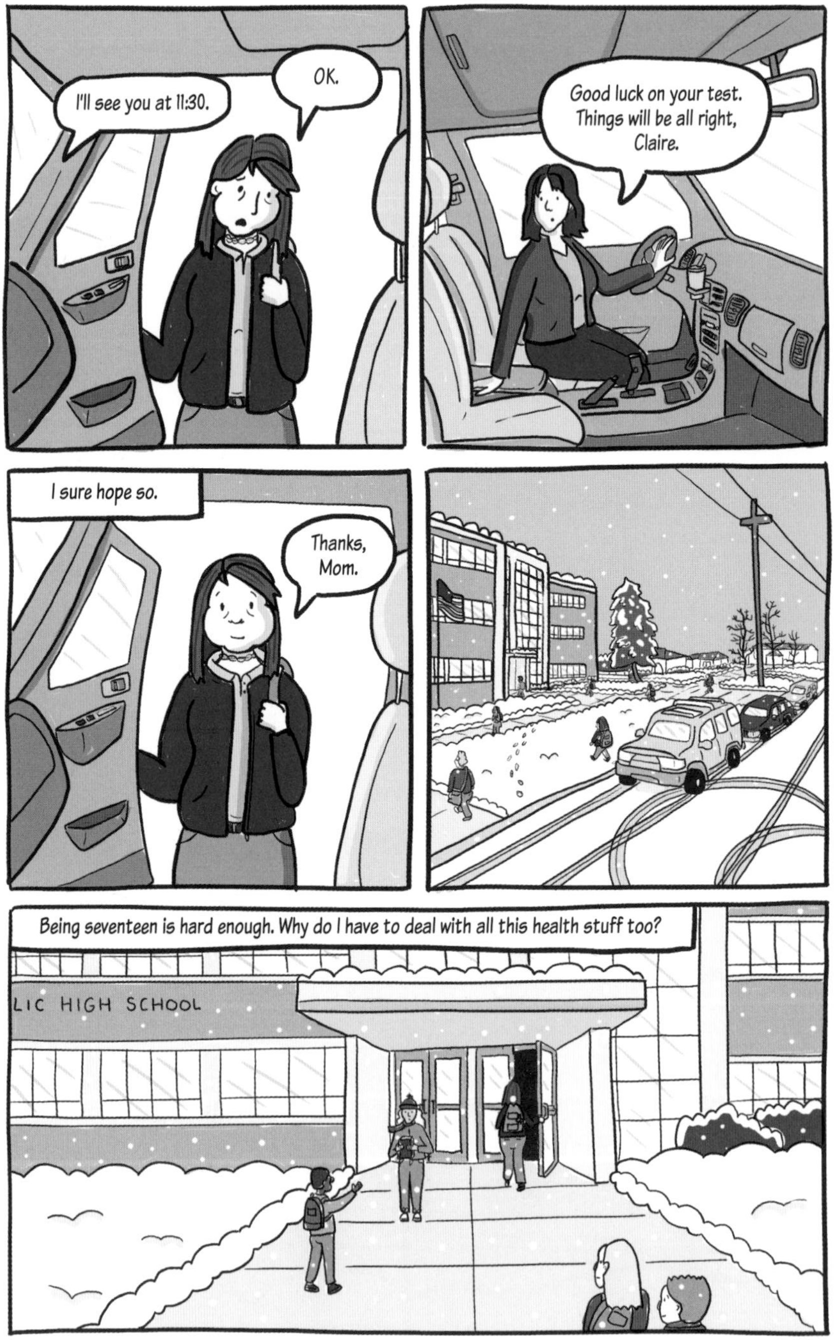
I'll see you at 11:30.
OK.
Good luck on your test. Things will be all right, Claire.
I sure hope so.
Thanks, Mom.
Being seventeen is hard enough. Why do I have to deal with all this health stuff too?
LIC HIGH SCHOOL

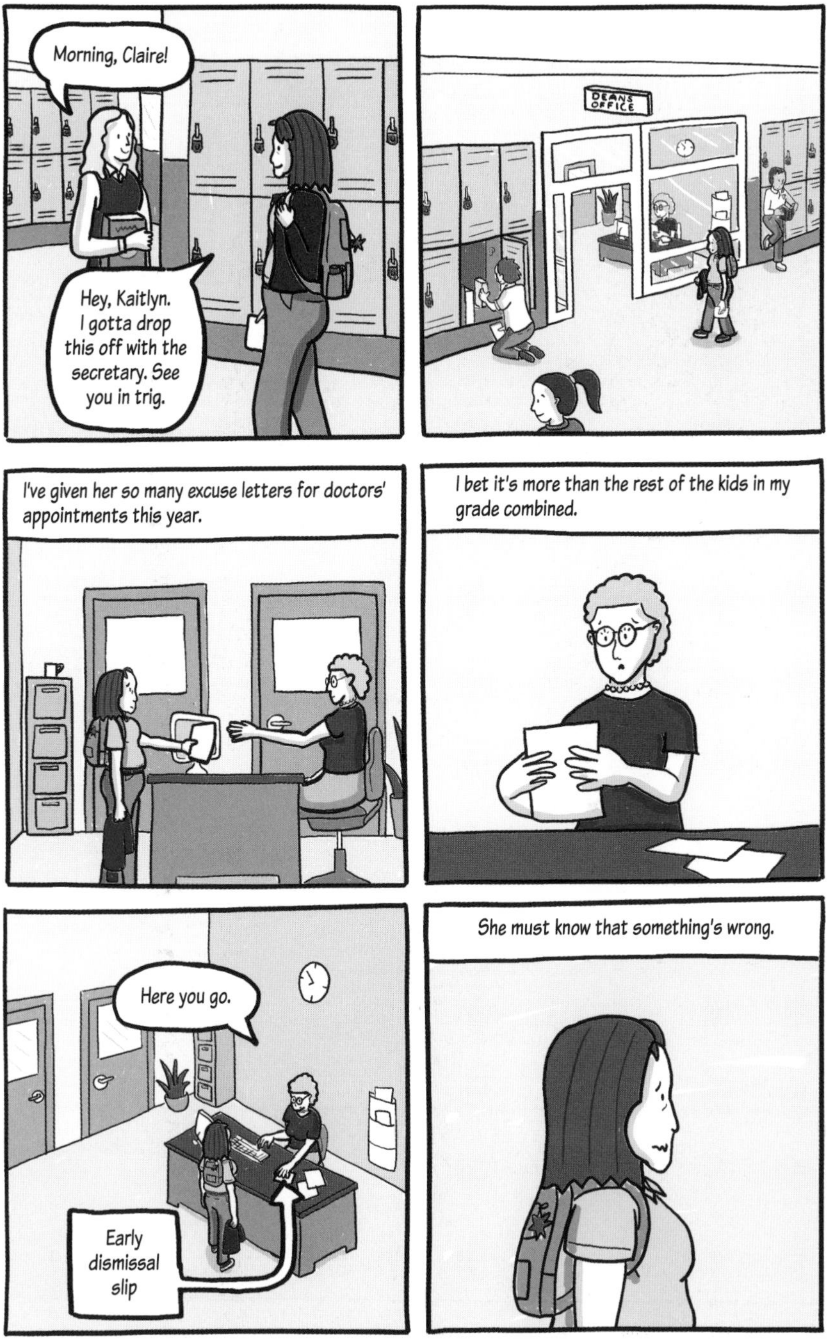
Morning, Claire!
Hey, Kaitlyn. I gotta drop this off with the secretary. See you in trig.
DEANS OFFICE
I've given her so many excuse letters for doctors' appointments this year.
I bet it's more than the rest of the kids in my grade combined.
Here you go.
Early dismissal slip
She must know that something's wrong.

GO BULLDOGS!
38-17-5
RING!!
AP US
AP ECON

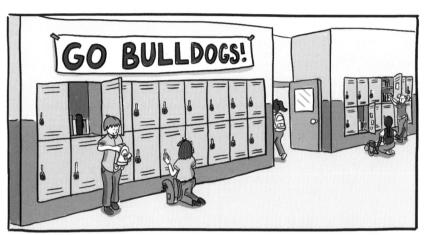

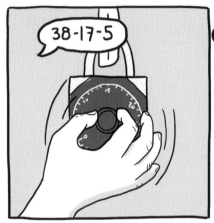

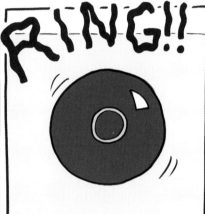

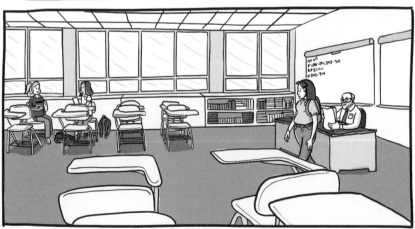

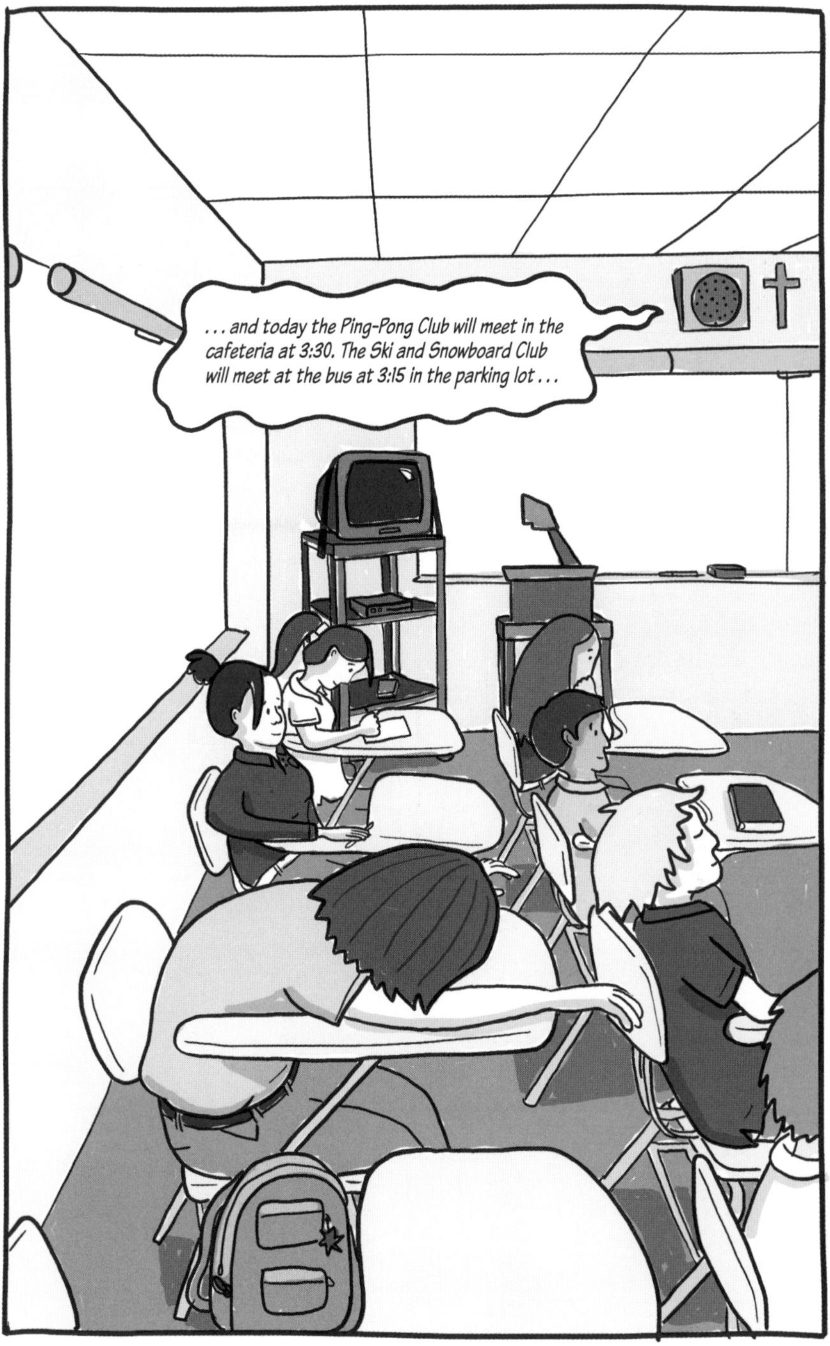
. . . and today the Ping-Pong Club will meet in the cafeteria at 3:30. The Ski and Snowboard Club will meet at the bus at 3:15 in the parking lot . . .

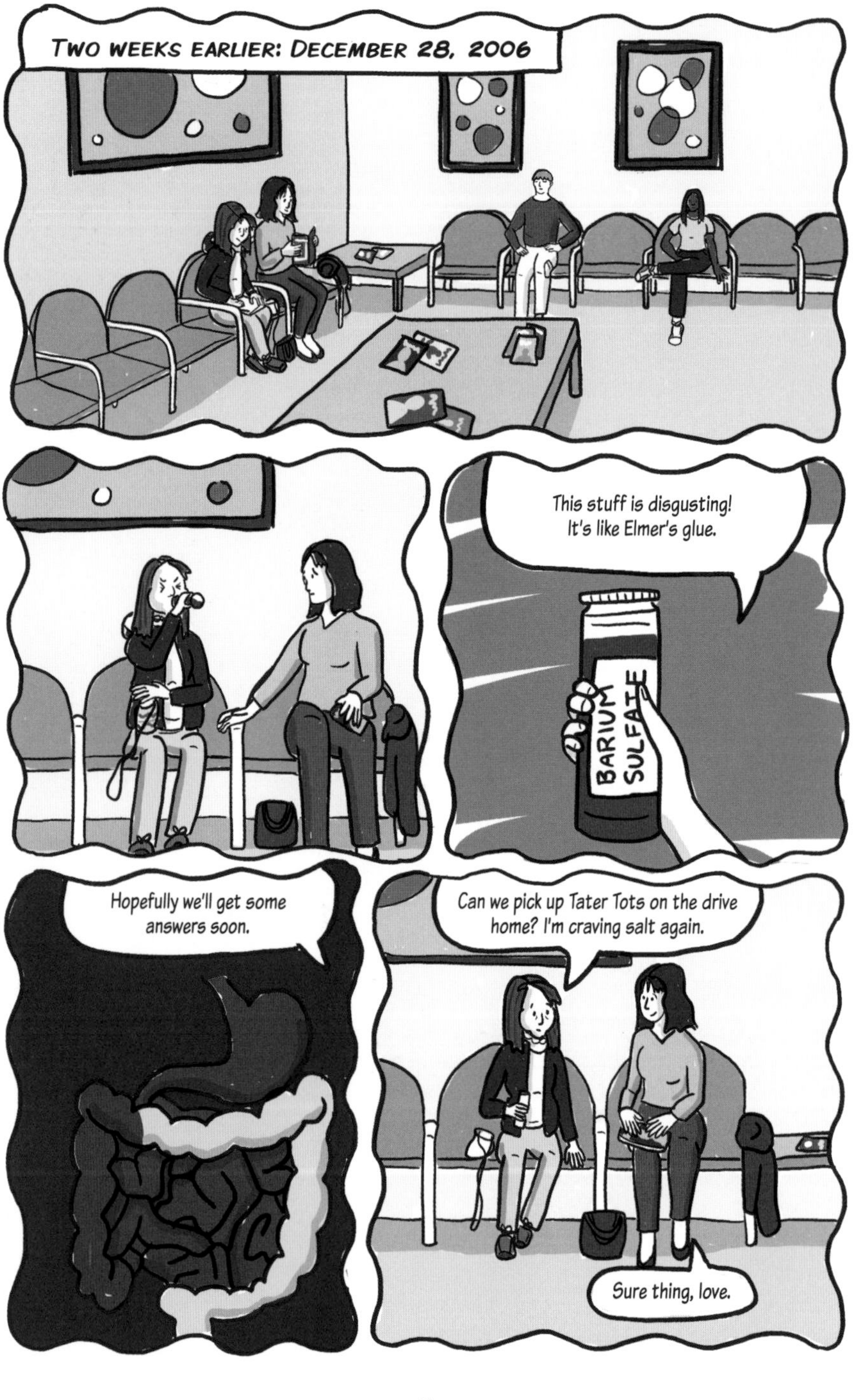
TWO WEEKS EARLIER: DECEMBER 28, 2006
This stuff is disgusting! It's like Elmer's glue.
BARIUM SULFATE
Hopefully we'll get some answers soon.
Can we pick up Tater Tots on the drive home? I'm craving salt again.
Sure thing, love.

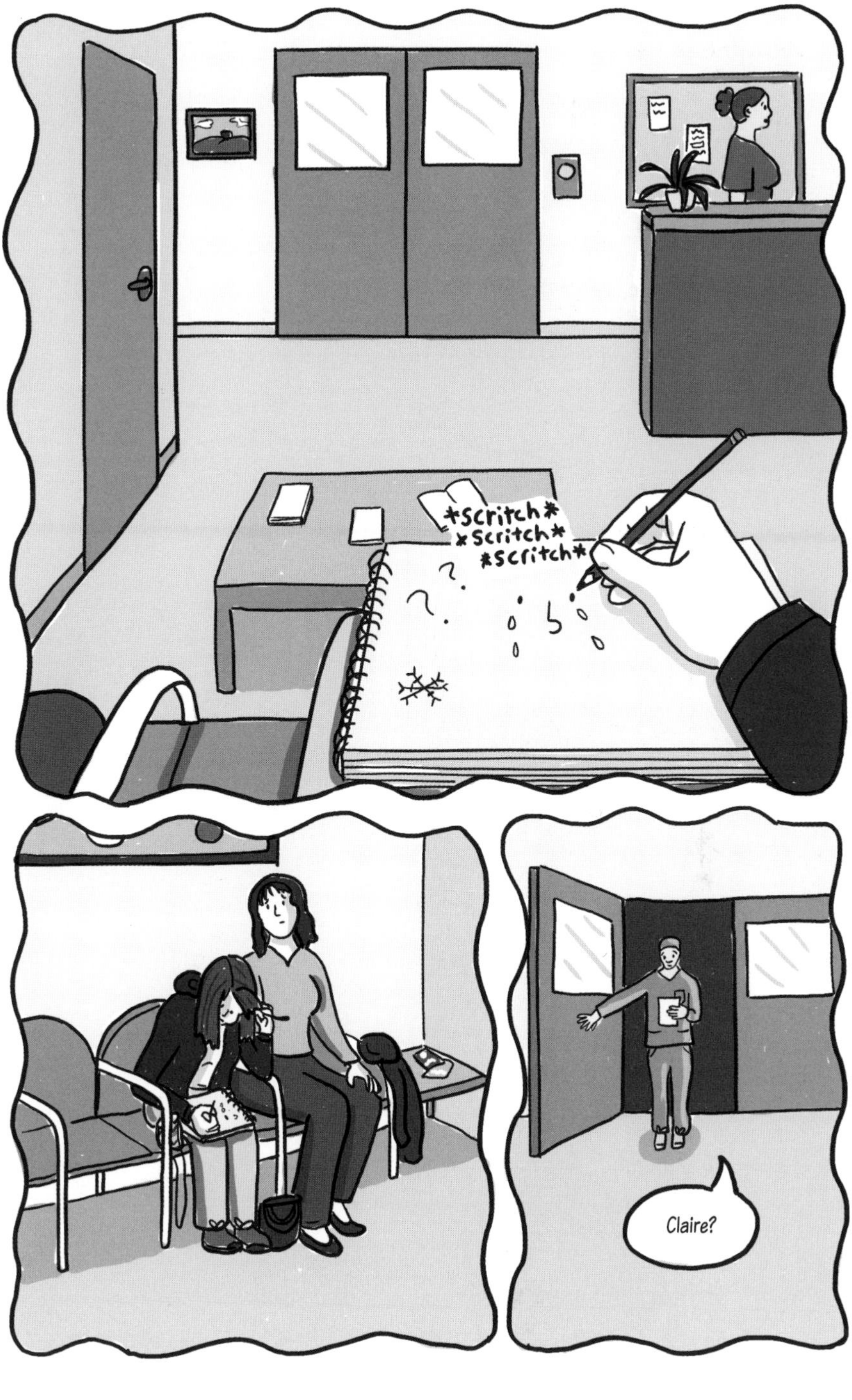
scritch
scritch
scritch
Claire?

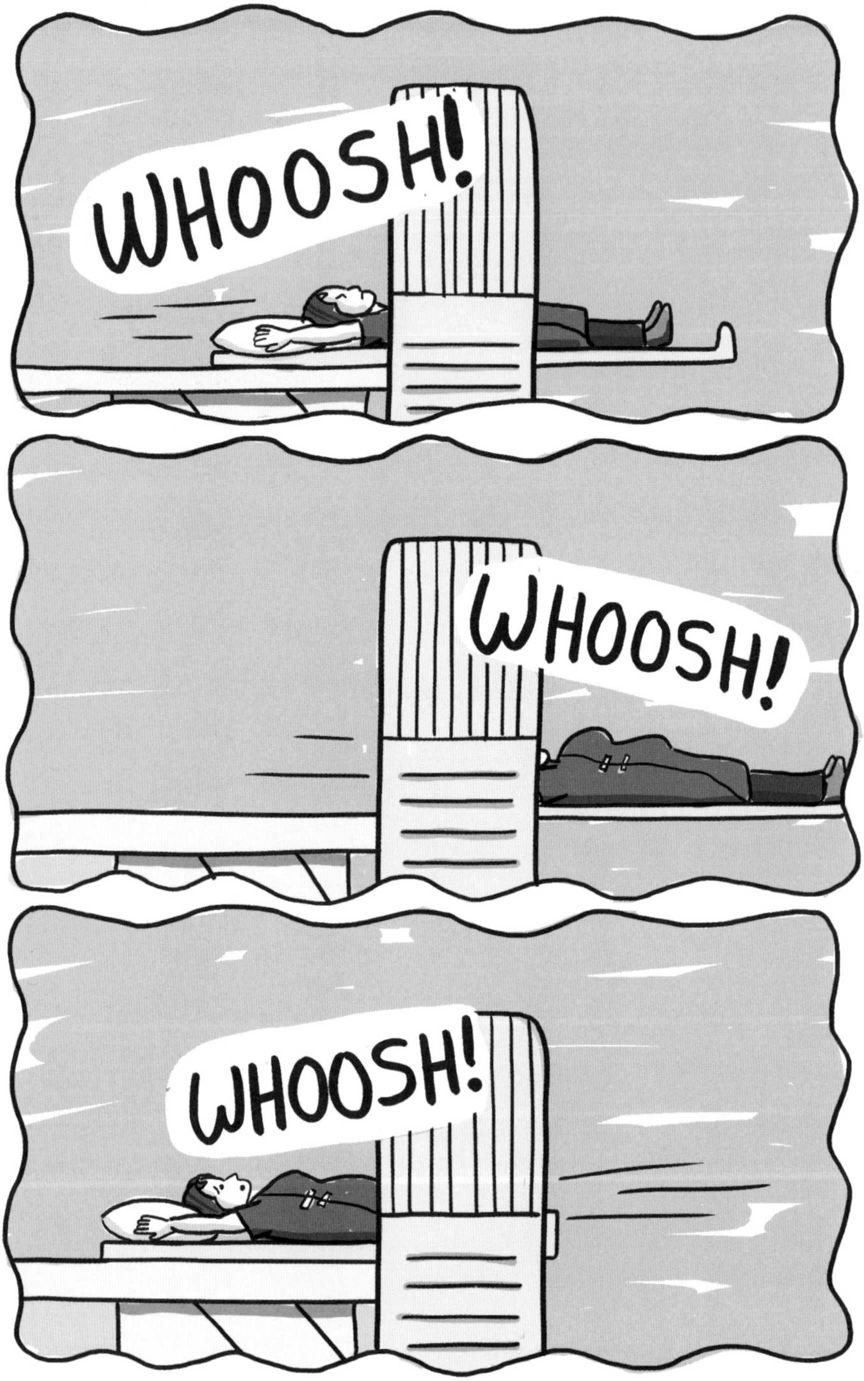
WHOOSH!
WHOOSH!
WHOOSH!

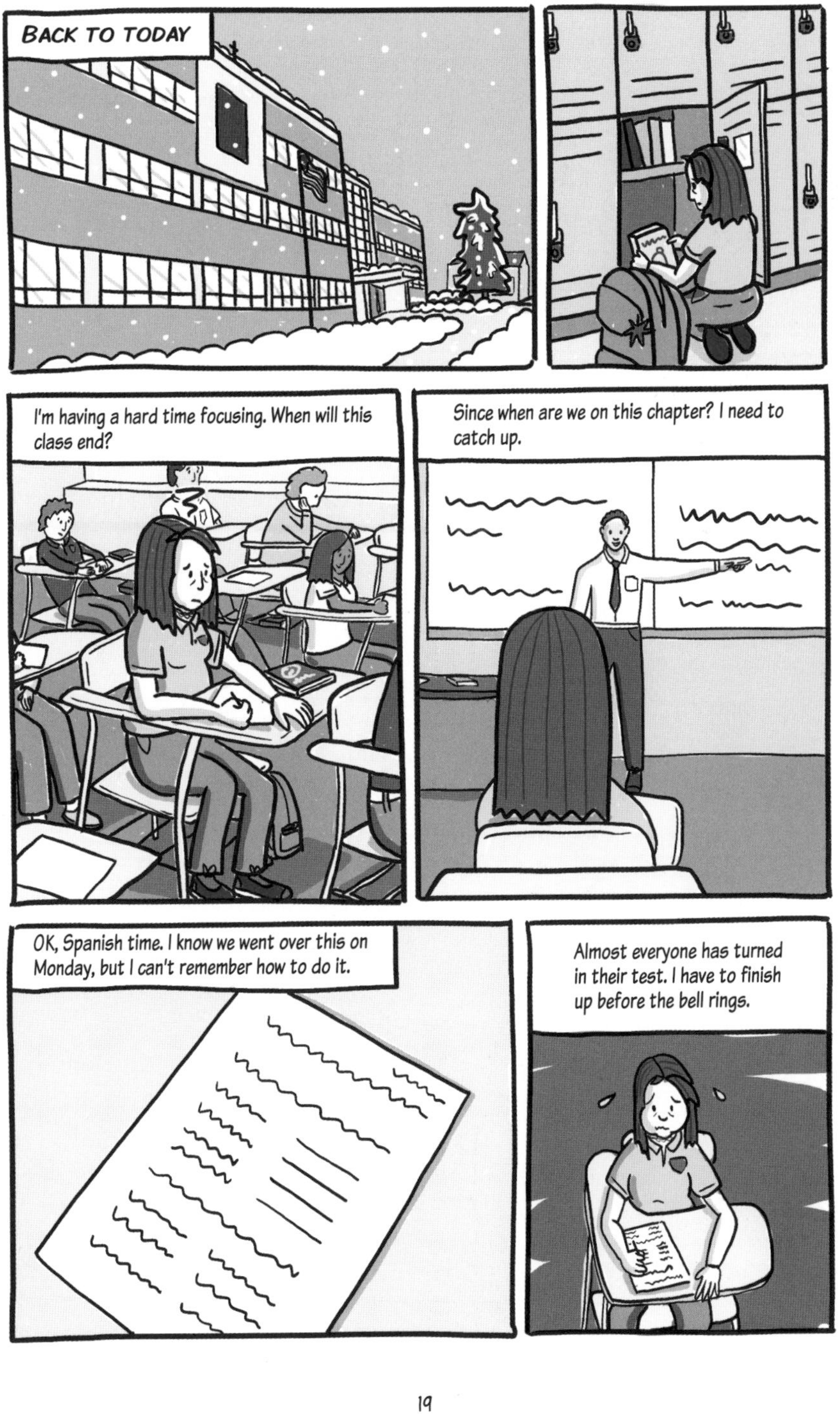
BACK TO TODAY
I'm having a hard time focusing. When will this class end?
Since when are we on this chapter? I need to catch up.
OK, Spanish time. I know we went over this on Monday, but I can't remember how to do it.
Almost everyone has turned in their test. I have to finish up before the bell rings.

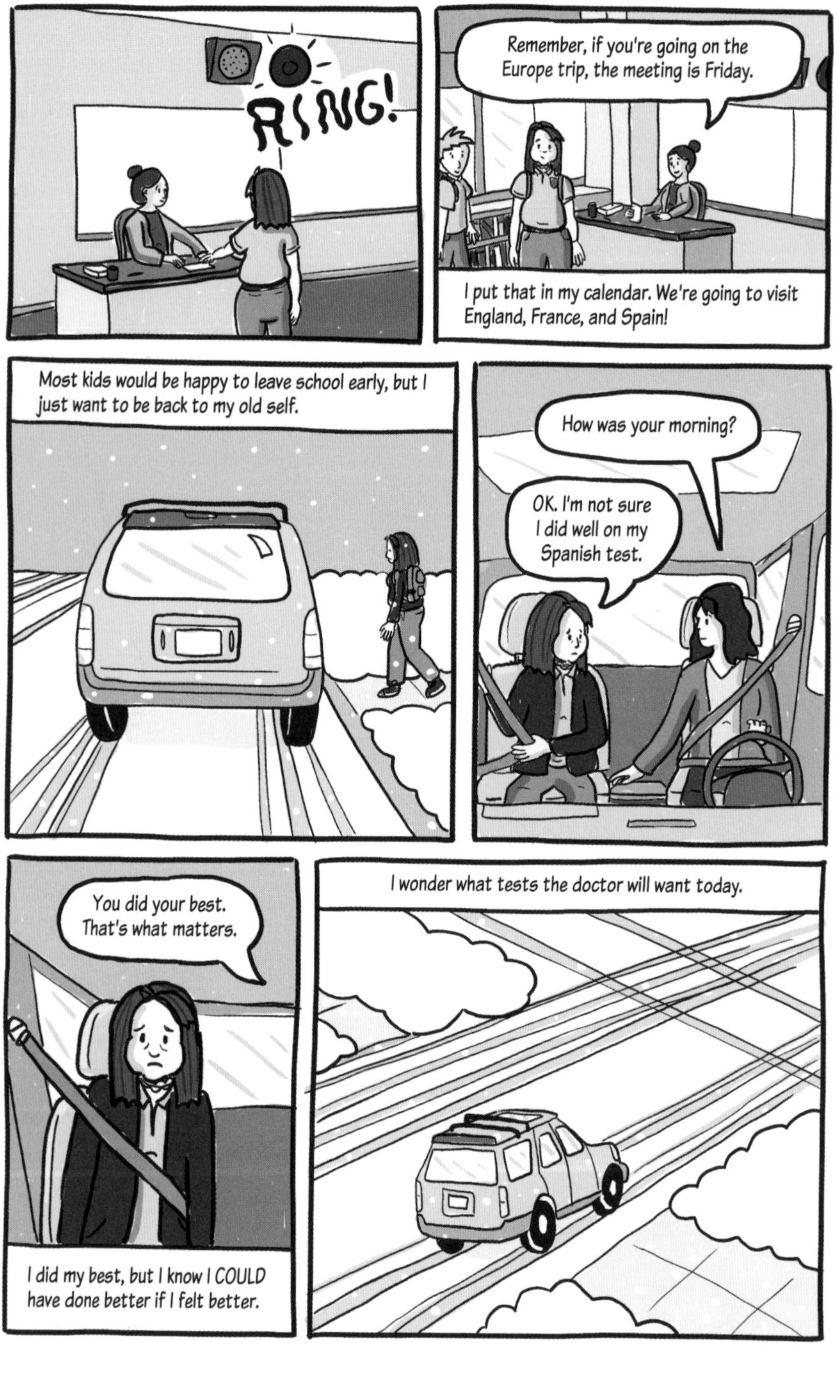
RING!
Remember, if you're going on the Europe trip, the meeting is Friday.
I put that in my calendar. We're going to visit England, France, and Spain!
Most kids would be happy to leave school early, but I just want to be back to my old self.
How was your morning?
OK. I'm not sure I did well on my Spanish test.
You did your best. That's what matters.
I did my best, but I know I COULD have done better if I felt better.
I wonder what tests the doctor will want today.

One, two, three.

POKE

If for any reason you need help, just squeeze the ball.

What music would you like to listen to?

Umm . . . pop?

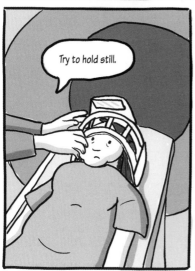

Try to hold still.

Claire, do you hear me?

Yes.

Great. Then we'll start with our first scan.

At least there's a mirror where I can see a tiny bit.

DO DO DO DO

WAH WAH WAH WAH

WUGGA WUGGA WUGGA

WUGGA CRANK

WUGGA CRANK

25 MINUTES LATER

OK, Claire, we're going to inject that dye now.

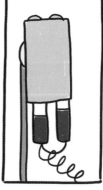

PWSSSH

22

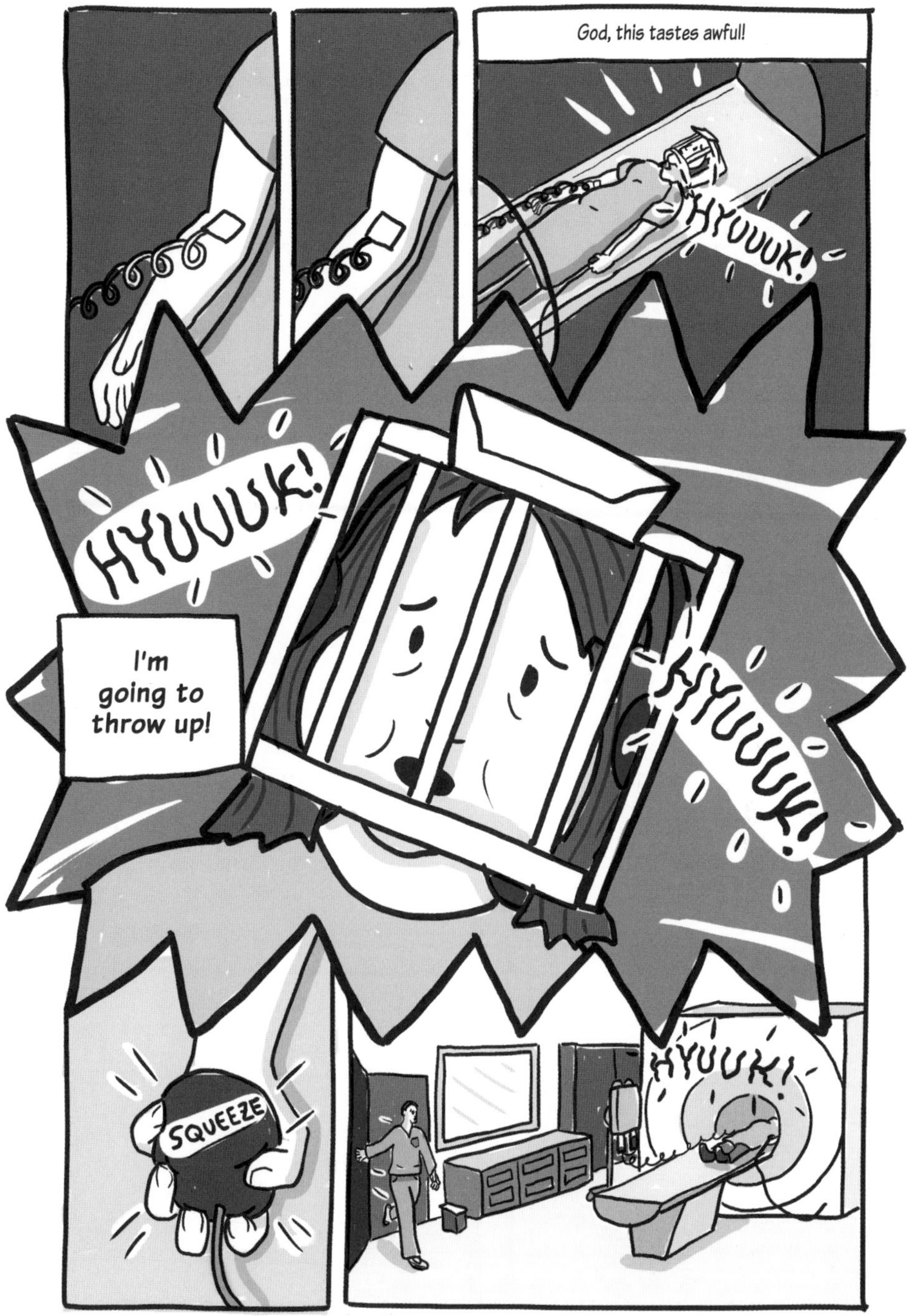
God, this tastes awful!
HYUUUK!
HYUUUK!
I'm going to throw up!
HYUUUK!
SQUEEZE
HYUUK!

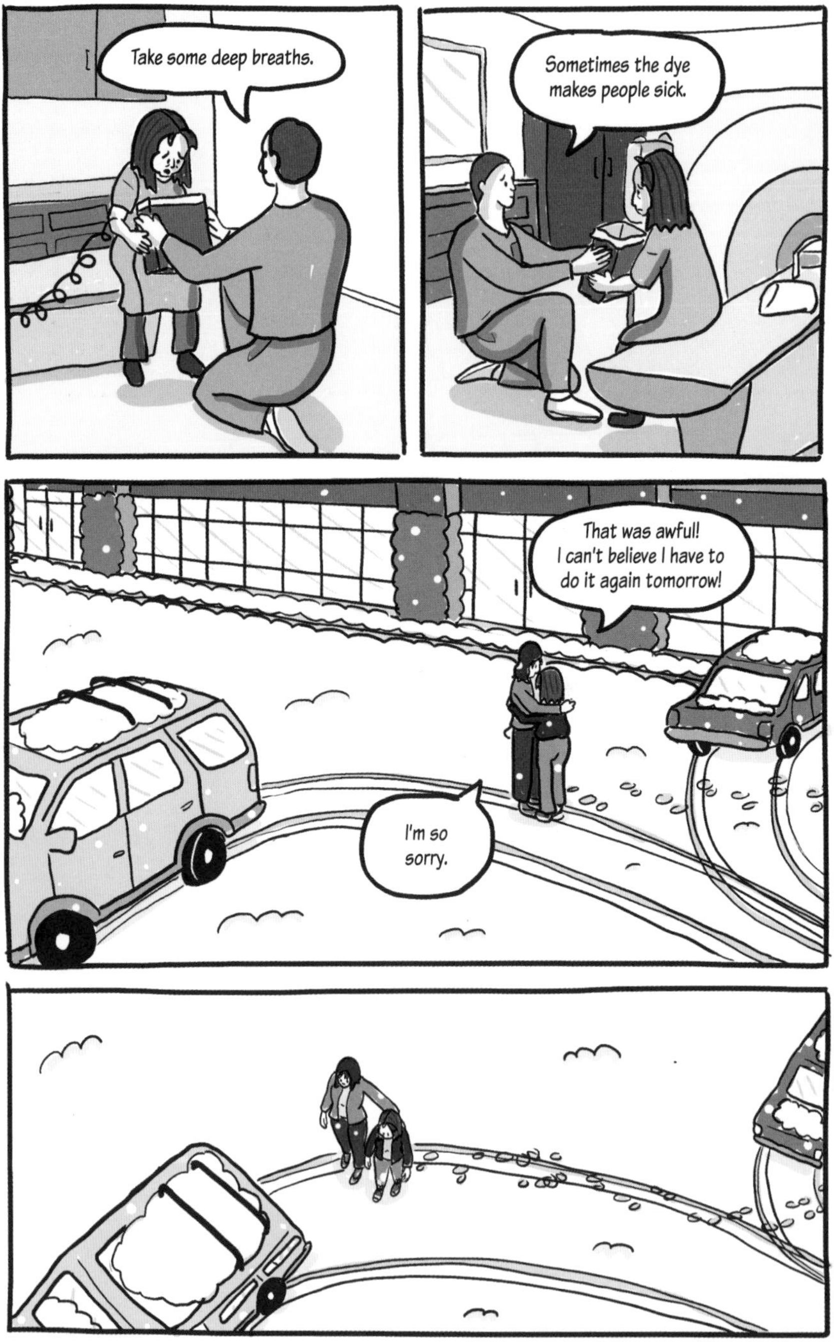
Take some deep breaths.
Sometimes the dye makes people sick.
That was awful! I can't believe I have to do it again tomorrow!
I'm so sorry.

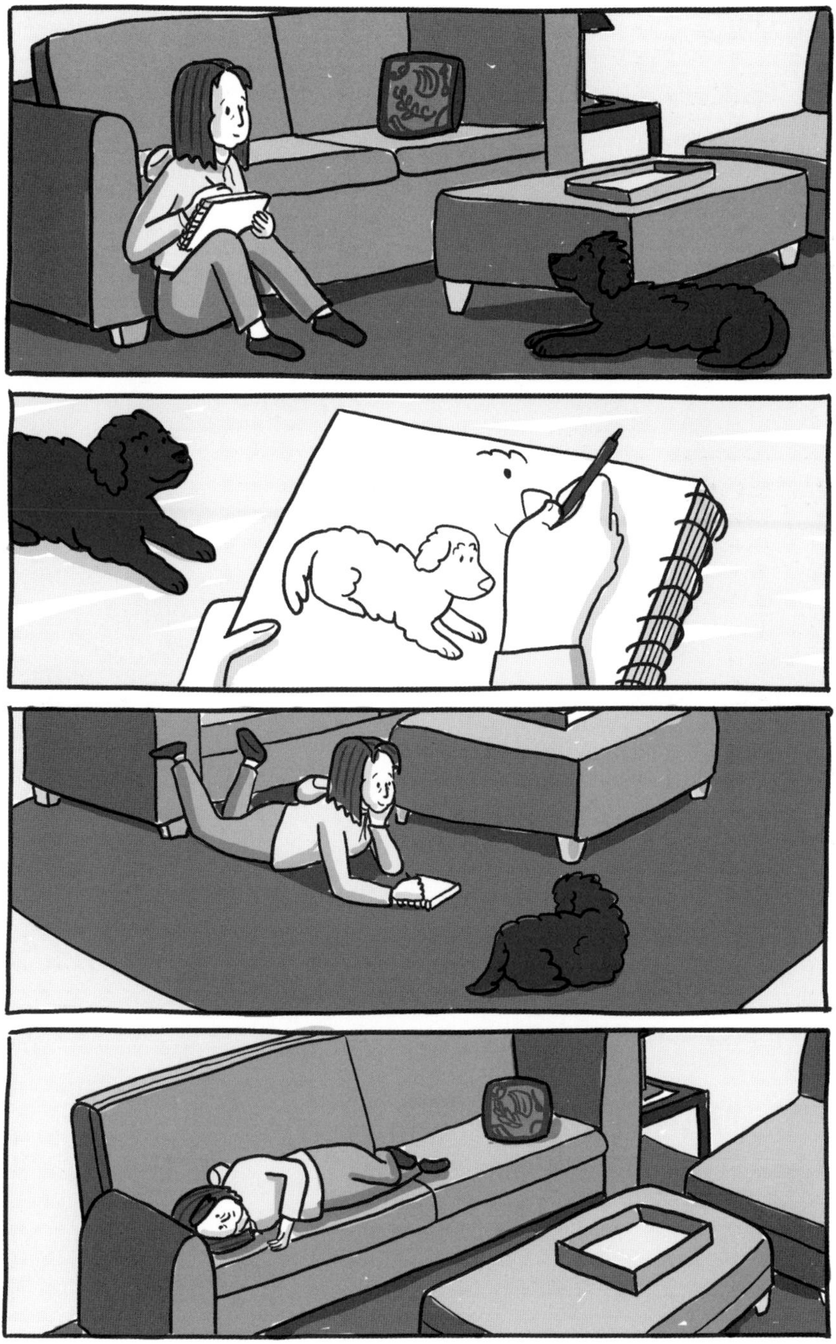

THE NEXT DAY

MOUNTAIN OAKS
IMAGING CENTER

I don't even know what they're looking for at this point . . .

WUGGA

The tests were so long, I felt like I was sinking into the floor!

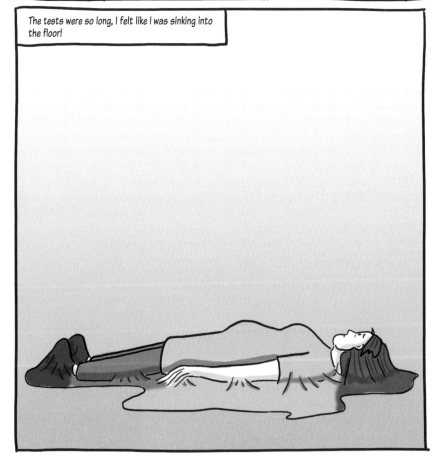

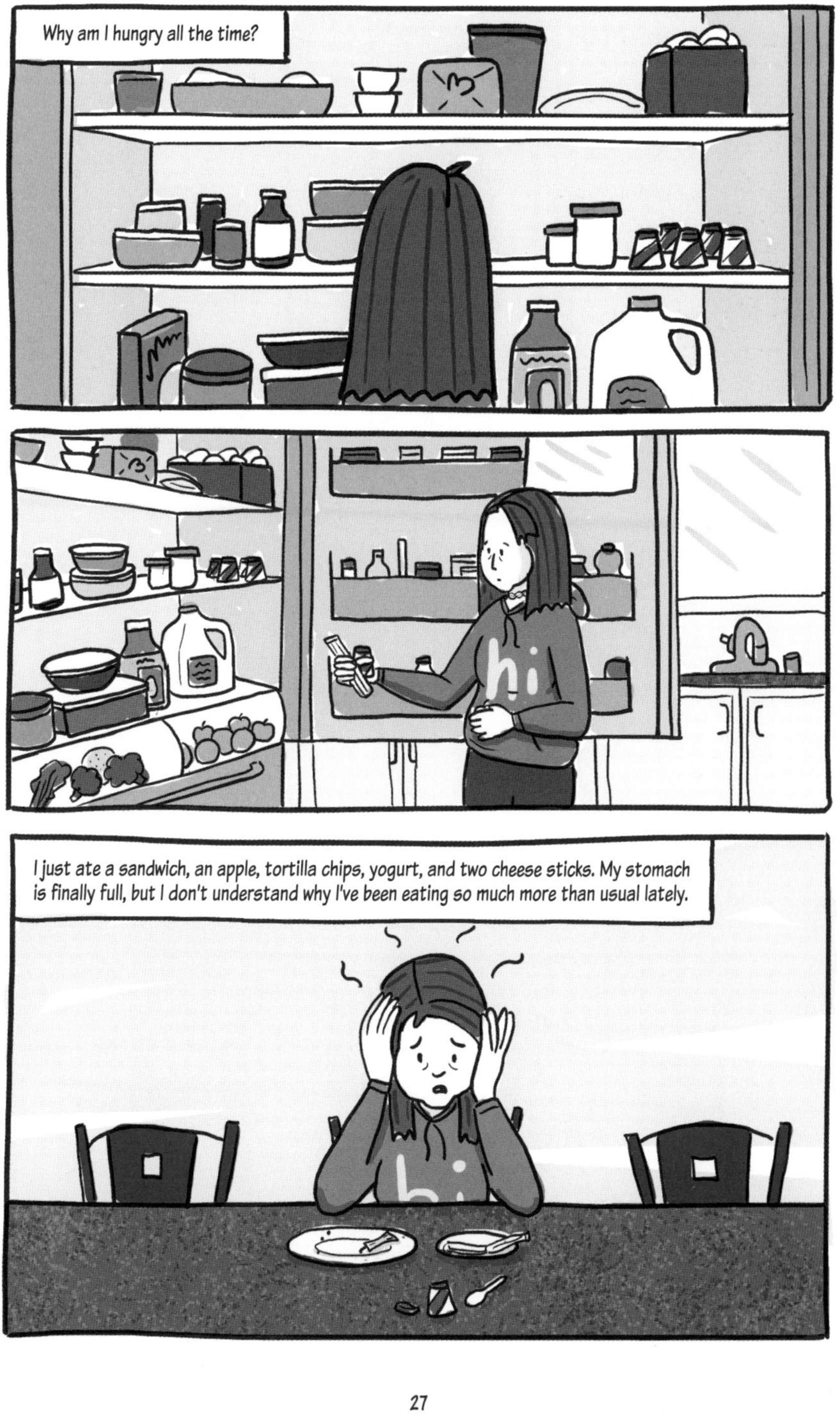
Why am I hungry all the time?
I just ate a sandwich, an apple, tortilla chips, yogurt, and two cheese sticks. My stomach is finally full, but I don't understand why I've been eating so much more than usual lately.
hi
hi

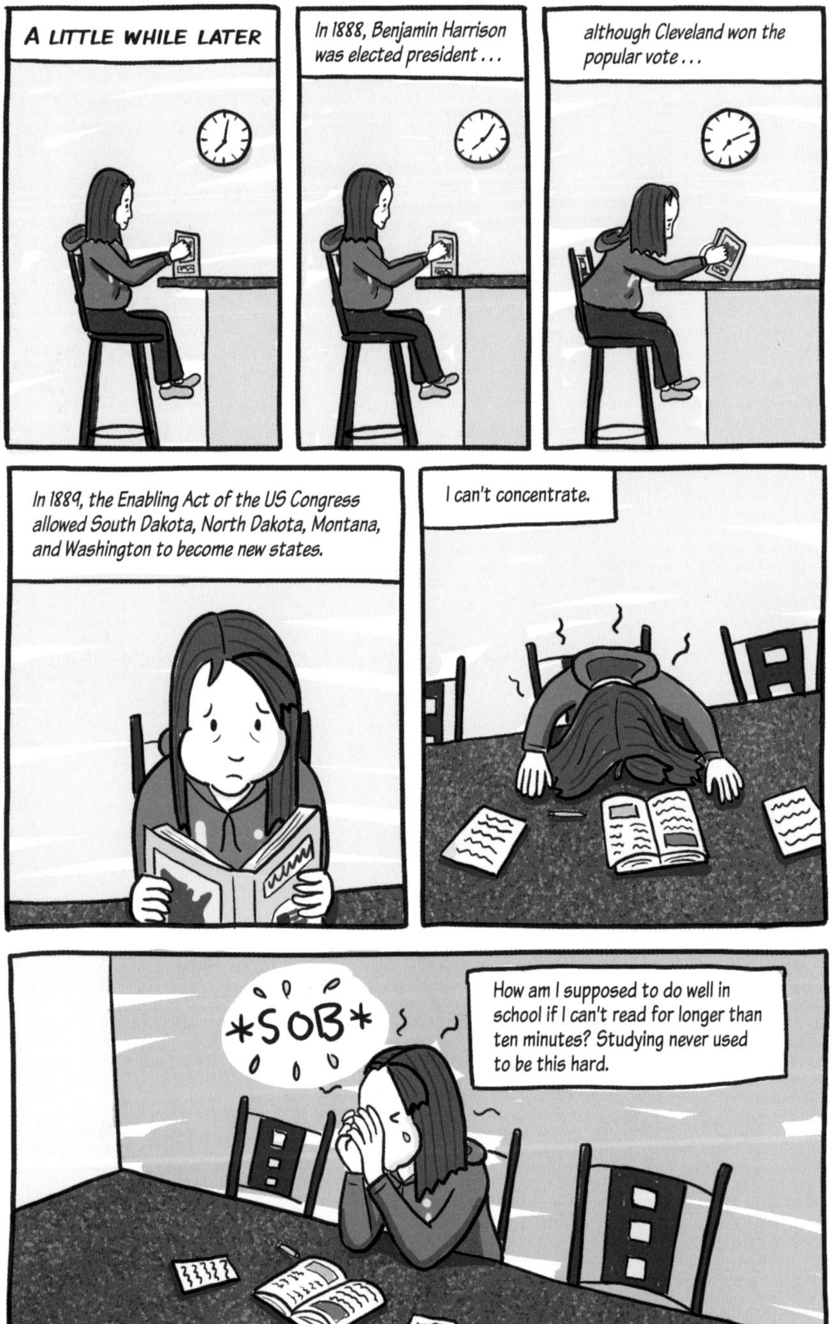
A LITTLE WHILE LATER
In 1888, Benjamin Harrison was elected president . . .
although Cleveland won the popular vote . . .
In 1889, the Enabling Act of the US Congress allowed South Dakota, North Dakota, Montana, and Washington to become new states.
I can't concentrate.
SOB
How am I supposed to do well in school if I can't read for longer than ten minutes? Studying never used to be this hard.

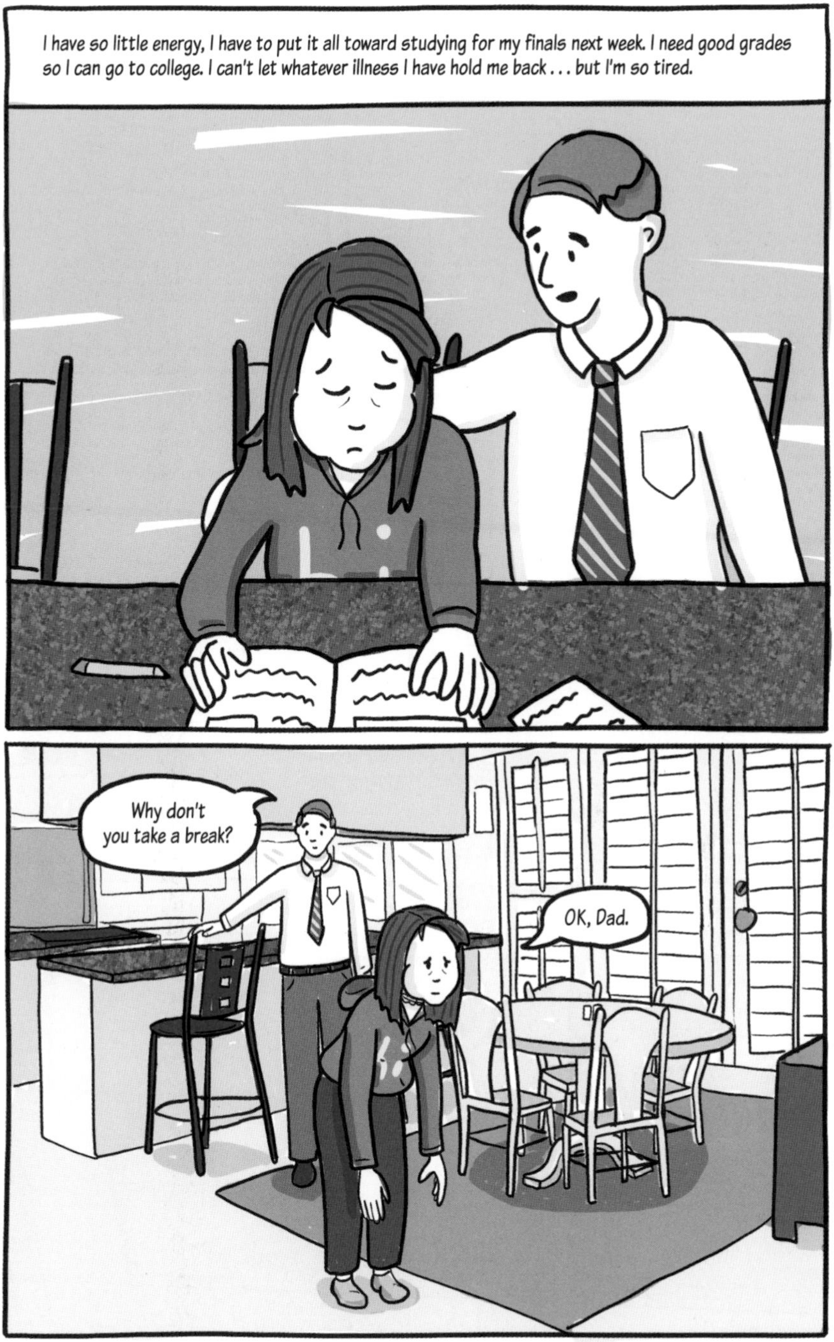
I have so little energy, I have to put it all toward studying for my finals next week. I need good grades so I can go to college. I can't let whatever illness I have hold me back . . . but I'm so tired.
Why don't you take a break?
OK, Dad.

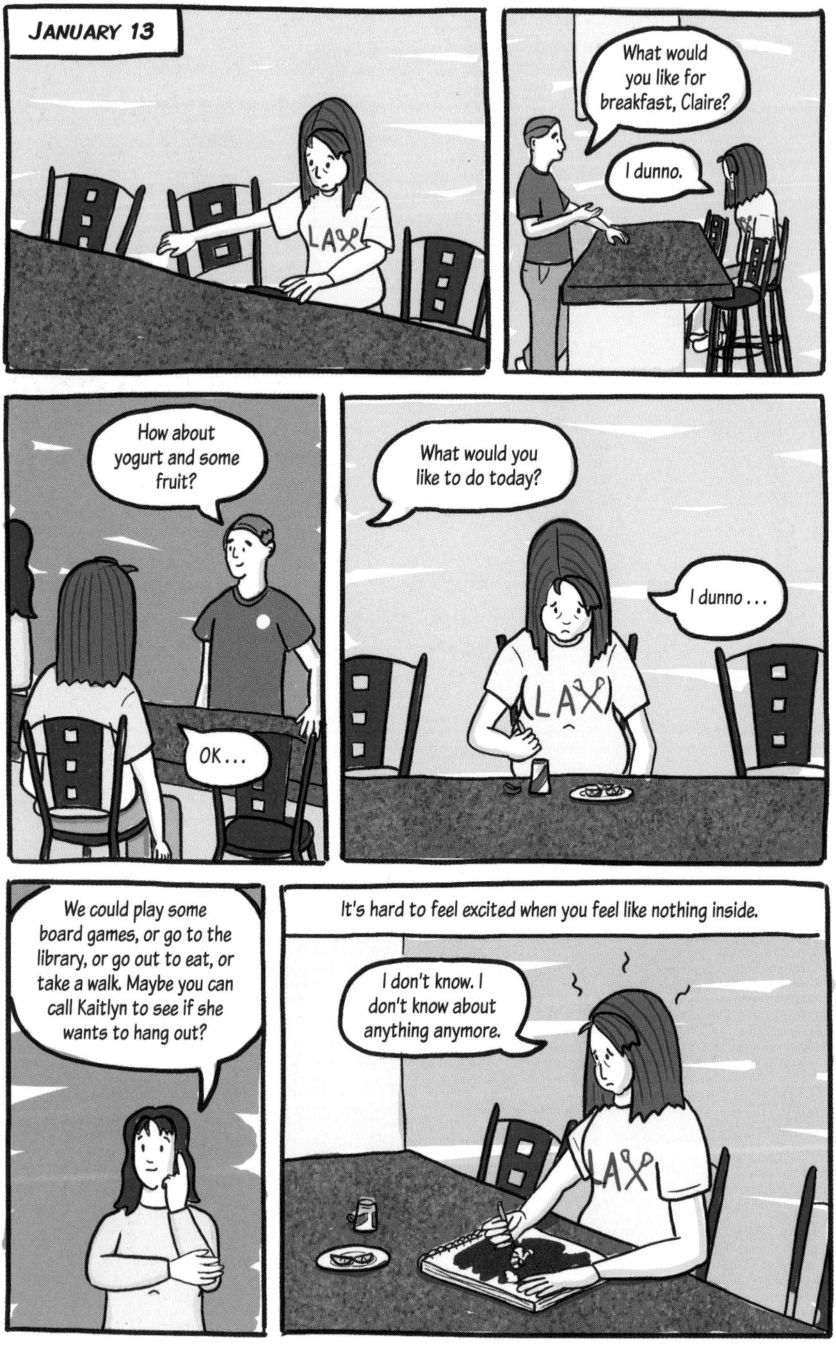
JANUARY 13
What would you like for breakfast, Claire?
I dunno.
How about yogurt and some fruit?
OK...
What would you like to do today?
I dunno...
We could play some board games, or go to the library, or go out to eat, or take a walk. Maybe you can call Kaitlyn to see if she wants to hang out?
It's hard to feel excited when you feel like nothing inside.
I don't know. I don't know about anything anymore.

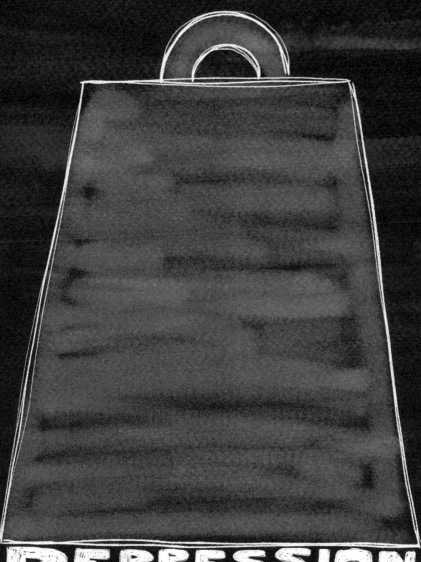

DEPRESSION

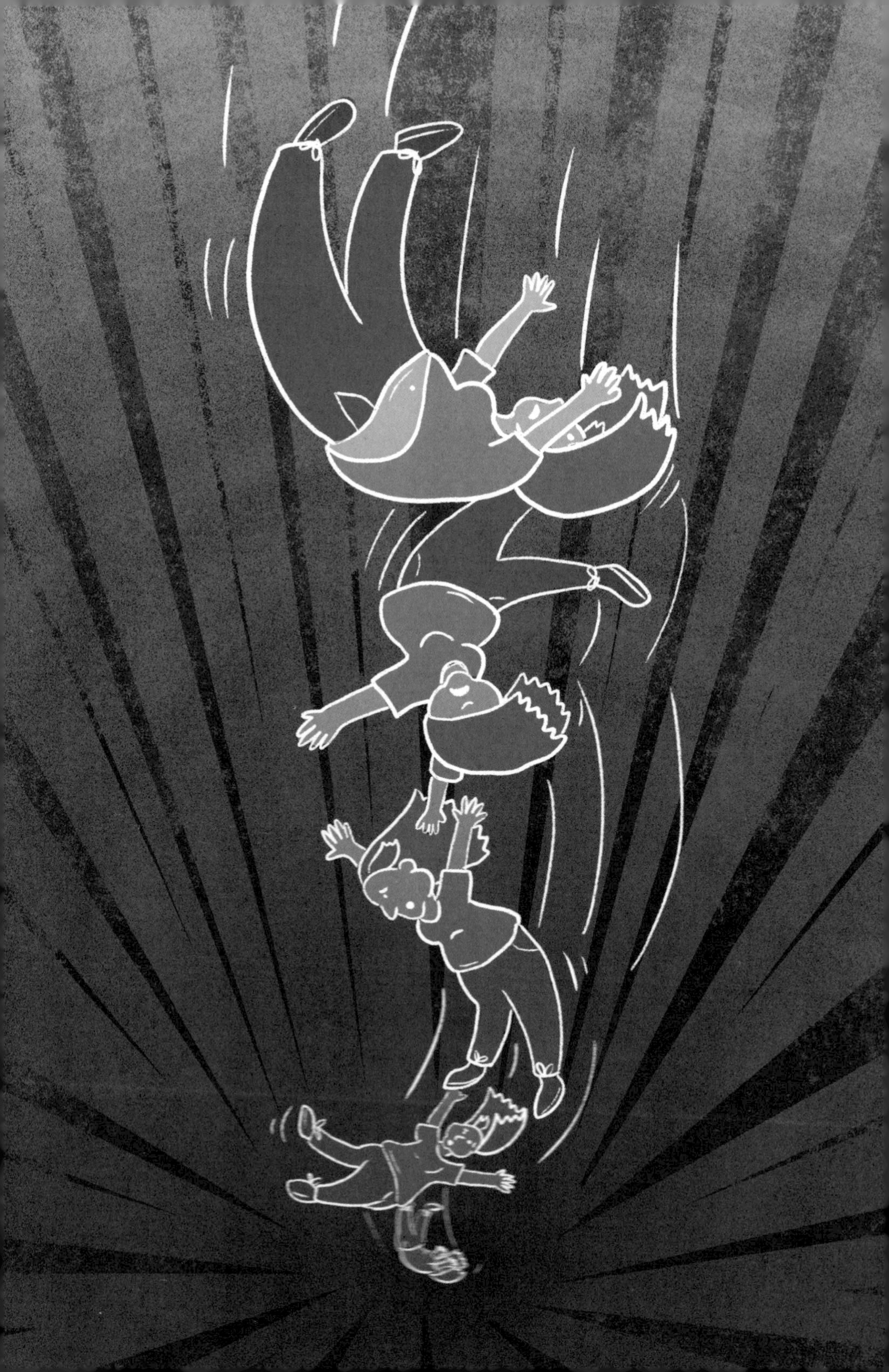

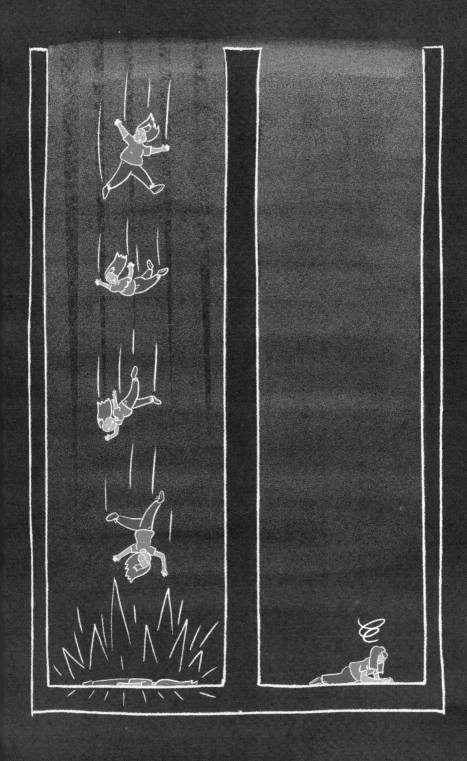

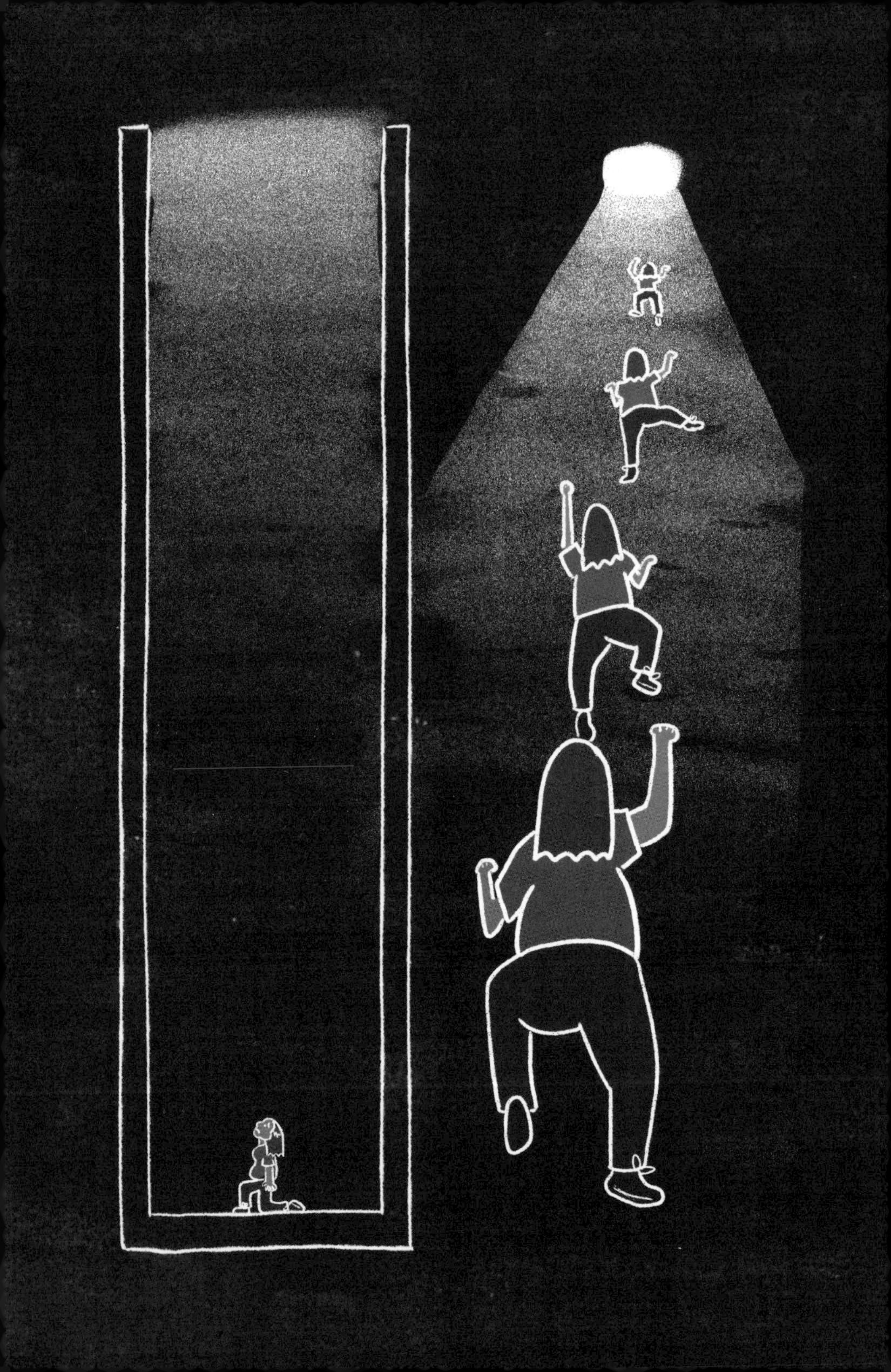

I am
OK*

* I am definitely not OK.
Please, for the love of God, help me!

I AM OK
I AM OK
I AM OK

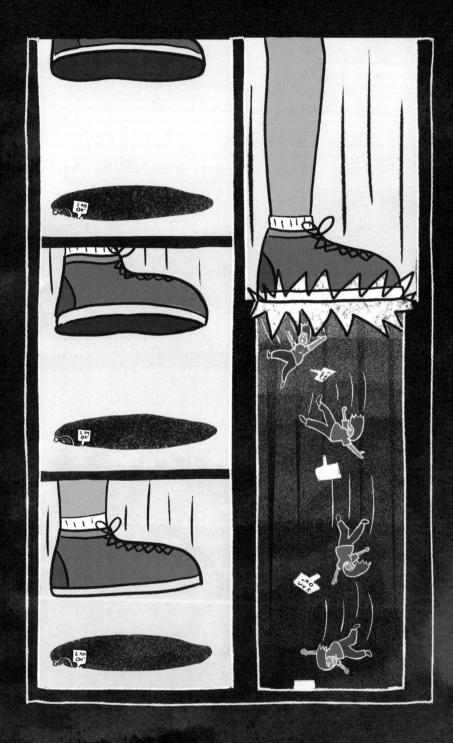

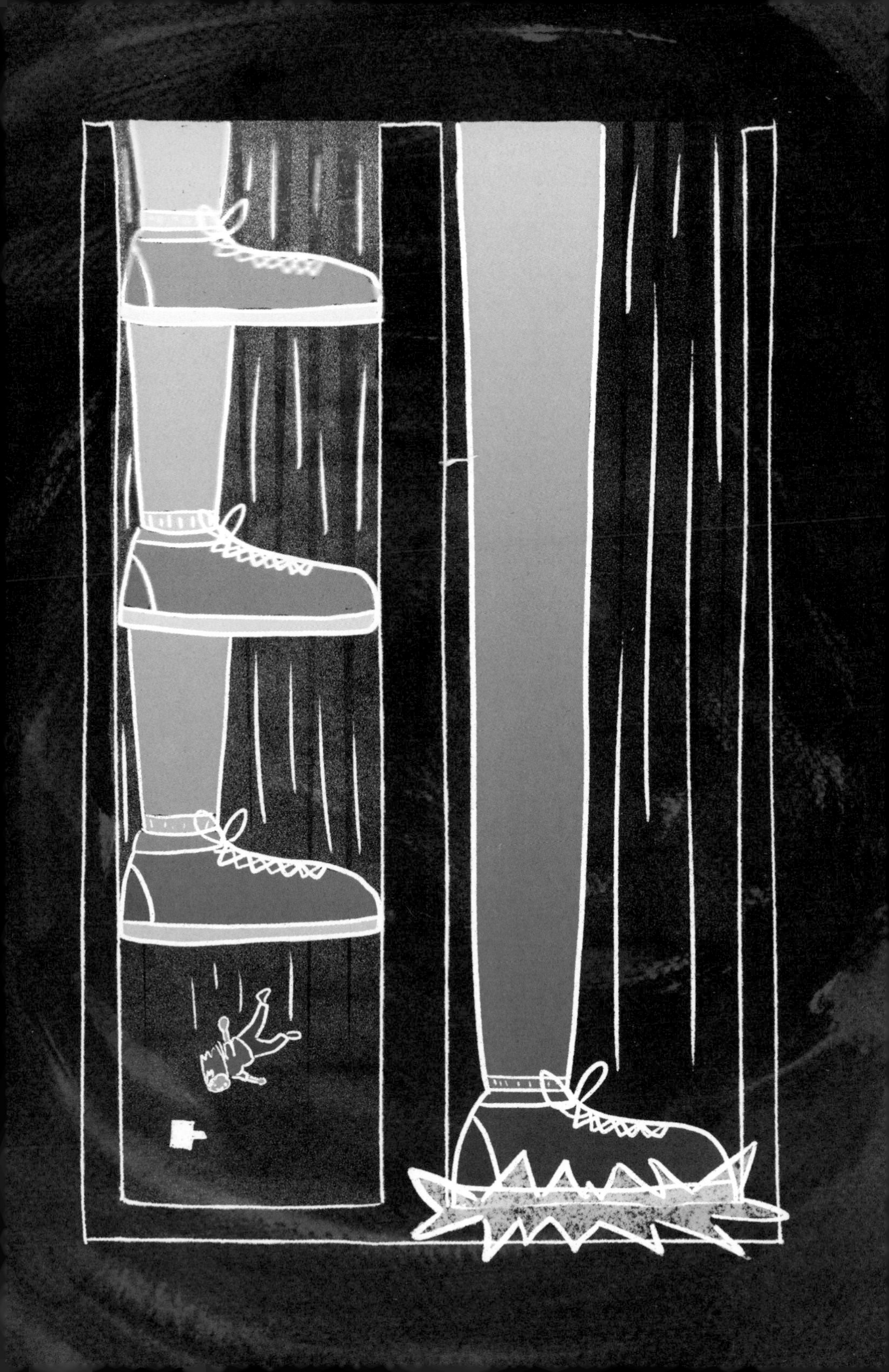

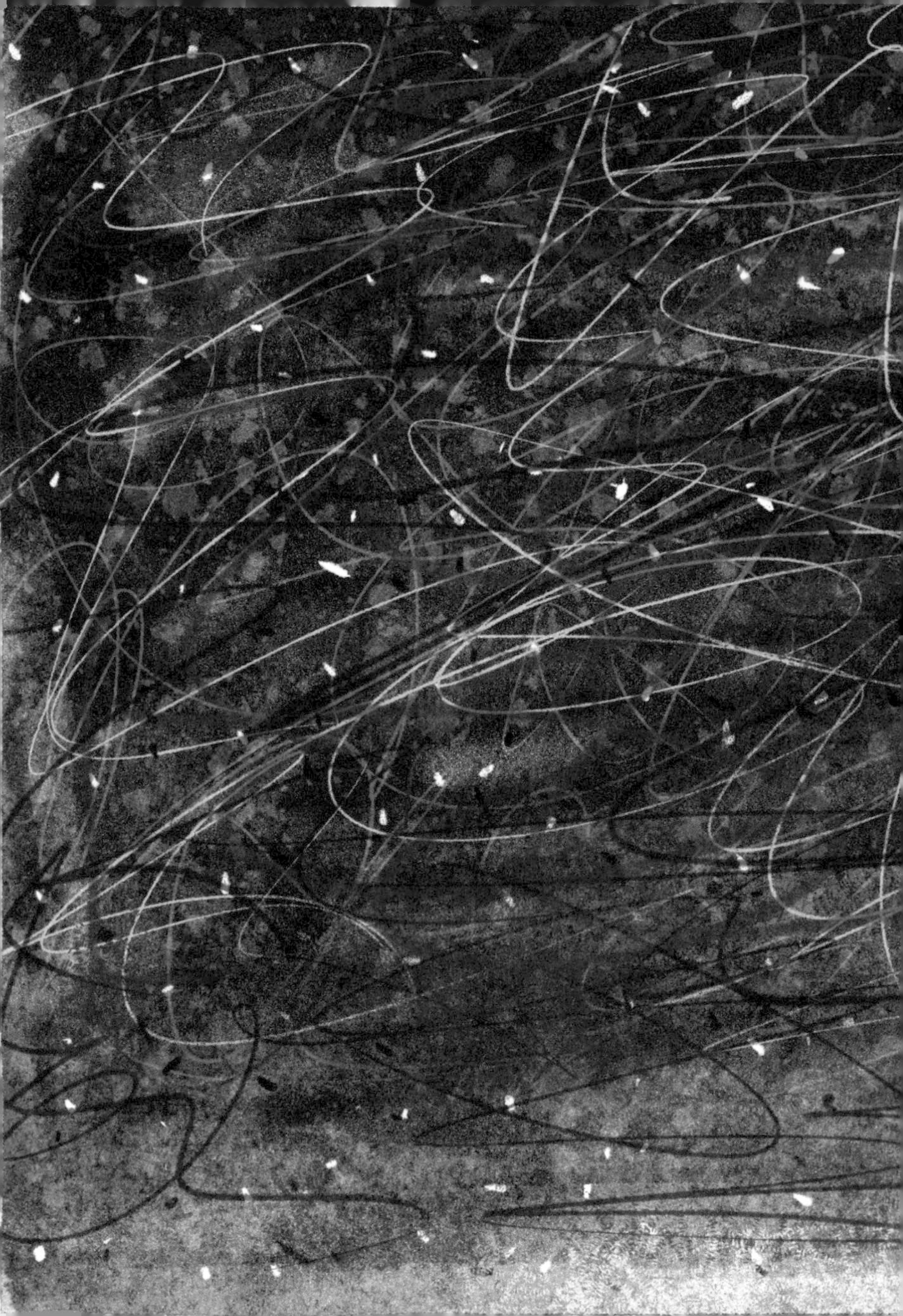

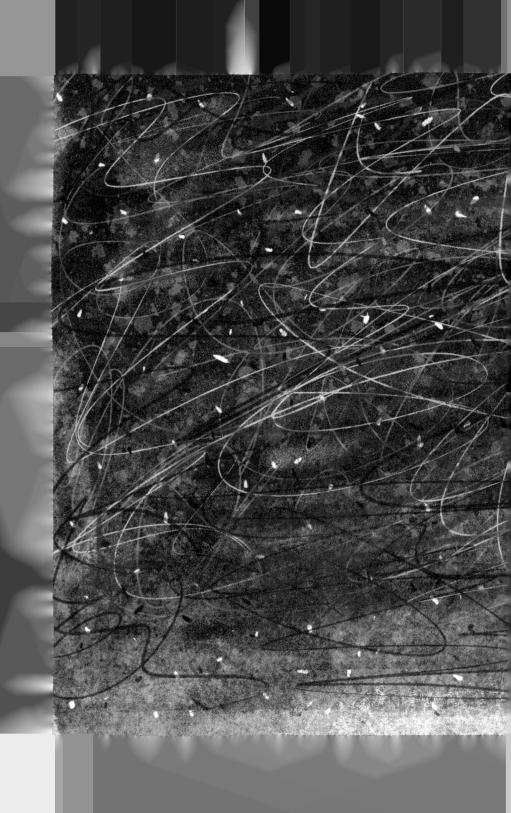

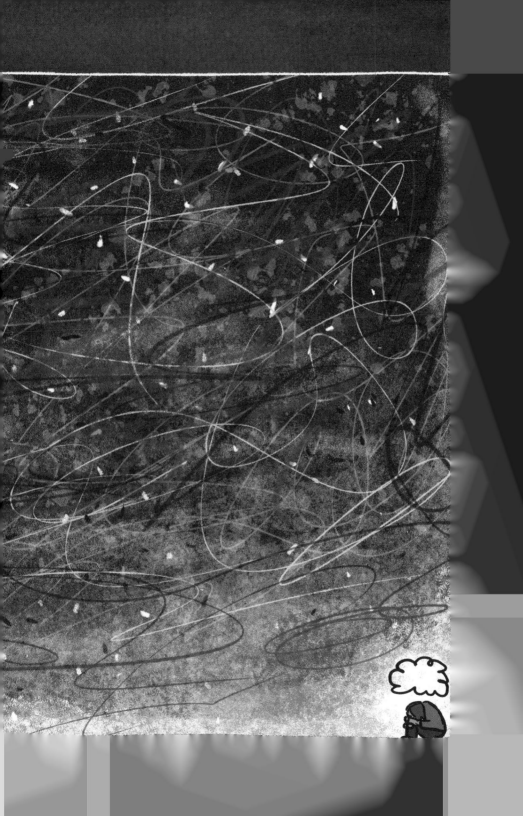

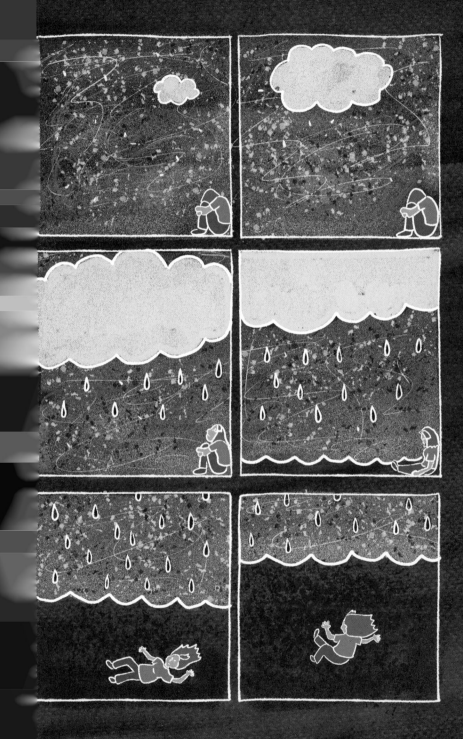

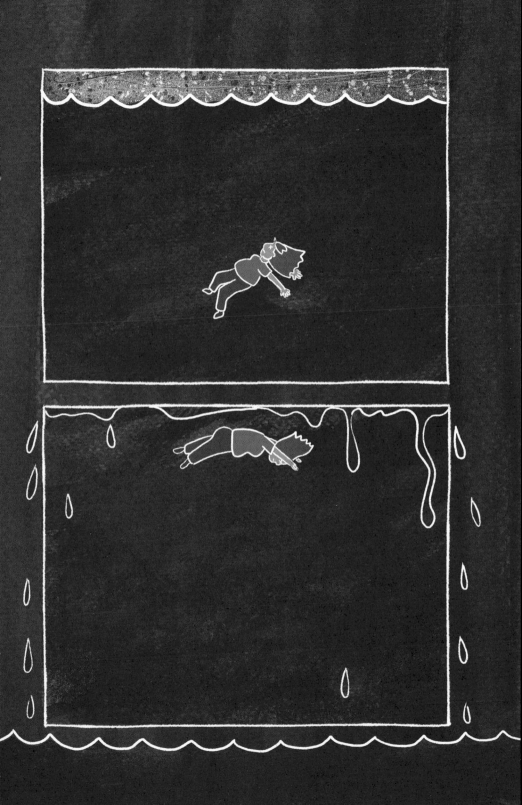

JANUARY 15
Another blood draw today?

How was your Christmas?

It was fine. My brother came back from college to visit. How was yours?

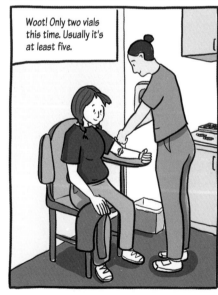

Woot! Only two vials this time. Usually it's at least five.

Thanks. See you next week.

You're welcome. Take care.

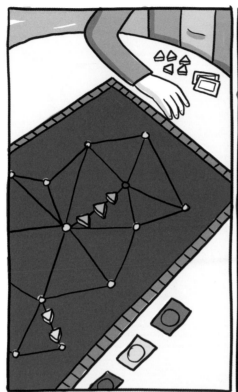

Your turn.

OK, I'm going from Kansas City to Denver.

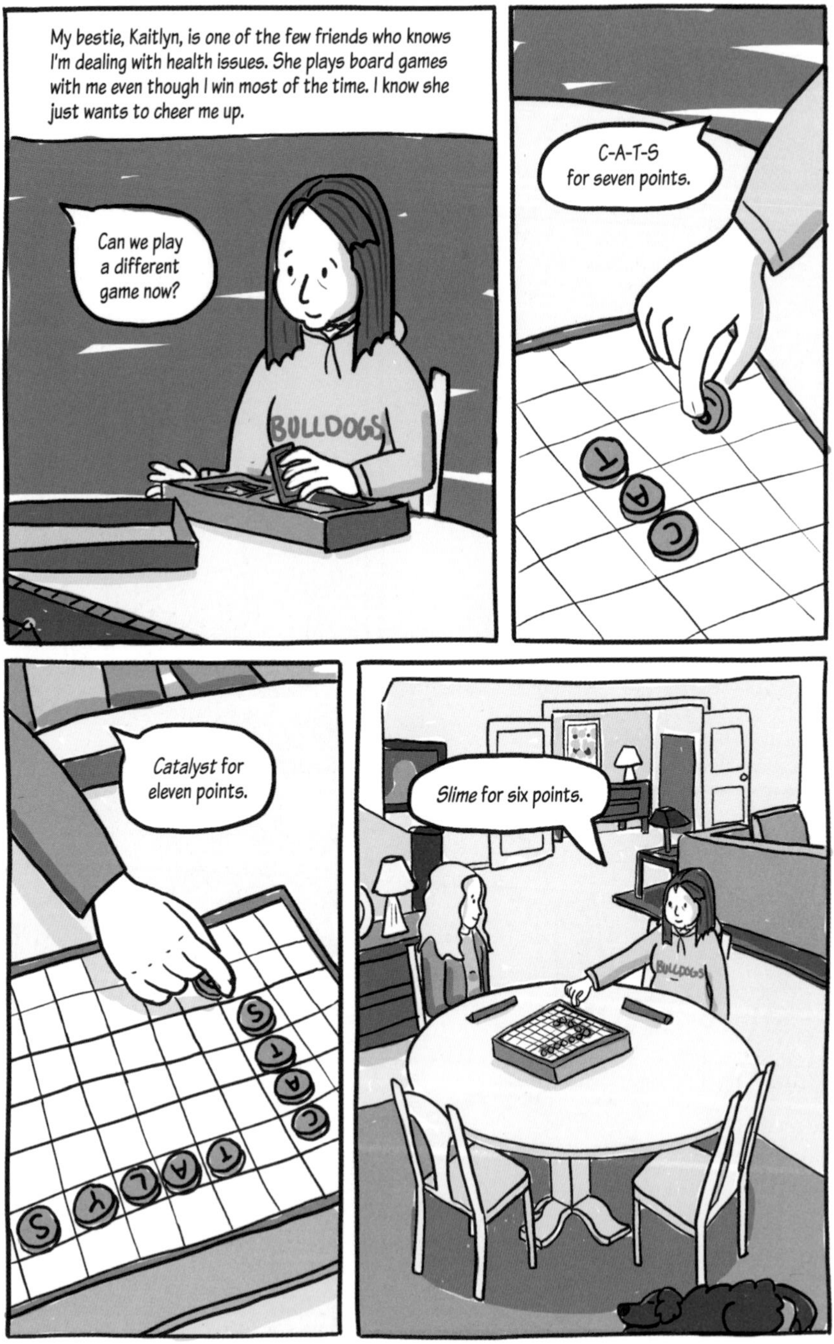
My bestie, Kaitlyn, is one of the few friends who knows I'm dealing with health issues. She plays board games with me even though I win most of the time. I know she just wants to cheer me up.
Can we play a different game now?
BULLDOGS
C-A-T-S for seven points.
Catalyst for eleven points.
Slime for six points.
BULLDOGS

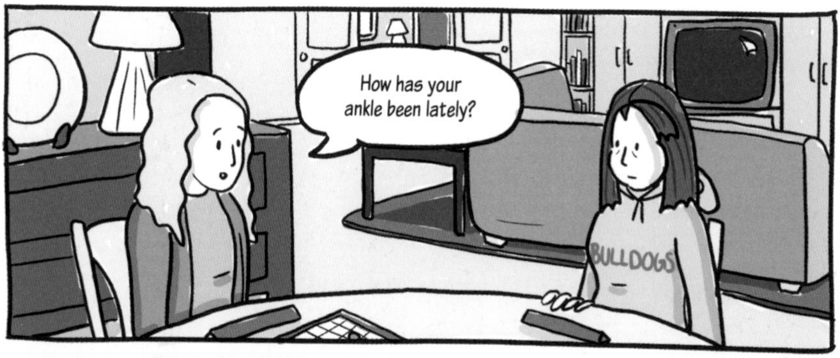
How has your ankle been lately?
BULLDOGS

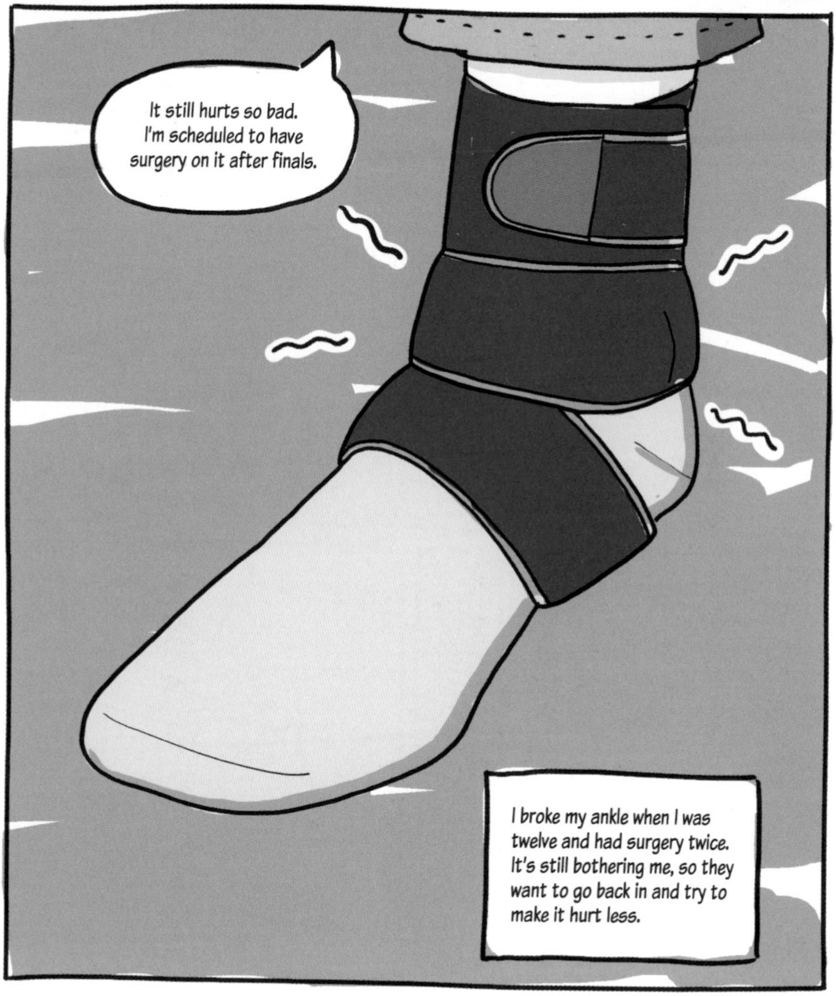
It still hurts so bad. I'm scheduled to have surgery on it after finals.
I broke my ankle when I was twelve and had surgery twice. It's still bothering me, so they want to go back in and try to make it hurt less.

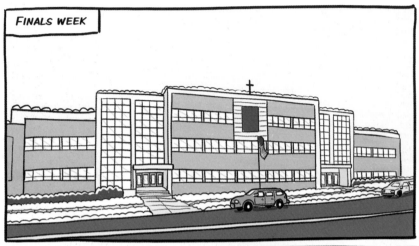

FINALS WEEK

My concentration is kaput and I have the worst headache right now.

OK, time is up.

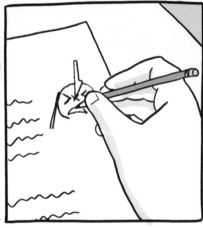

46

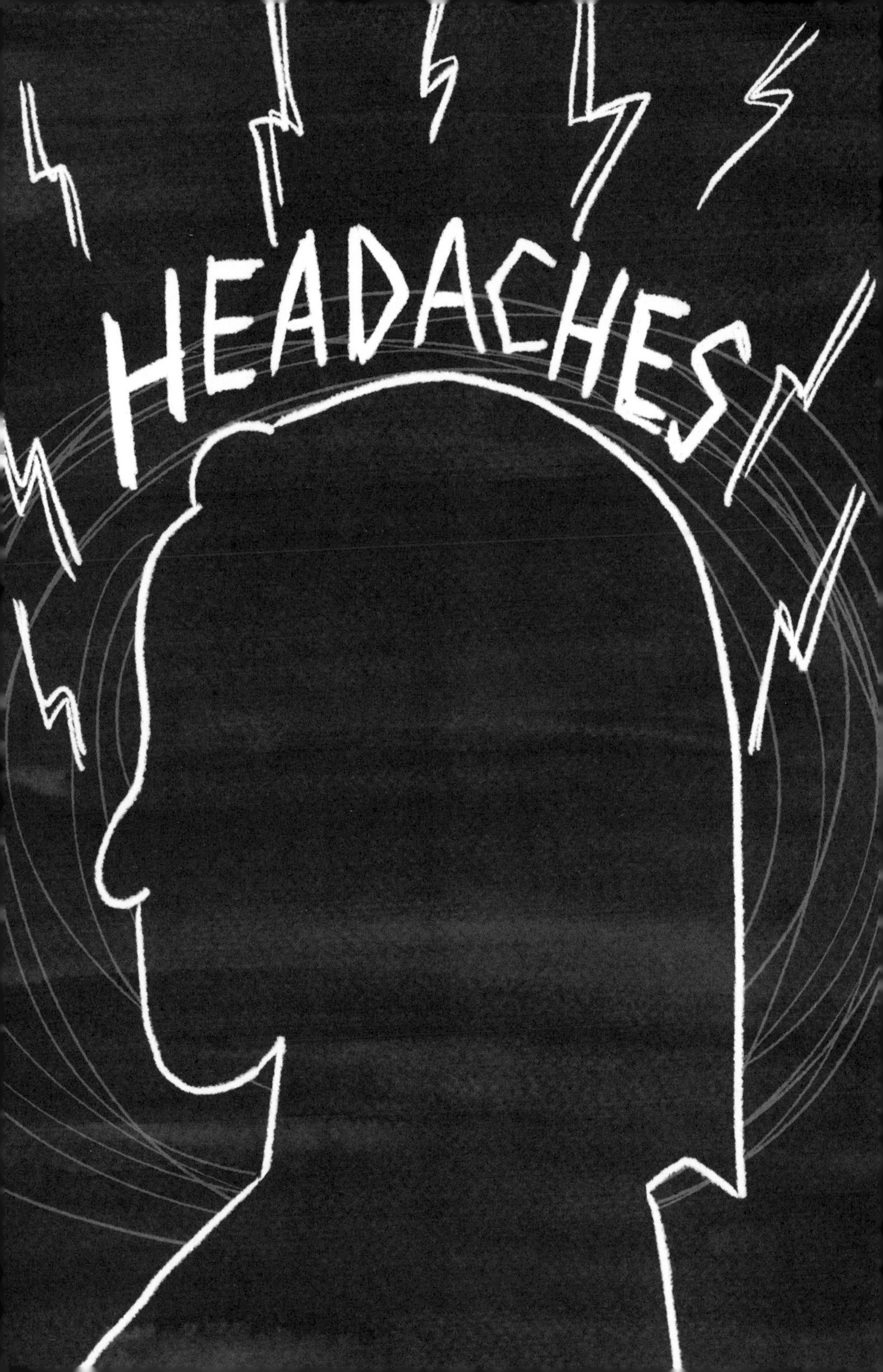
HEADACHES

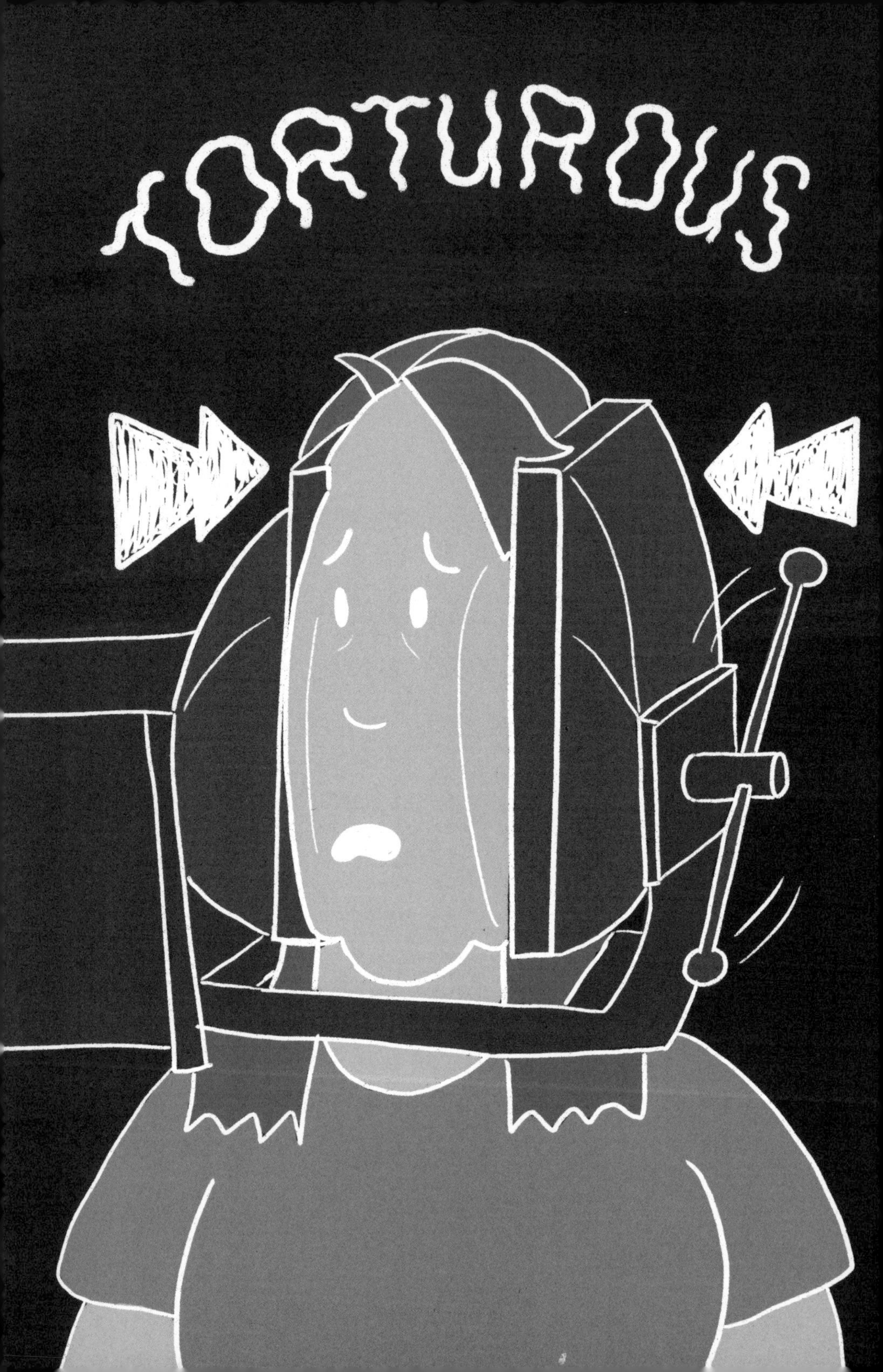
TORTUROUS

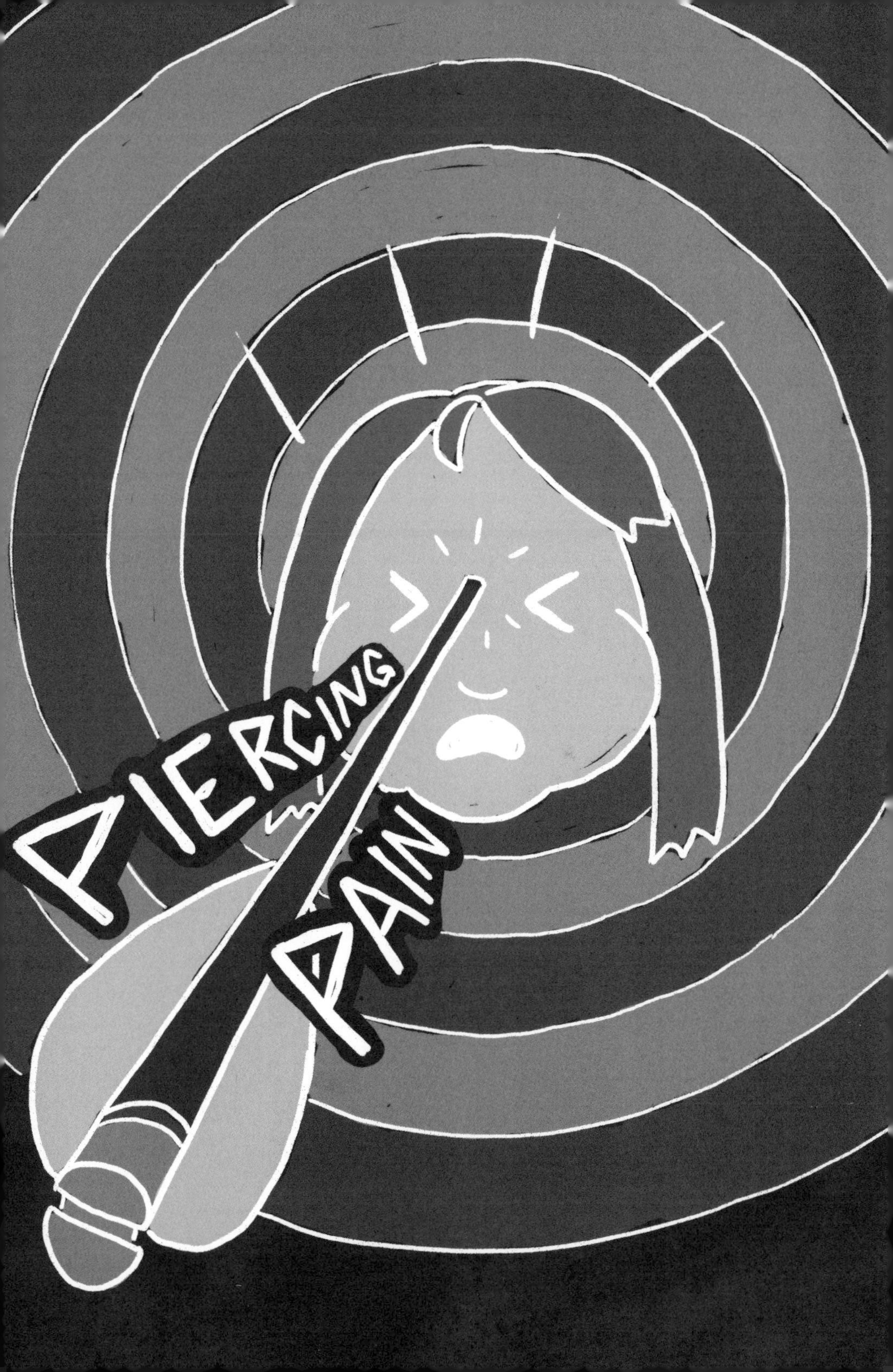
PIERCING
PAIN

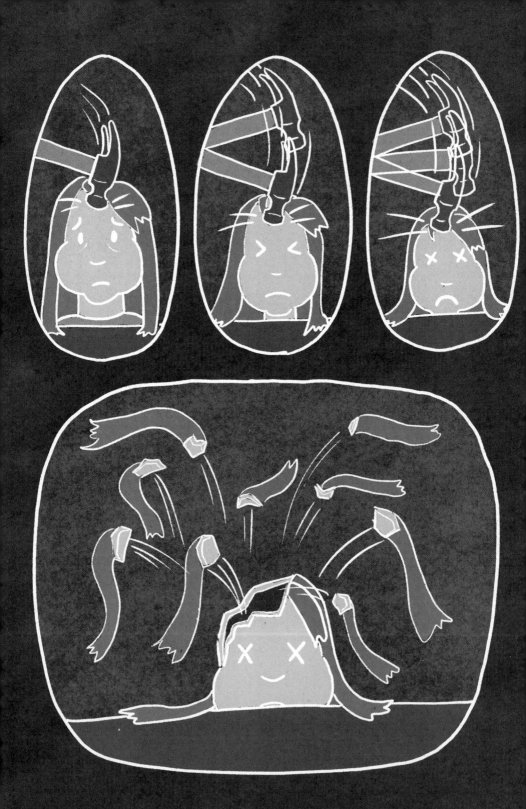

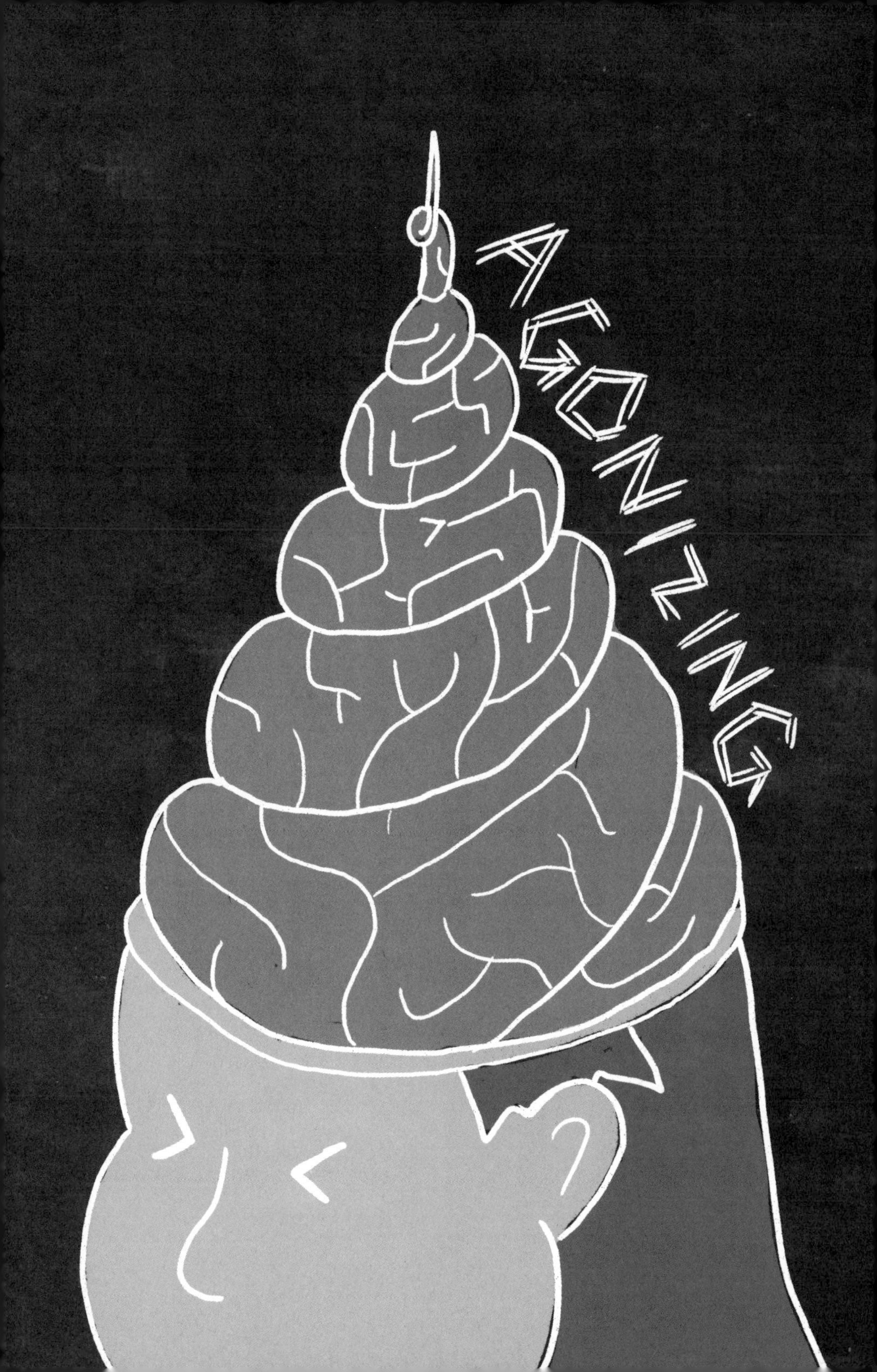
AGONIZING

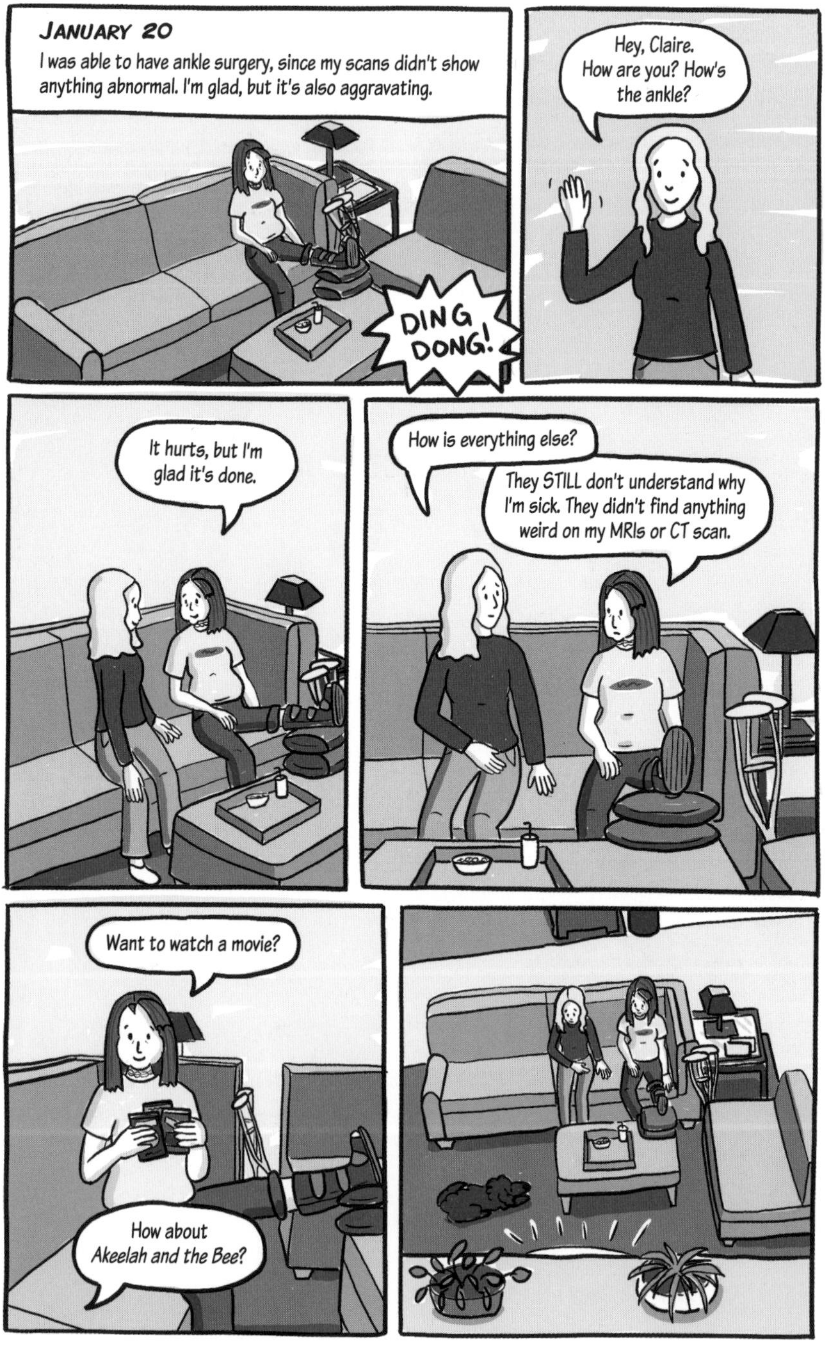
JANUARY 20
I was able to have ankle surgery, since my scans didn't show anything abnormal. I'm glad, but it's also aggravating.
DING DONG!
Hey, Claire. How are you? How's the ankle?
It hurts, but I'm glad it's done.
How is everything else?
They STILL don't understand why I'm sick. They didn't find anything weird on my MRIs or CT scan.
Want to watch a movie?
How about Akeelah and the Bee?

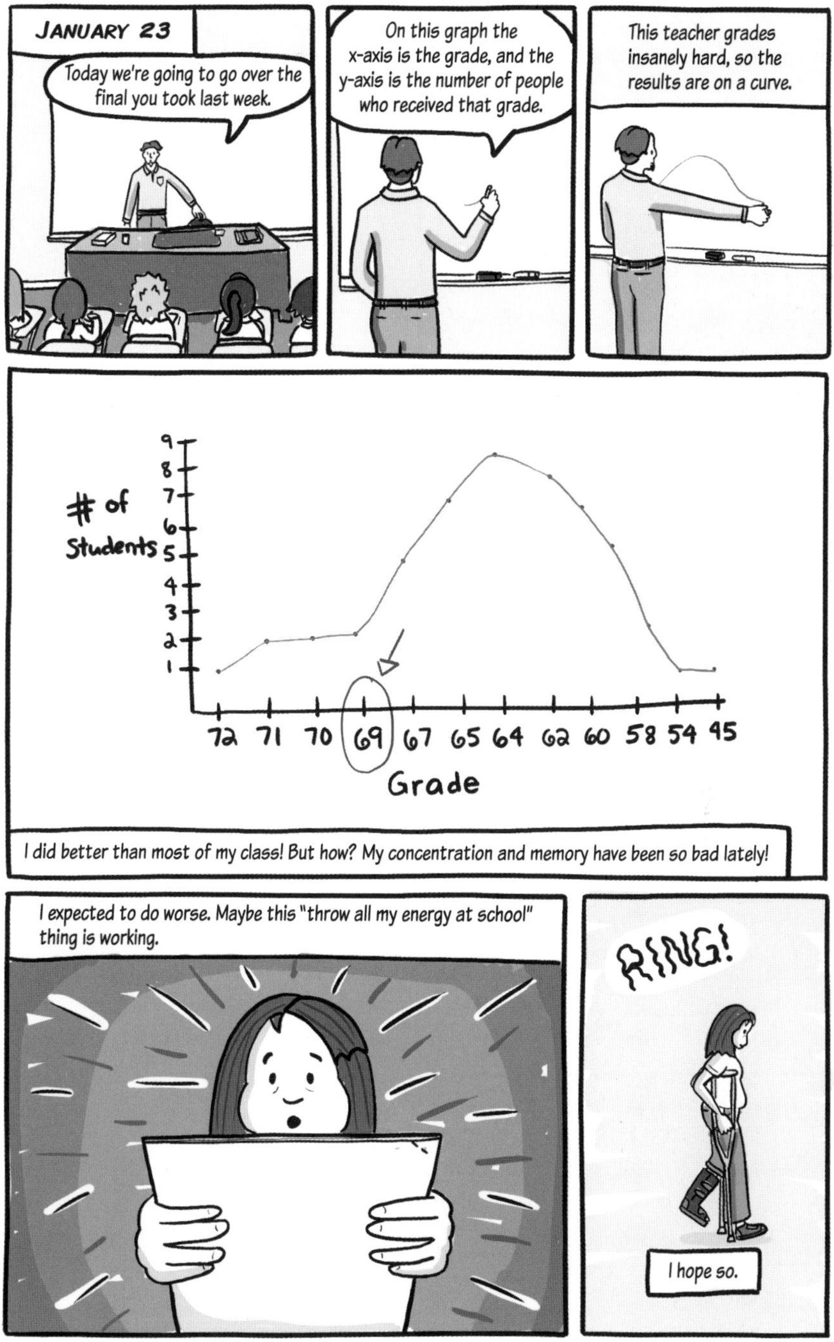

JANUARY 23
Today we're going to go over the final you took last week.
On this graph the x-axis is the grade, and the y-axis is the number of people who received that grade.
This teacher grades insanely hard, so the results are on a curve.
# of Students
9
8
7
6
5
4
3
2
1
72 71 70 69 67 65 64 62 60 58 54 45
Grade
I did better than most of my class! But how? My concentration and memory have been so bad lately!
I expected to do worse. Maybe this "throw all my energy at school" thing is working.
RING!
I hope so.

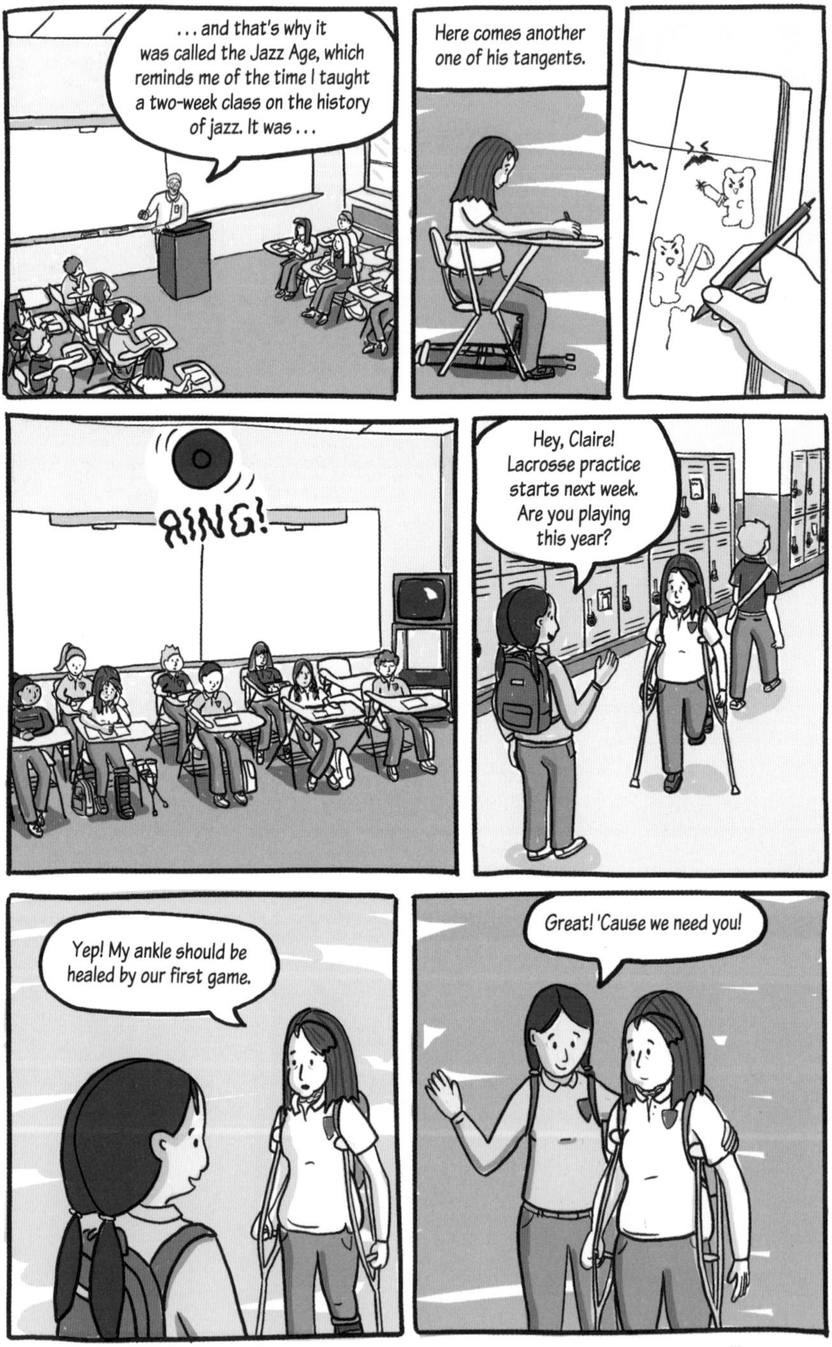

. . . and that's why it was called the Jazz Age, which reminds me of the time I taught a two-week class on the history of jazz. It was . . .
Here comes another one of his tangents.
RING!
Hey, Claire! Lacrosse practice starts next week. Are you playing this year?
Yep! My ankle should be healed by our first game.
Great! 'Cause we need you!

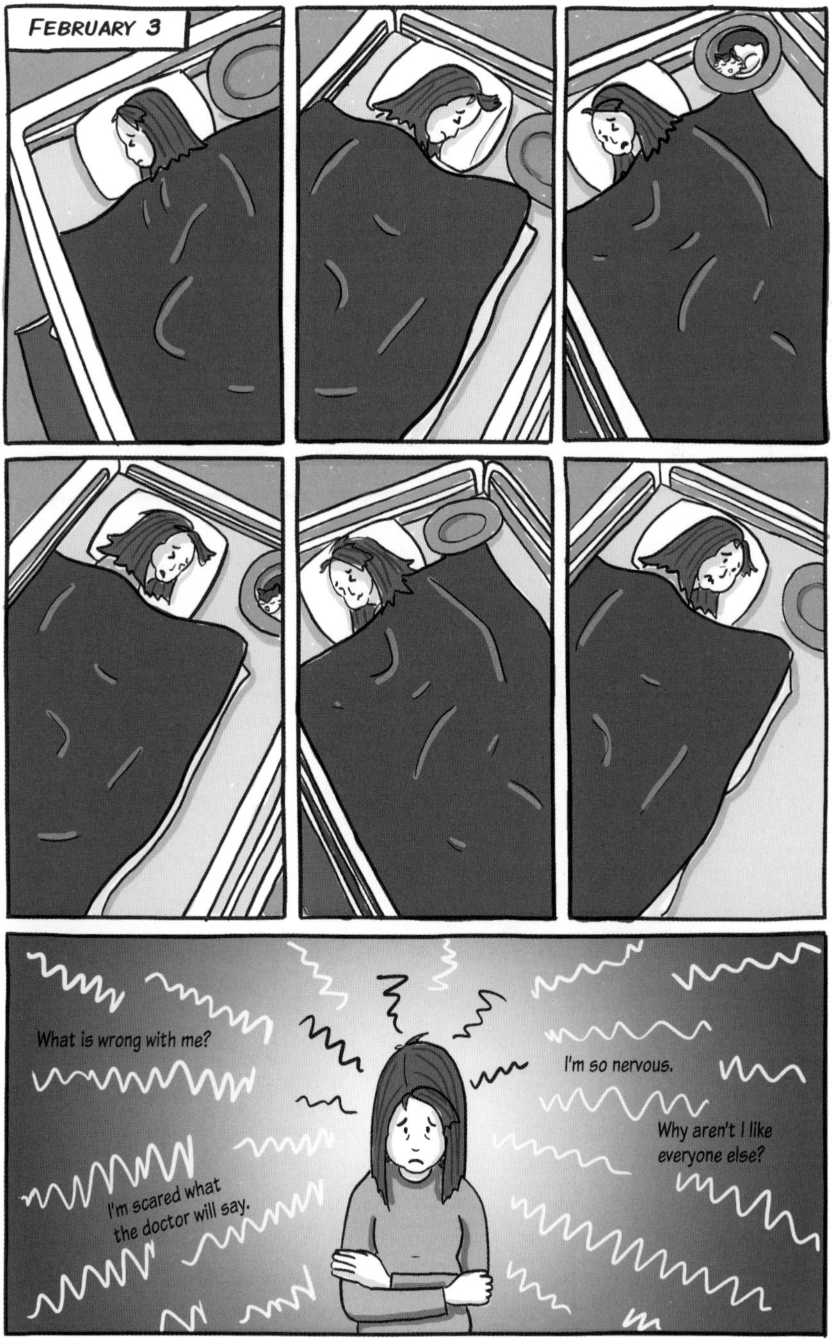
FEBRUARY 3
What is wrong with me?
I'm scared what the doctor will say.
I'm so nervous.
Why aren't I like everyone else?

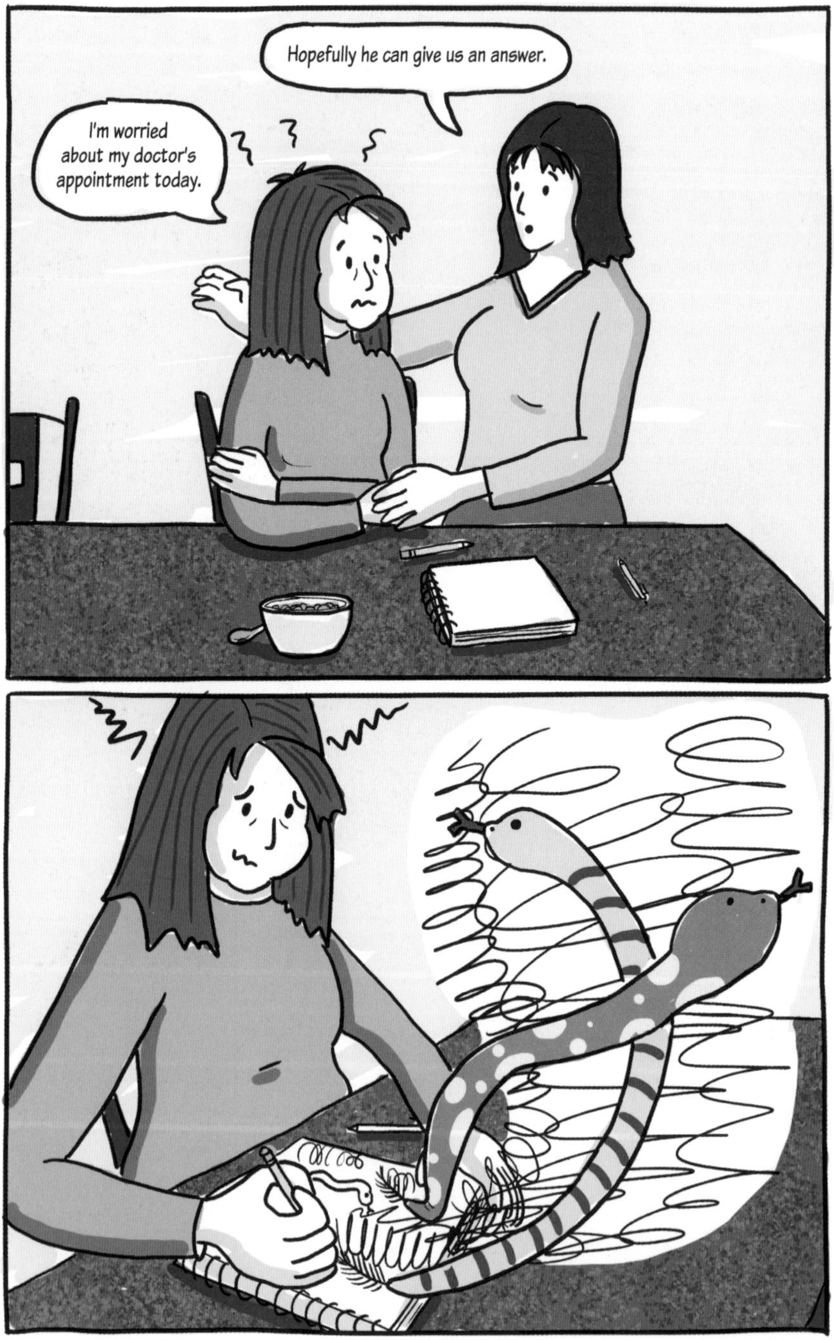
I'm worried about my doctor's appointment today.
Hopefully he can give us an answer.

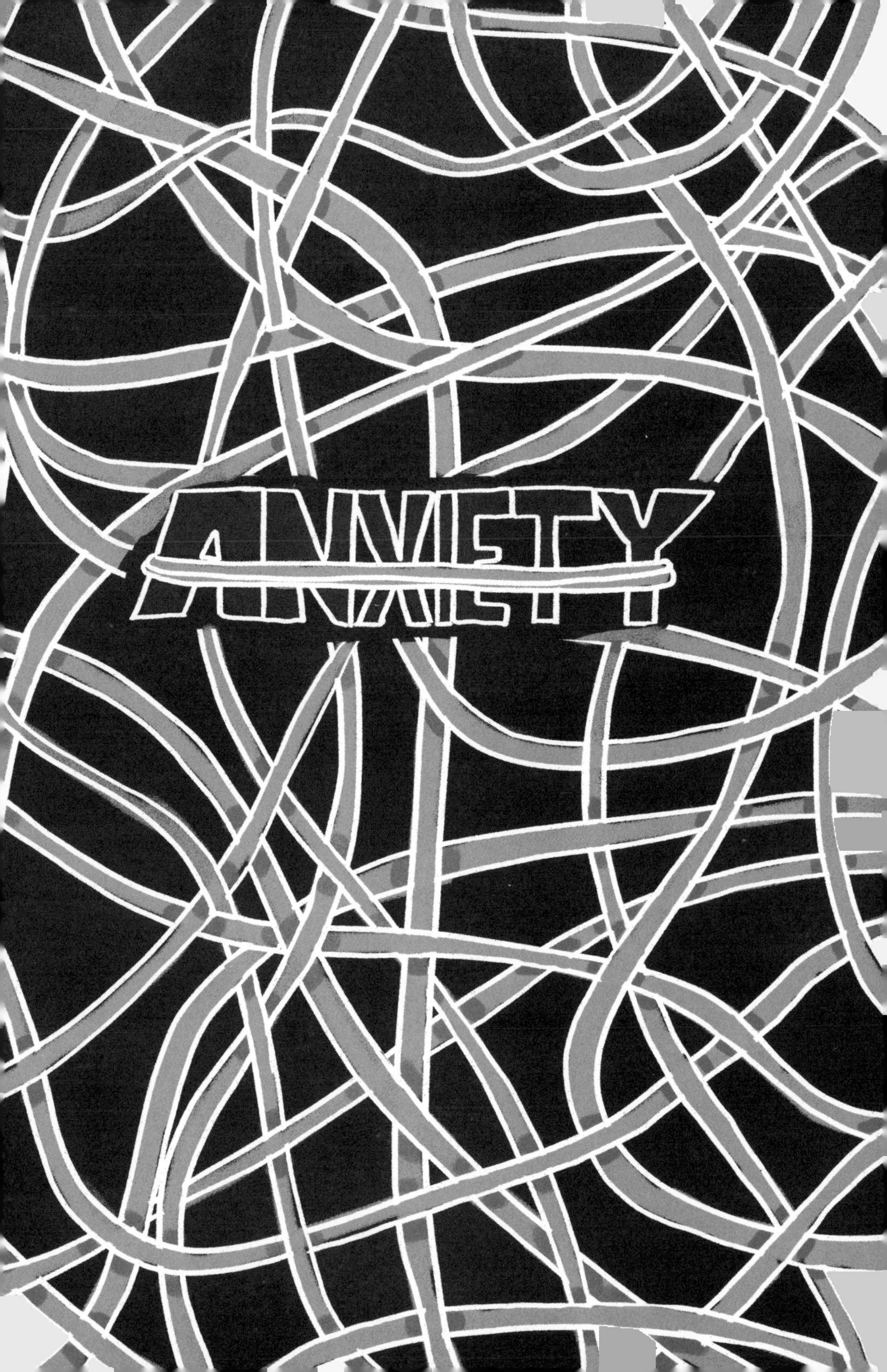
ANXIETY

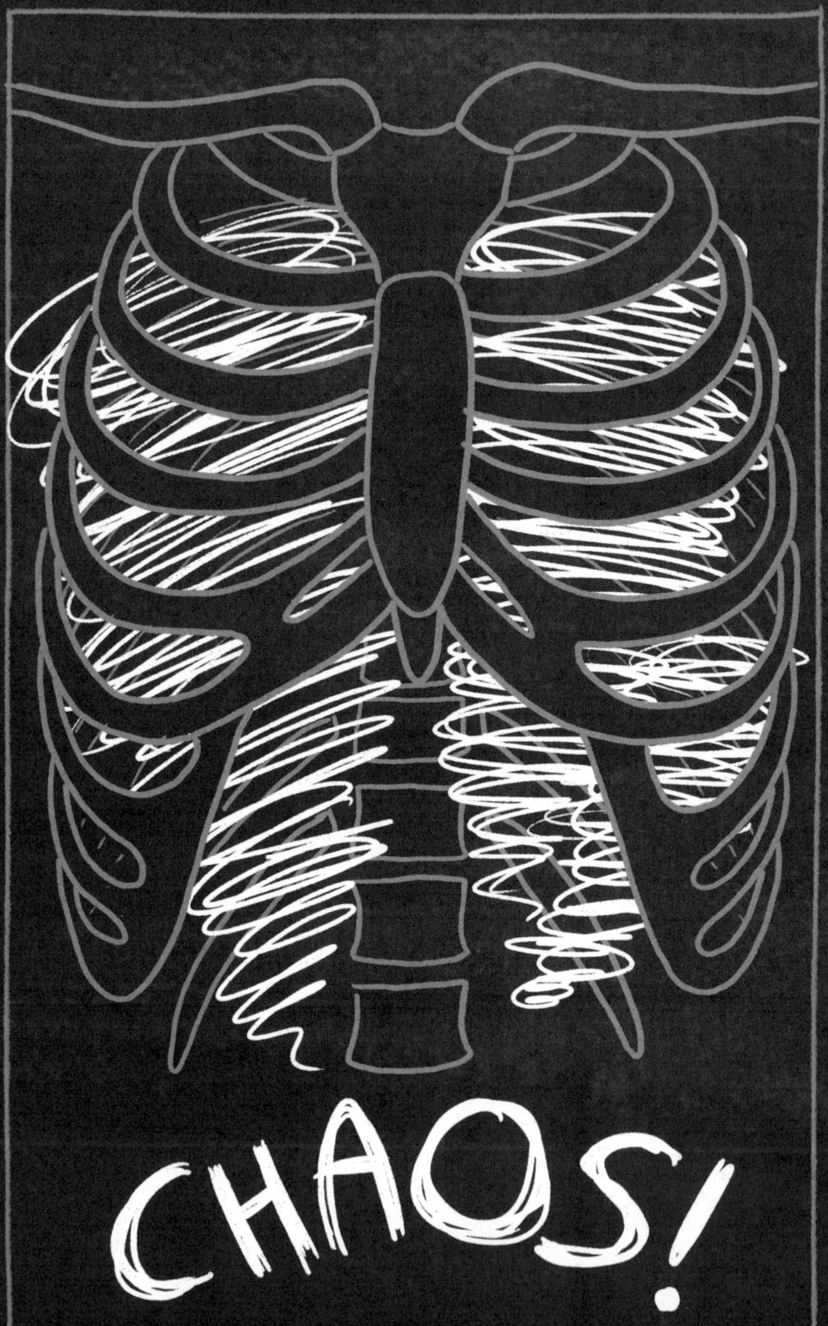
CHAOS!

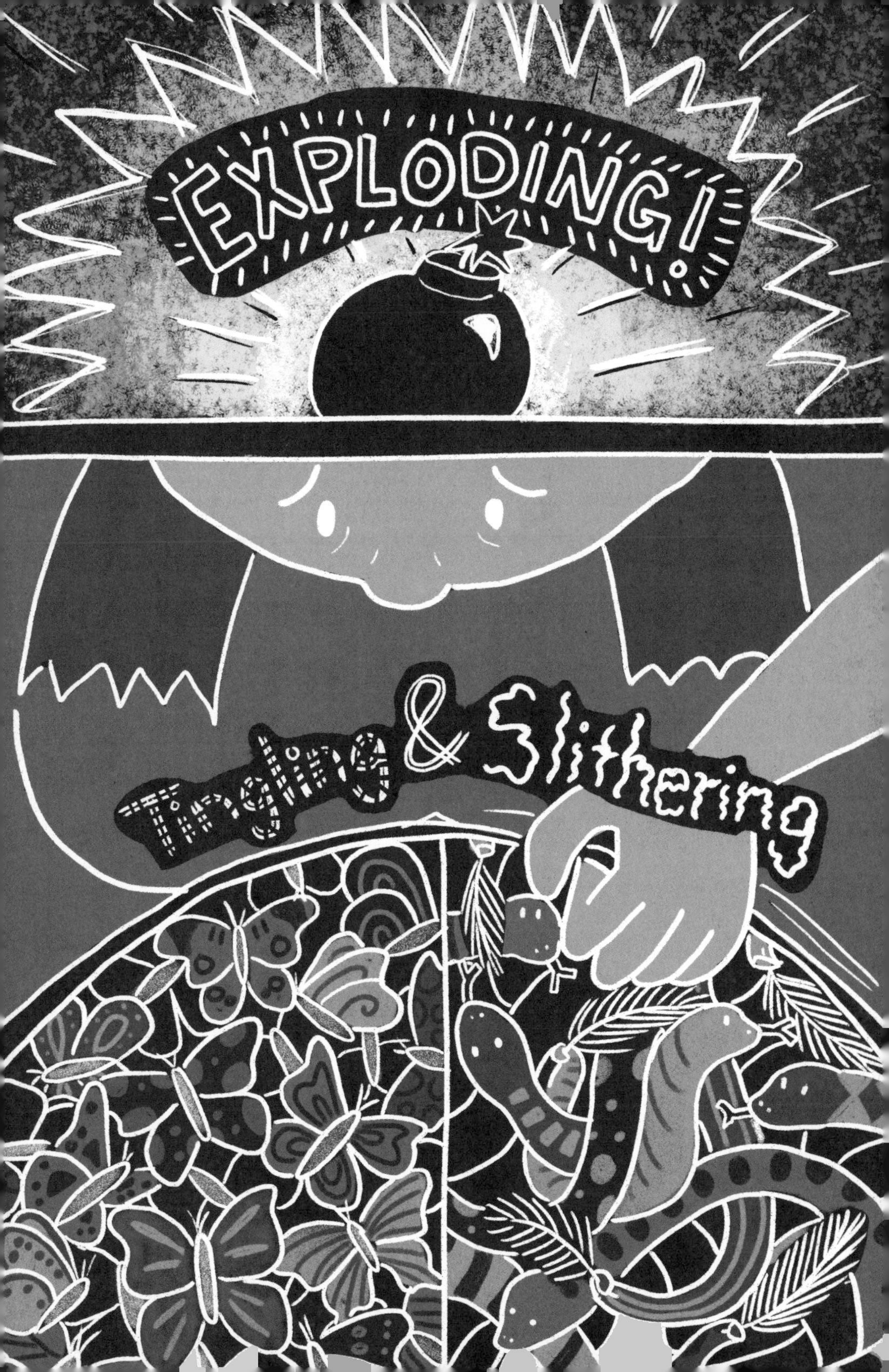
EXPLODING!
Tingling & Slithering

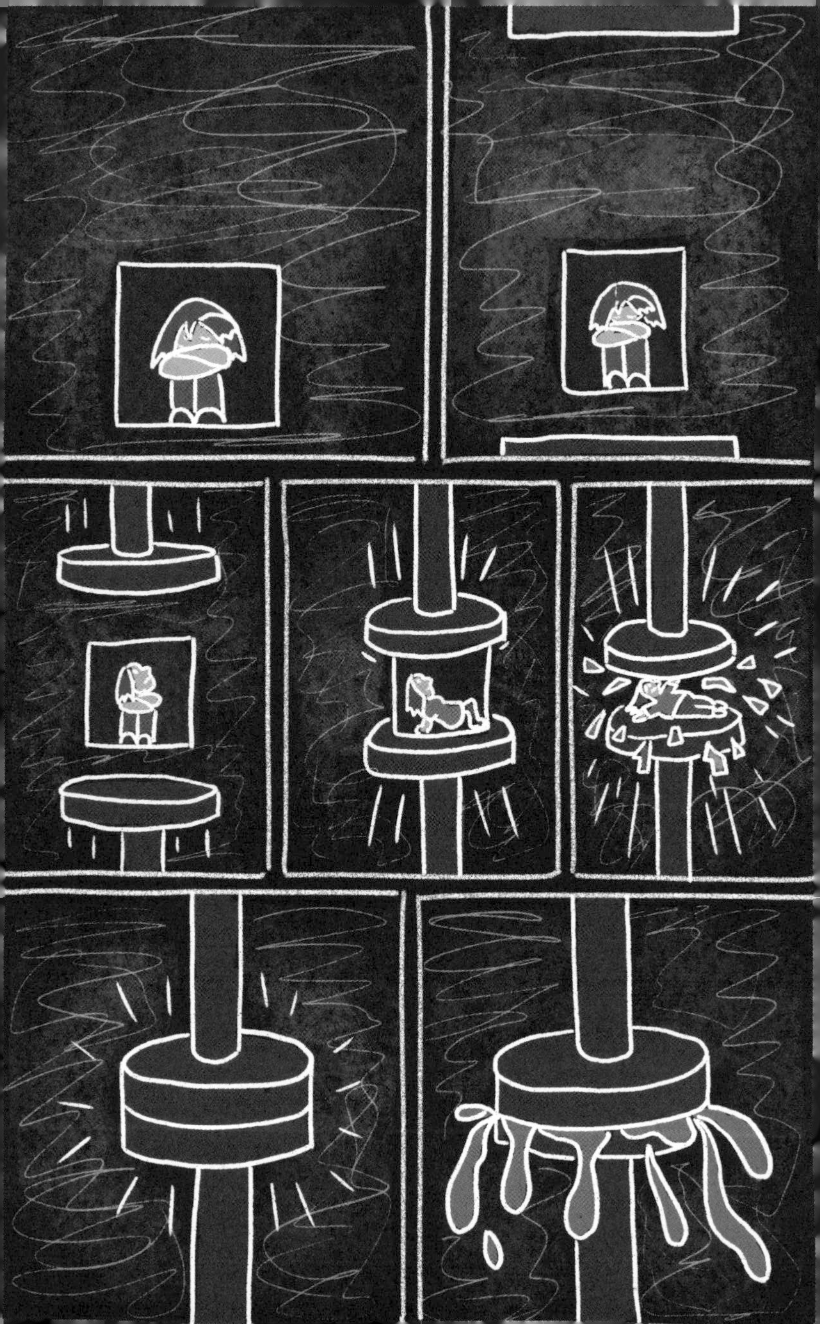

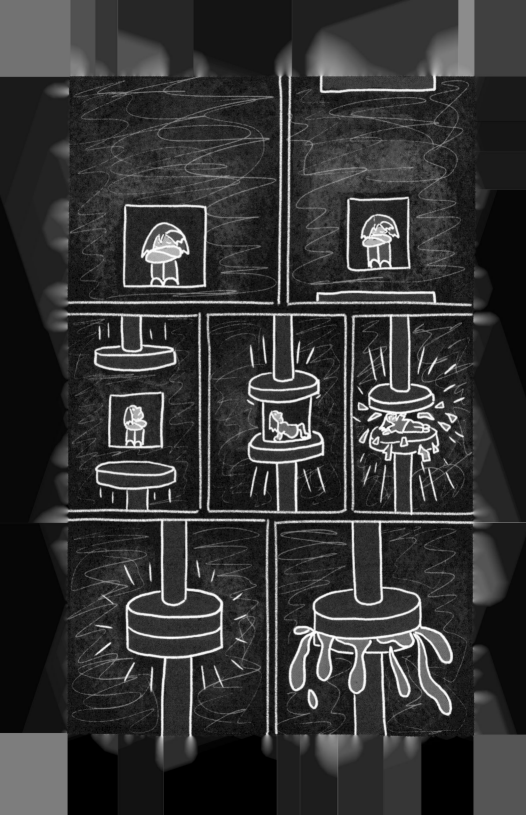

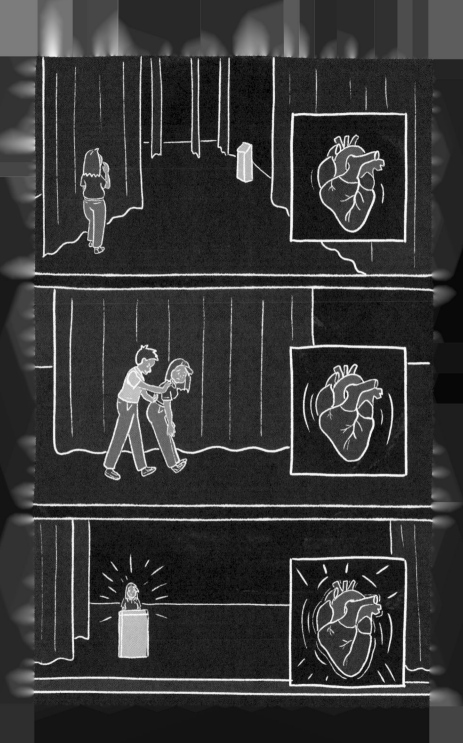

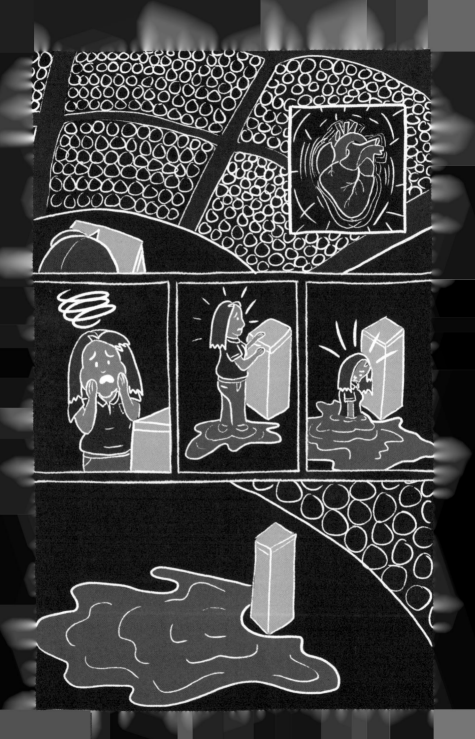

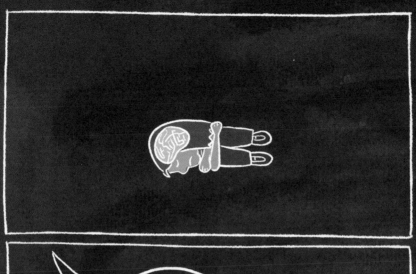

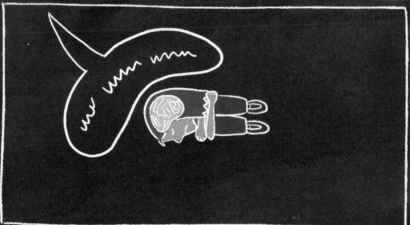

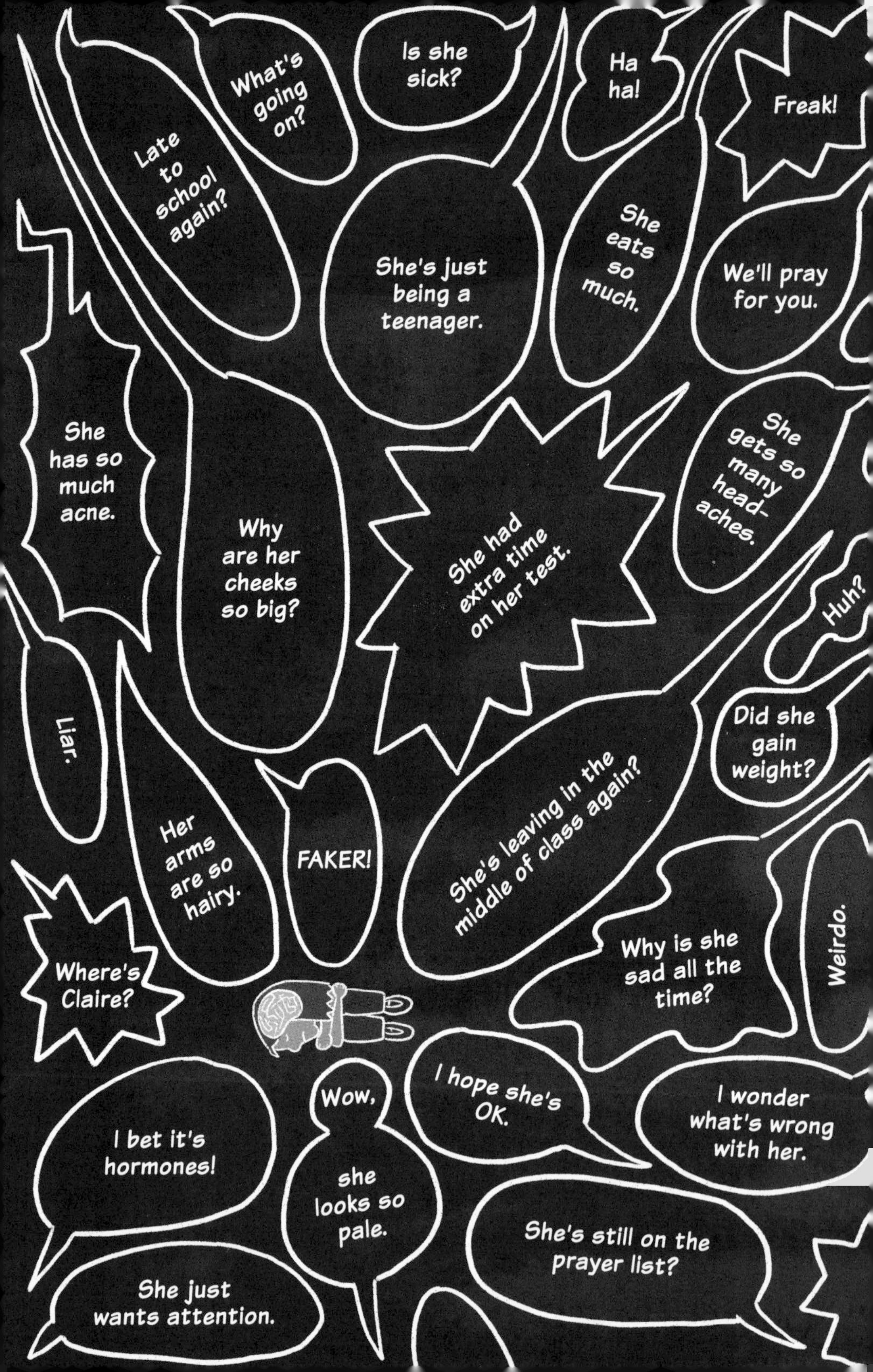
Late to school again?
What's going on?
Is she sick?
Ha ha!
Freak!
She's just being a teenager.
She eats so much.
We'll pray for you.
She has so much acne.
Why are her cheeks so big?
She had extra time on her test.
She gets so many head-aches.
Huh?
Liar.
Did she gain weight?
Her arms are so hairy.
FAKER!
She's leaving in the middle of class again?
Weirdo.
Why is she sad all the time?
Where's Claire?
I hope she's OK.
I wonder what's wrong with her.
Wow,
she looks so pale.
I bet it's hormones!
She's still on the prayer list?
She just wants attention.

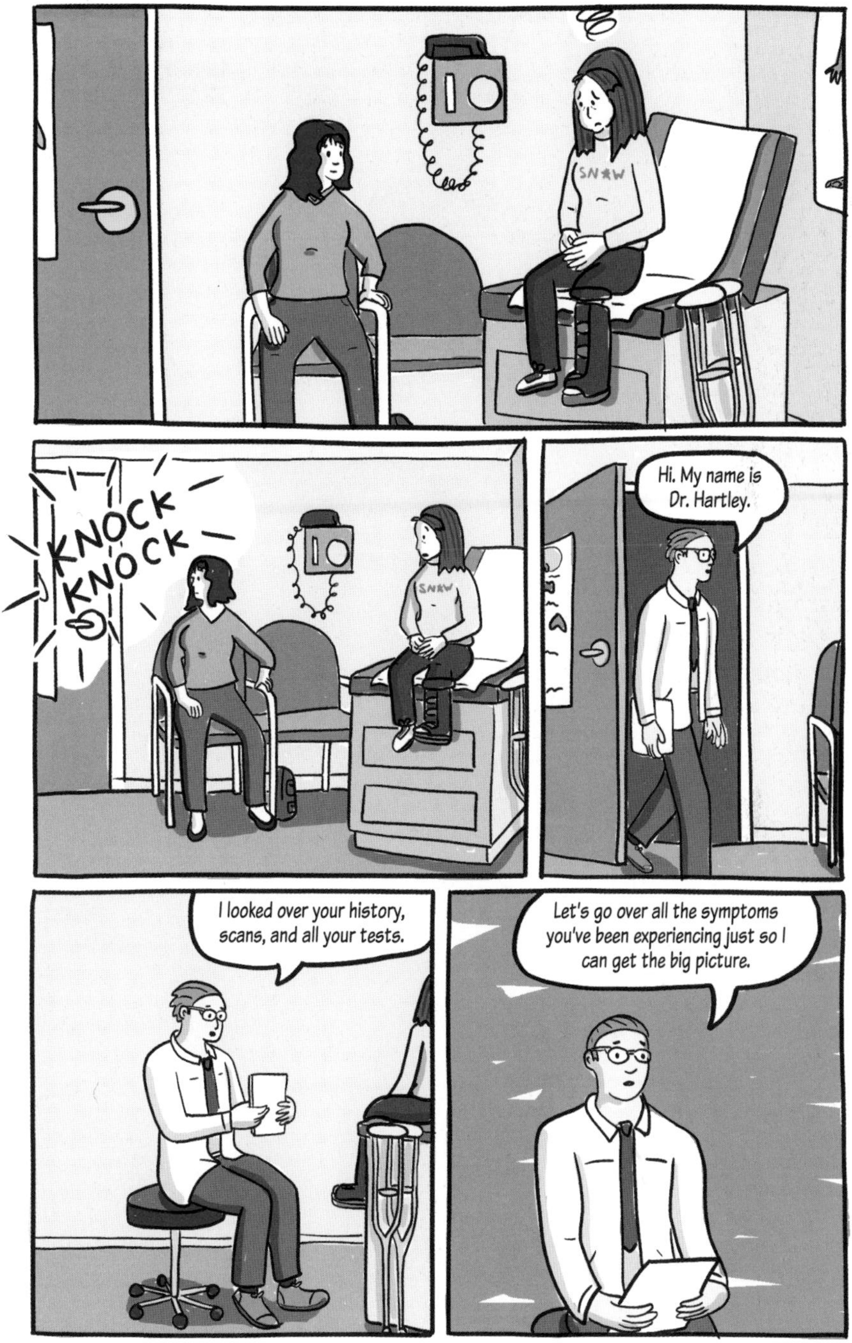
SNOW
KNOCK KNOCK
Hi. My name is Dr. Hartley.
I looked over your history, scans, and all your tests.
Let's go over all the symptoms you've been experiencing just so I can get the big picture.

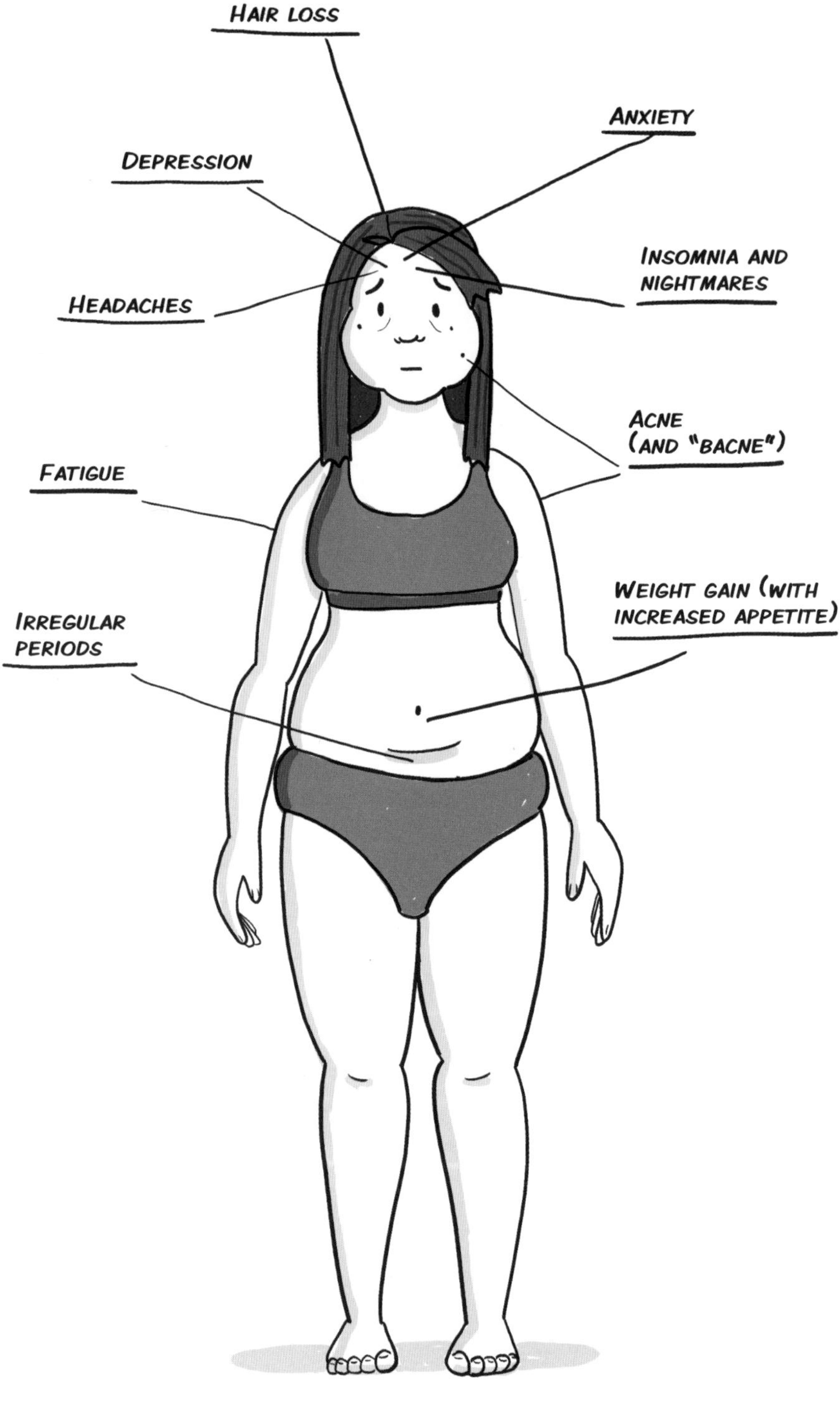
Hair loss
Anxiety
Depression
Insomnia and nightmares
Headaches
Acne (and "bacne")
Fatigue
Weight gain (with increased appetite)
Irregular periods

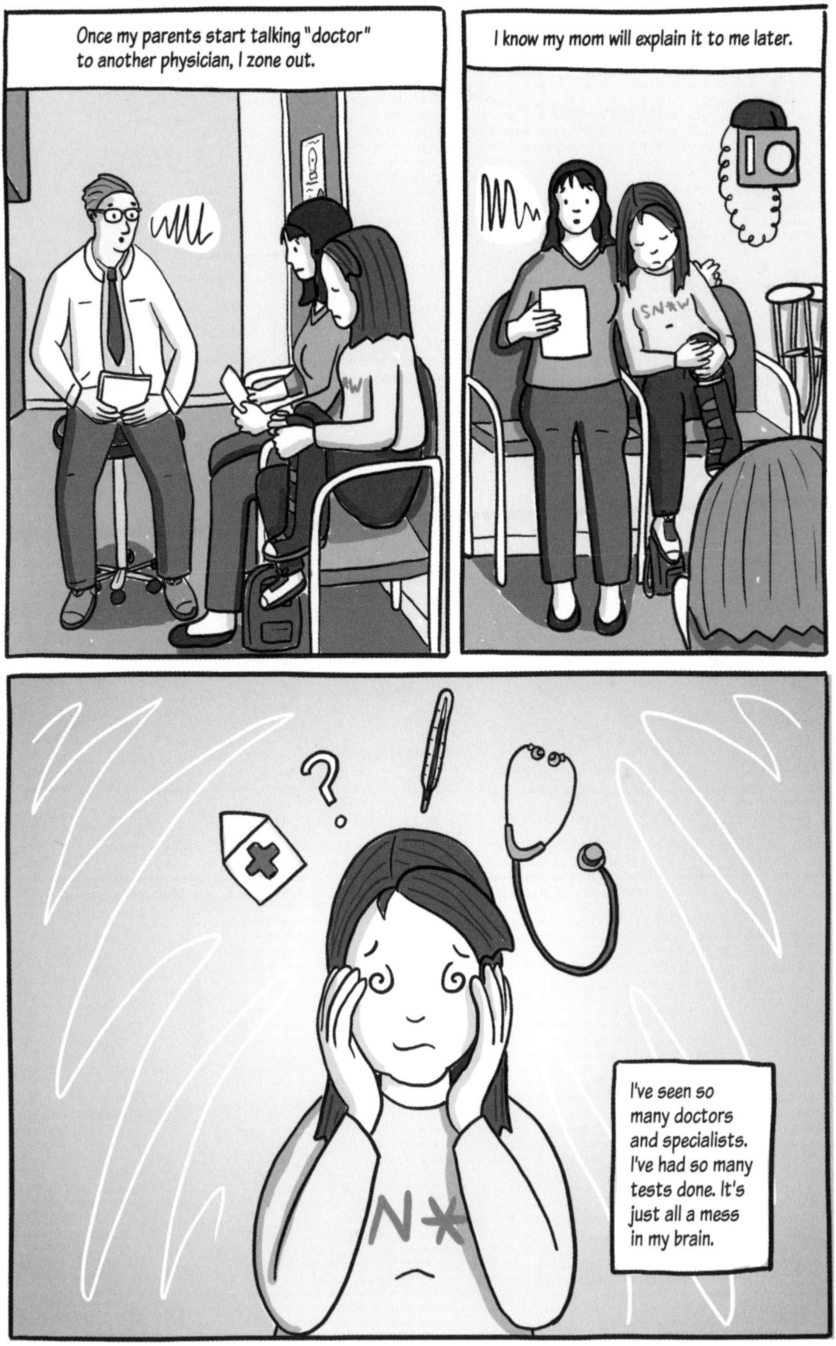
Once my parents start talking "doctor" to another physician, I zone out.
I know my mom will explain it to me later.
SN*W
I've seen so many doctors and specialists. I've had so many tests done. It's just all a mess in my brain.

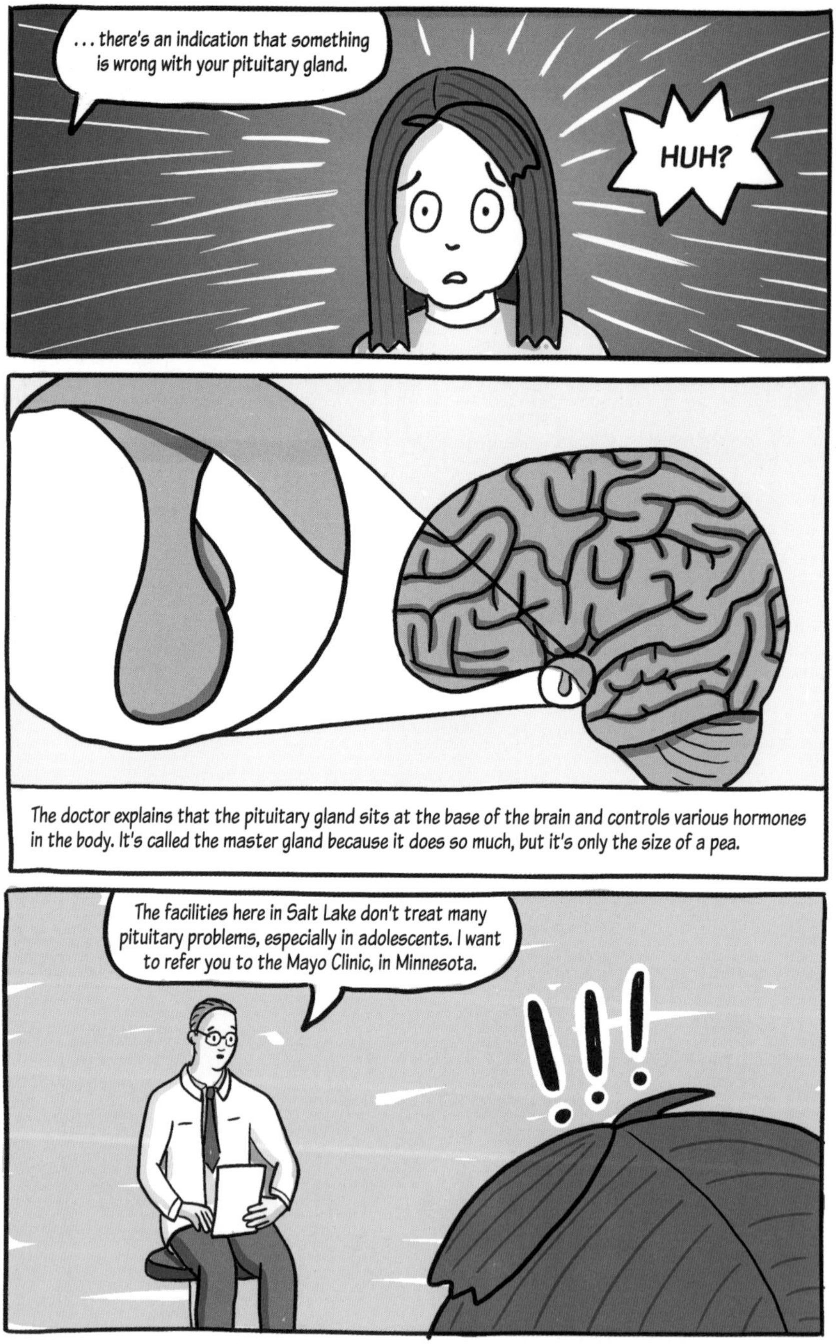

... there's an indication that something is wrong with your pituitary gland.
HUH?
The doctor explains that the pituitary gland sits at the base of the brain and controls various hormones in the body. It's called the master gland because it does so much, but it's only the size of a pea.
The facilities here in Salt Lake don't treat many pituitary problems, especially in adolescents. I want to refer you to the Mayo Clinic, in Minnesota.
!!!

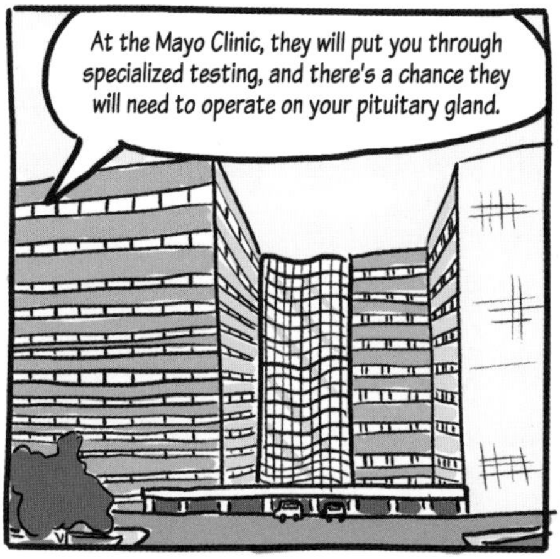
At the Mayo Clinic, they will put you through specialized testing, and there's a chance they will need to operate on your pituitary gland.

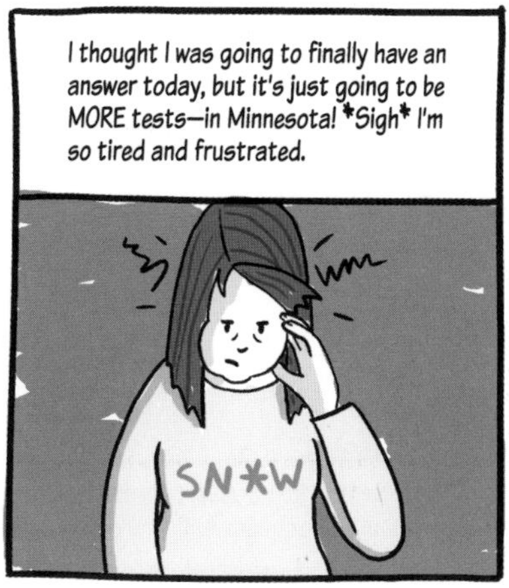
I thought I was going to finally have an answer today, but it's just going to be MORE tests—in Minnesota! *Sigh* I'm so tired and frustrated.
SN*W

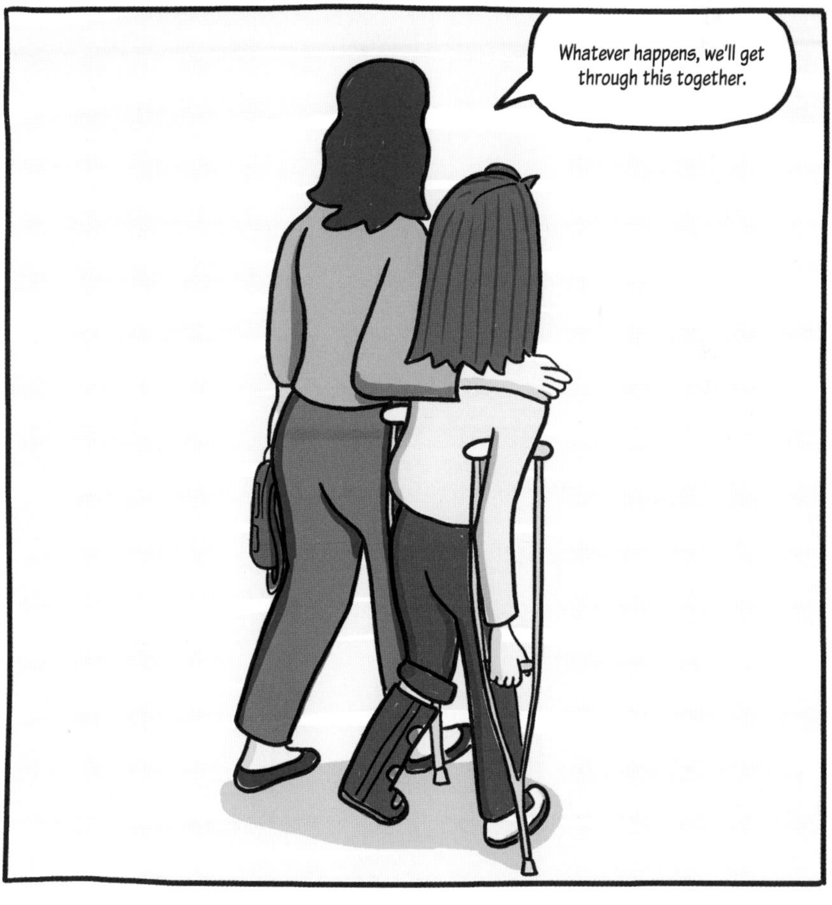
Whatever happens, we'll get through this together.

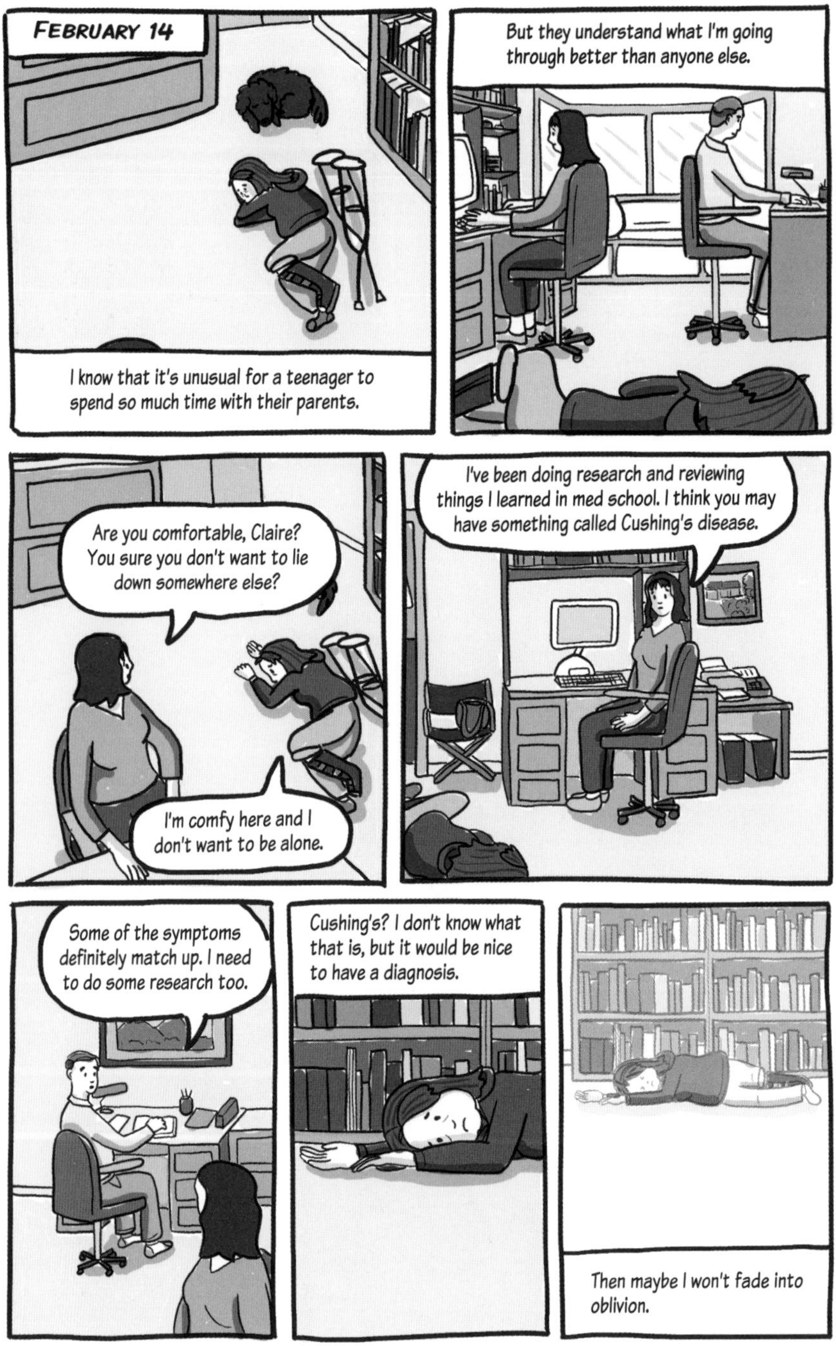
FEBRUARY 14
I know that it's unusual for a teenager to spend so much time with their parents.
But they understand what I'm going through better than anyone else.
Are you comfortable, Claire? You sure you don't want to lie down somewhere else?
I'm comfy here and I don't want to be alone.
I've been doing research and reviewing things I learned in med school. I think you may have something called Cushing's disease.
Some of the symptoms definitely match up. I need to do some research too.
Cushing's? I don't know what that is, but it would be nice to have a diagnosis.
Then maybe I won't fade into oblivion.

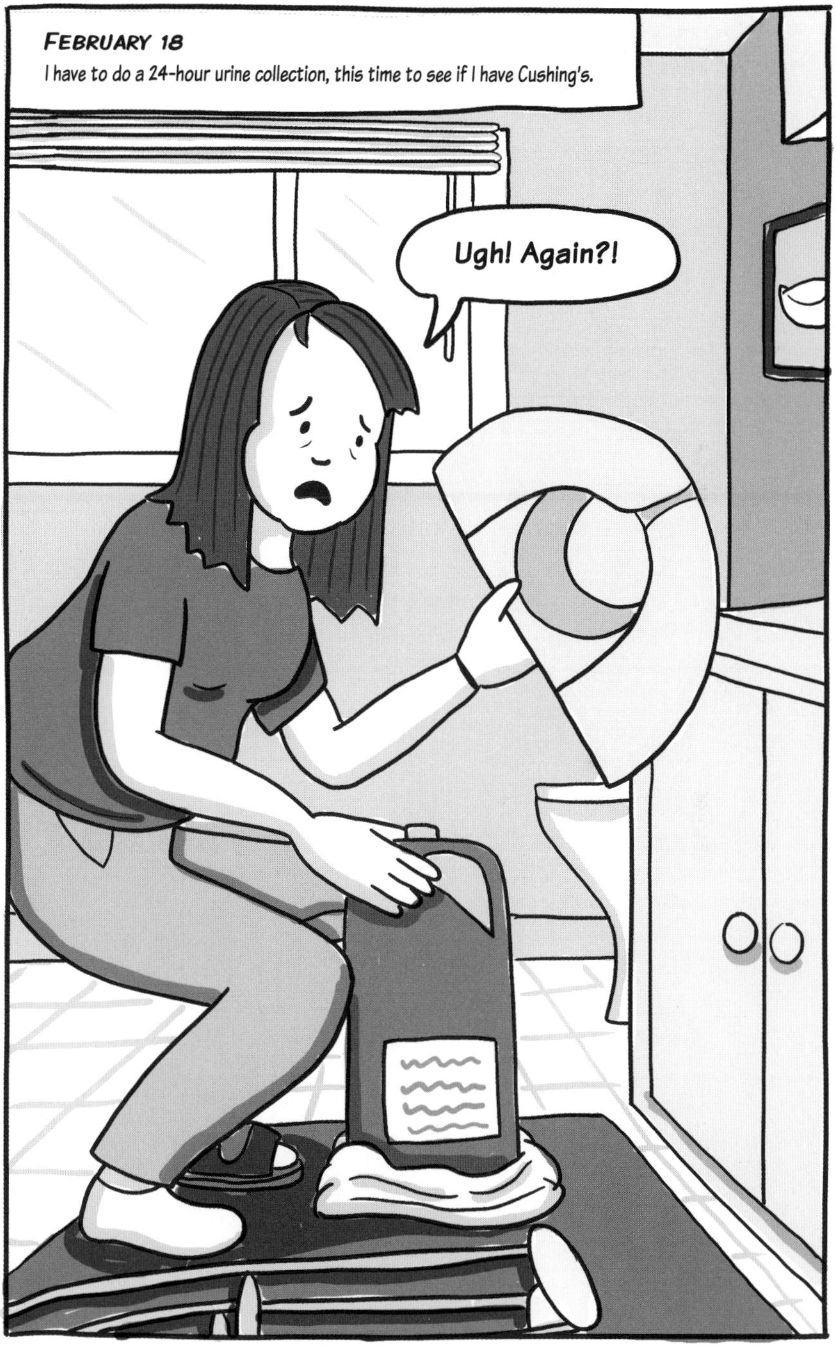
FEBRUARY 18
I have to do a 24-hour urine collection, this time to see if I have Cushing's.
Ugh! Again?!

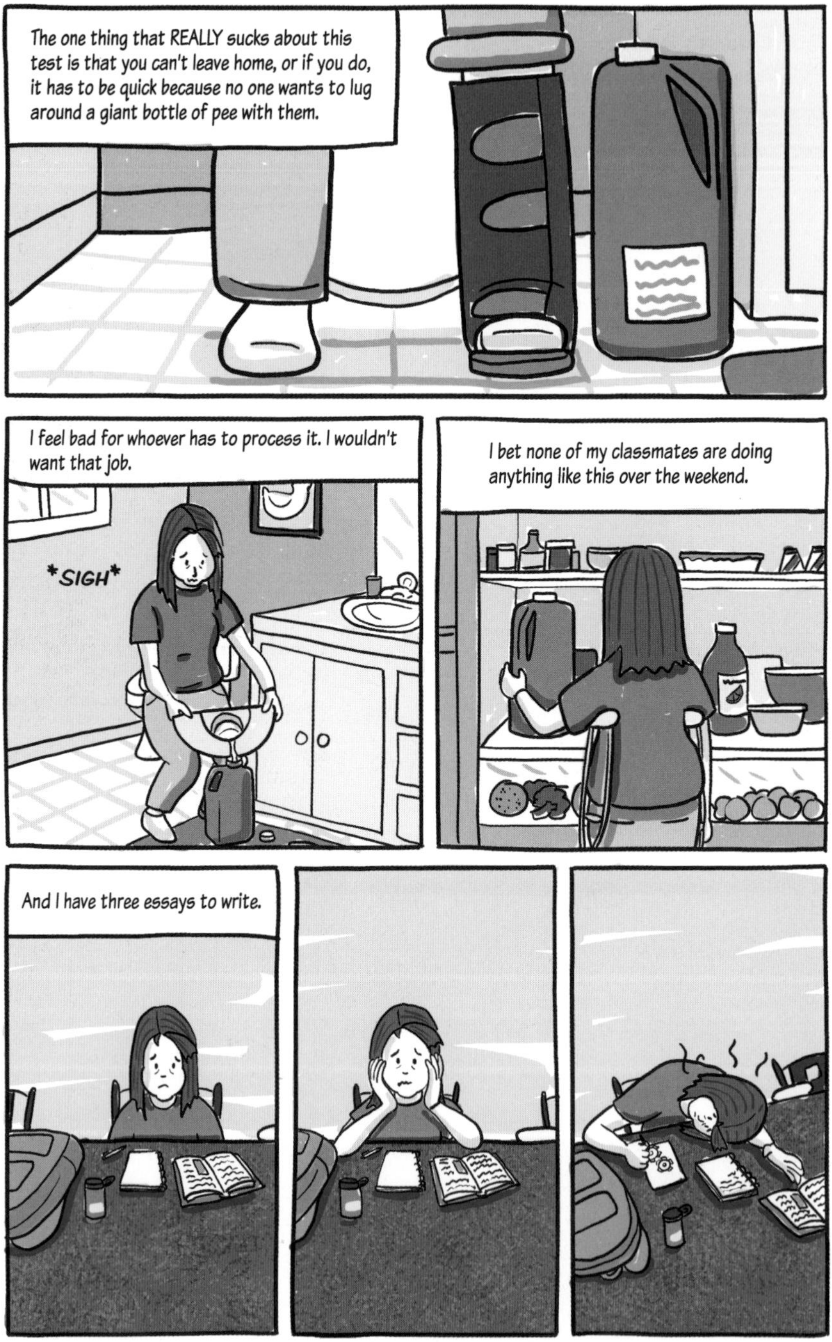
The one thing that REALLY sucks about this test is that you can't leave home, or if you do, it has to be quick because no one wants to lug around a giant bottle of pee with them.
I feel bad for whoever has to process it. I wouldn't want that job.
SIGH
I bet none of my classmates are doing anything like this over the weekend.
And I have three essays to write.

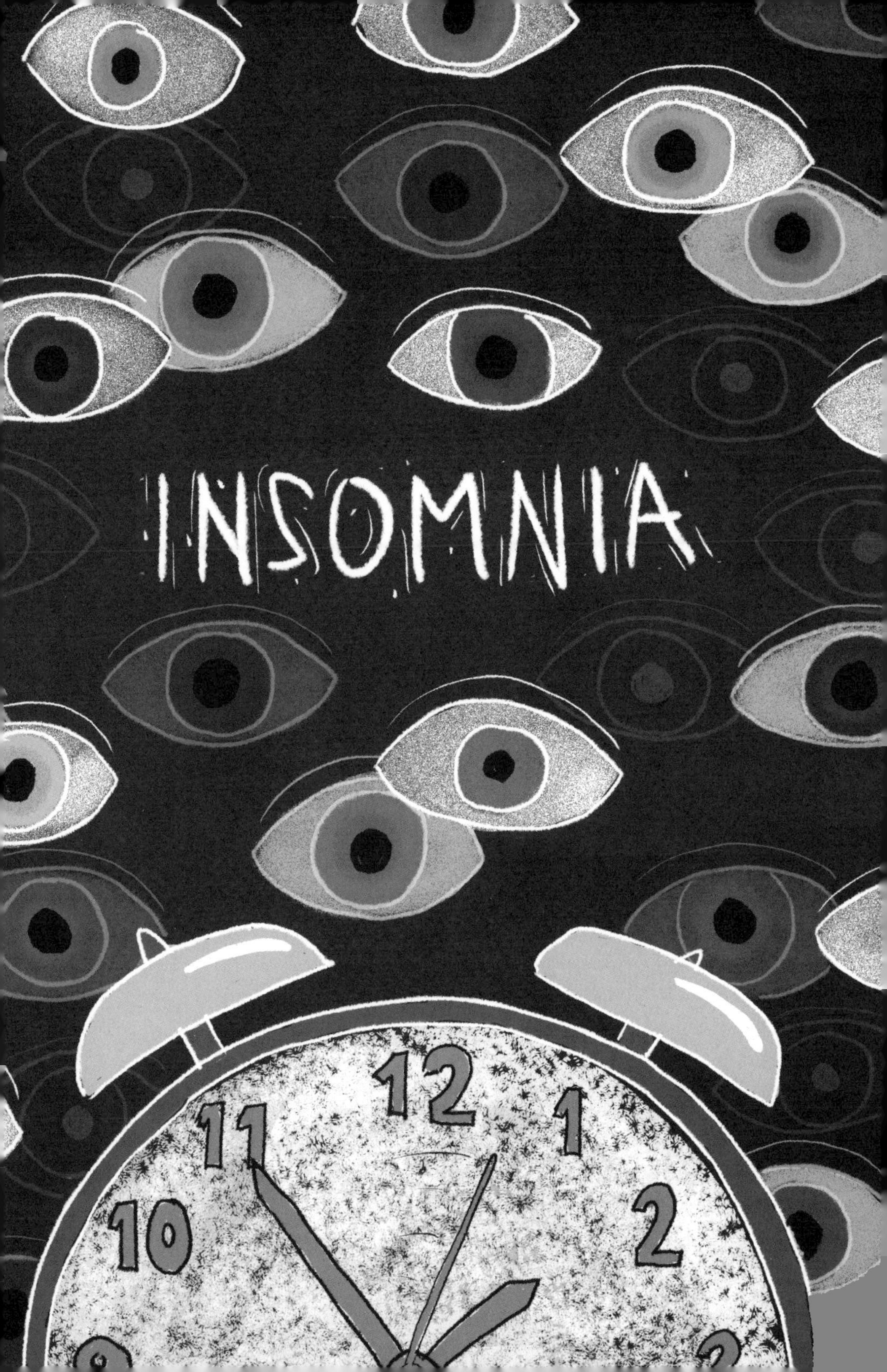
INSOMNIA
12
11
1
10
2

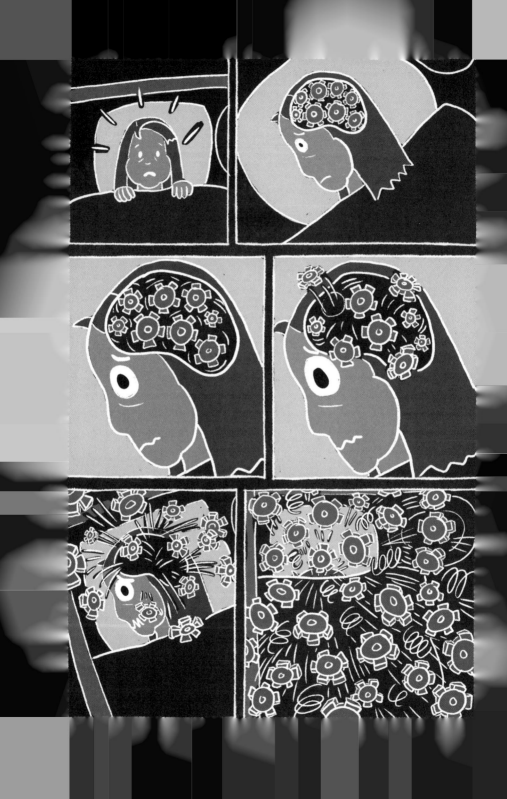

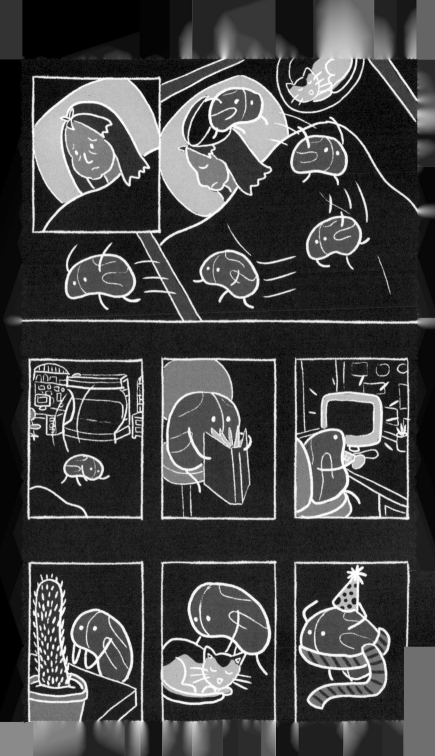

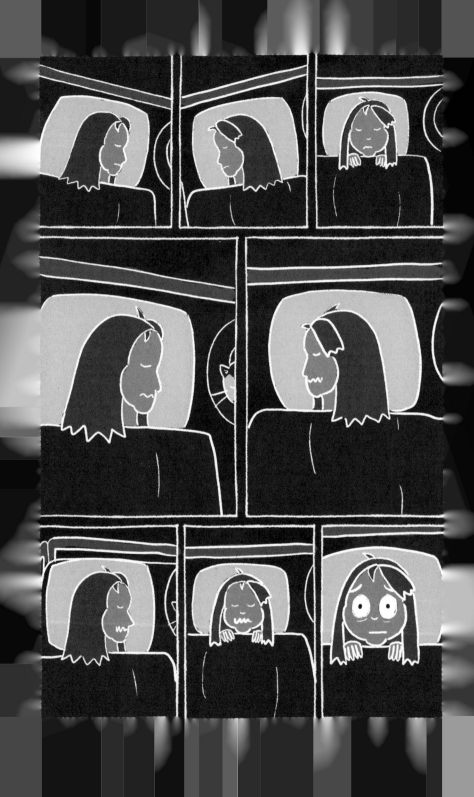

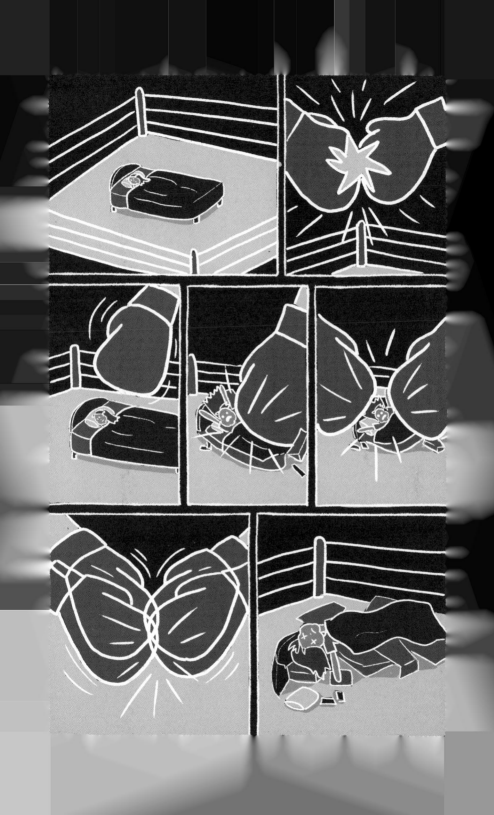

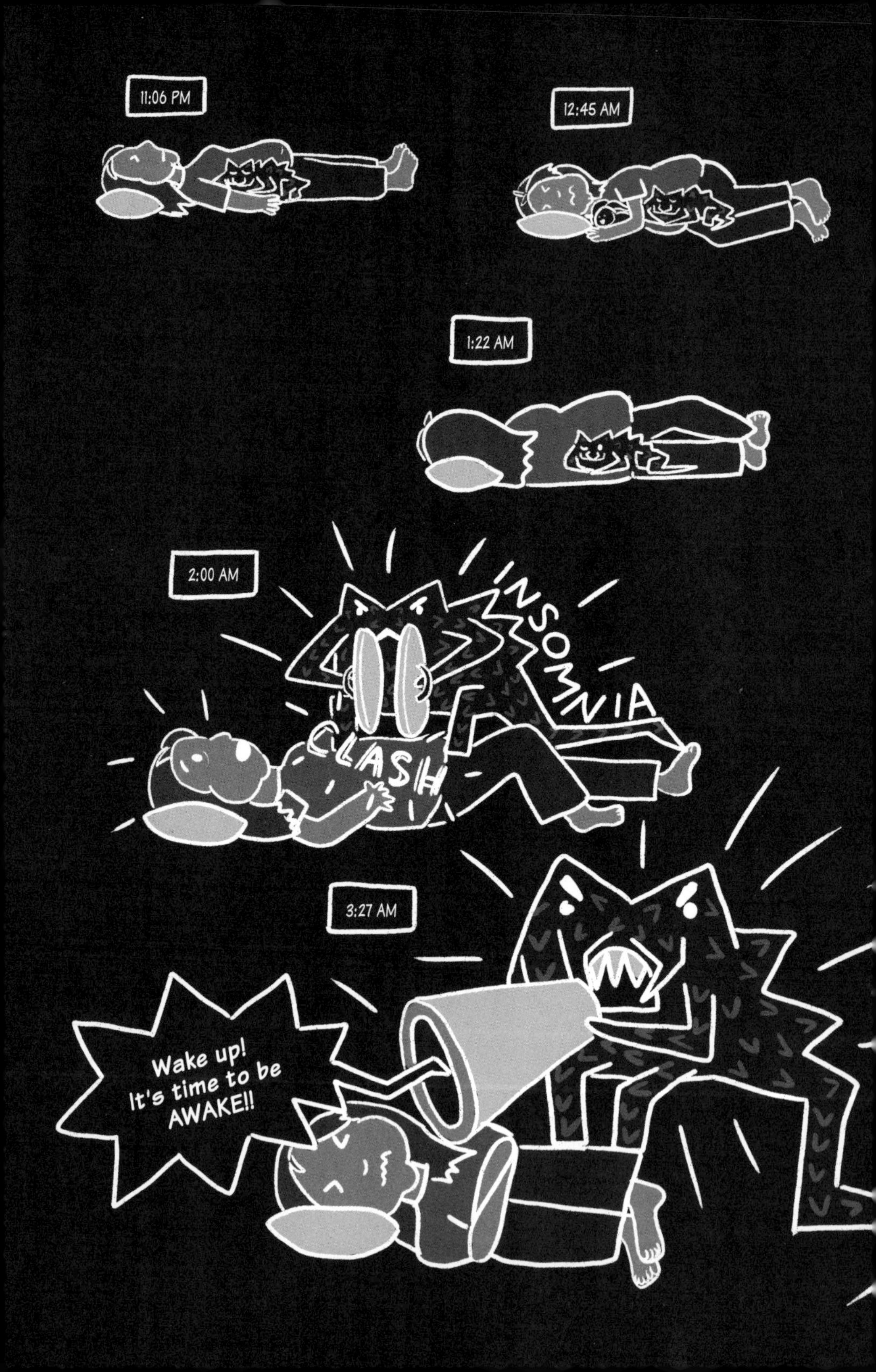
11:06 PM
12:45 AM
1:22 AM
2:00 AM
INSOMNIA
CLASH
3:27 AM
Wake up!
It's time to be
AWAKE!!

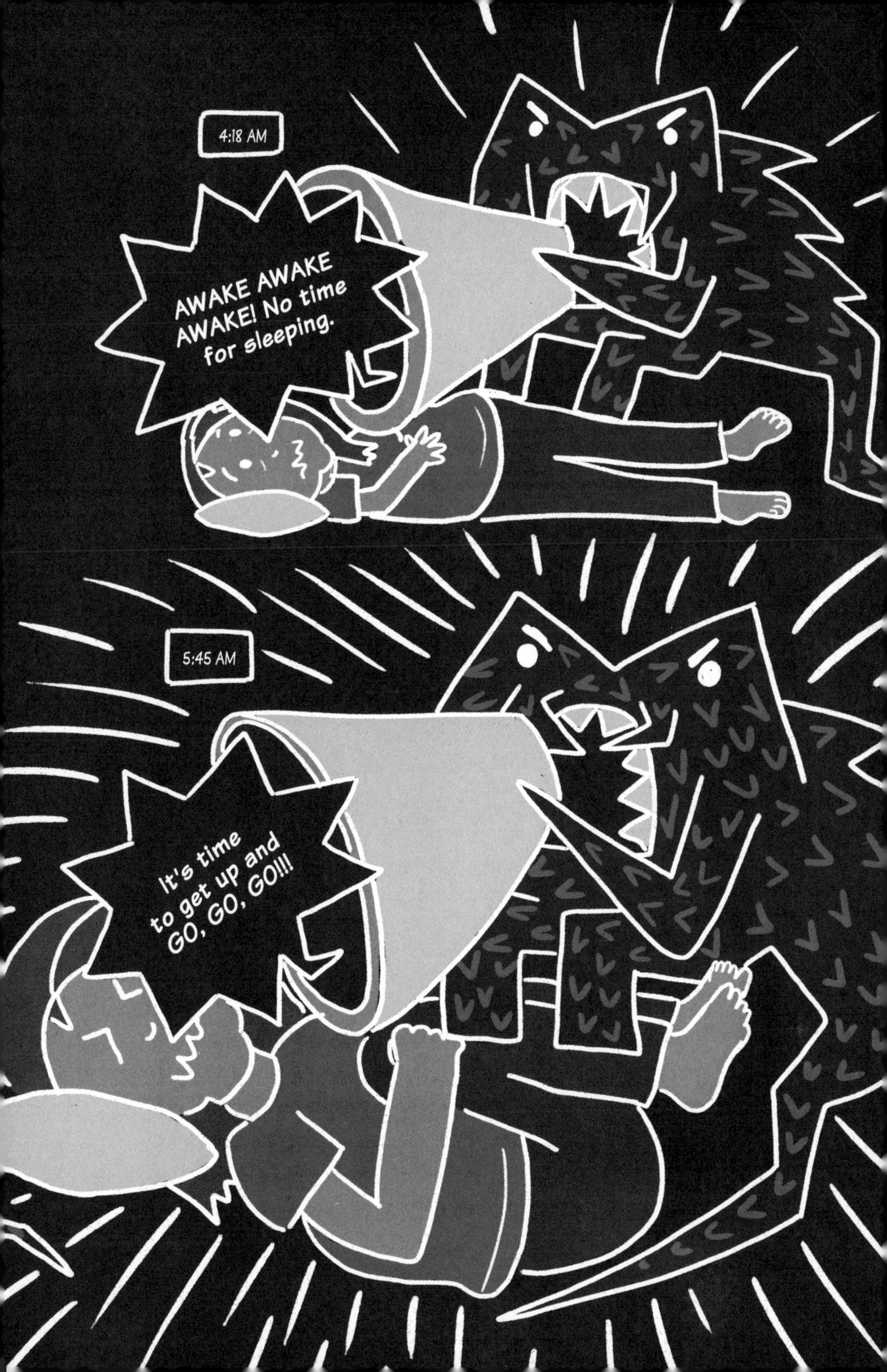
4:18 AM
AWAKE AWAKE AWAKE! No time for sleeping.
5:45 AM
It's time to get up and GO, GO, GO!!!

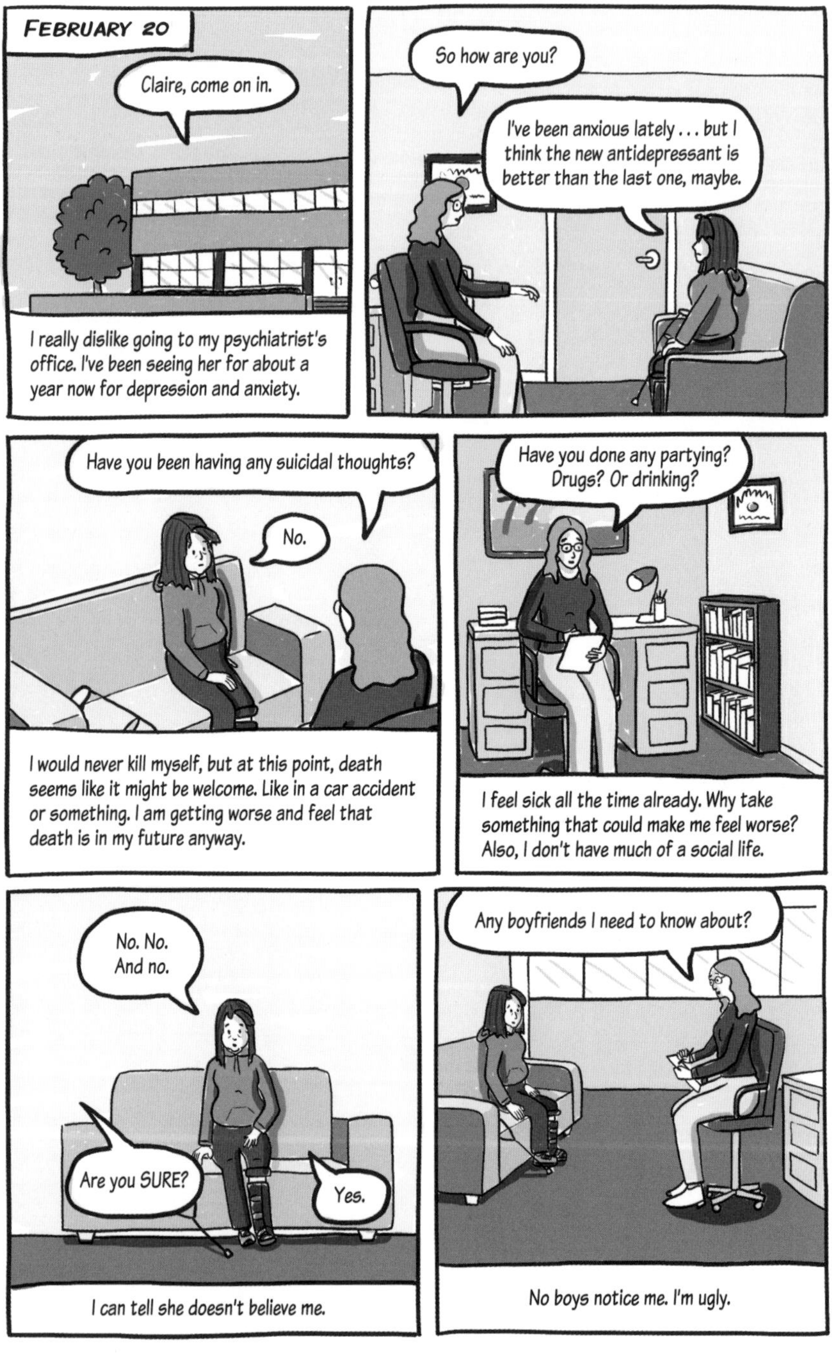
FEBRUARY 20
Claire, come on in.
I really dislike going to my psychiatrist's office. I've been seeing her for about a year now for depression and anxiety.
So how are you?
I've been anxious lately . . . but I think the new antidepressant is better than the last one, maybe.
Have you been having any suicidal thoughts?
No.
I would never kill myself, but at this point, death seems like it might be welcome. Like in a car accident or something. I am getting worse and feel that death is in my future anyway.
Have you done any partying? Drugs? Or drinking?
I feel sick all the time already. Why take something that could make me feel worse? Also, I don't have much of a social life.
No. No. And no.
Are you SURE?
Yes.
I can tell she doesn't believe me.
Any boyfriends I need to know about?
No boys notice me. I'm ugly.

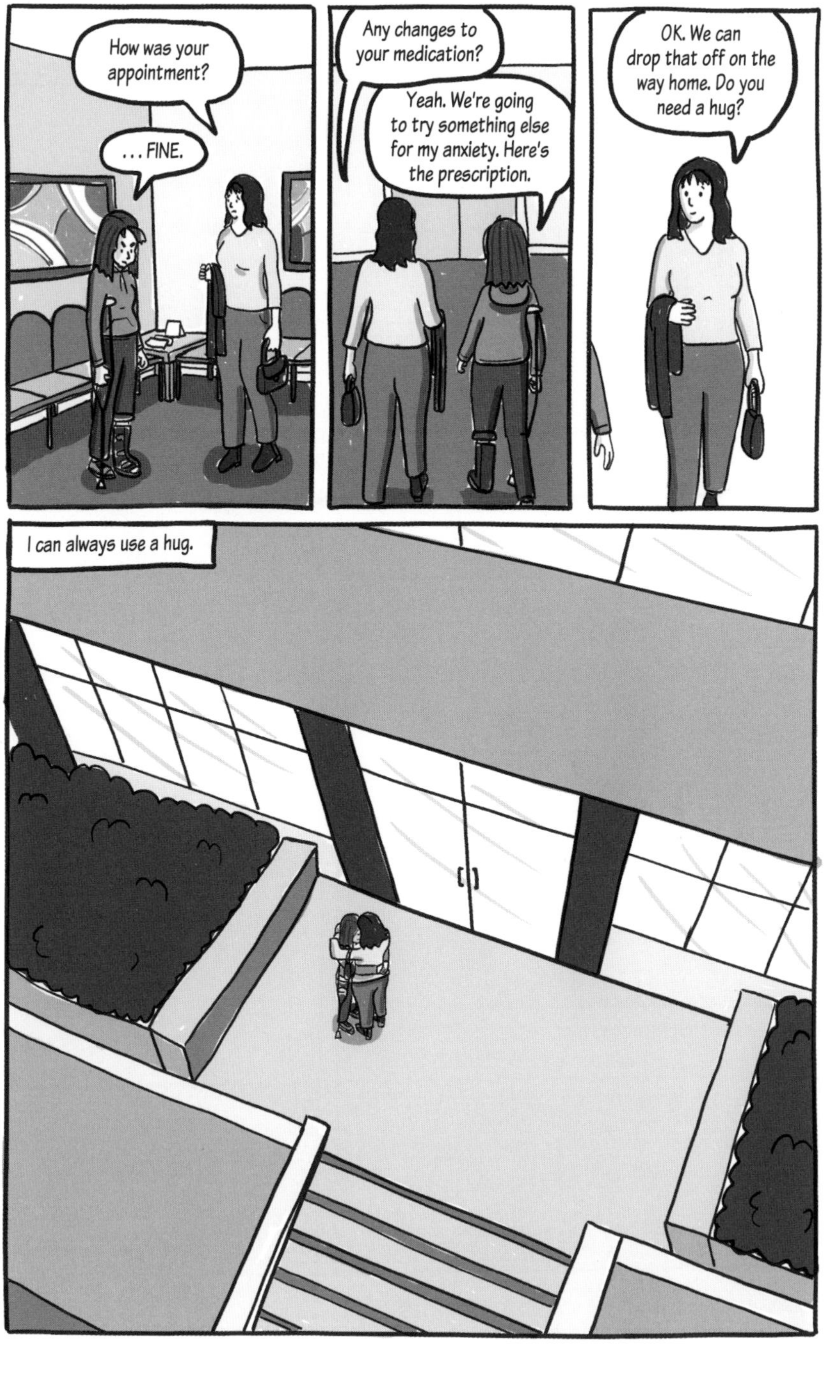
How was your appointment?
. . . FINE.
Any changes to your medication?
Yeah. We're going to try something else for my anxiety. Here's the prescription.
OK. We can drop that off on the way home. Do you need a hug?
I can always use a hug.

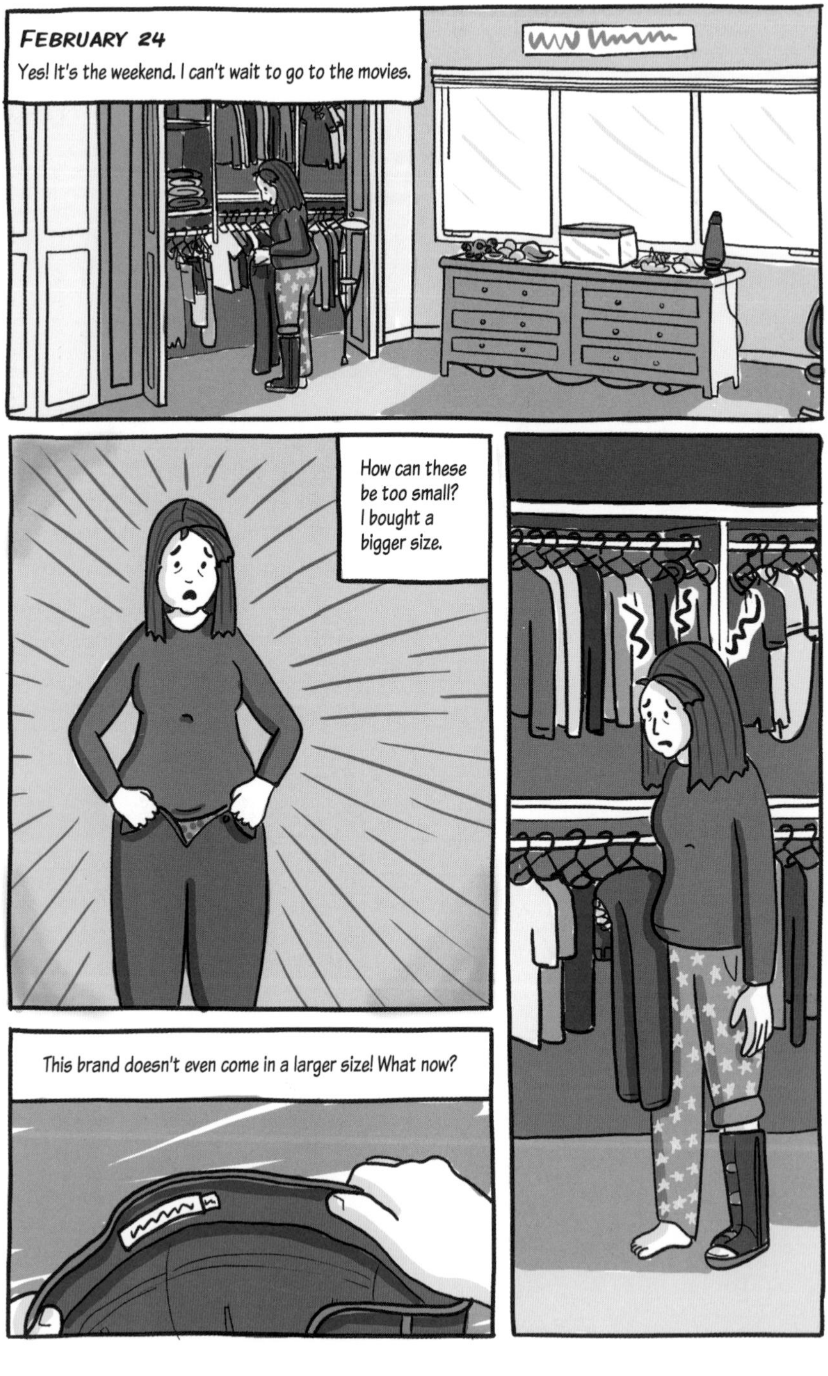
FEBRUARY 24
Yes! It's the weekend. I can't wait to go to the movies.
How can these be too small? I bought a bigger size.
This brand doesn't even come in a larger size! What now?

I despise my body.

It's unrecognizable.

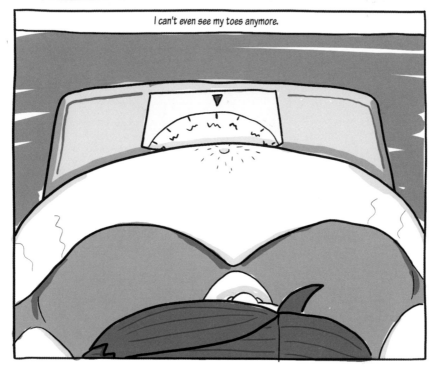

I can't even see my toes anymore.

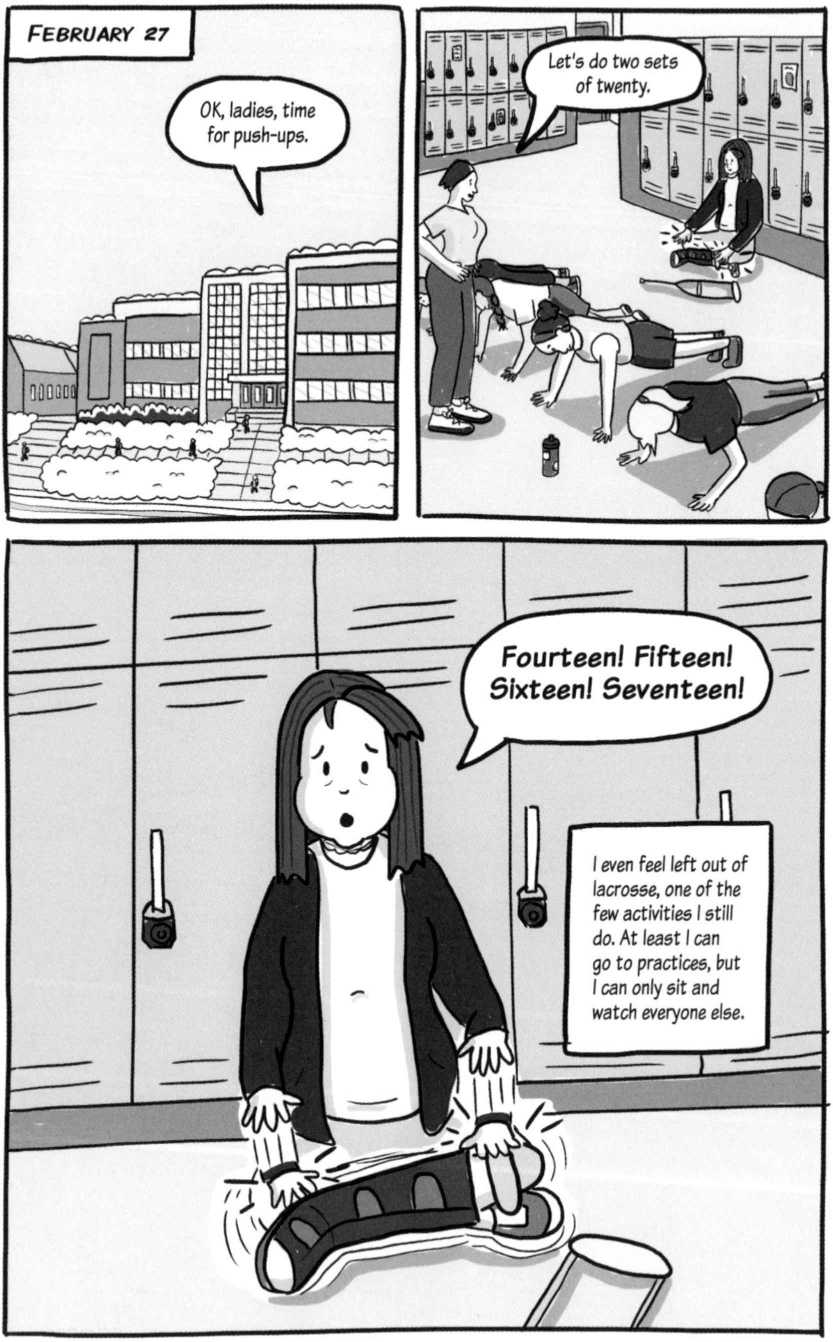
FEBRUARY 27
OK, ladies, time for push-ups.
Let's do two sets of twenty.
Fourteen! Fifteen! Sixteen! Seventeen!
I even feel left out of lacrosse, one of the few activities I still do. At least I can go to practices, but I can only sit and watch everyone else.

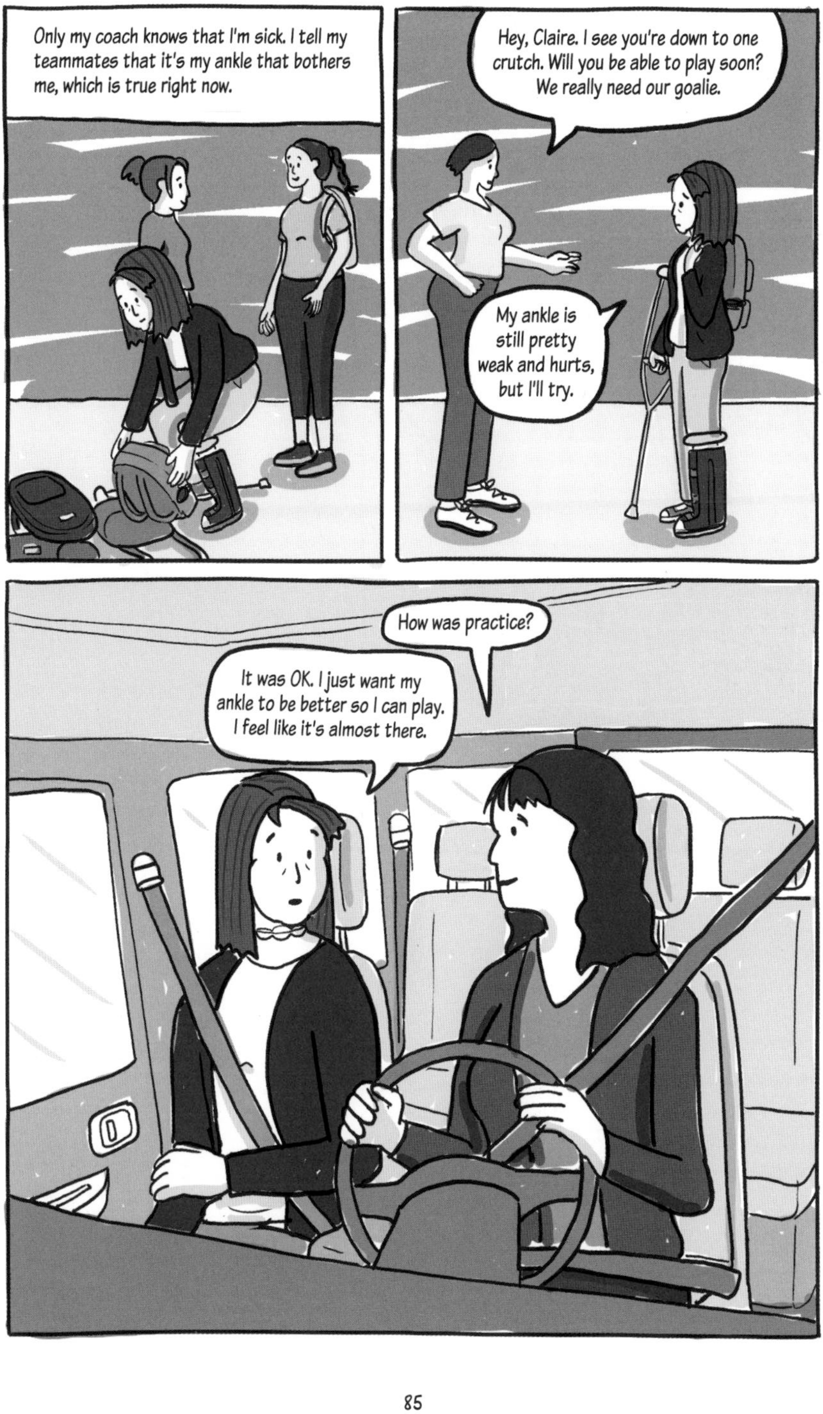
Only my coach knows that I'm sick. I tell my teammates that it's my ankle that bothers me, which is true right now.
Hey, Claire. I see you're down to one crutch. Will you be able to play soon? We really need our goalie.
My ankle is still pretty weak and hurts, but I'll try.
How was practice?
It was OK. I just want my ankle to be better so I can play. I feel like it's almost there.

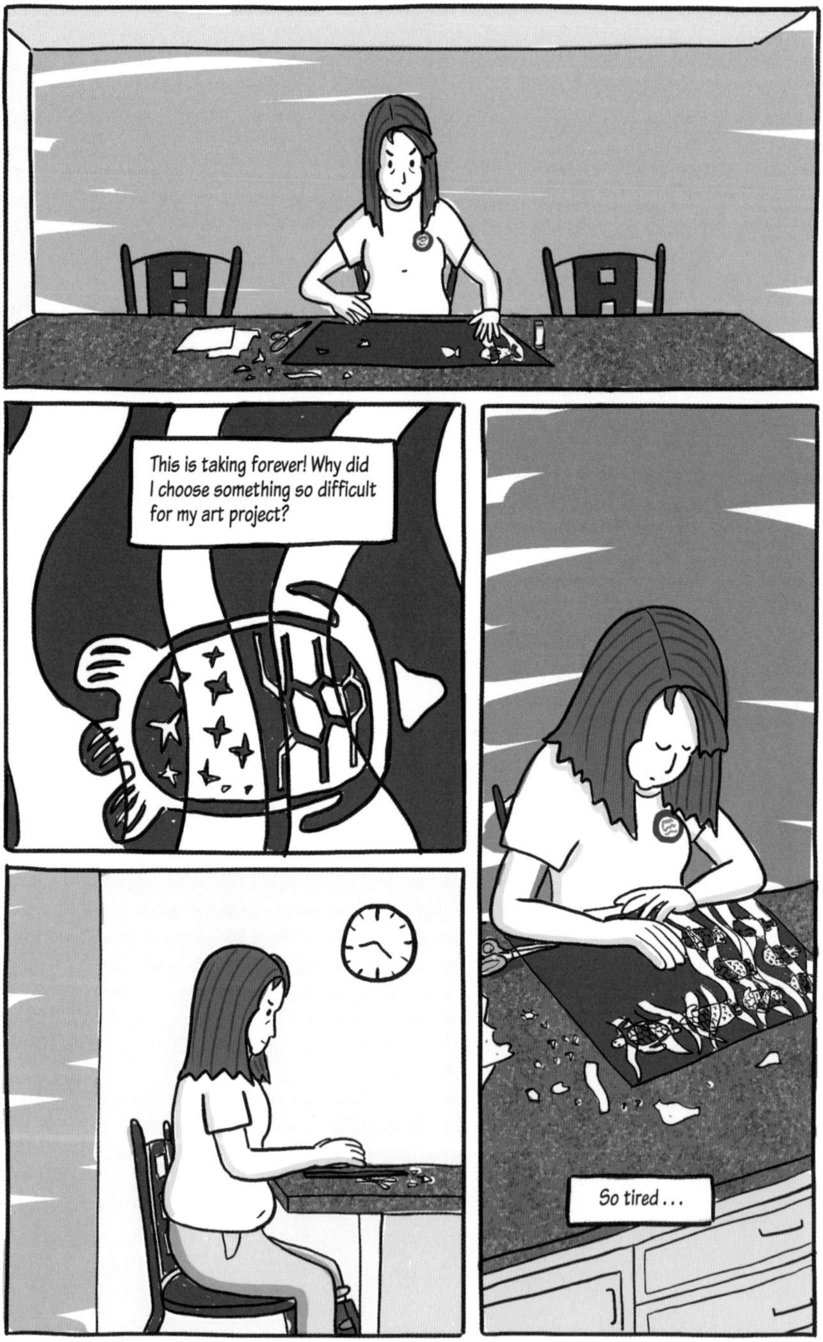
This is taking forever! Why did I choose something so difficult for my art project?
So tired . . .

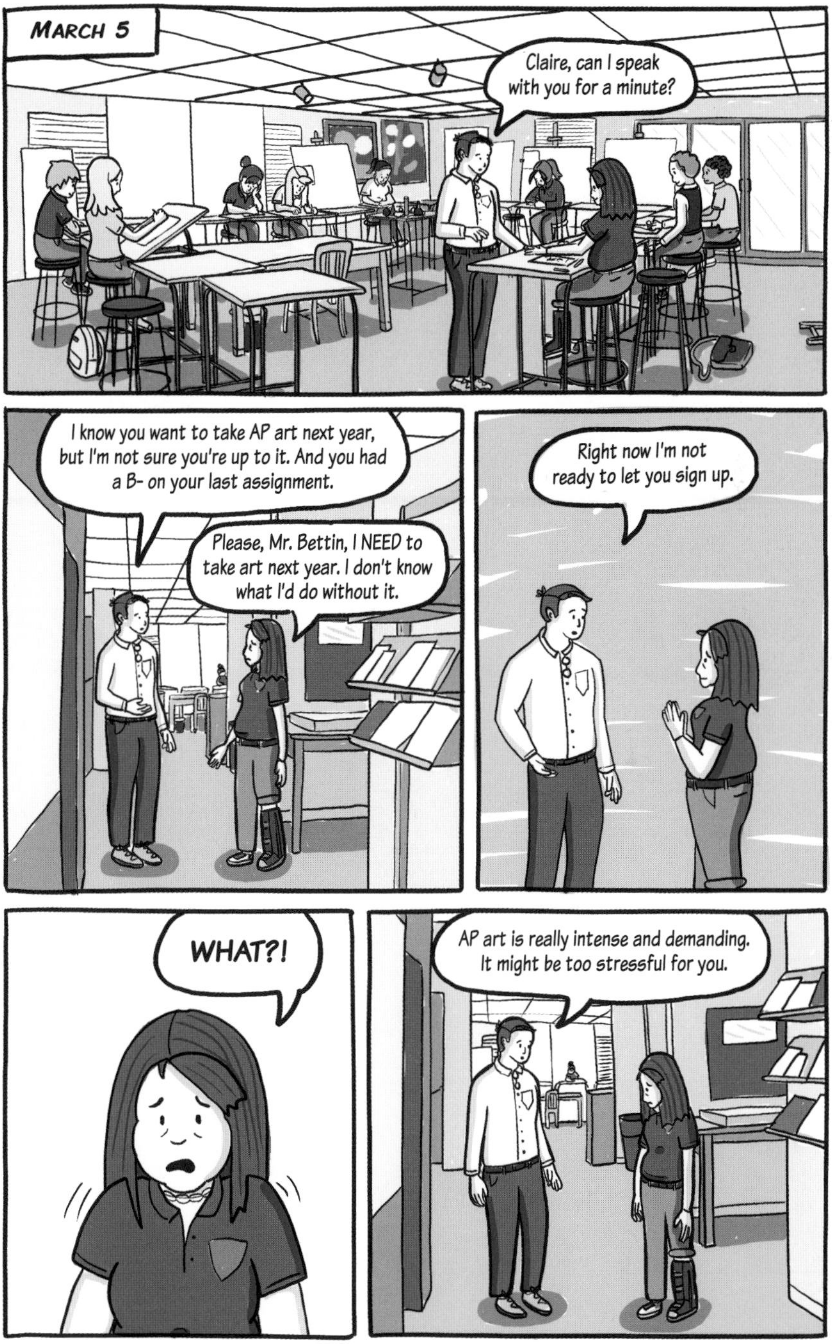
March 5
Claire, can I speak with you for a minute?
I know you want to take AP art next year, but I'm not sure you're up to it. And you had a B- on your last assignment.
Please, Mr. Bettin, I NEED to take art next year. I don't know what I'd do without it.
Right now I'm not ready to let you sign up.
WHAT?!
AP art is really intense and demanding. It might be too stressful for you.

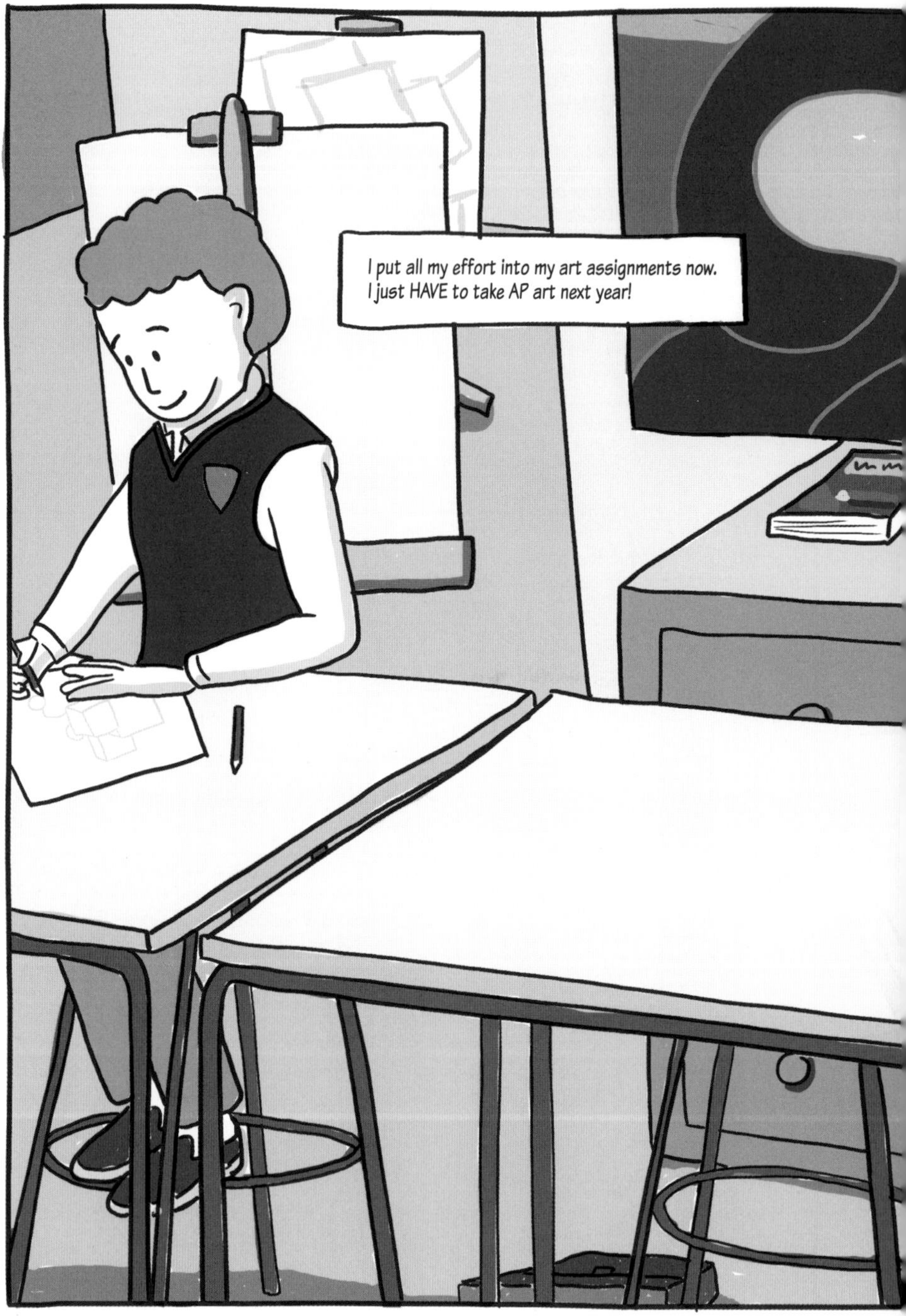
I put all my effort into my art assignments now. I just HAVE to take AP art next year!

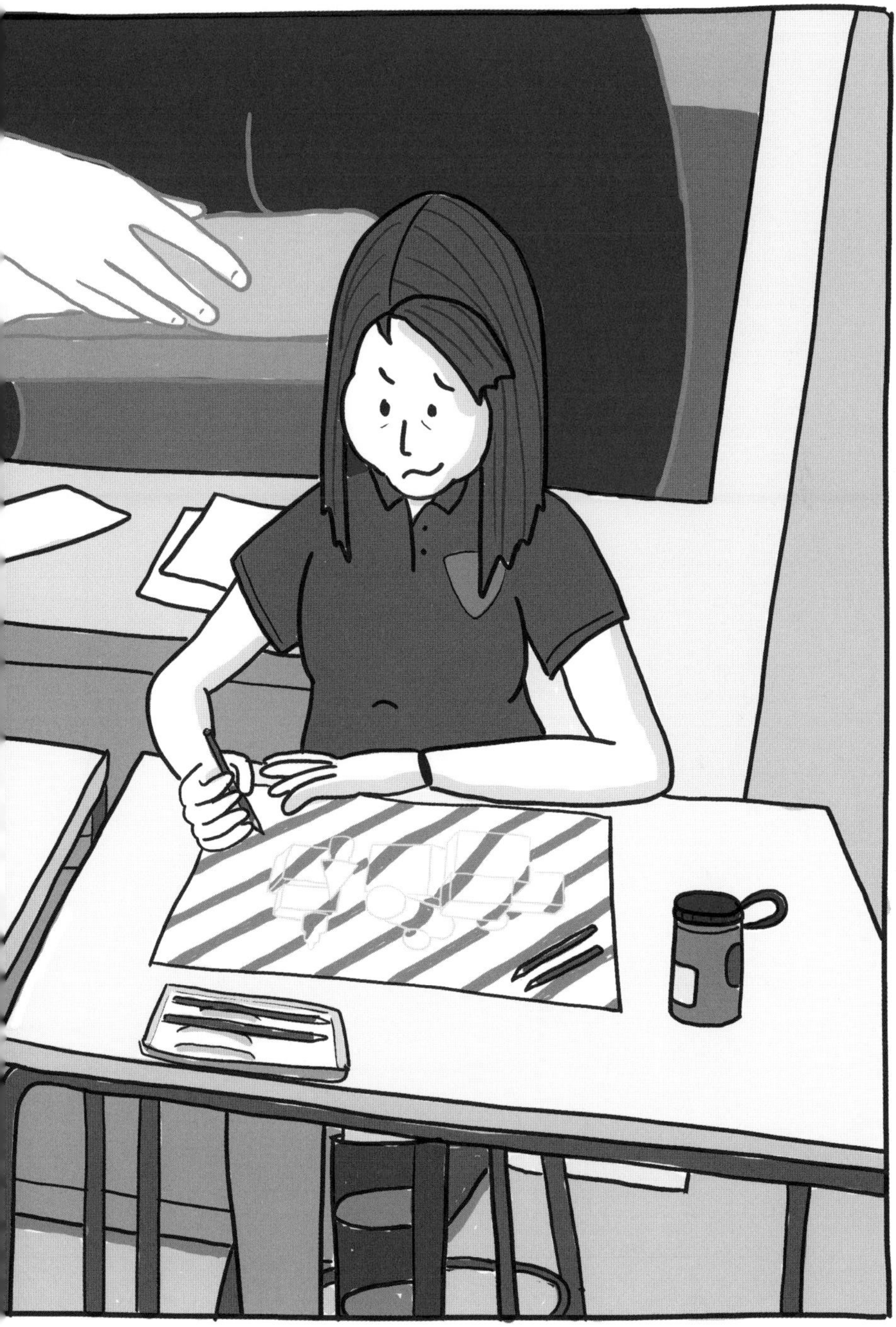

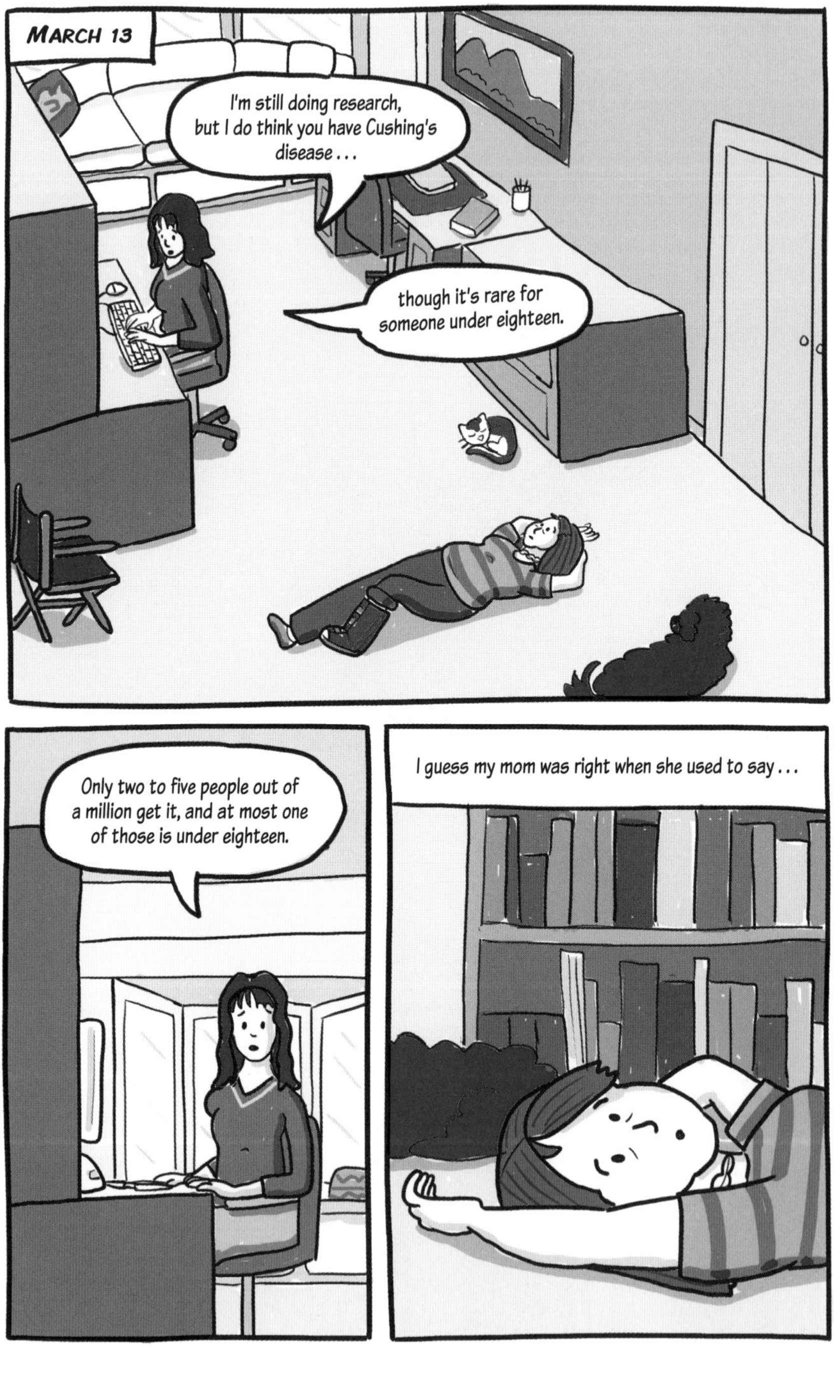
MARCH 13
I'm still doing research, but I do think you have Cushing's disease . . .
though it's rare for someone under eighteen.
Only two to five people out of a million get it, and at most one of those is under eighteen.
I guess my mom was right when she used to say . . .

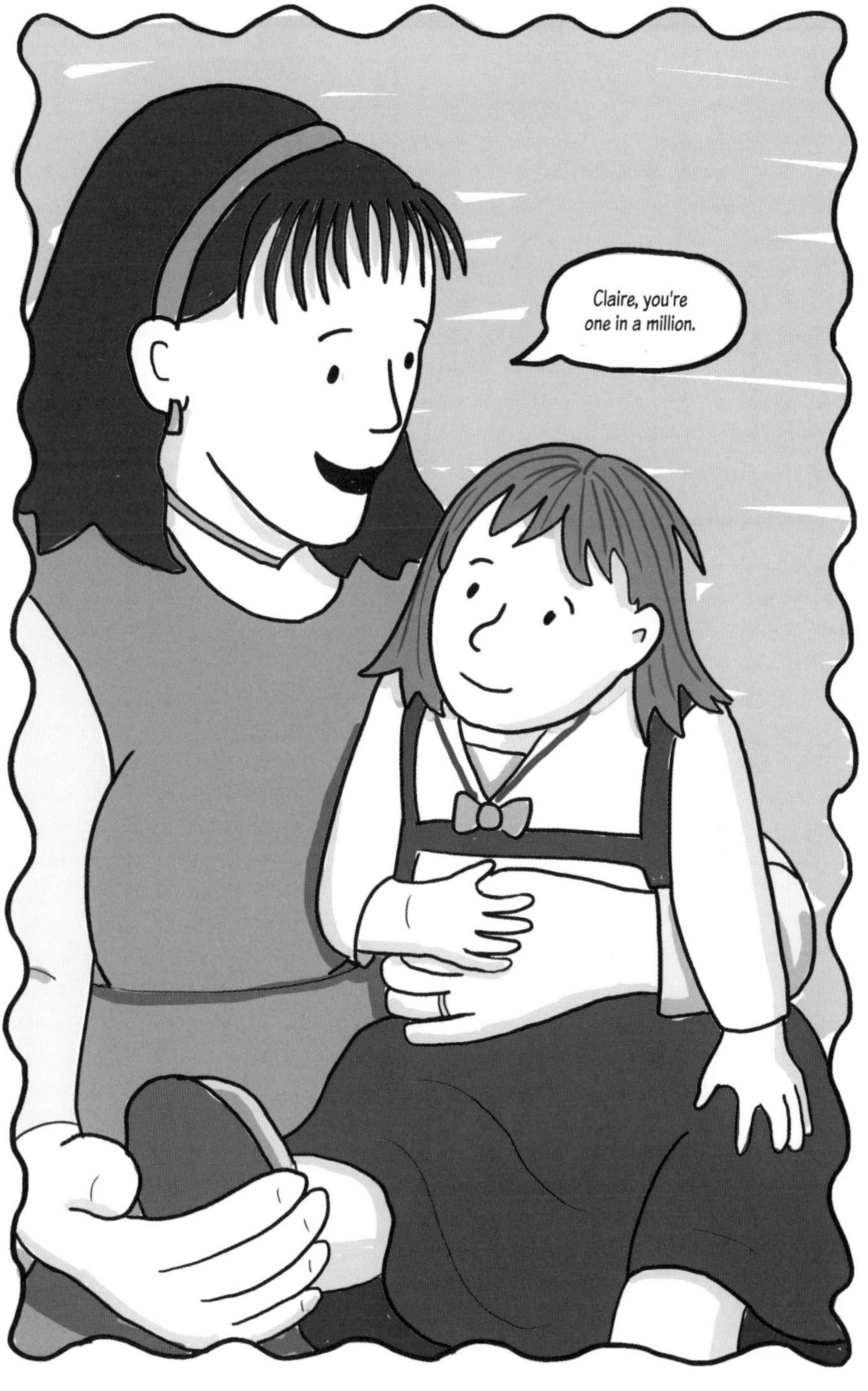
Claire, you're one in a million.

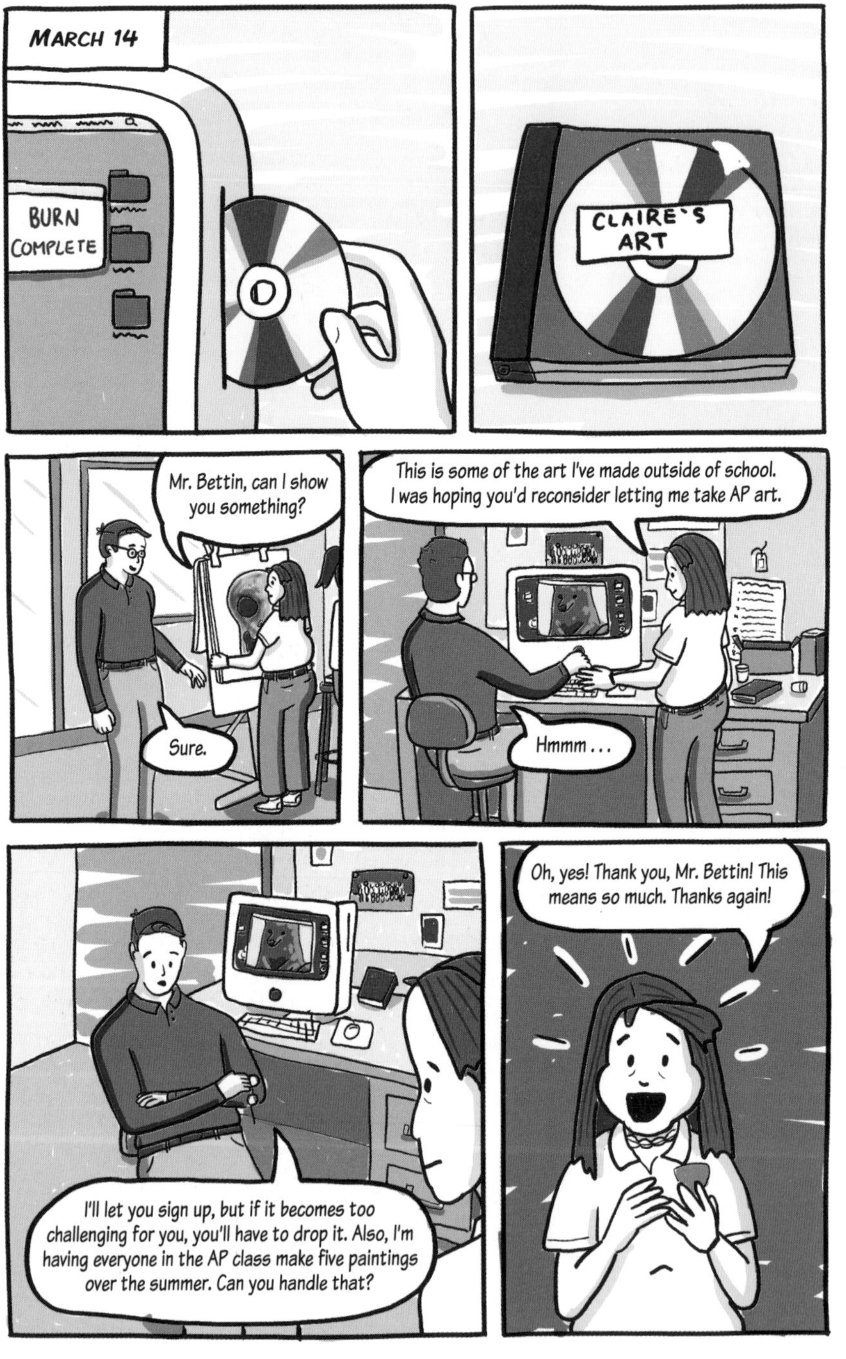
MARCH 14
BURN COMPLETE
CLAIRE'S ART
Mr. Bettin, can I show you something?
Sure.
This is some of the art I've made outside of school. I was hoping you'd reconsider letting me take AP art.
Hmmm . . .
I'll let you sign up, but if it becomes too challenging for you, you'll have to drop it. Also, I'm having everyone in the AP class make five paintings over the summer. Can you handle that?
Oh, yes! Thank you, Mr. Bettin! This means so much. Thanks again!

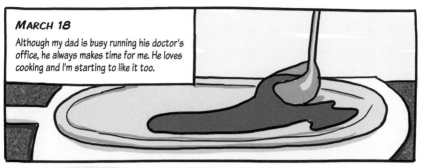

MARCH 18

Although my dad is busy running his doctor's office, he always makes time for me. He loves cooking and I'm starting to like it too.

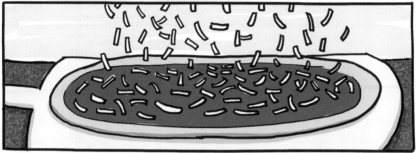

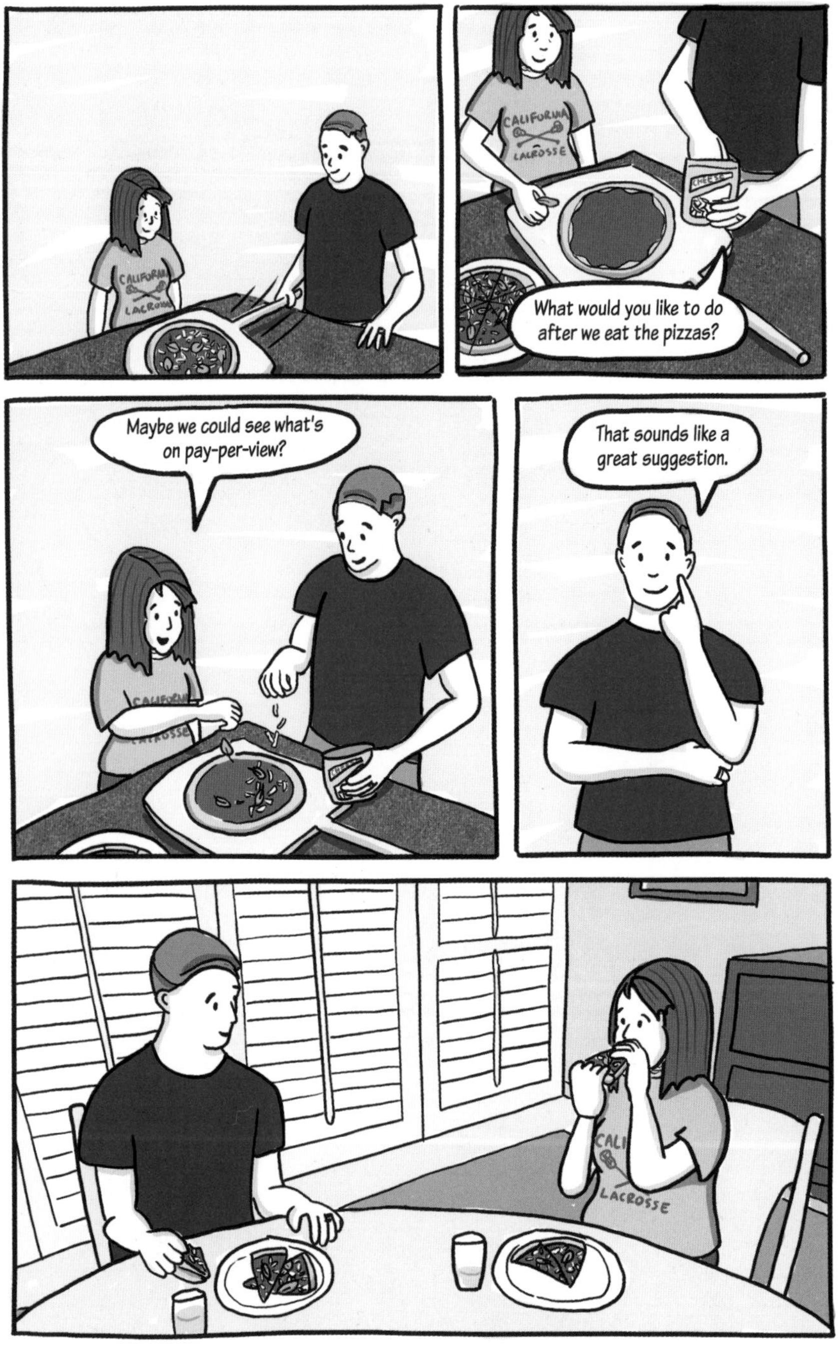

CALIFORNIA LACROSSE
CALIFORNIA LACROSSE
CHEESE
What would you like to do after we eat the pizzas?
Maybe we could see what's on pay-per-view?
That sounds like a great suggestion.
LACROSSE

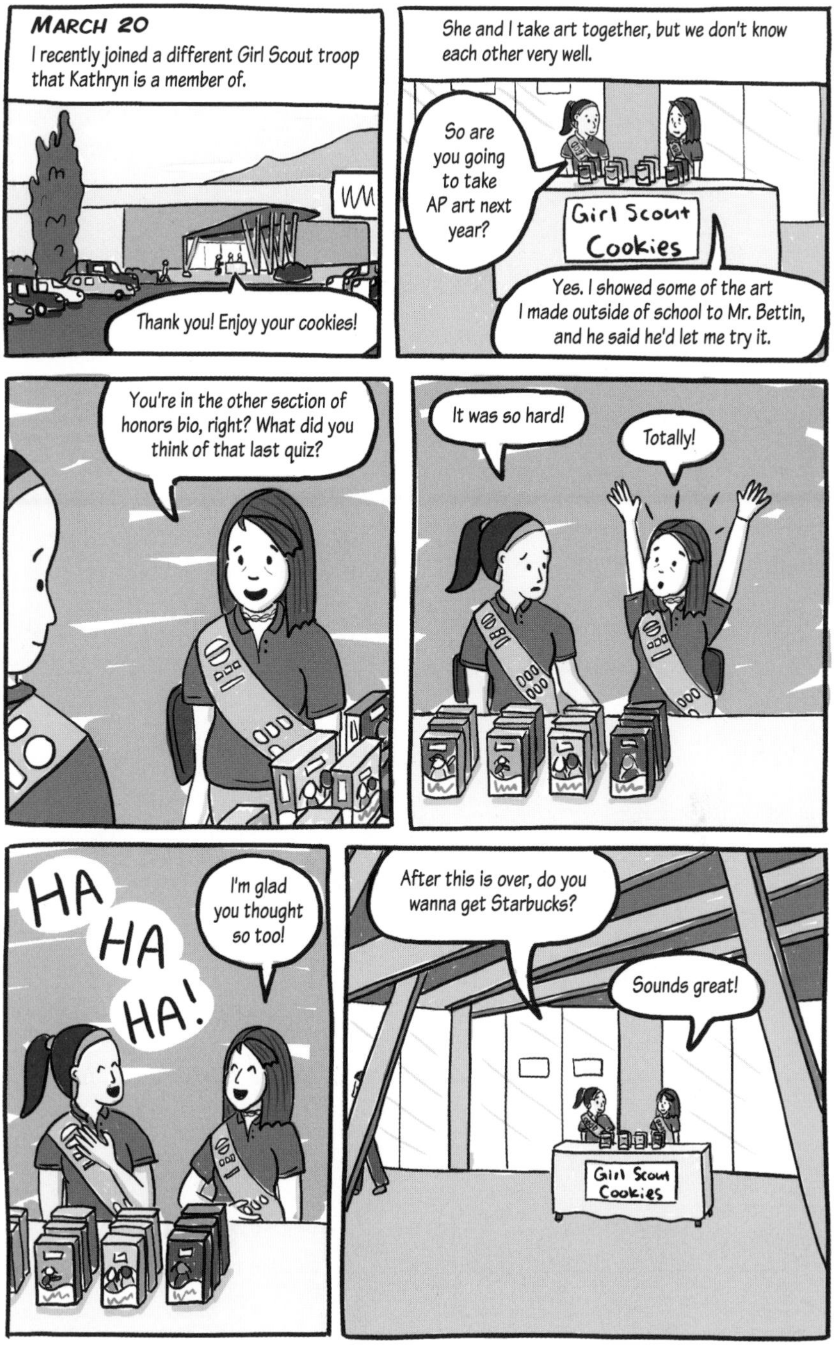
MARCH 20
I recently joined a different Girl Scout troop that Kathryn is a member of.
Thank you! Enjoy your cookies!
She and I take art together, but we don't know each other very well.
So are you going to take AP art next year?
Girl Scout Cookies
Yes. I showed some of the art I made outside of school to Mr. Bettin, and he said he'd let me try it.
You're in the other section of honors bio, right? What did you think of that last quiz?
It was so hard!
Totally!
HA HA HA!
I'm glad you thought so too!
After this is over, do you wanna get Starbucks?
Sounds great!
Girl Scout Cookies

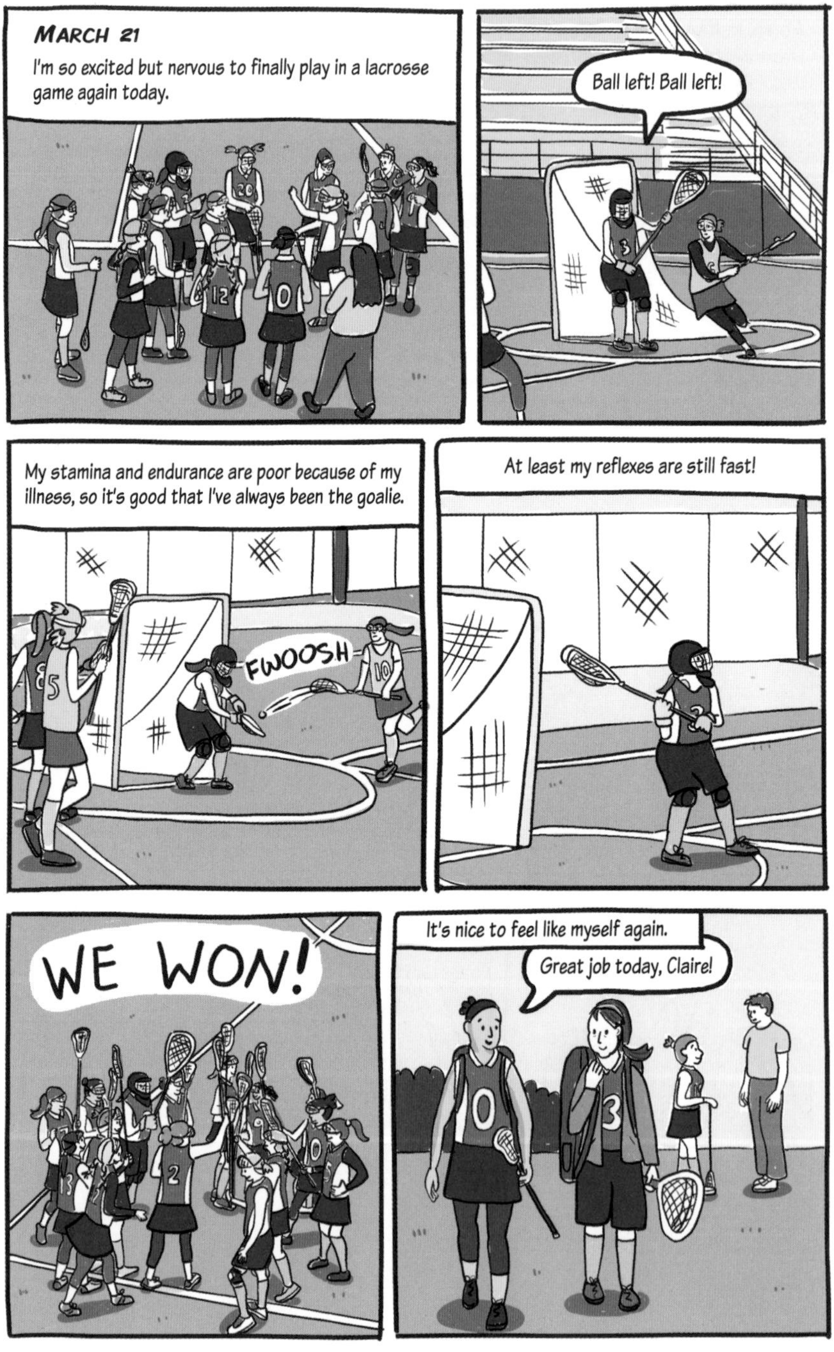
MARCH 21
I'm so excited but nervous to finally play in a lacrosse game again today.
Ball left! Ball left!
My stamina and endurance are poor because of my illness, so it's good that I've always been the goalie.
FWOOSH
At least my reflexes are still fast!
WE WON!
It's nice to feel like myself again.
Great job today, Claire!

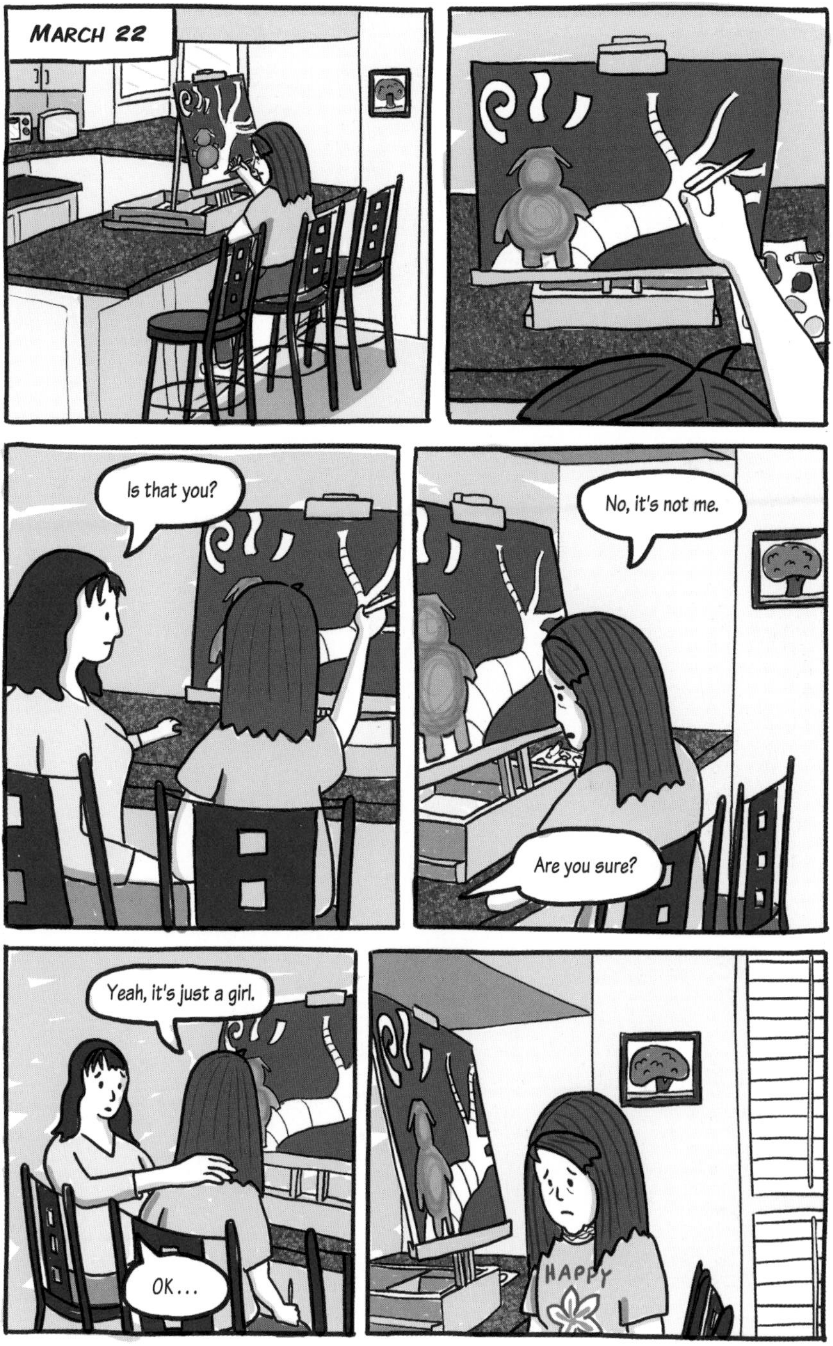
MARCH 22
Is that you?
No, it's not me.
Are you sure?
Yeah, it's just a girl.
OK...
HAPPY

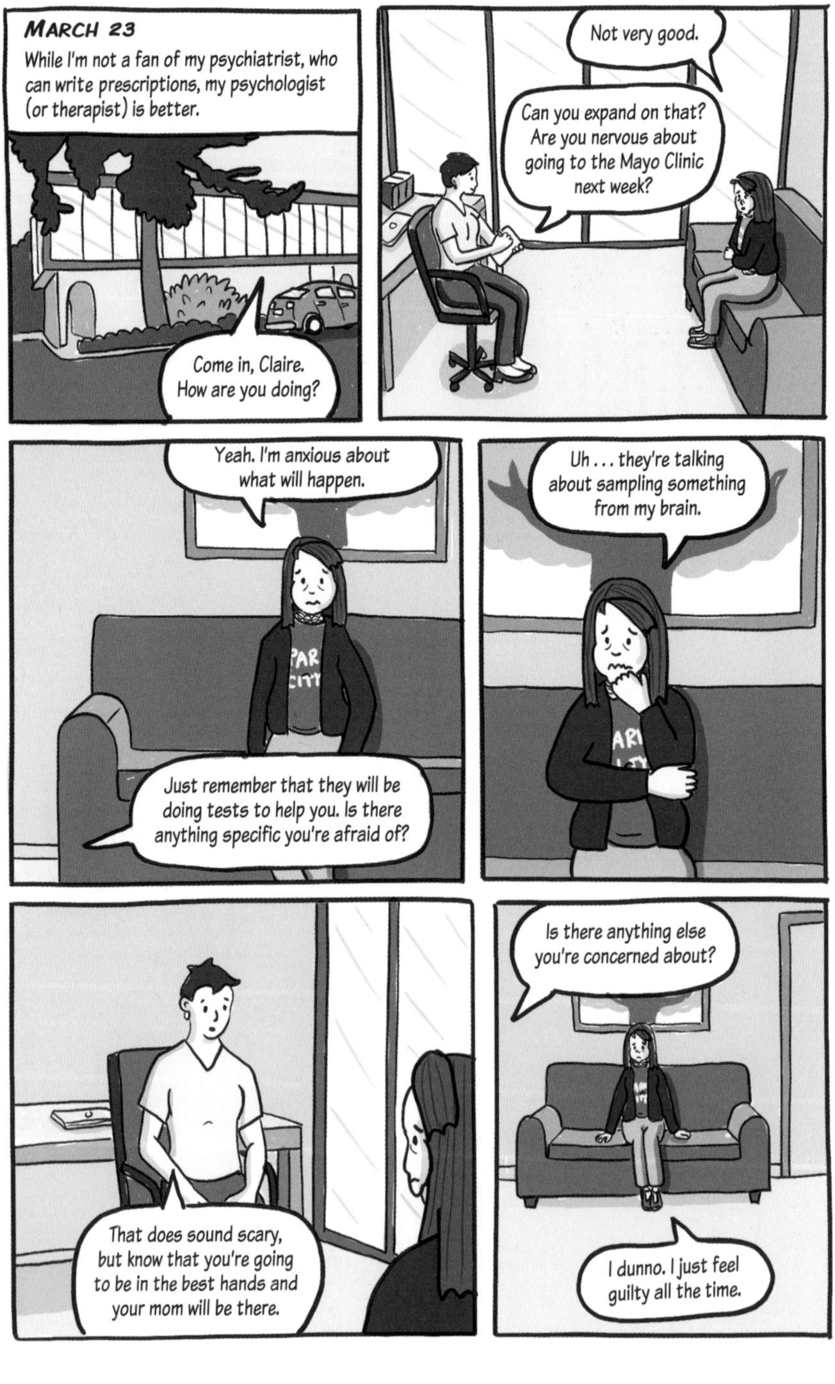
MARCH 23
While I'm not a fan of my psychiatrist, who can write prescriptions, my psychologist (or therapist) is better.
Come in, Claire. How are you doing?
Not very good.
Can you expand on that? Are you nervous about going to the Mayo Clinic next week?
Yeah. I'm anxious about what will happen.
Just remember that they will be doing tests to help you. Is there anything specific you're afraid of?
Uh . . . they're talking about sampling something from my brain.
That does sound scary, but know that you're going to be in the best hands and your mom will be there.
Is there anything else you're concerned about?
I dunno. I just feel guilty all the time.

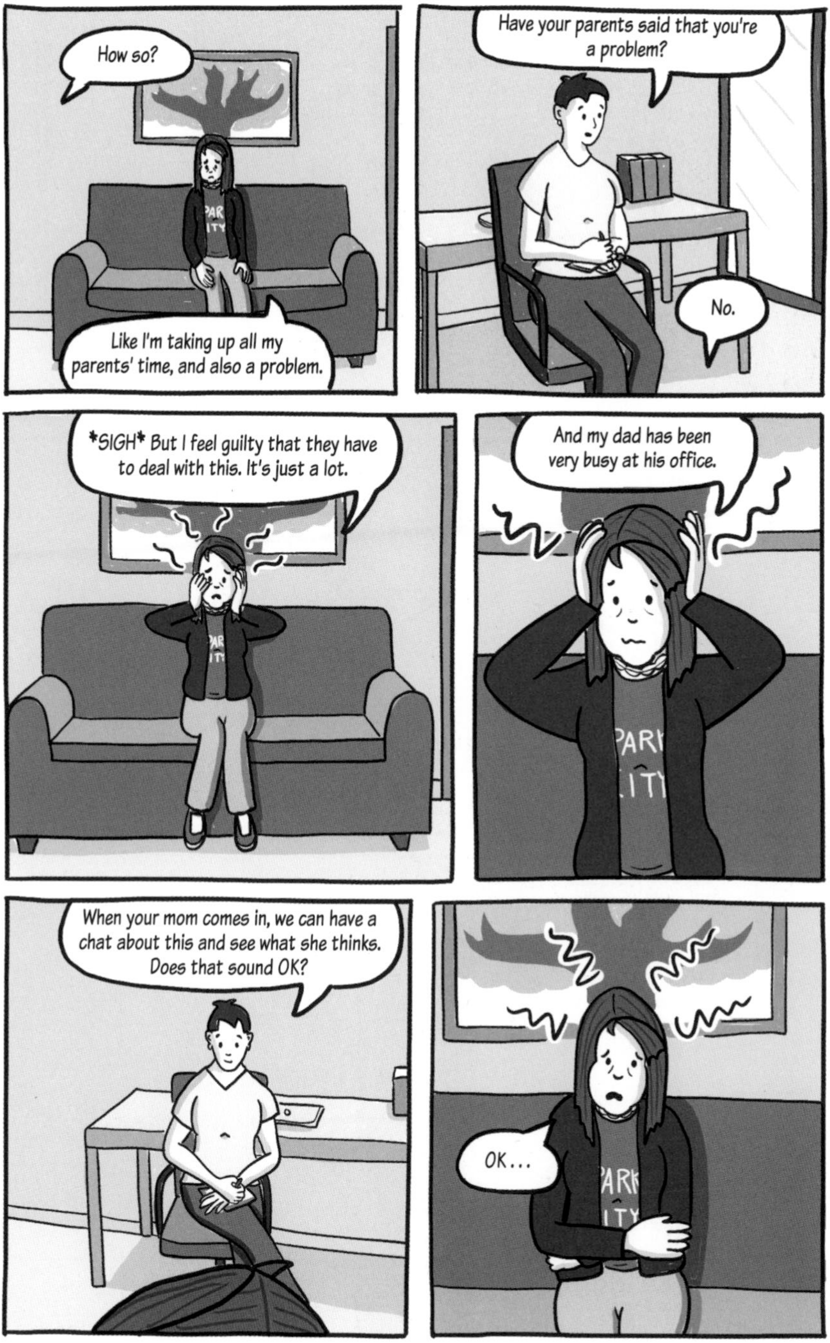
How so?
Like I'm taking up all my parents' time, and also a problem.
Have your parents said that you're a problem?
No.
SIGH But I feel guilty that they have to deal with this. It's just a lot.
And my dad has been very busy at his office.
When your mom comes in, we can have a chat about this and see what she thinks. Does that sound OK?
OK...

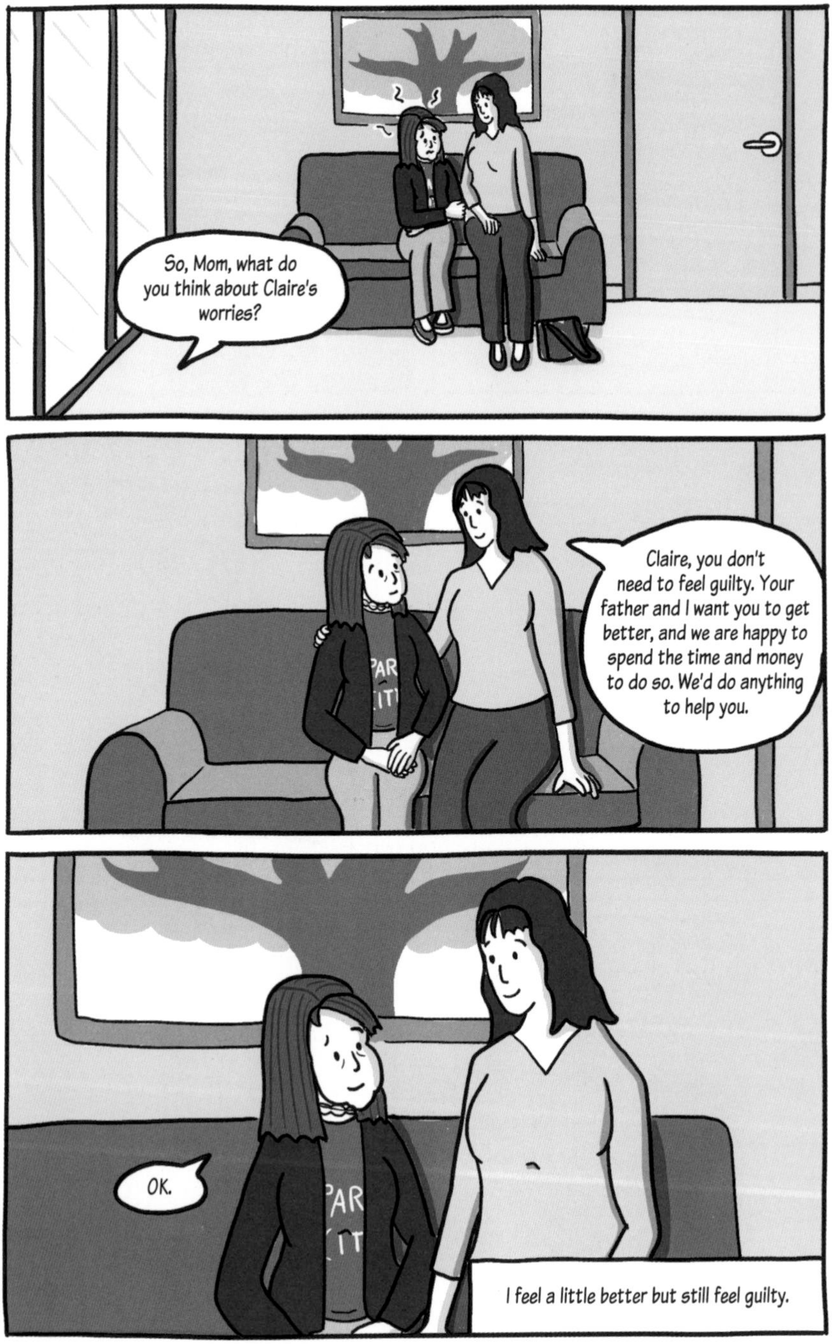
So, Mom, what do you think about Claire's worries?
Claire, you don't need to feel guilty. Your father and I want you to get better, and we are happy to spend the time and money to do so. We'd do anything to help you.
OK.
I feel a little better but still feel guilty.

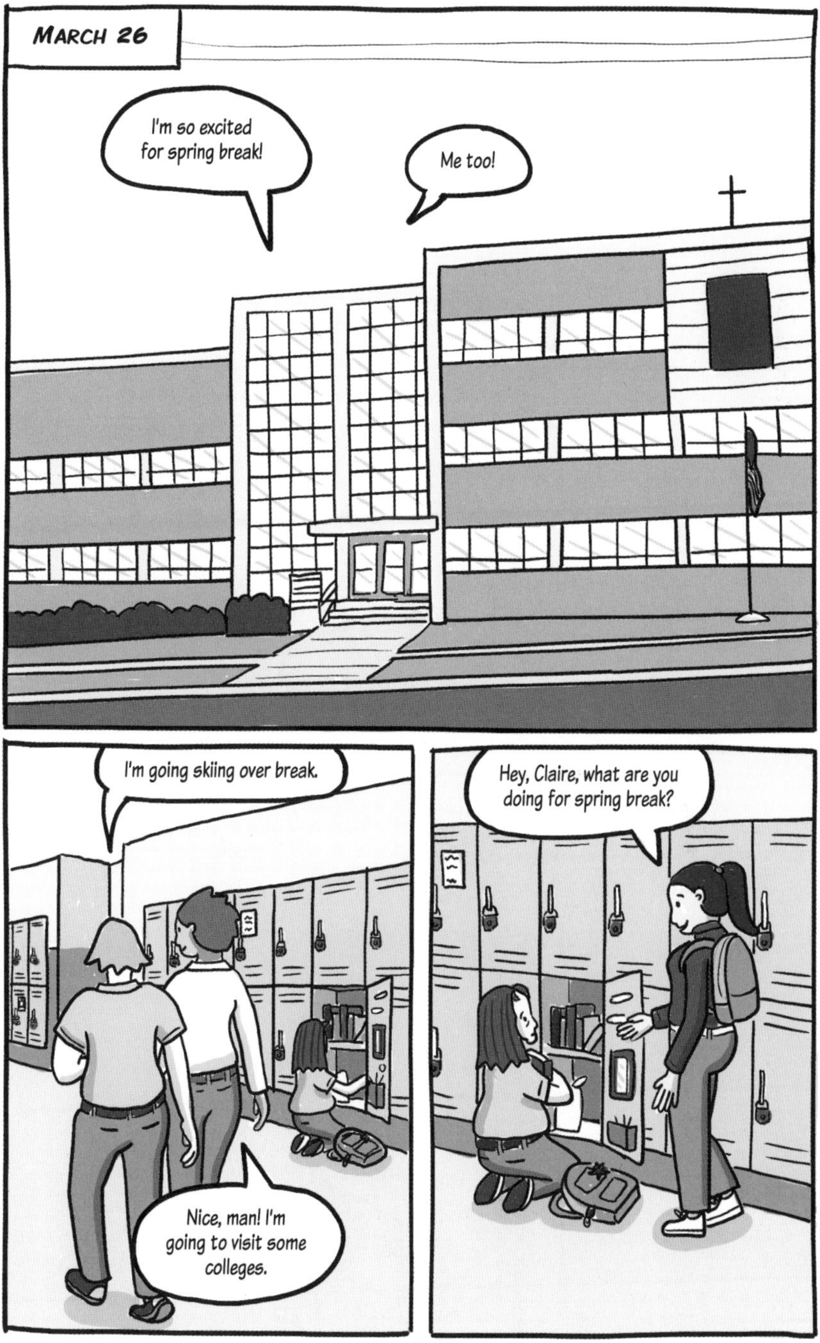
MARCH 26
I'm so excited for spring break!
Me too!
I'm going skiing over break.
Nice, man! I'm going to visit some colleges.
Hey, Claire, what are you doing for spring break?

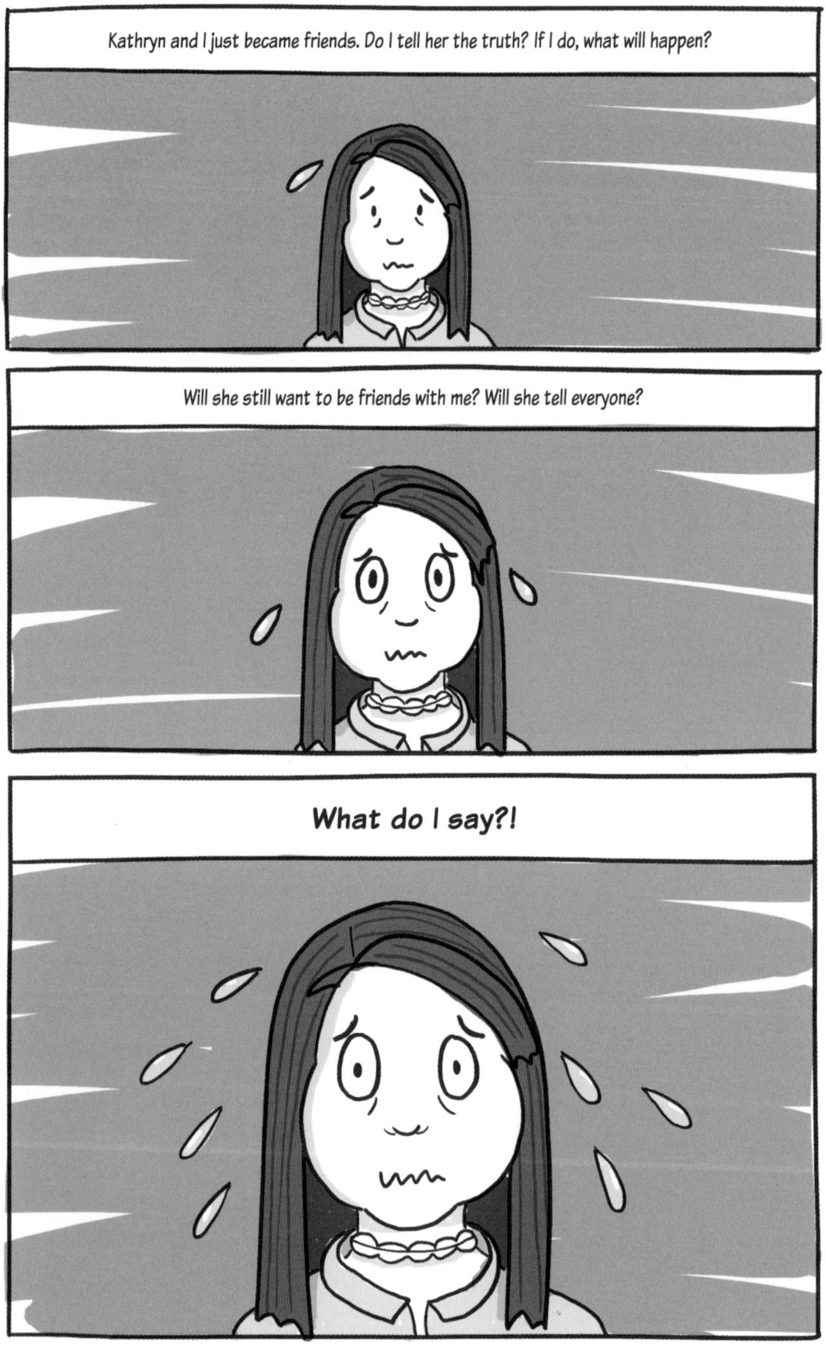

Kathryn and I just became friends. Do I tell her the truth? If I do, what will happen?
Will she still want to be friends with me? Will she tell everyone?
What do I say?!

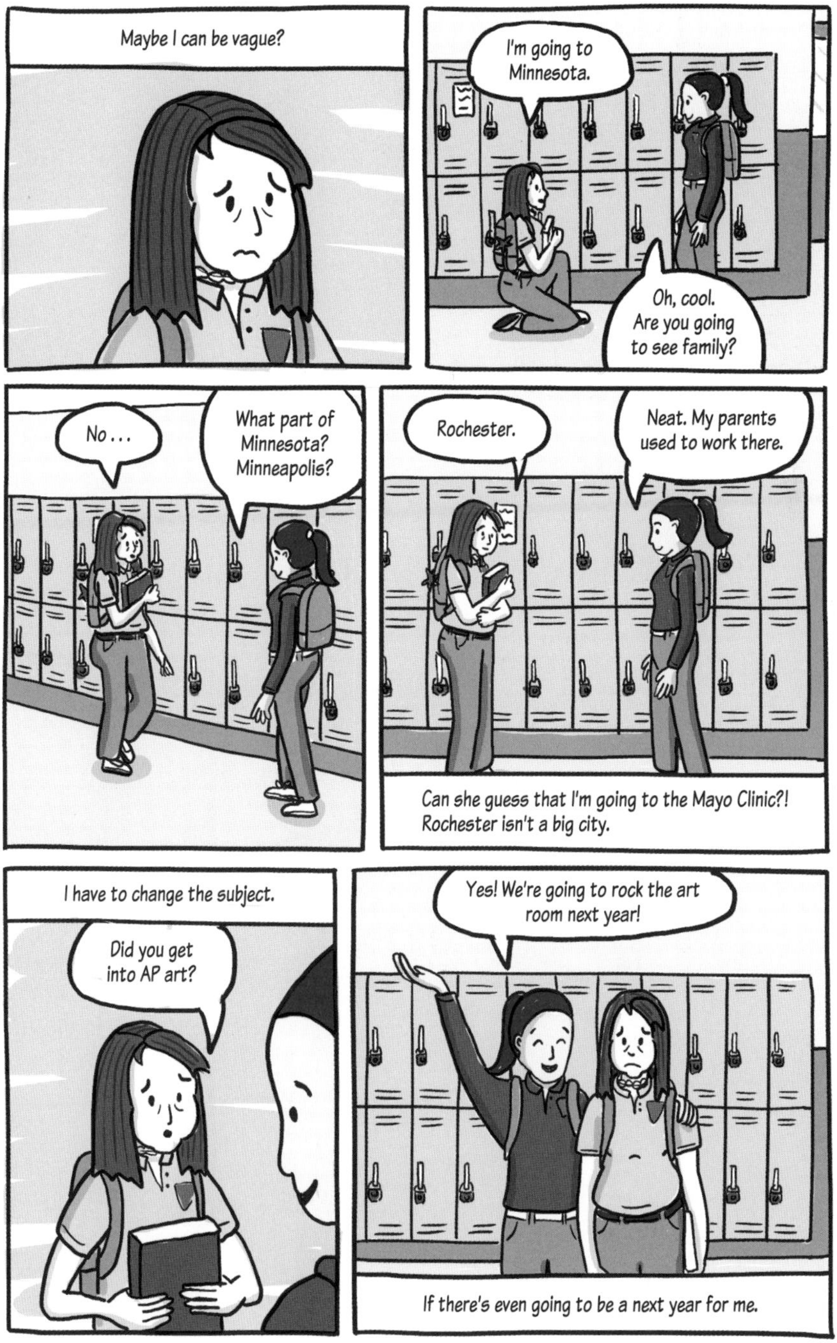
Maybe I can be vague?
I'm going to Minnesota.
Oh, cool. Are you going to see family?
No . . .
What part of Minnesota? Minneapolis?
Rochester.
Neat. My parents used to work there.
Can she guess that I'm going to the Mayo Clinic?! Rochester isn't a big city.
I have to change the subject.
Did you get into AP art?
Yes! We're going to rock the art room next year!
If there's even going to be a next year for me.

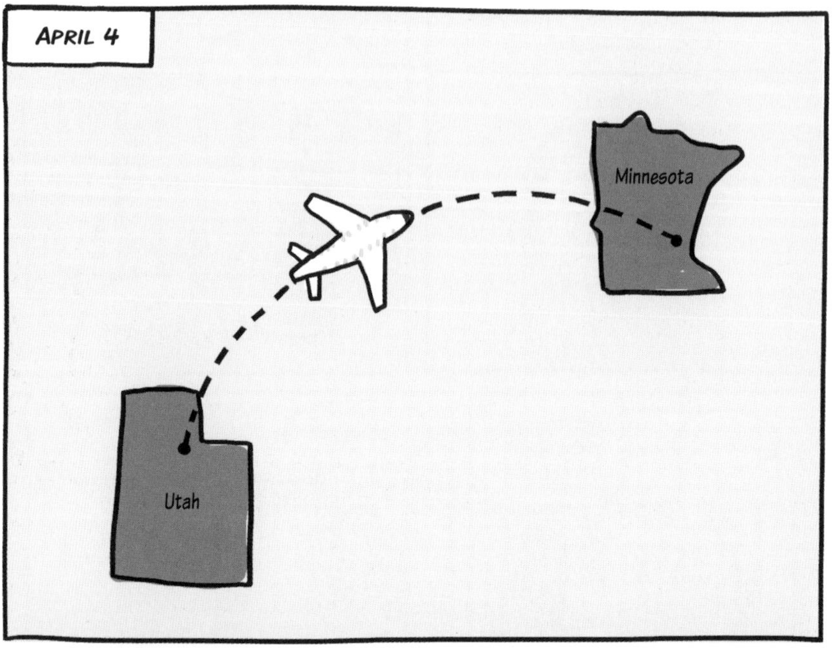
APRIL 4
Minnesota
Utah

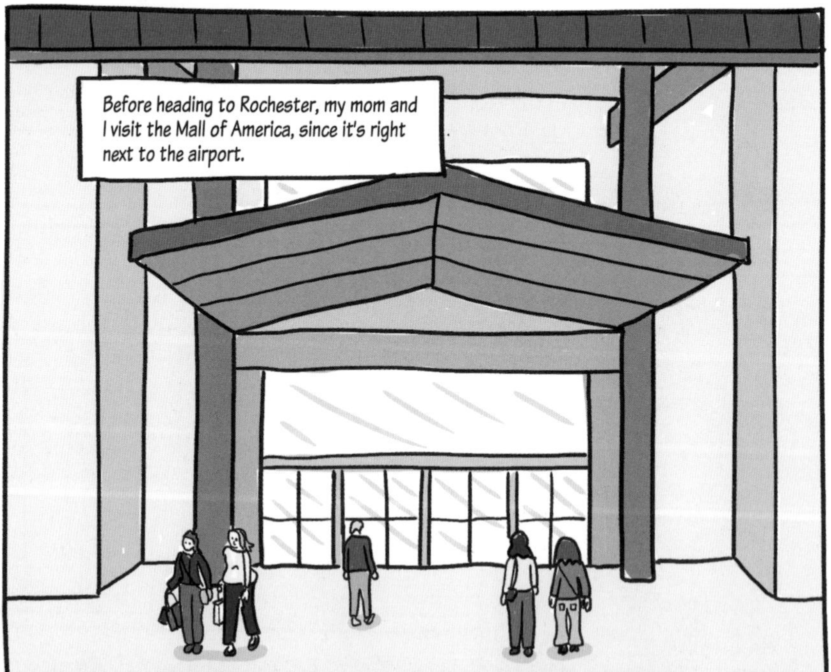
Before heading to Rochester, my mom and I visit the Mall of America, since it's right next to the airport.

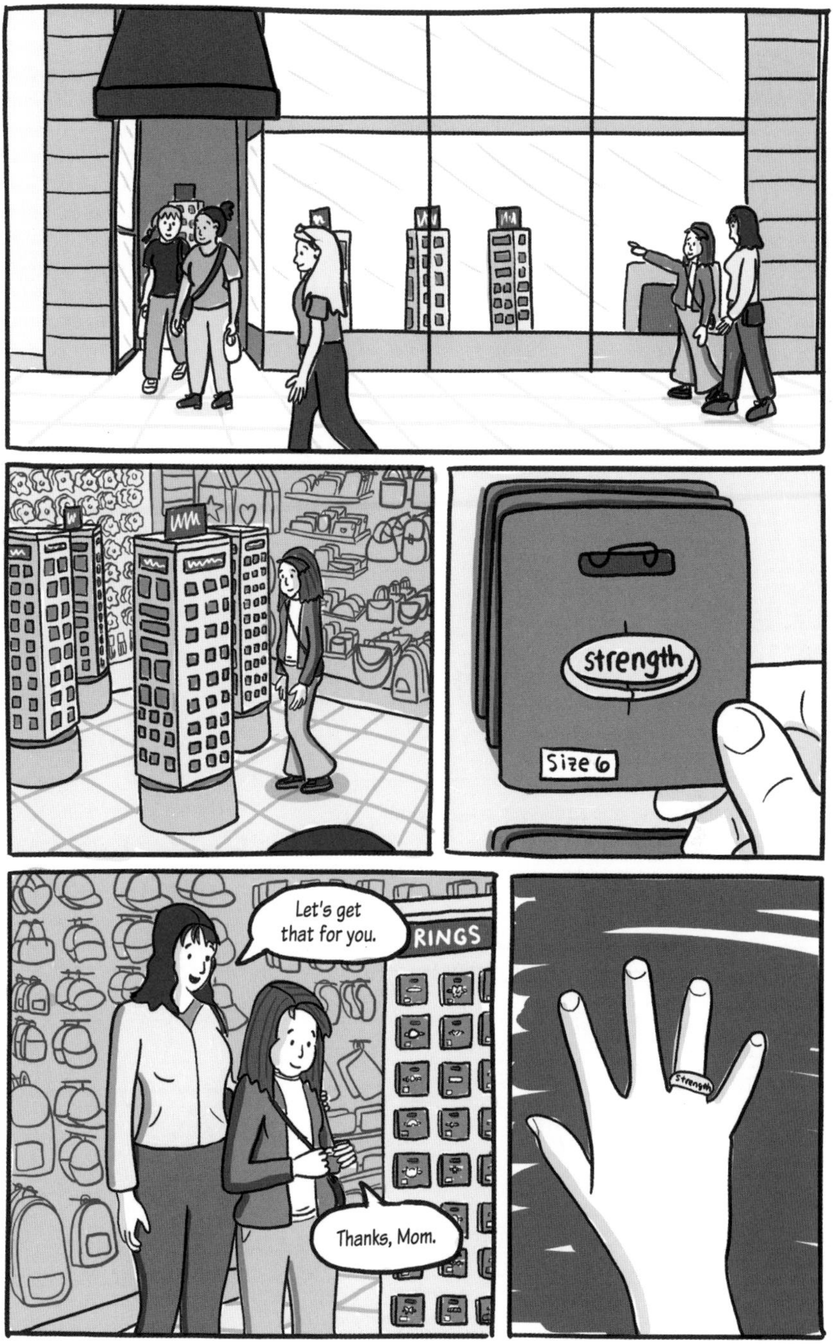
strength
Size 6
Let's get that for you.
RINGS
Thanks, Mom.
strength

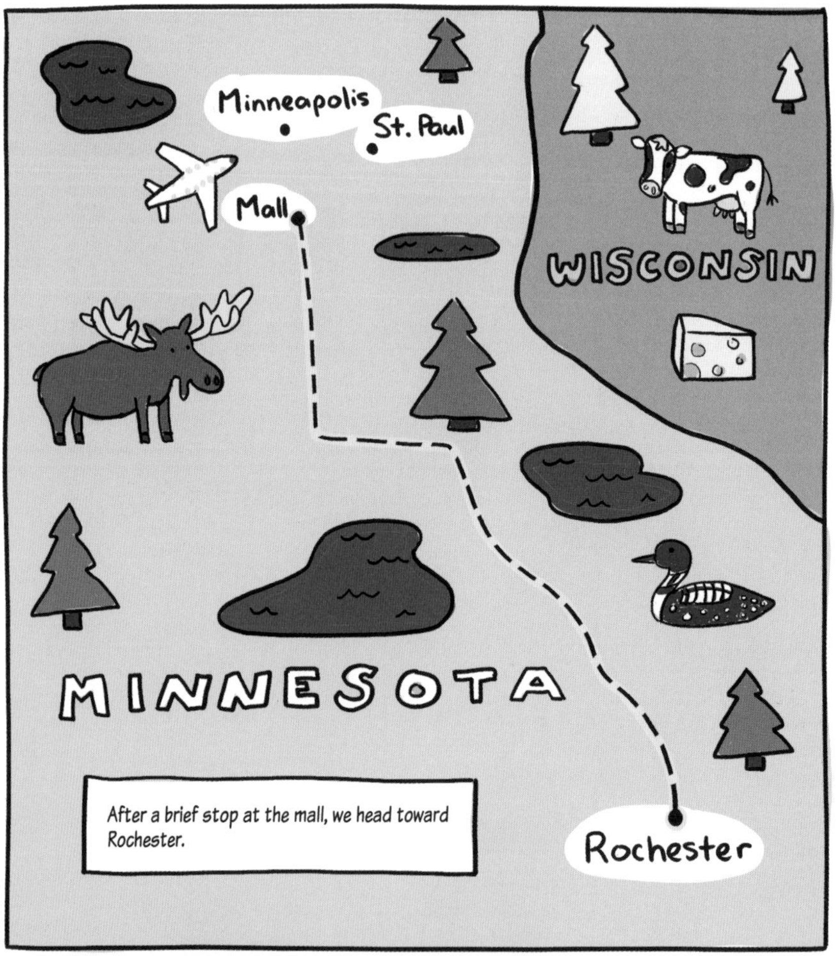
Minneapolis
St. Paul
Mall
WISCONSIN
MINNESOTA
After a brief stop at the mall, we head toward Rochester.
Rochester

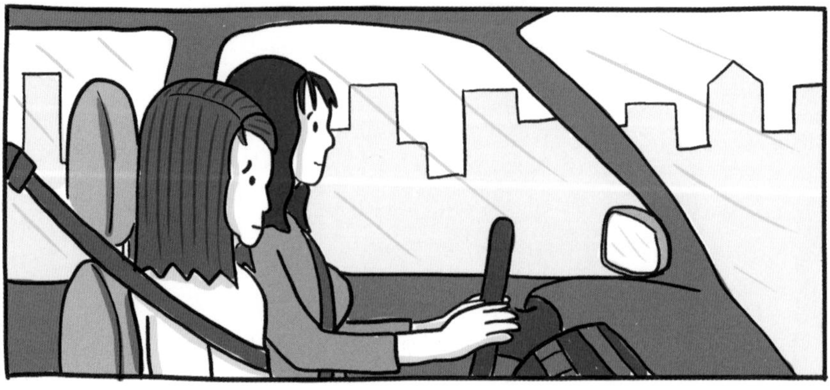

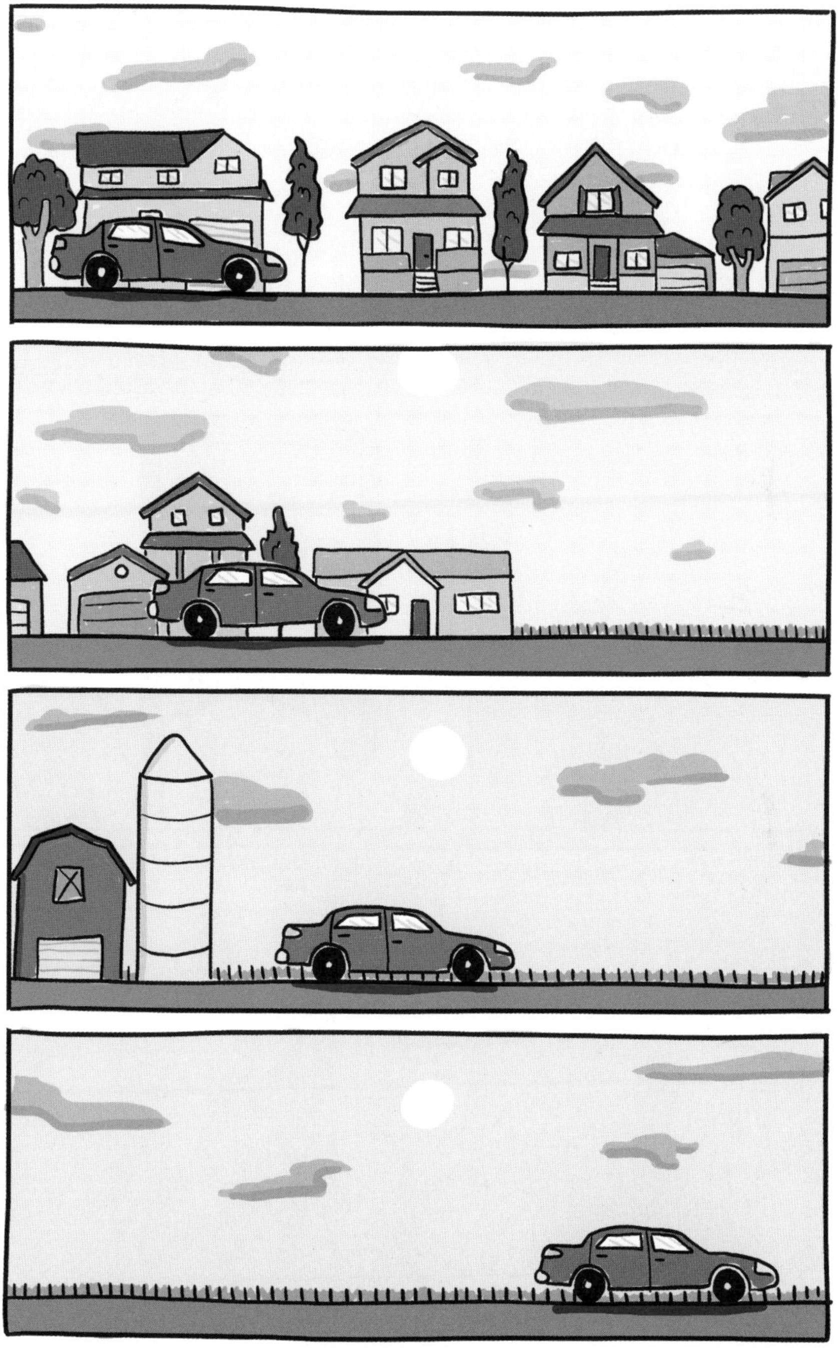

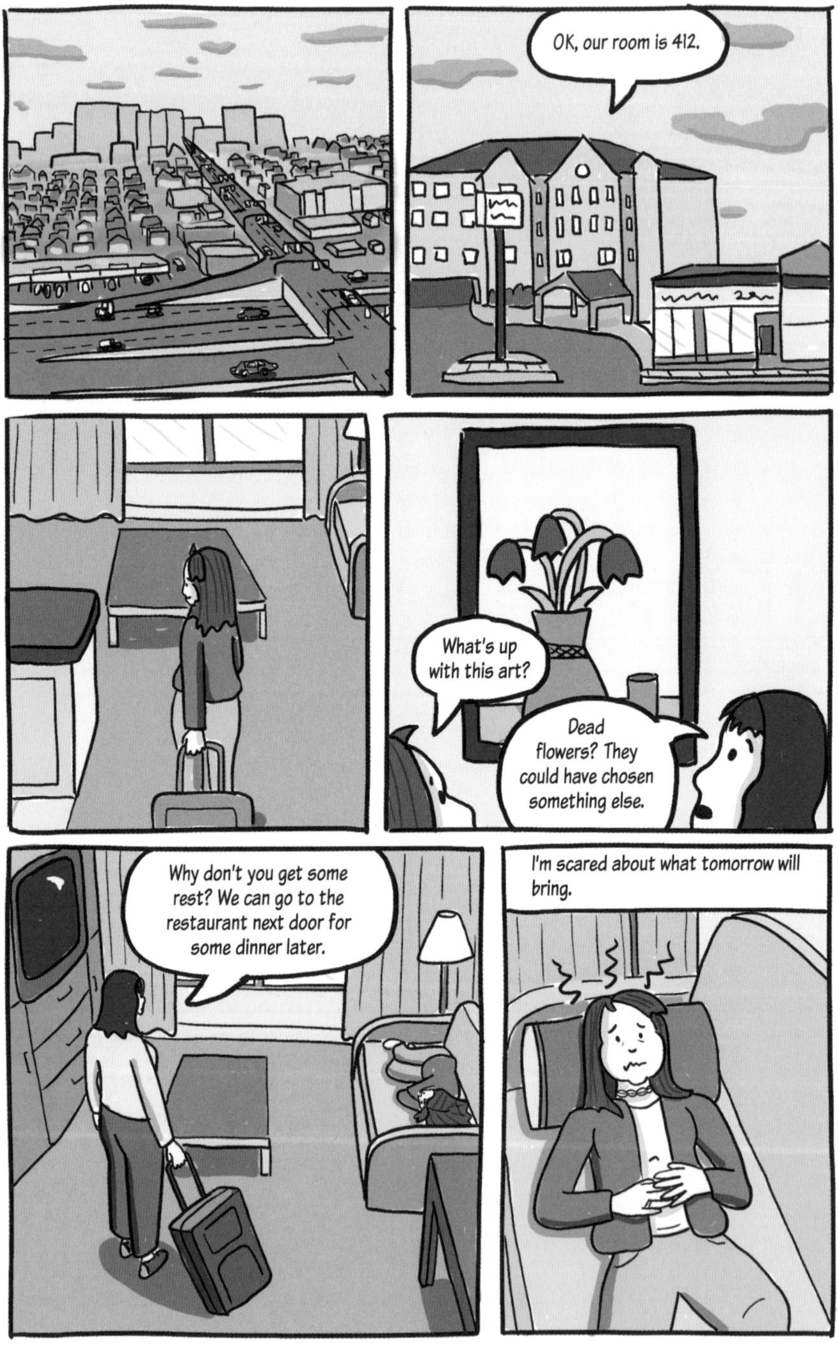
OK, our room is 412.
What's up with this art?
Dead flowers? They could have chosen something else.
Why don't you get some rest? We can go to the restaurant next door for some dinner later.
I'm scared about what tomorrow will bring.

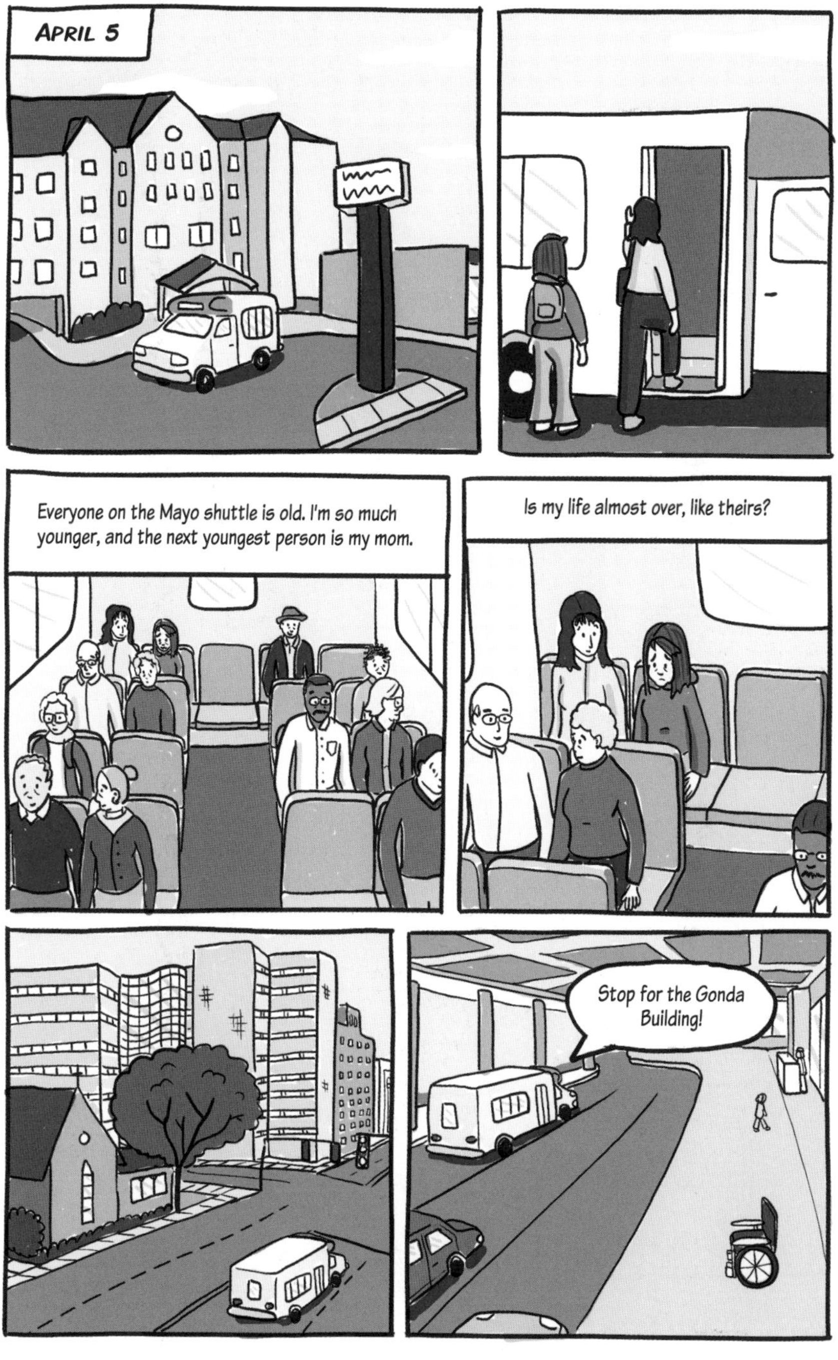
April 5
Everyone on the Mayo shuttle is old. I'm so much younger, and the next youngest person is my mom.
Is my life almost over, like theirs?
Stop for the Gonda Building!

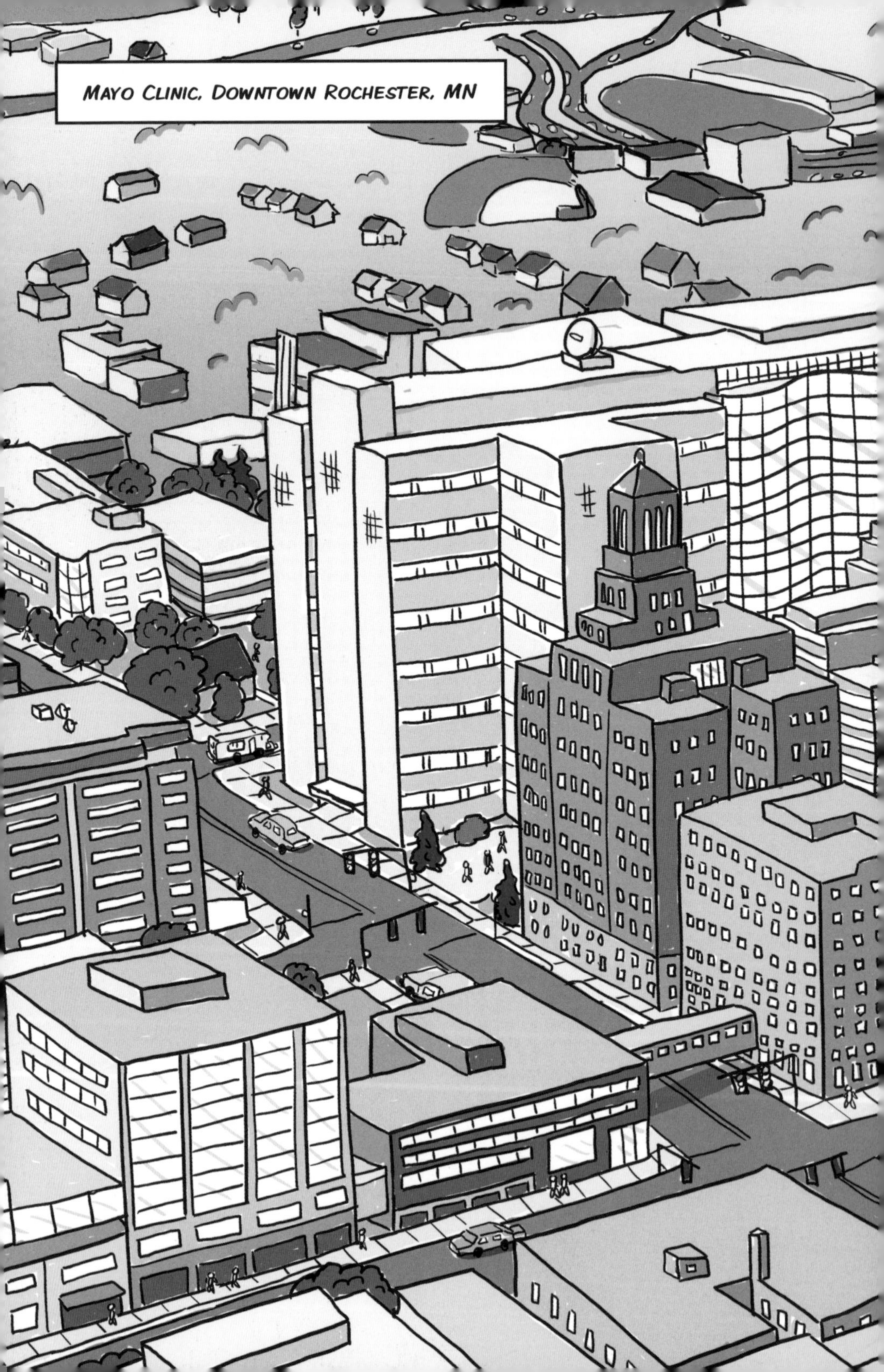
Mayo Clinic, Downtown Rochester, MN

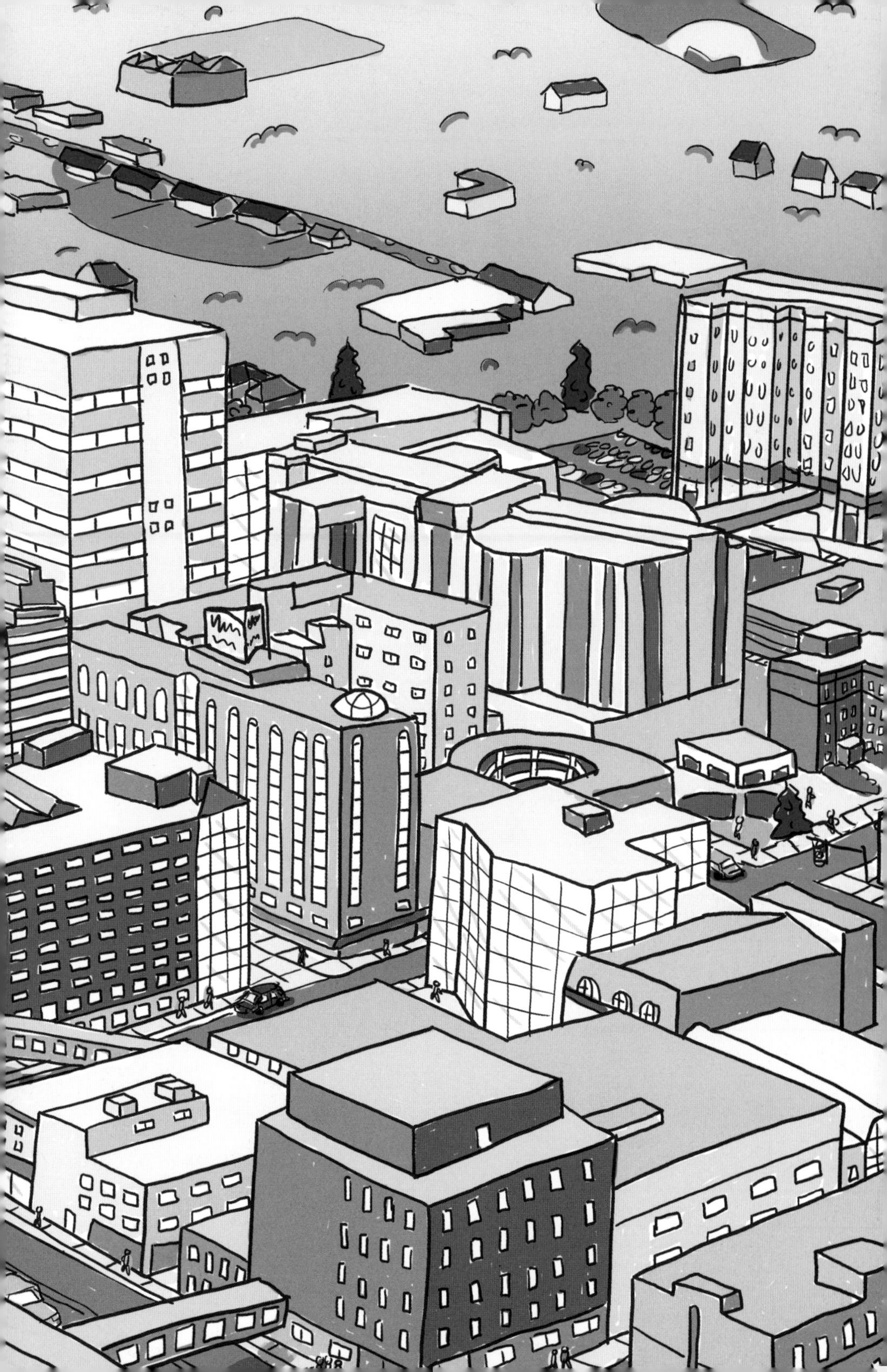

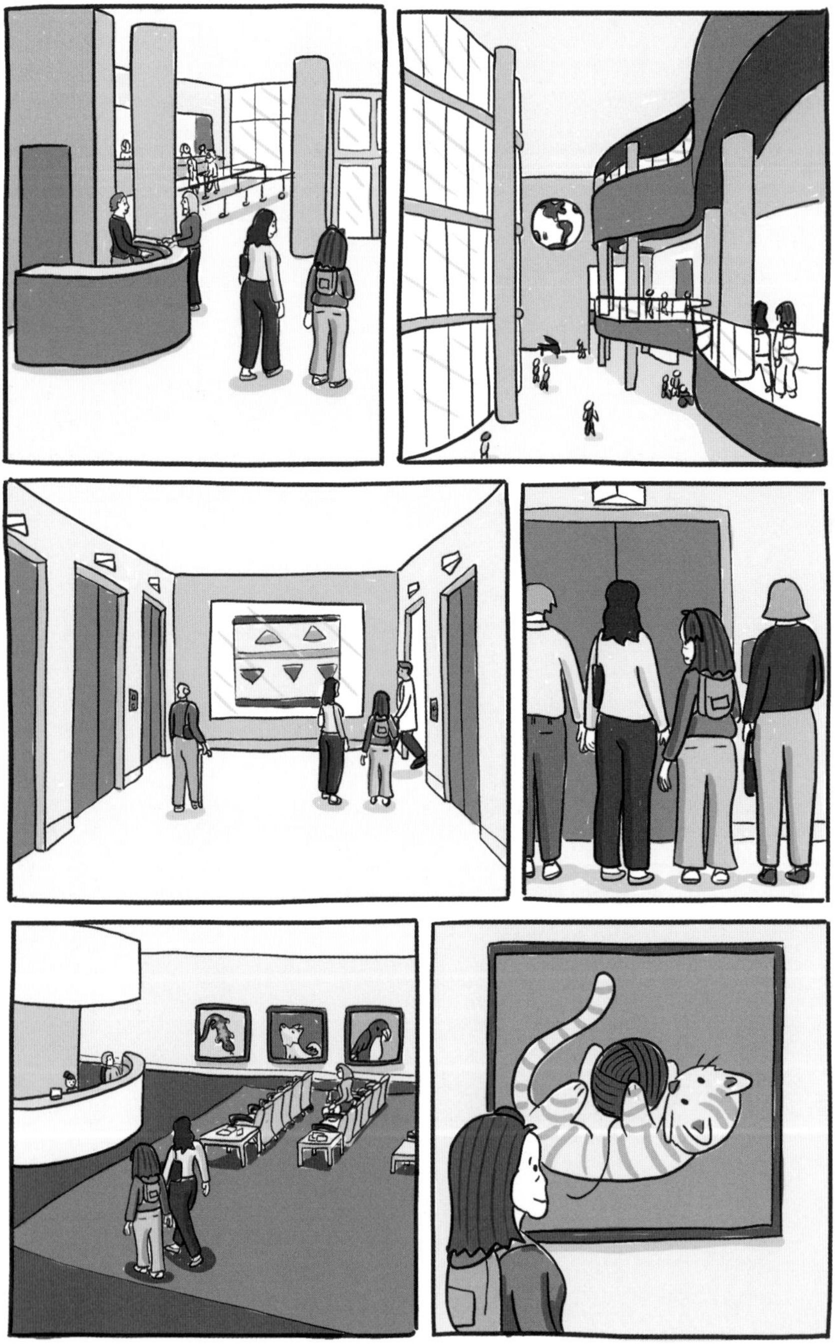

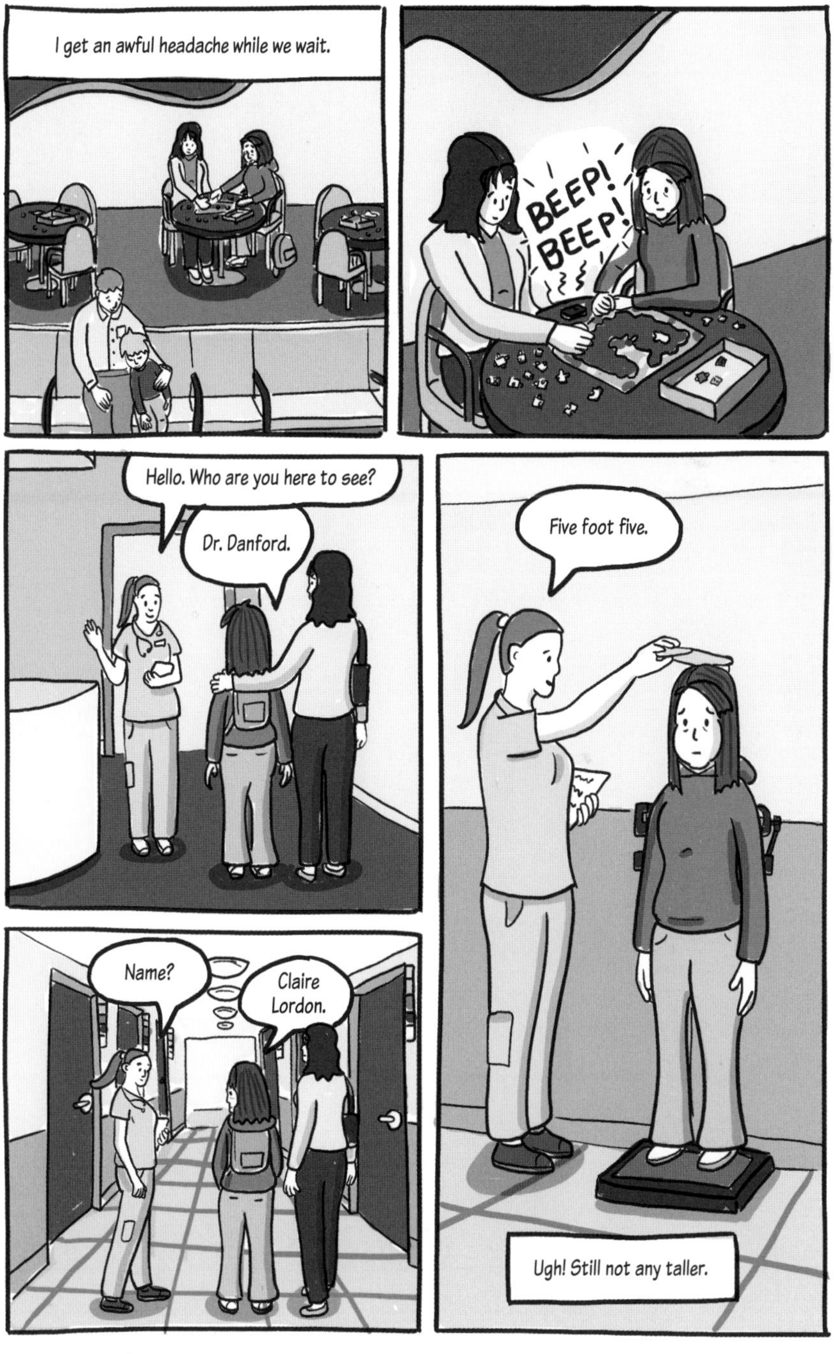
I get an awful headache while we wait.
BEEP! BEEP!
Hello. Who are you here to see?
Dr. Danford.
Five foot five.
Name?
Claire Lordon.
Ugh! Still not any taller.

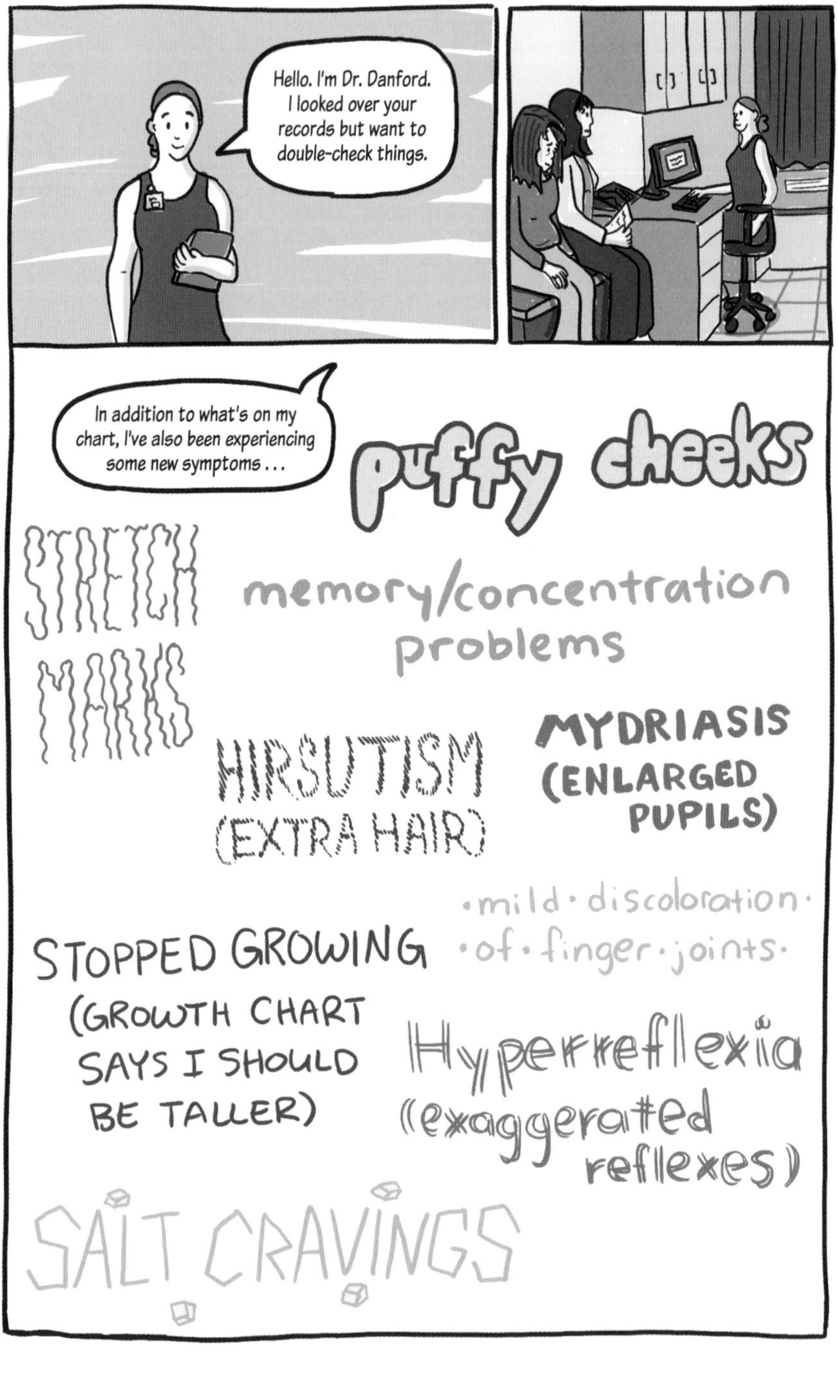
Hello. I'm Dr. Danford. I looked over your records but want to double-check things.
In addition to what's on my chart, I've also been experiencing some new symptoms . . .
puffy cheeks
STRETCH MARKS
memory/concentration problems
HIRSUTISM (EXTRA HAIR)
MYDRIASIS (ENLARGED PUPILS)
·mild·discoloration· ·of·finger·joints·
STOPPED GROWING (GROWTH CHART SAYS I SHOULD BE TALLER)
Hyperreflexia (exaggerated reflexes)
SALT CRAVINGS

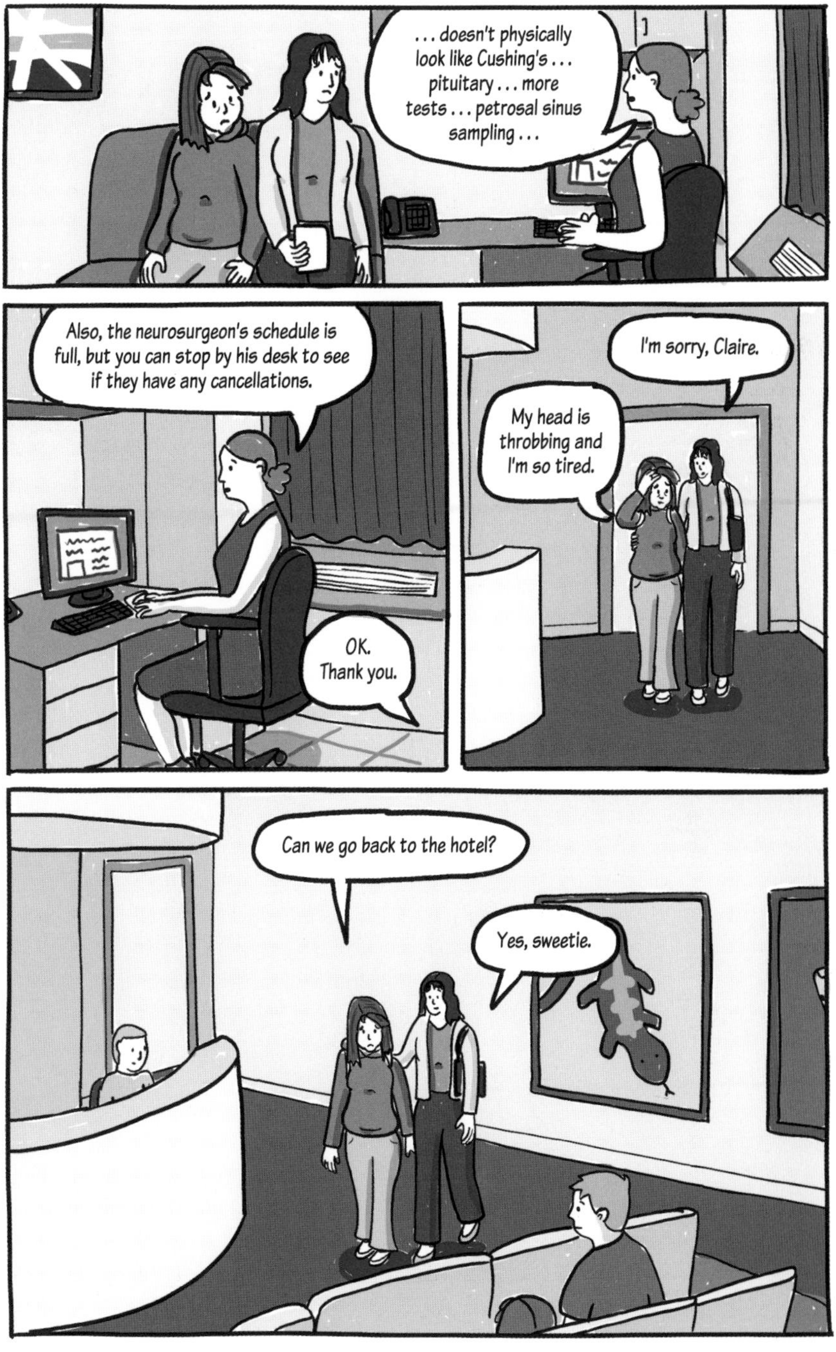
. . . doesn't physically look like Cushing's . . . pituitary . . . more tests . . . petrosal sinus sampling . . .
Also, the neurosurgeon's schedule is full, but you can stop by his desk to see if they have any cancellations.
OK. Thank you.
I'm sorry, Claire.
My head is throbbing and I'm so tired.
Can we go back to the hotel?
Yes, sweetie.

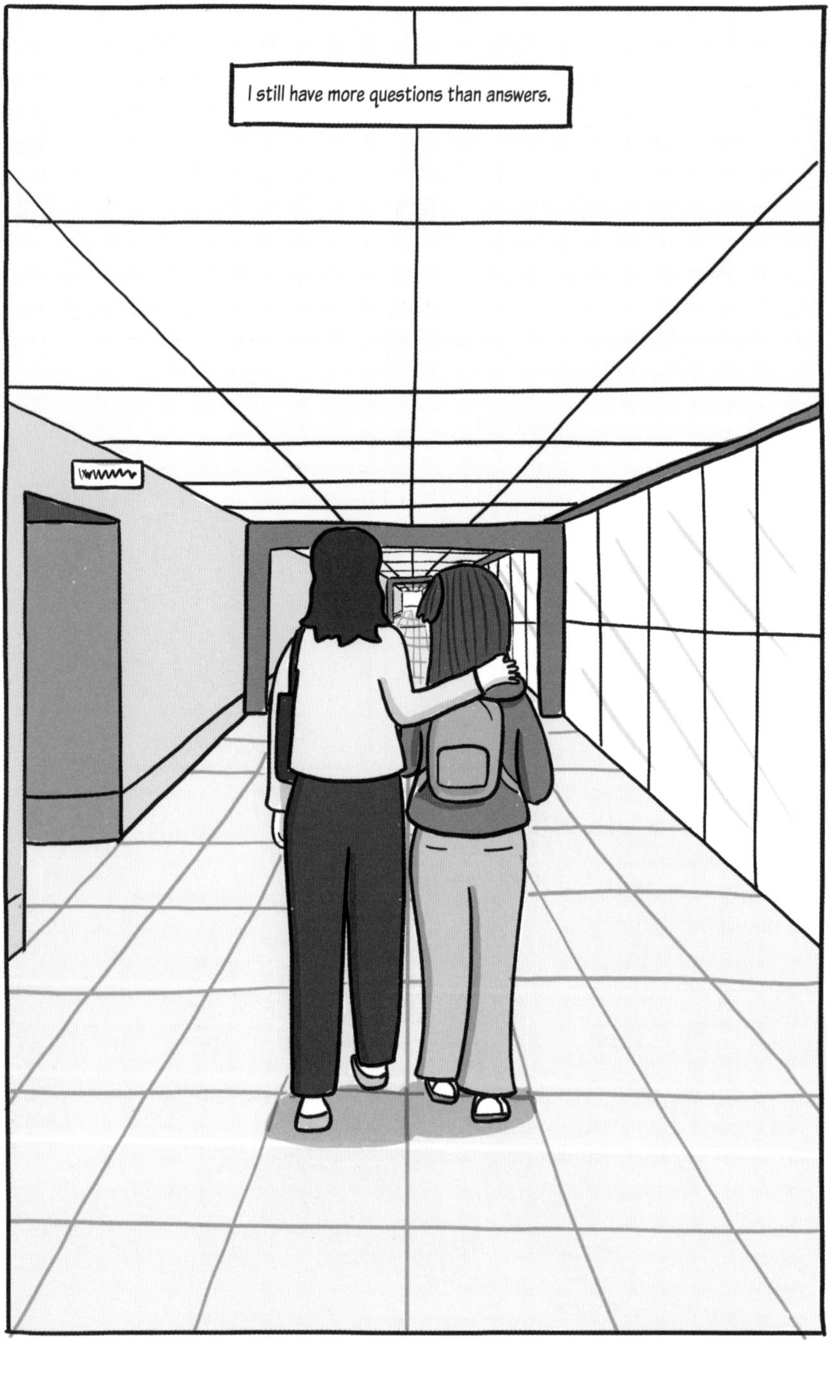
I still have more questions than answers.

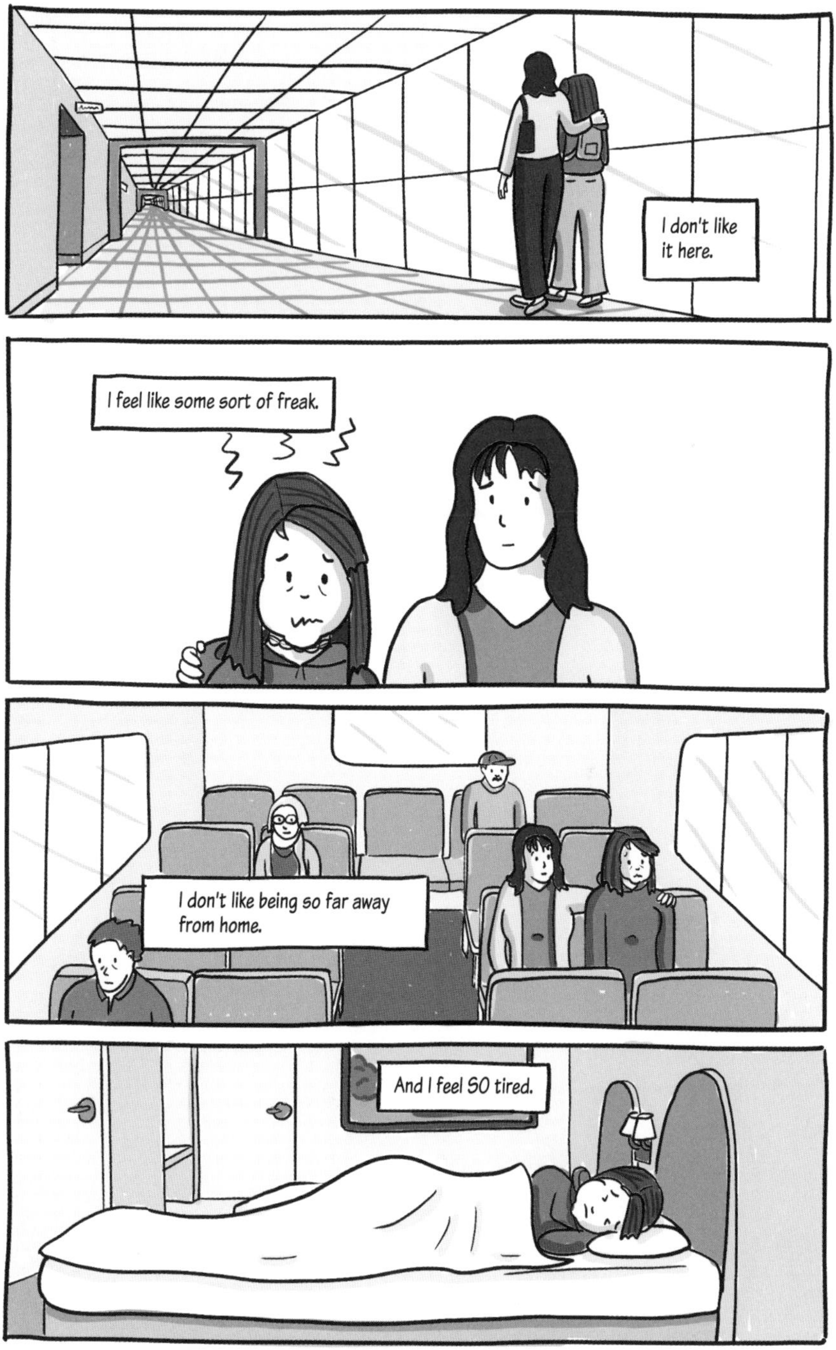
I don't like it here.
I feel like some sort of freak.
I don't like being so far away from home.
And I feel SO tired.

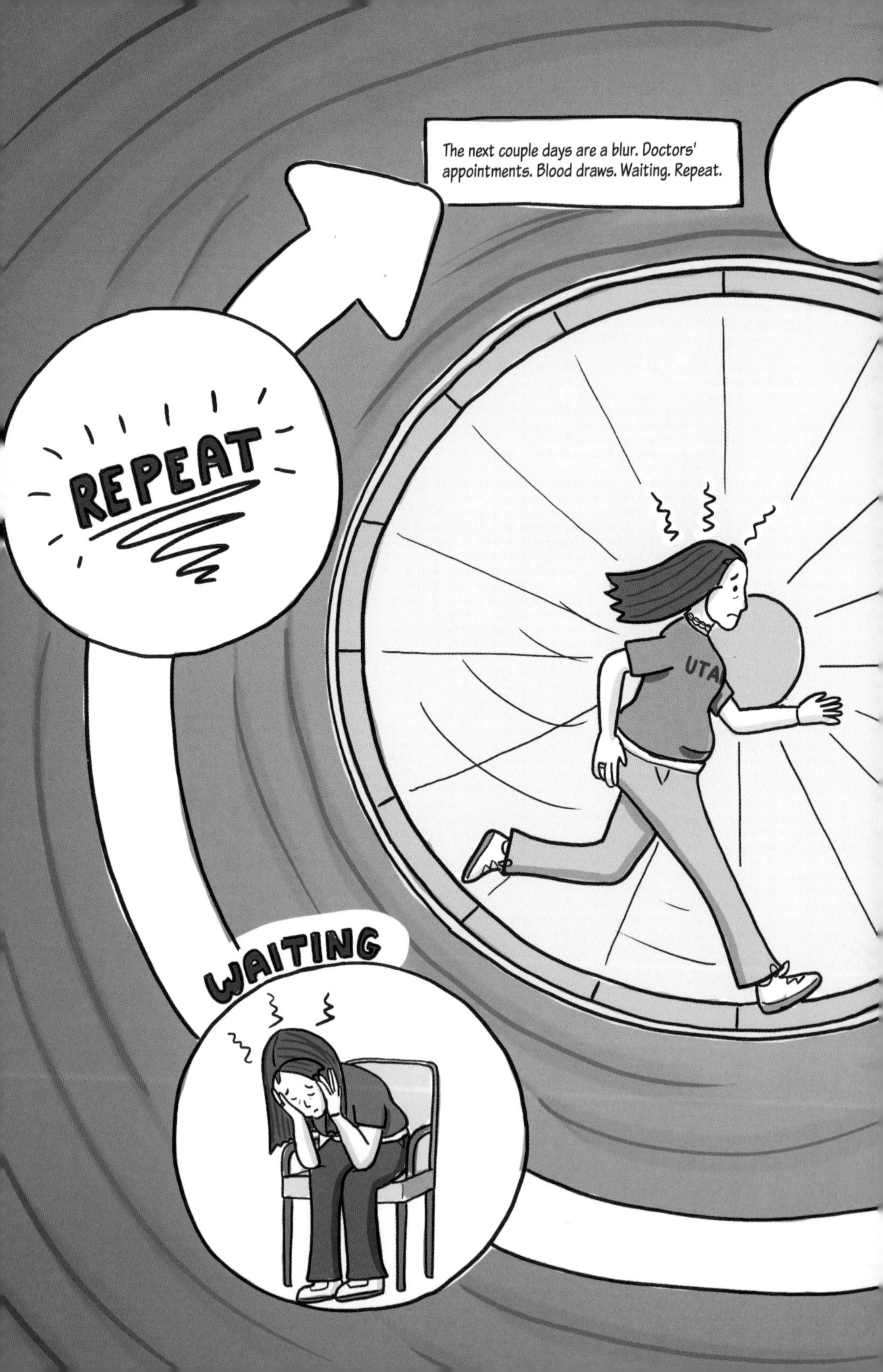
The next couple days are a blur. Doctors' appointments. Blood draws. Waiting. Repeat.
REPEAT
UTA
WAITING

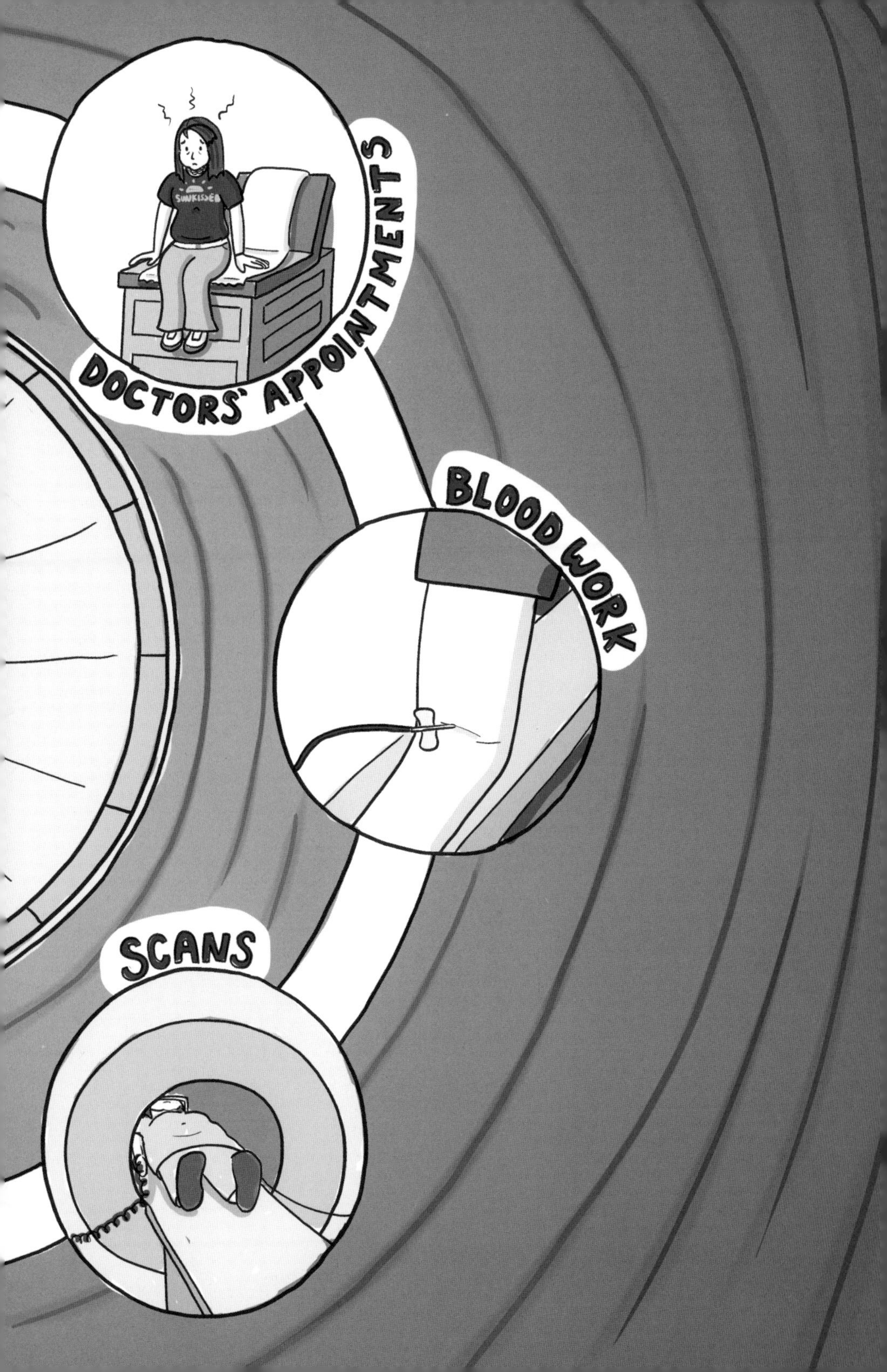
SUNKISSED
DOCTORS' APPOINTMENTS
BLOOD WORK
SCANS

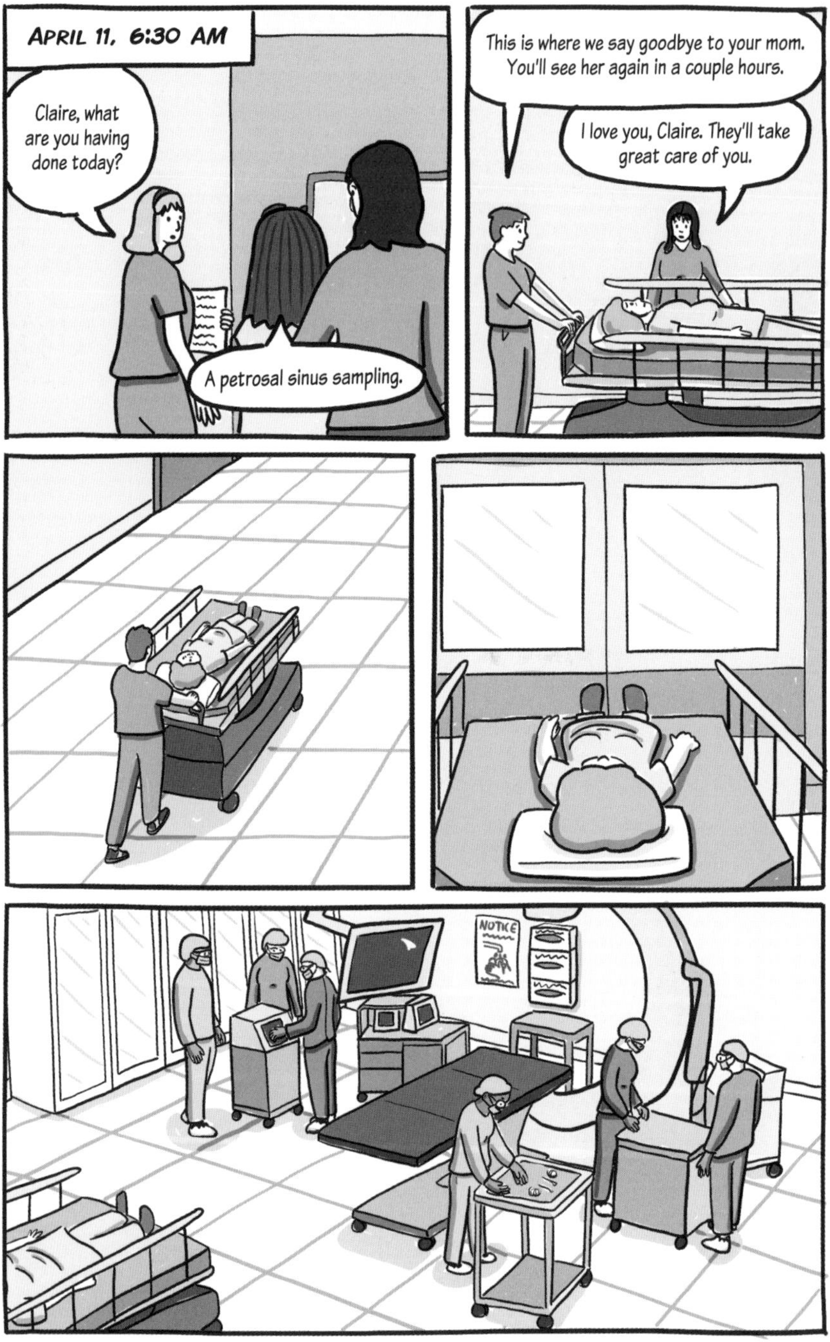
APRIL 11, 6:30 AM
Claire, what are you having done today?
A petrosal sinus sampling.
This is where we say goodbye to your mom. You'll see her again in a couple hours.
I love you, Claire. They'll take great care of you.
NOTICE

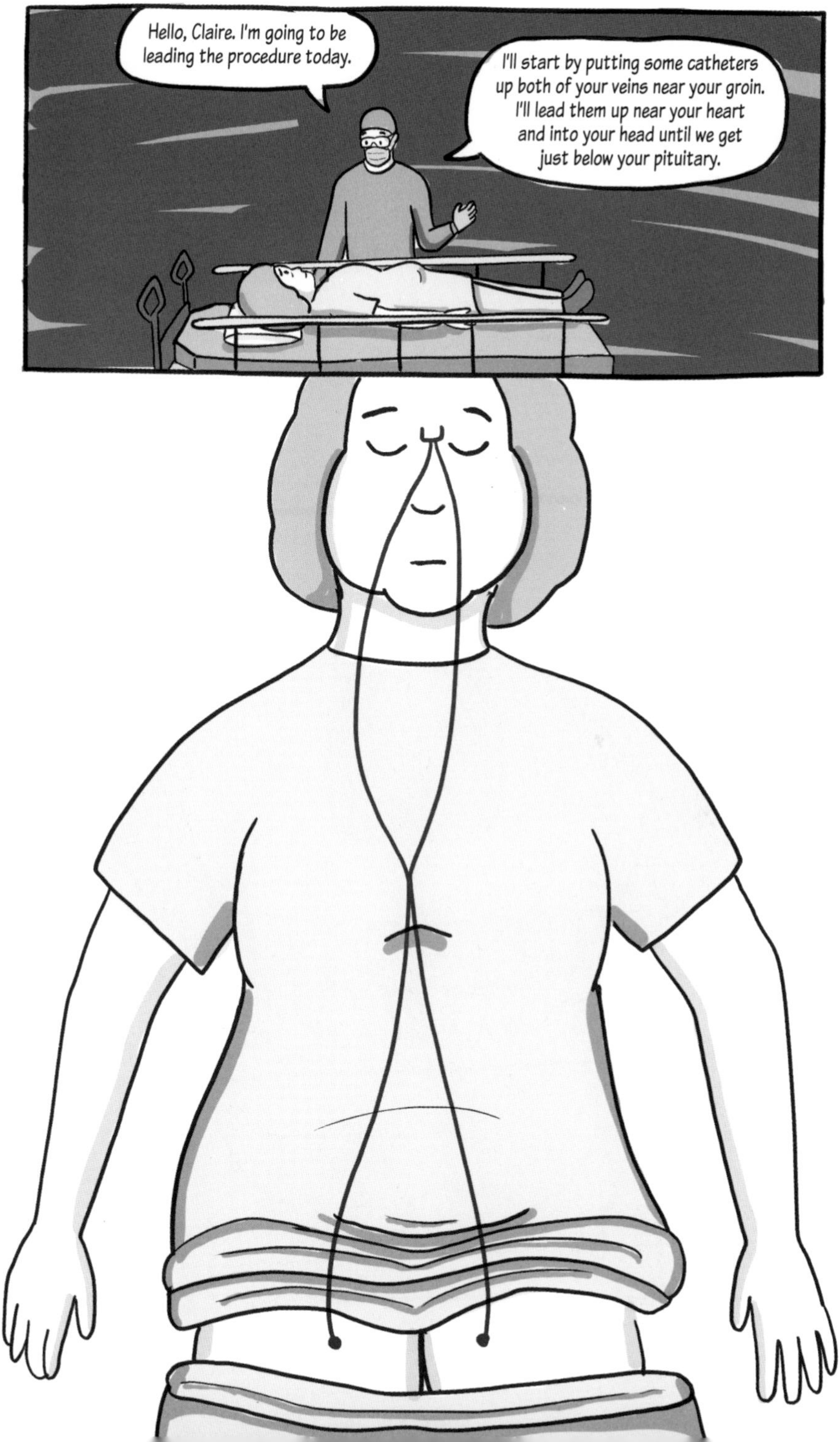
Hello, Claire. I'm going to be leading the procedure today.
I'll start by putting some catheters up both of your veins near your groin. I'll lead them up near your heart and into your head until we get just below your pituitary.

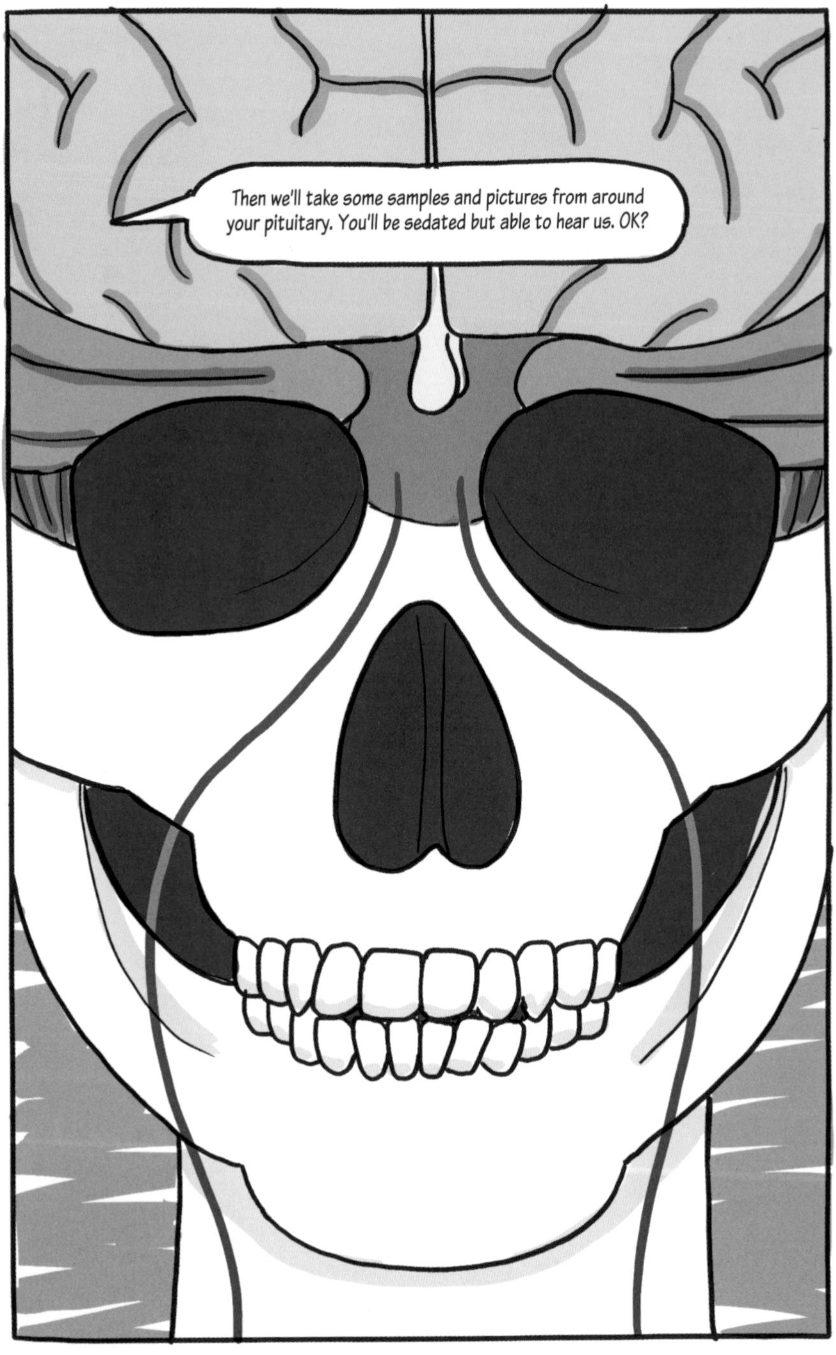
Then we'll take some samples and pictures from around your pituitary. You'll be sedated but able to hear us. OK?

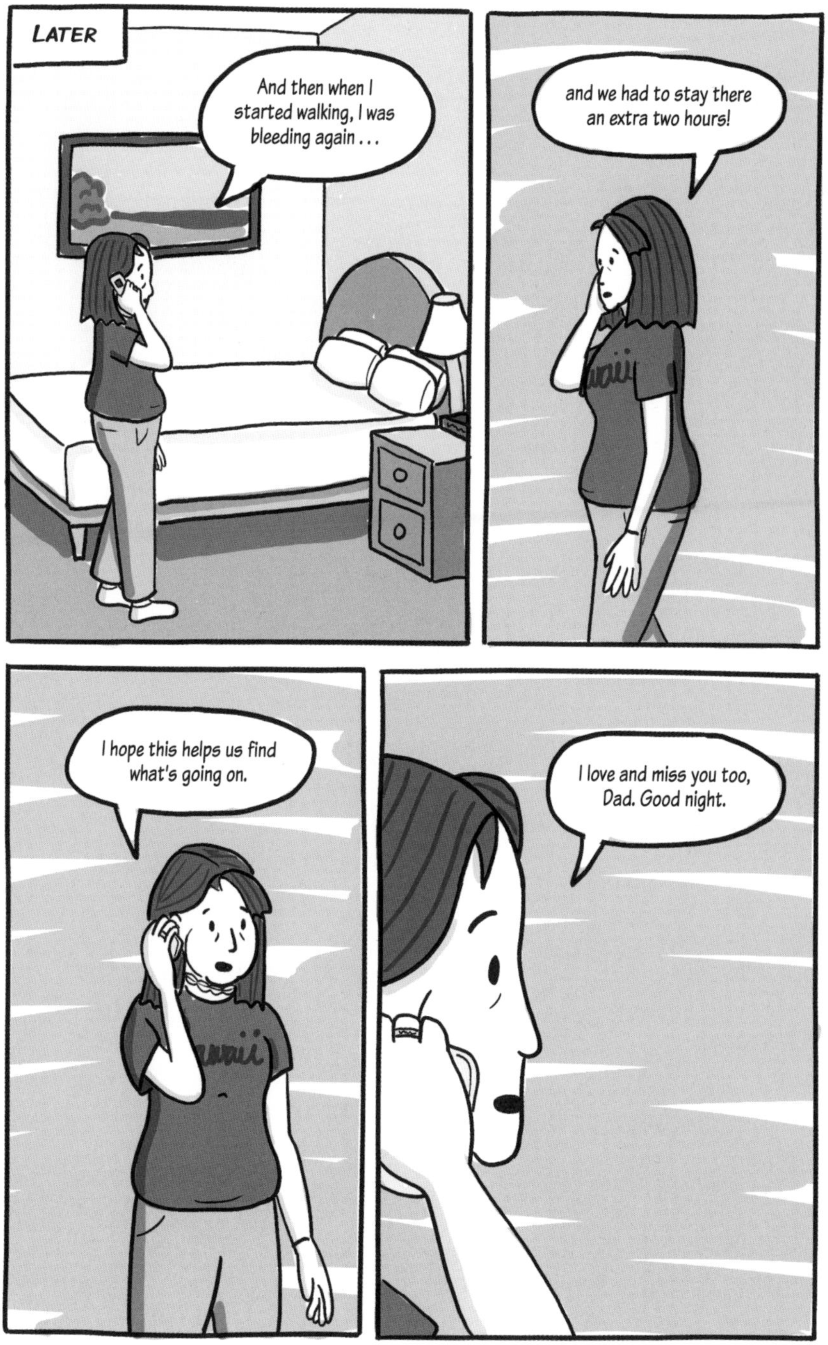
LATER
And then when I started walking, I was bleeding again . . .
and we had to stay there an extra two hours!
I hope this helps us find what's going on.
I love and miss you too, Dad. Good night.

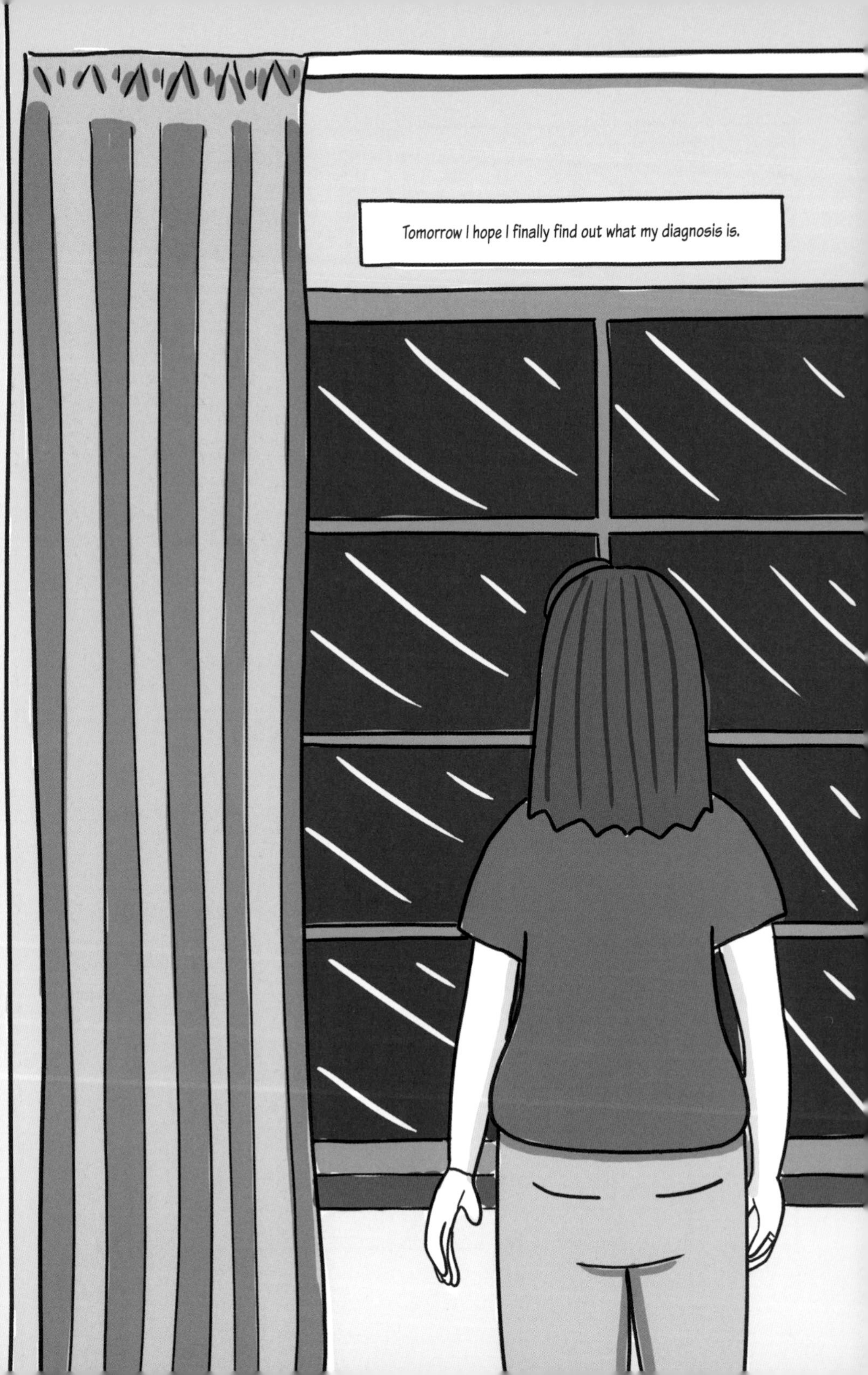
Tomorrow I hope I finally find out what my diagnosis is.

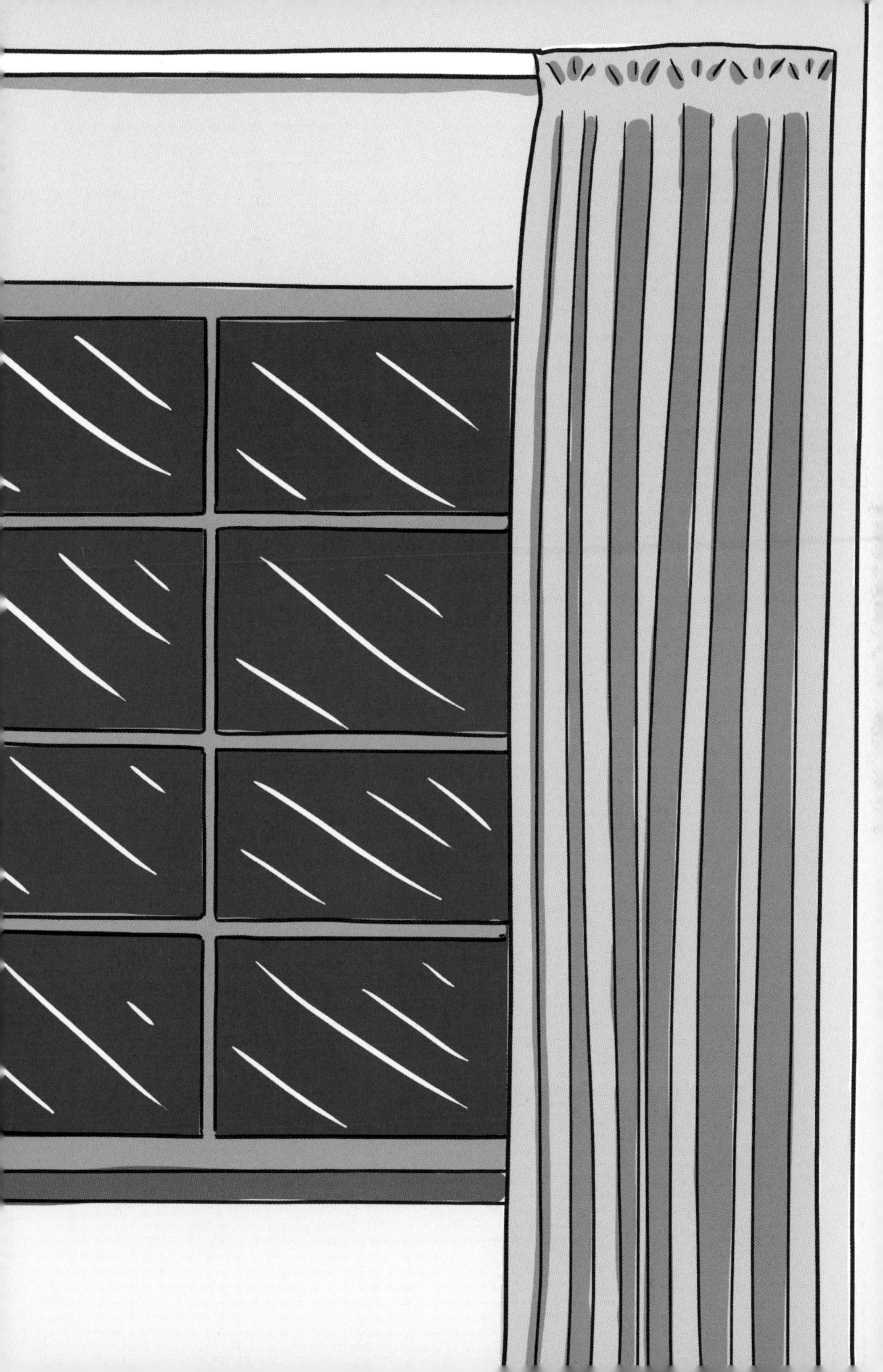

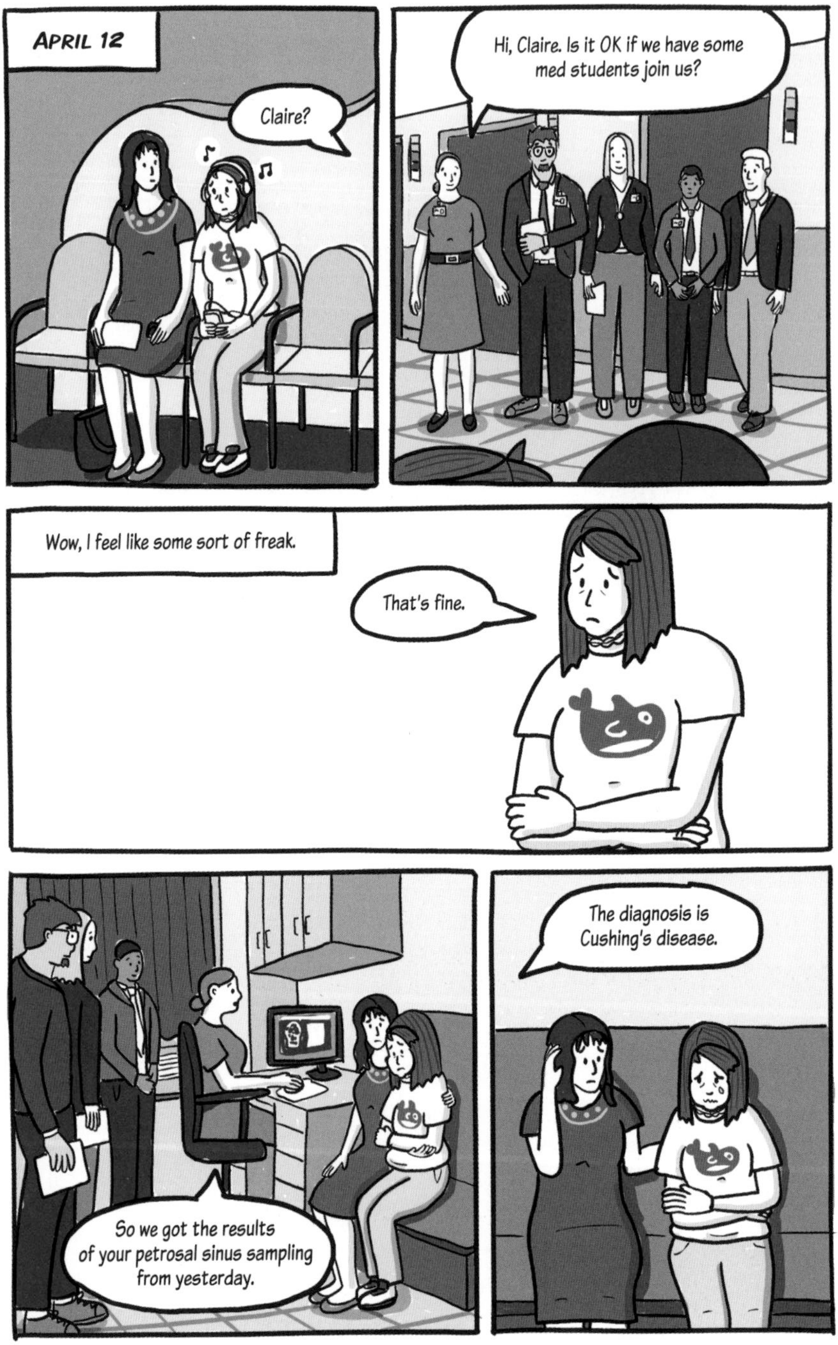
APRIL 12
Claire?
Hi, Claire. Is it OK if we have some med students join us?
Wow, I feel like some sort of freak.
That's fine.
So we got the results of your petrosal sinus sampling from yesterday.
The diagnosis is Cushing's disease.

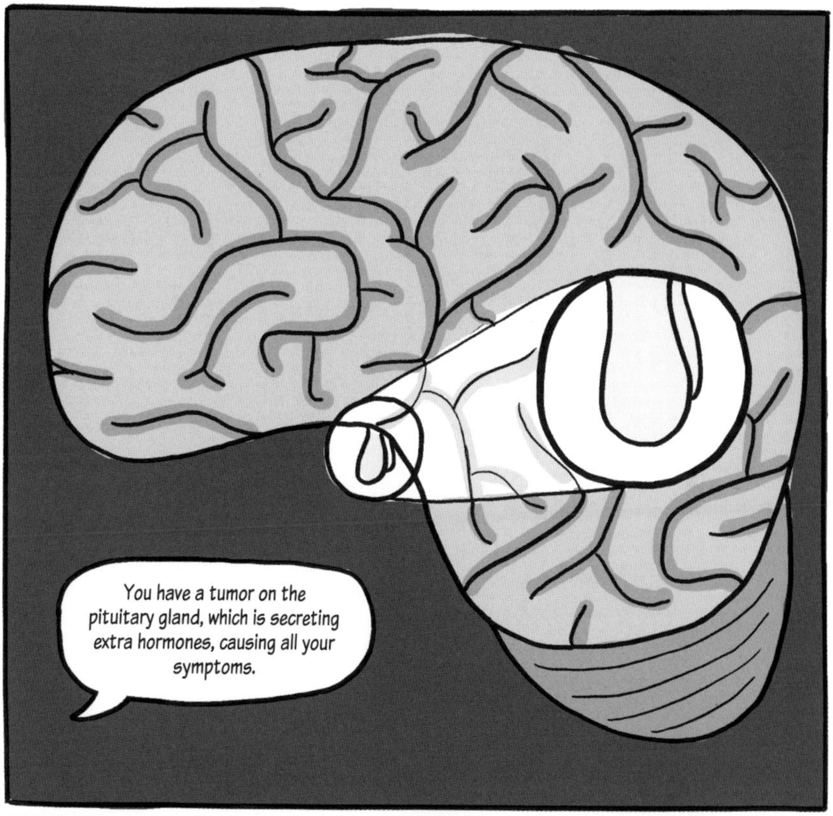
You have a tumor on the pituitary gland, which is secreting extra hormones, causing all your symptoms.

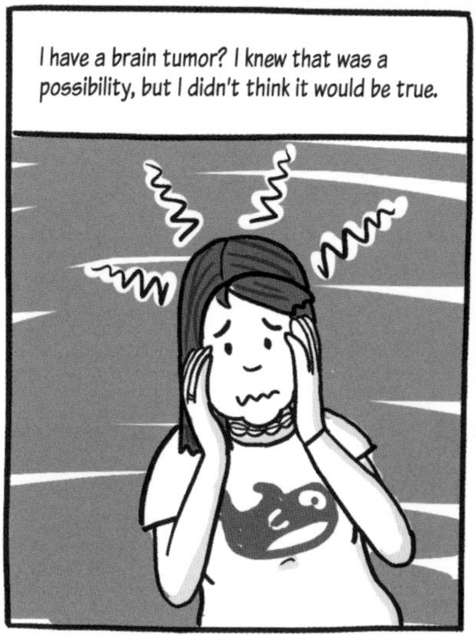
I have a brain tumor? I knew that was a possibility, but I didn't think it would be true.

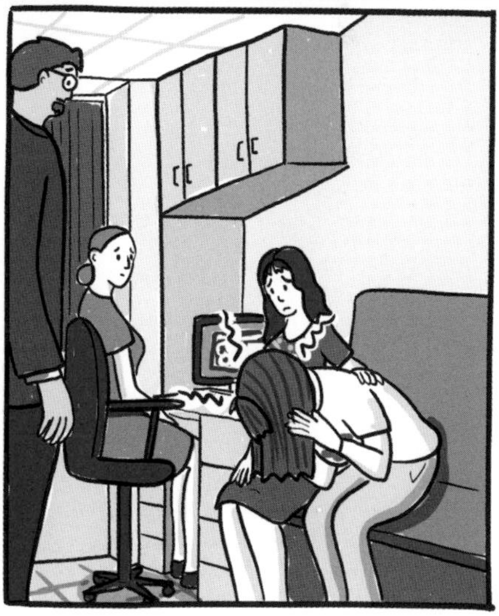

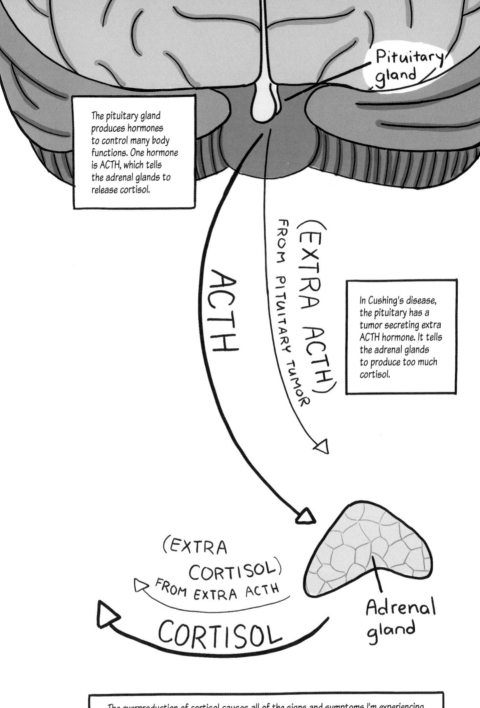

The pituitary gland produces hormones to control many body functions. One hormone is ACTH, which tells the adrenal glands to release cortisol.

Pituitary gland

ACTH

(EXTRA ACTH) FROM PITUITARY TUMOR

In Cushing's disease, the pituitary has a tumor secreting extra ACTH hormone. It tells the adrenal glands to produce too much cortisol.

(EXTRA CORTISOL) FROM EXTRA ACTH

CORTISOL

Adrenal gland

The overproduction of cortisol causes all of the signs and symptoms I'm experiencing (weight gain, hair growth, depression, etc.).

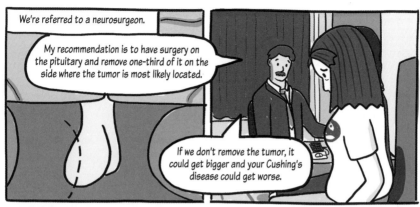

We're referred to a neurosurgeon.

My recommendation is to have surgery on the pituitary and remove one-third of it on the side where the tumor is most likely located.

If we don't remove the tumor, it could get bigger and your Cushing's disease could get worse.

You could start having vision problems, high blood pressure, diabetes, and other serious issues.

To not conflict with school or your trip to Europe, we can schedule for the second week in July. Does that sound good?

Sure.

Expect to receive a full itinerary in the mail at least one month before then.

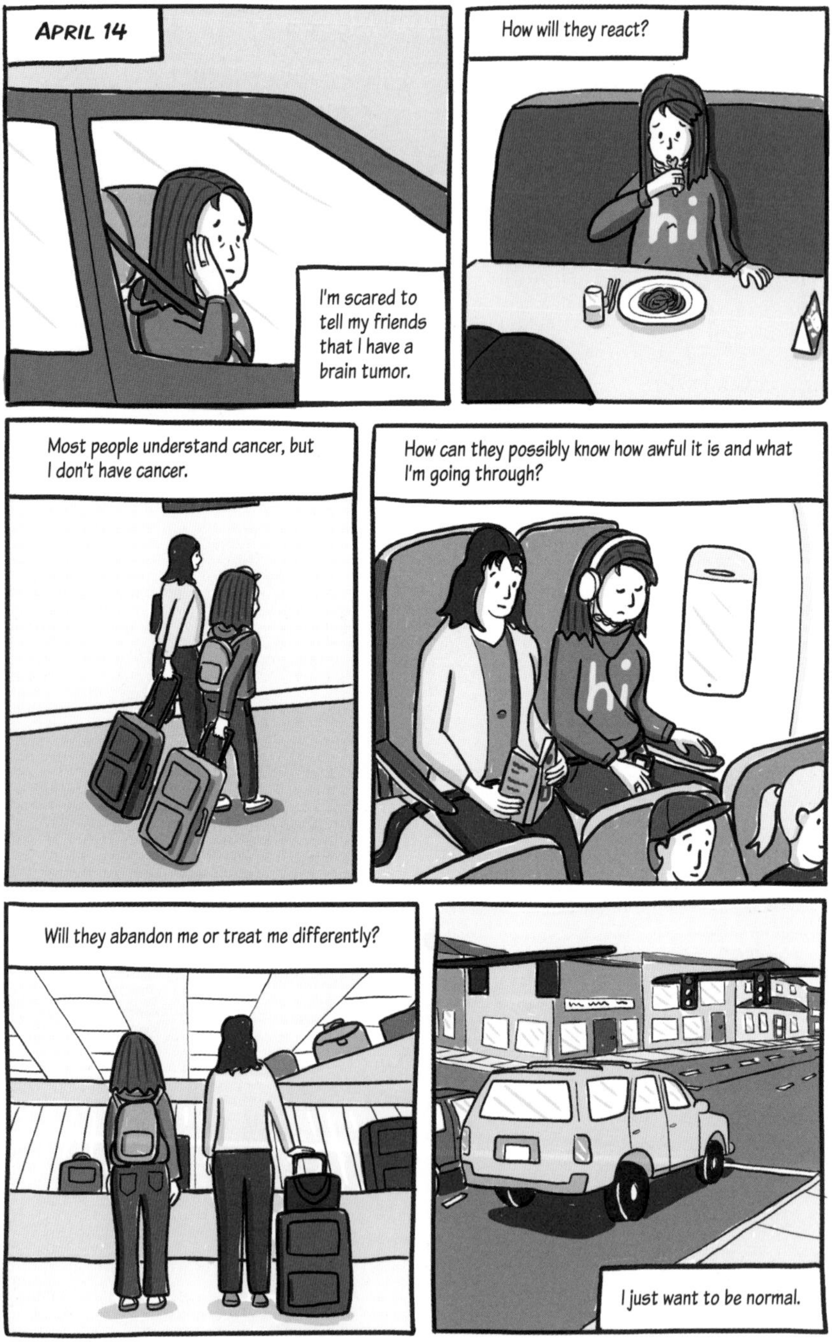
APRIL 14
I'm scared to tell my friends that I have a brain tumor.
How will they react?
Most people understand cancer, but I don't have cancer.
How can they possibly know how awful it is and what I'm going through?
Will they abandon me or treat me differently?
I just want to be normal.

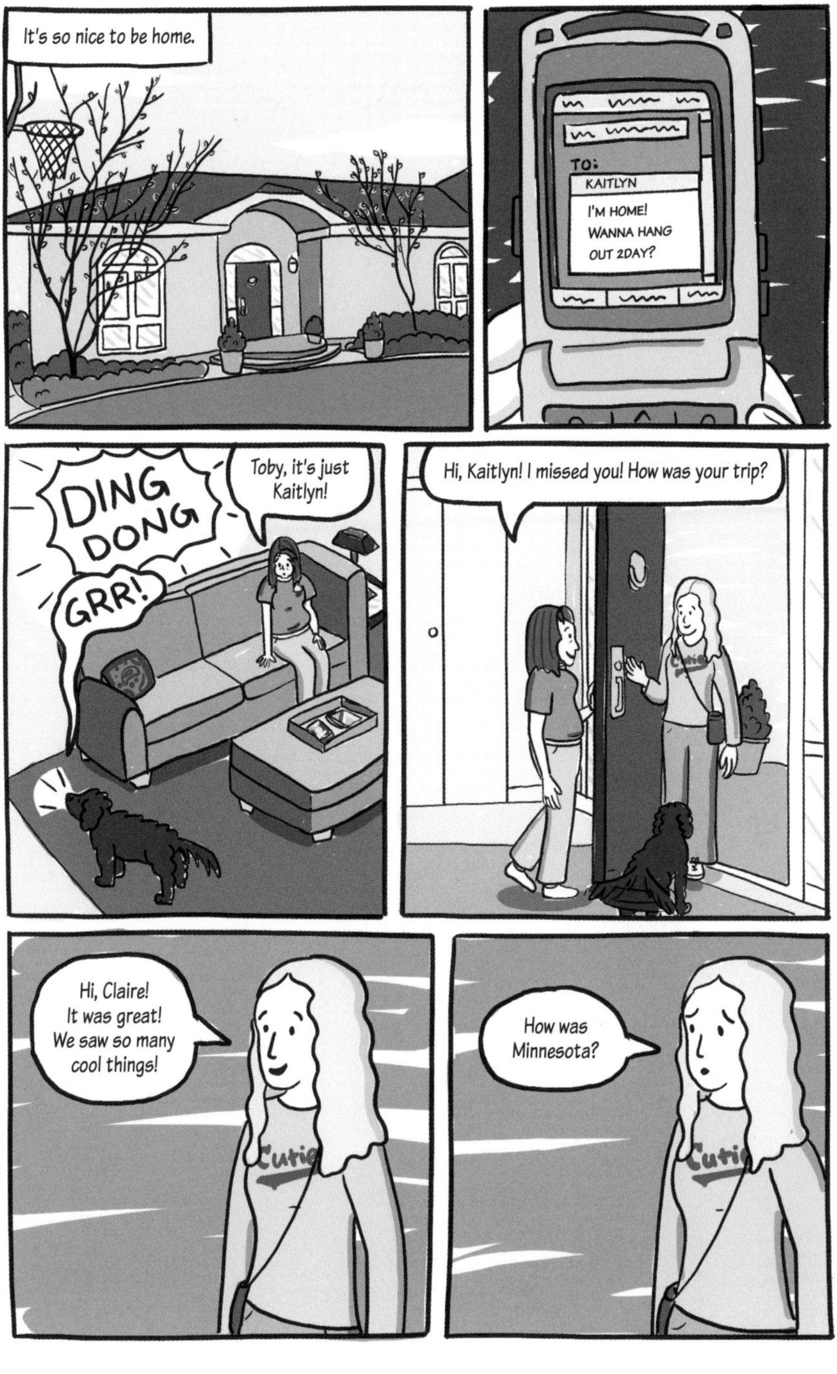
It's so nice to be home.
TO:
KAITLYN
I'M HOME! WANNA HANG OUT 2DAY?
DING DONG
GRR!
Toby, it's just Kaitlyn!
Hi, Kaitlyn! I missed you! How was your trip?
Cutie
Hi, Claire! It was great! We saw so many cool things!
How was Minnesota?

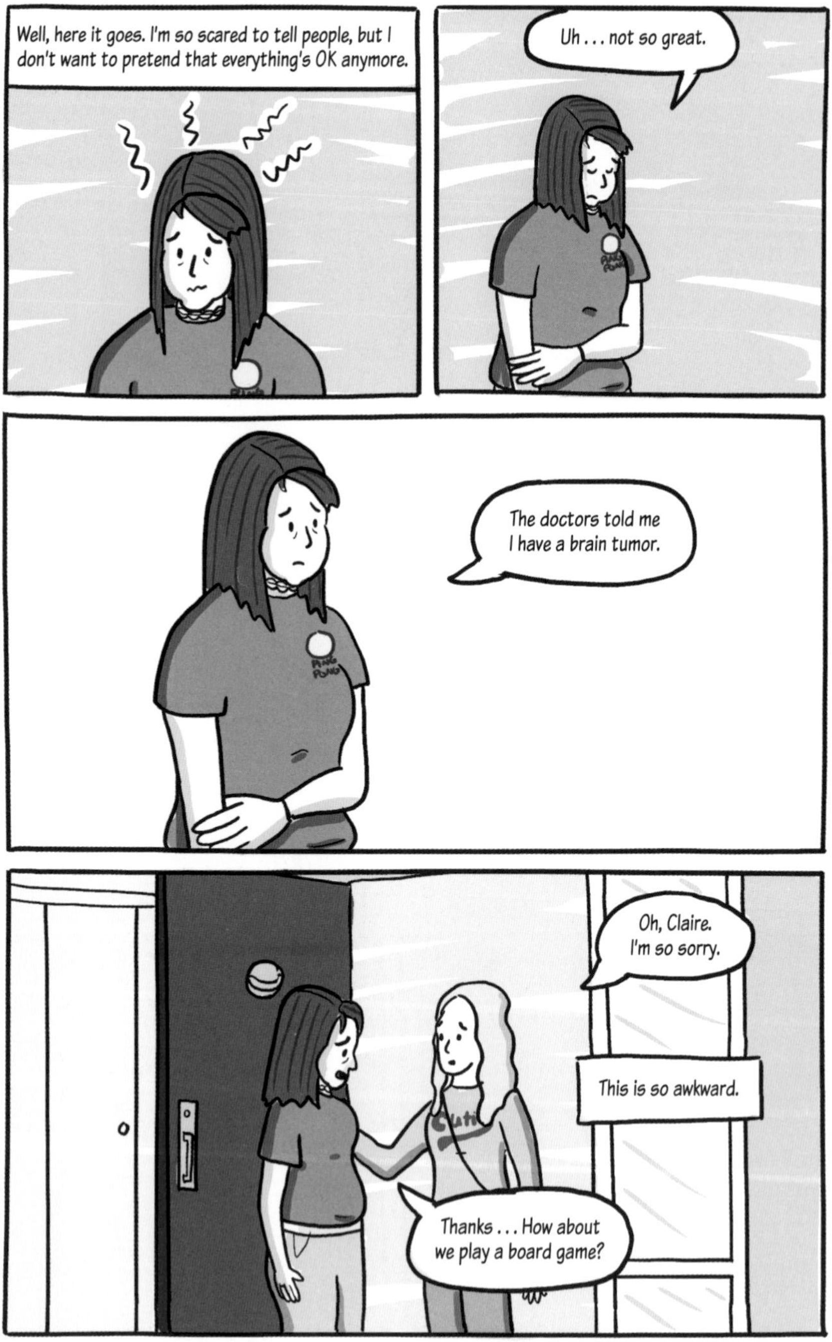

Well, here it goes. I'm so scared to tell people, but I don't want to pretend that everything's OK anymore.
Uh . . . not so great.
The doctors told me I have a brain tumor.
Oh, Claire. I'm so sorry.
This is so awkward.
Thanks . . . How about we play a board game?

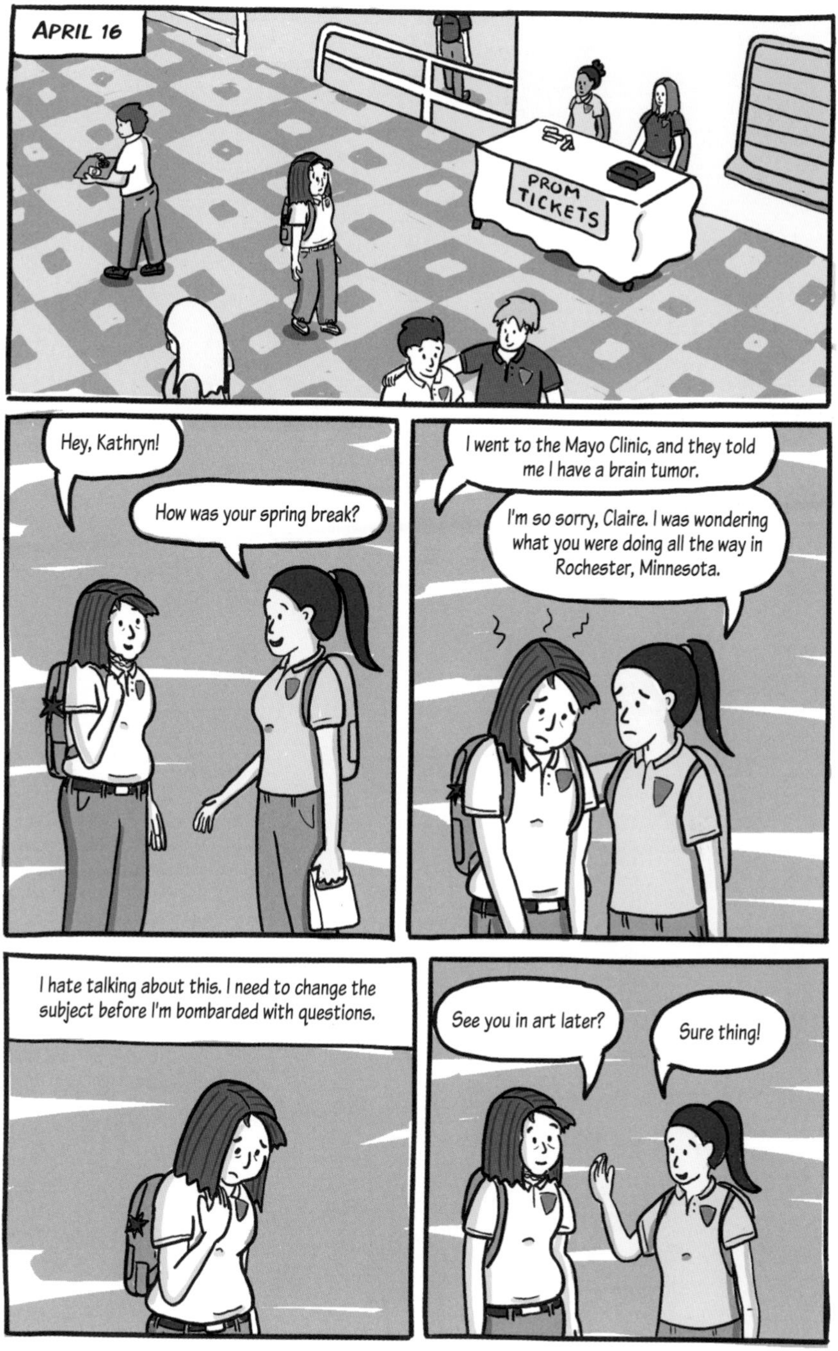

APRIL 16
PROM TICKETS
Hey, Kathryn!
How was your spring break?
I went to the Mayo Clinic, and they told me I have a brain tumor.
I'm so sorry, Claire. I was wondering what you were doing all the way in Rochester, Minnesota.
I hate talking about this. I need to change the subject before I'm bombarded with questions.
See you in art later?
Sure thing!

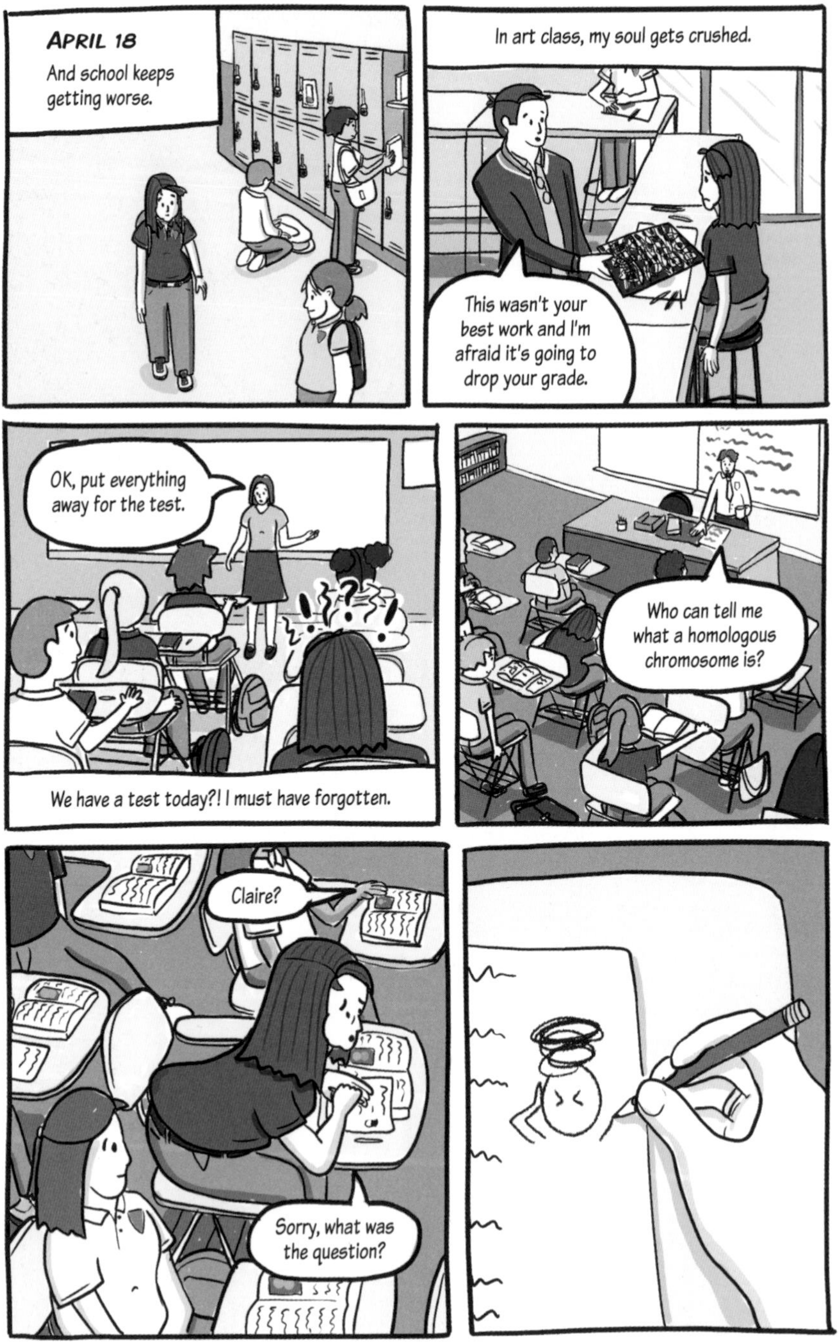
APRIL 18
And school keeps getting worse.
In art class, my soul gets crushed.
This wasn't your best work and I'm afraid it's going to drop your grade.
OK, put everything away for the test.
!?
We have a test today?! I must have forgotten.
Who can tell me what a homologous chromosome is?
Claire?
Sorry, what was the question?

BRAIN FOG

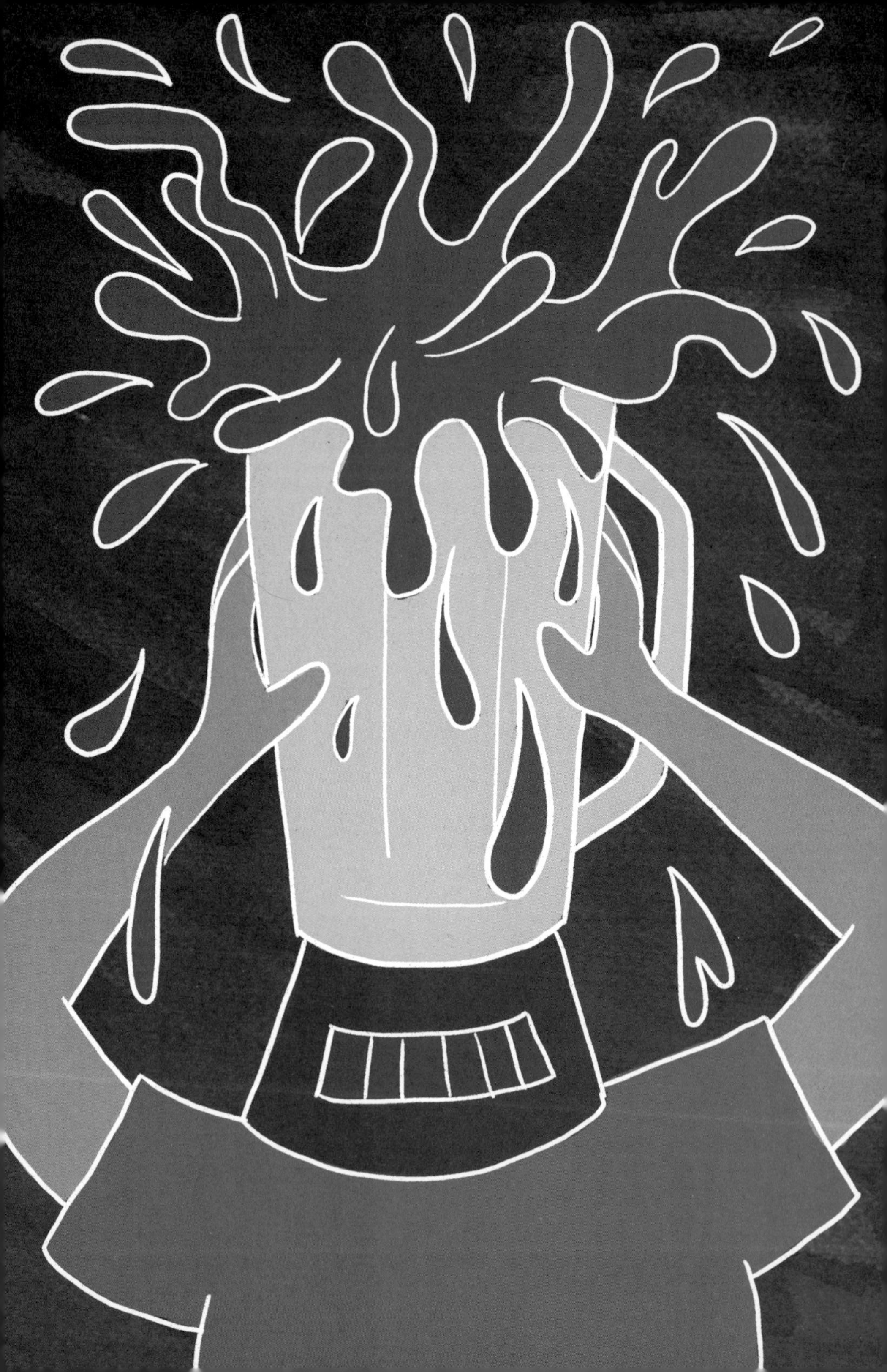

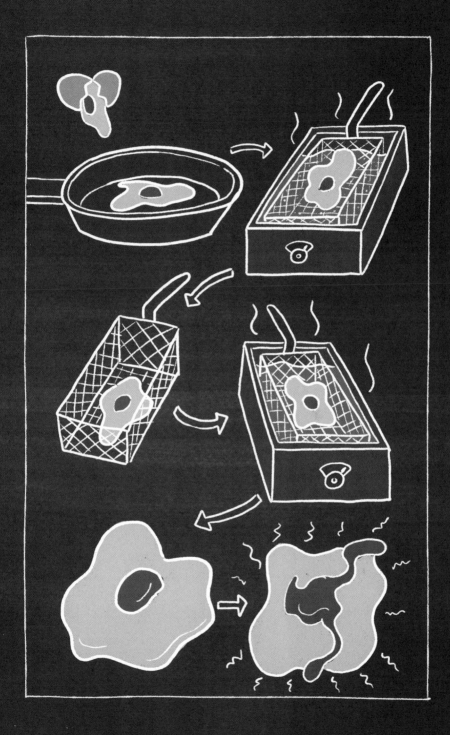

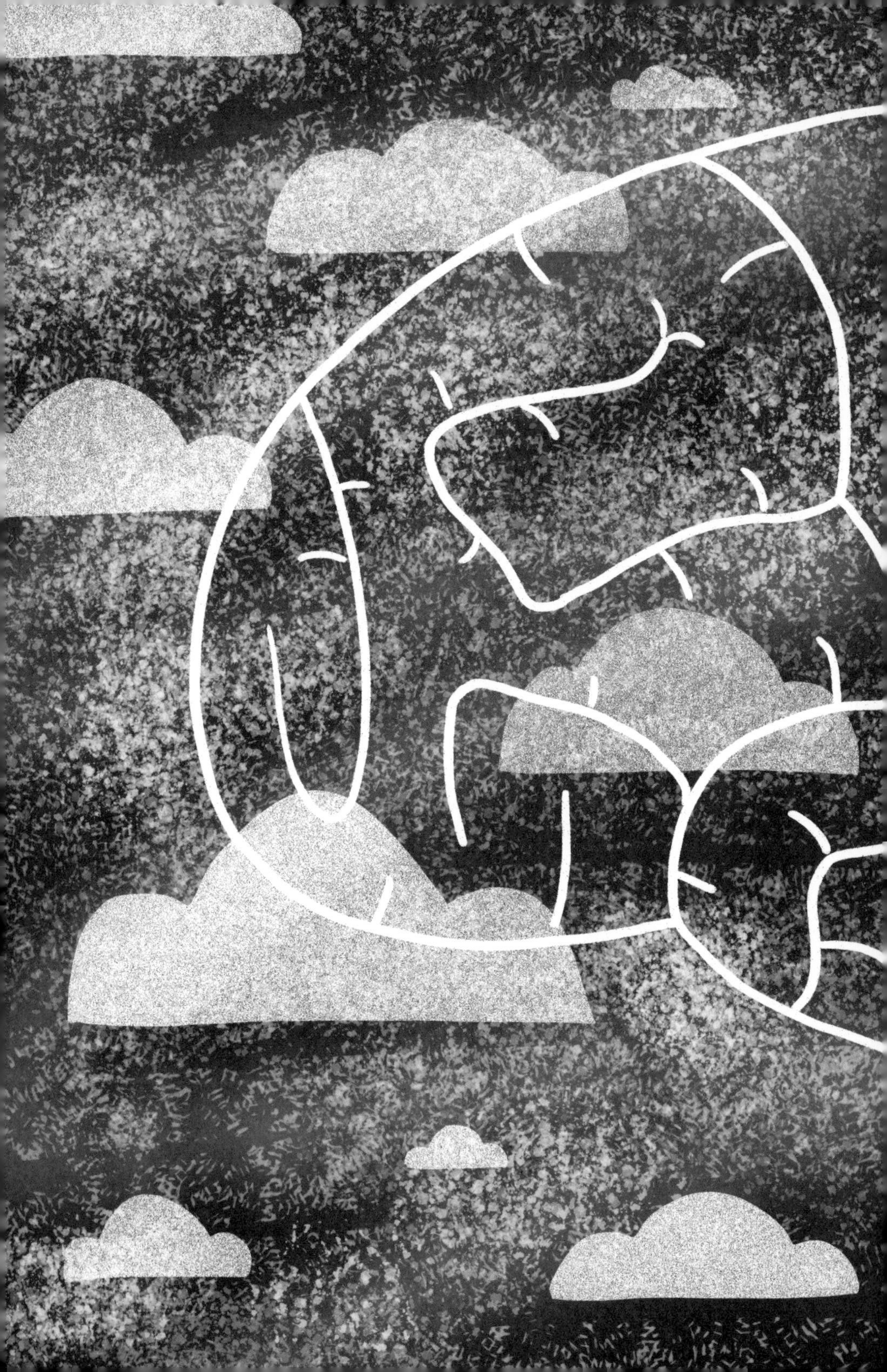

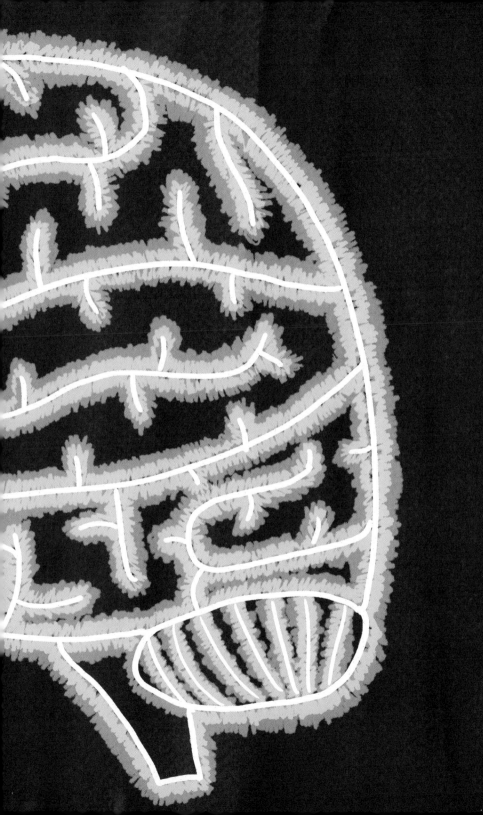

APRIL 25

And now when I'm playing lacrosse, I get confused.

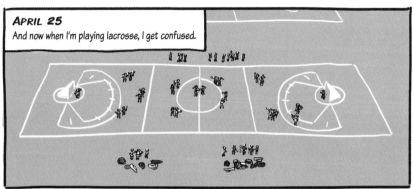

Is that left or right?

Ball right!
Ball right!

FWEET!

My concentration problems are making me a sucky goalie.

I'm letting my team down.

SNIFF
SNIFF

I can't believe I lost the game for us in double overtime.

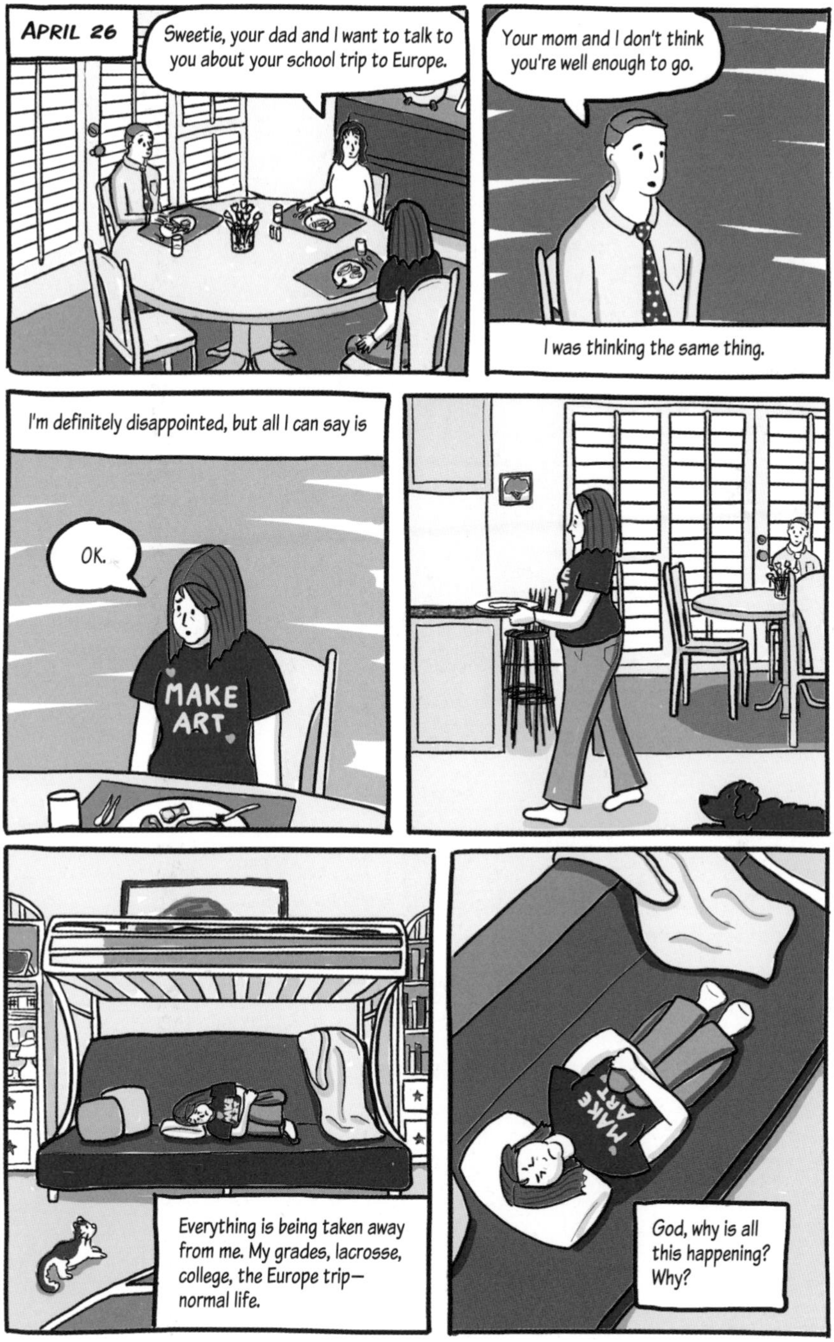
April 26
Sweetie, your dad and I want to talk to you about your school trip to Europe.
Your mom and I don't think you're well enough to go.
I was thinking the same thing.
I'm definitely disappointed, but all I can say is
OK.
MAKE ART
Everything is being taken away from me. My grades, lacrosse, college, the Europe trip—normal life.
God, why is all this happening? Why?

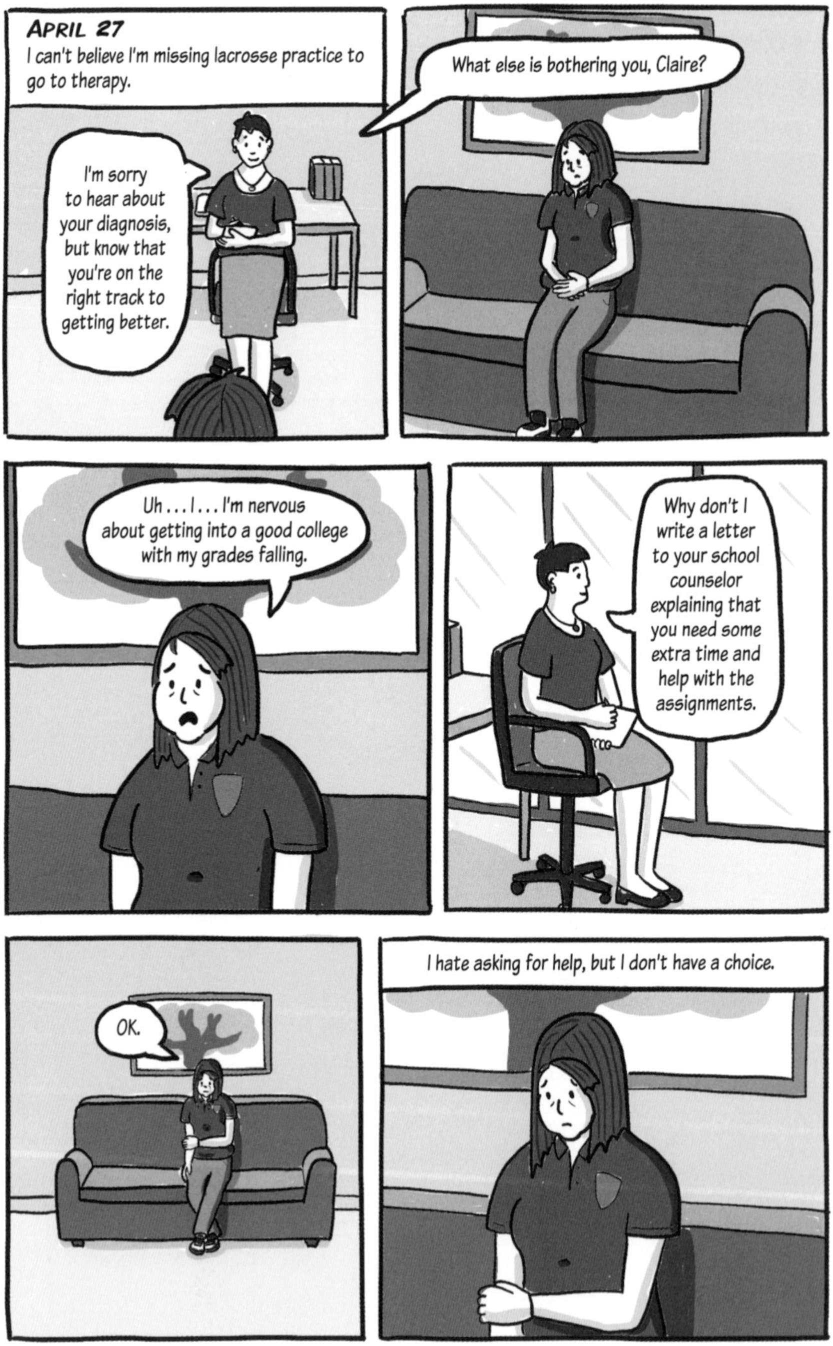
APRIL 27
I can't believe I'm missing lacrosse practice to go to therapy.
I'm sorry to hear about your diagnosis, but know that you're on the right track to getting better.
What else is bothering you, Claire?
Uh . . . I . . . I'm nervous about getting into a good college with my grades falling.
Why don't I write a letter to your school counselor explaining that you need some extra time and help with the assignments.
OK.
I hate asking for help, but I don't have a choice.

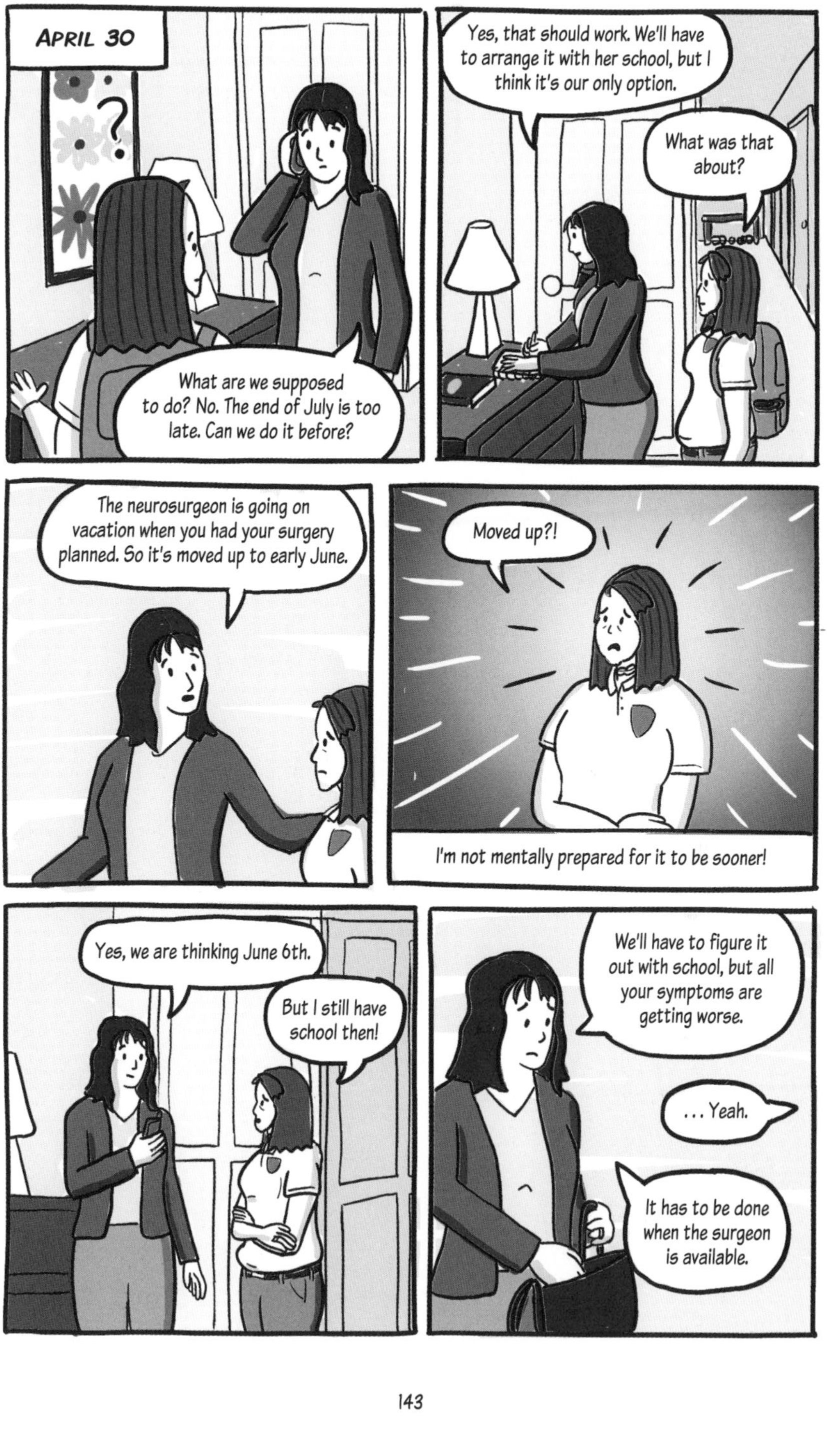
APRIL 30
?
What are we supposed to do? No. The end of July is too late. Can we do it before?
Yes, that should work. We'll have to arrange it with her school, but I think it's our only option.
What was that about?
The neurosurgeon is going on vacation when you had your surgery planned. So it's moved up to early June.
Moved up?!
I'm not mentally prepared for it to be sooner!
Yes, we are thinking June 6th.
But I still have school then!
We'll have to figure it out with school, but all your symptoms are getting worse.
. . . Yeah.
It has to be done when the surgeon is available.

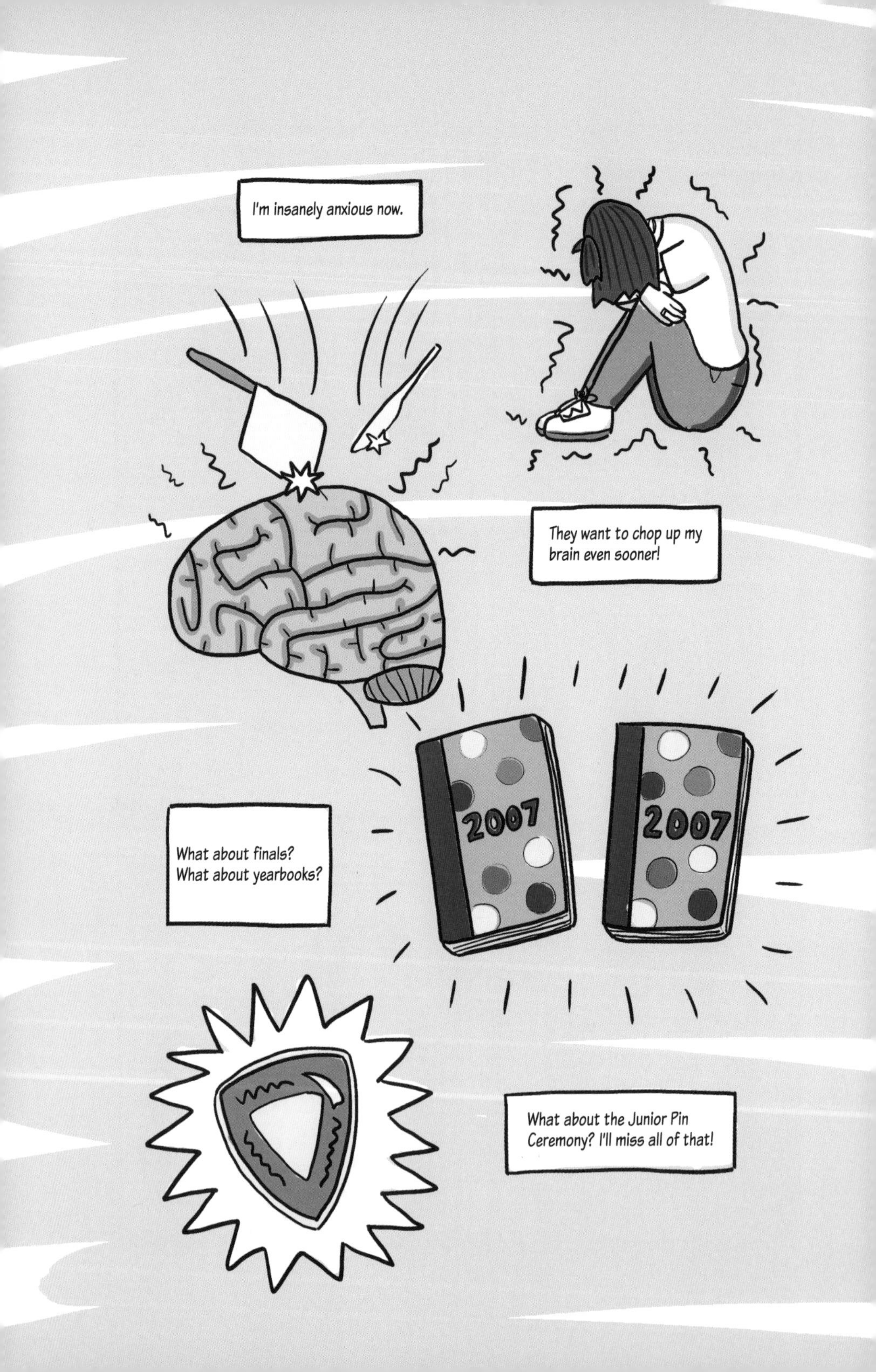
I'm insanely anxious now.
They want to chop up my brain even sooner!
What about finals? What about yearbooks?
2007
2007
What about the Junior Pin Ceremony? I'll miss all of that!

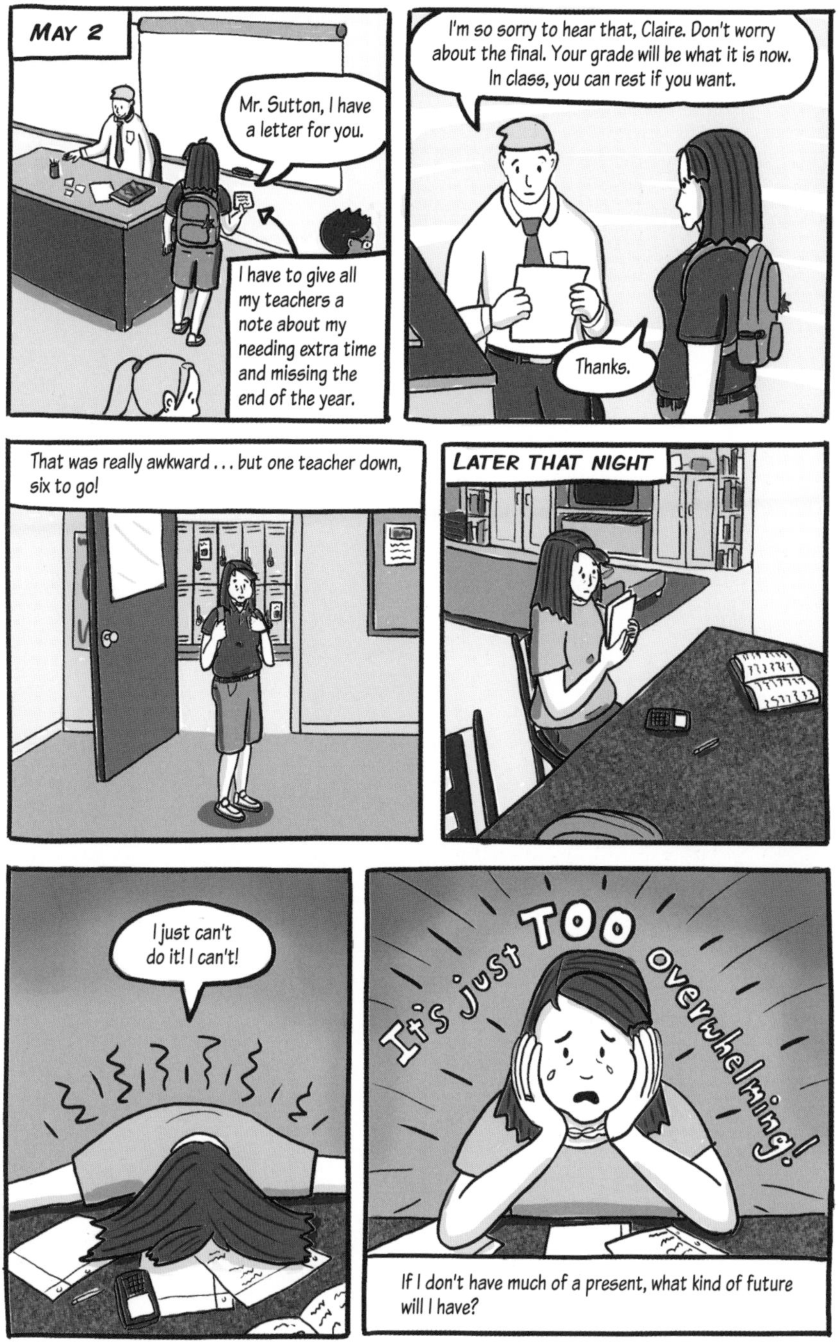
MAY 2
Mr. Sutton, I have a letter for you.
I have to give all my teachers a note about my needing extra time and missing the end of the year.
I'm so sorry to hear that, Claire. Don't worry about the final. Your grade will be what it is now. In class, you can rest if you want.
Thanks.
That was really awkward . . . but one teacher down, six to go!
LATER THAT NIGHT
I just can't do it! I can't!
It's just TOO overwhelming!
If I don't have much of a present, what kind of future will I have?

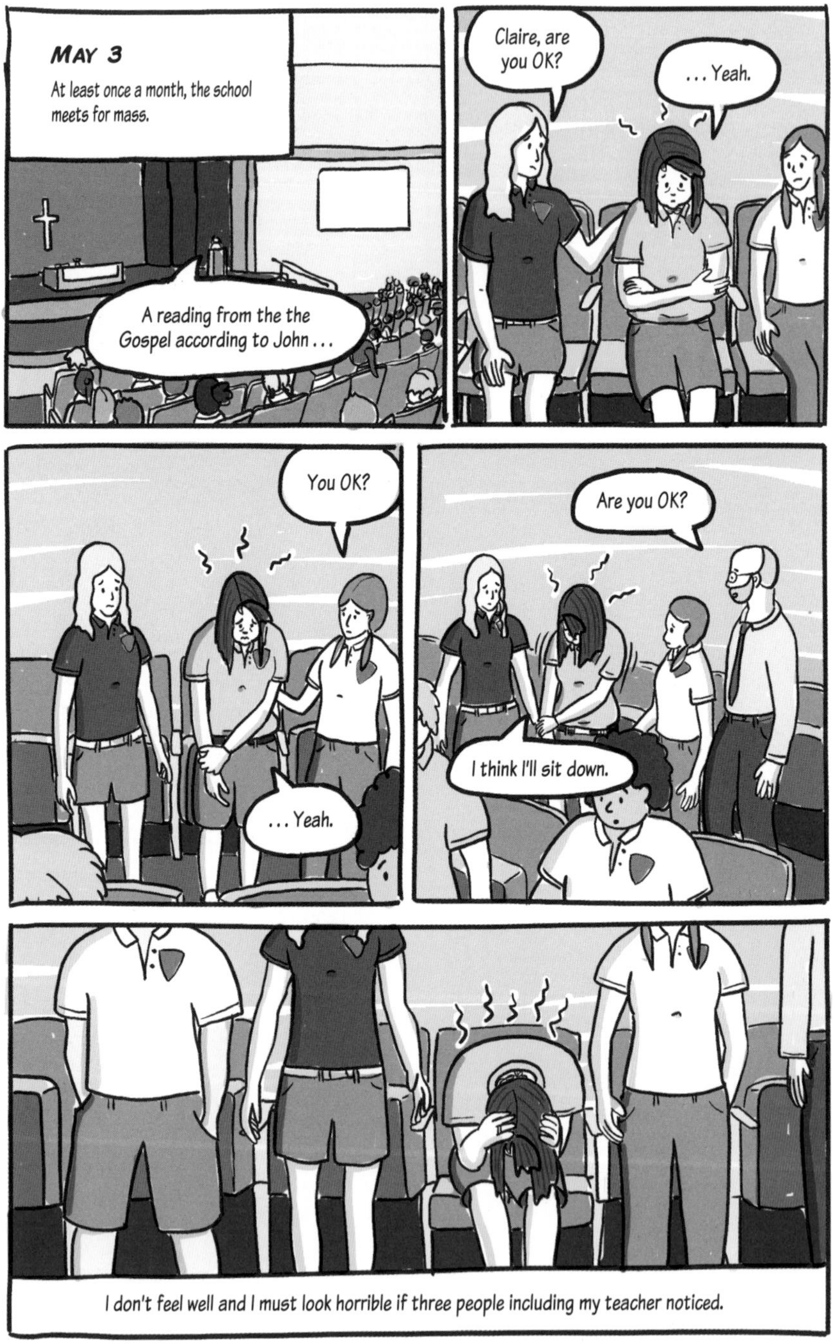
MAY 3
At least once a month, the school meets for mass.
A reading from the the Gospel according to John . . .
Claire, are you OK?
. . . Yeah.
You OK?
. . . Yeah.
Are you OK?
I think I'll sit down.
I don't feel well and I must look horrible if three people including my teacher noticed.

me. Why me? Why now? I
ffering. Oh please make it Stop! My Symptoms are getting
xious. I just got my Lit Mag and none of my art got in it! I feel like
ailure. I'm so sad... Should I even pursue art? Am I good enough?
pit. I want to be my old, happy self. My mom said that my tumor might
rse. I want to be successful, but currently I'm a failure. Now
aunting. I try SO hard to be Strong. I feel so weak. Juni

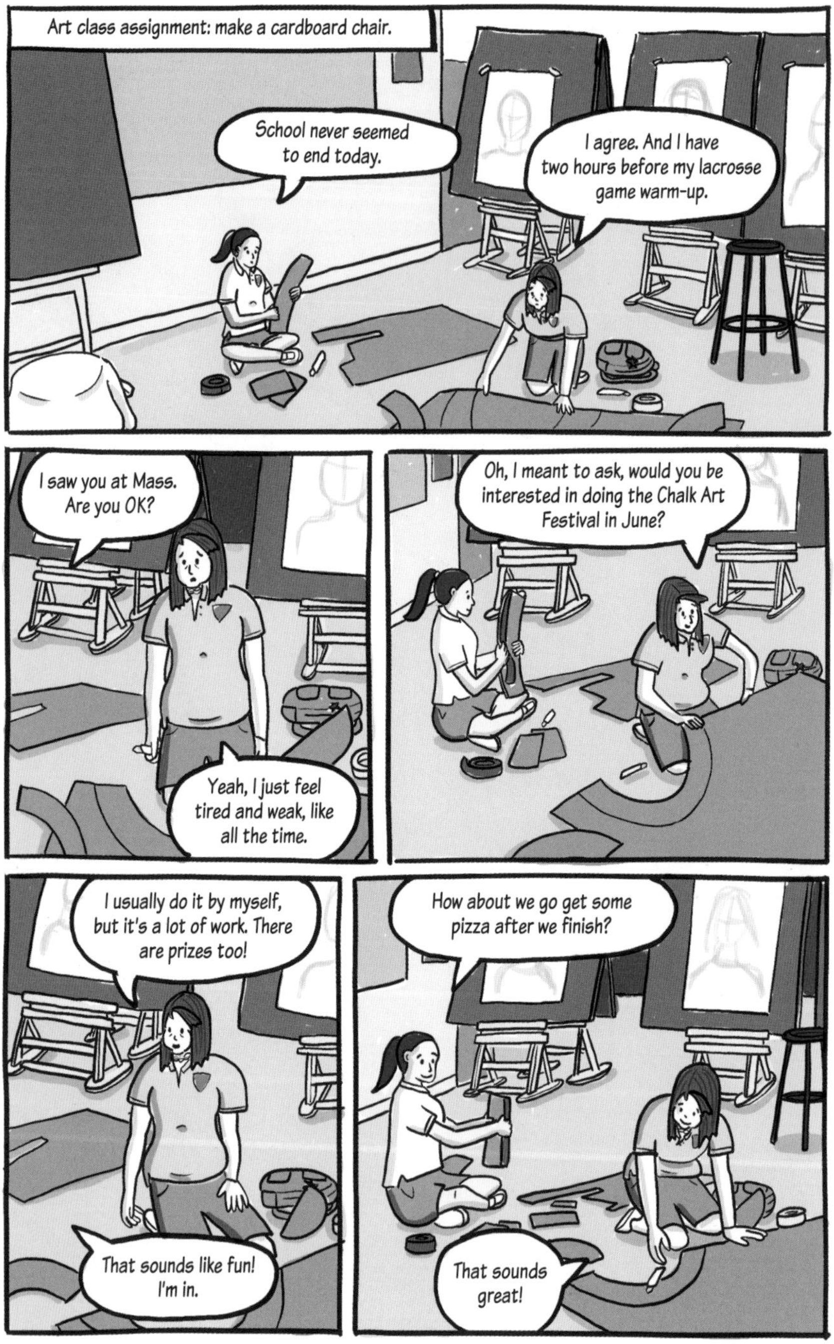

Art class assignment: make a cardboard chair.
School never seemed to end today.
I agree. And I have two hours before my lacrosse game warm-up.
I saw you at Mass. Are you OK?
Yeah, I just feel tired and weak, like all the time.
Oh, I meant to ask, would you be interested in doing the Chalk Art Festival in June?
I usually do it by myself, but it's a lot of work. There are prizes too!
That sounds like fun! I'm in.
How about we go get some pizza after we finish?
That sounds great!

MAY 10

Ever since I became sick, I feel myself being more drawn to making art.

Maybe it's because I'm having a hard time concentrating on anything else right now.

Maybe it's because I can let my feelings out through it.

Or because it's one of the few things I still enjoy.

In any case, it's nice having one thing that I look forward to in the school day.

I just have to make sure I finish this chair before I leave for my surgery. I need to show Mr. Bettin that I'm still serious about AP next year.

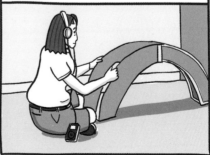

149

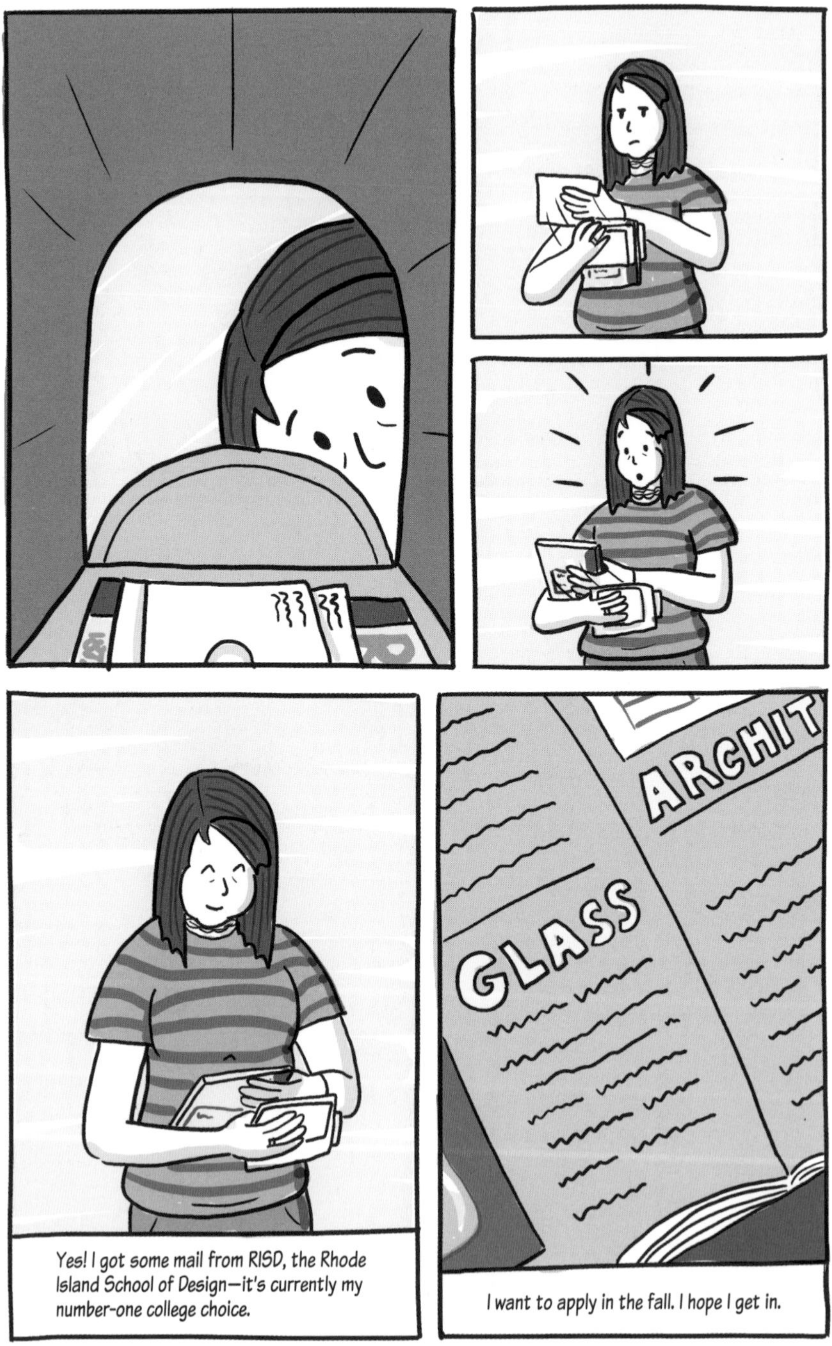

ARCHIT
GLASS
Yes! I got some mail from RISD, the Rhode Island School of Design—it's currently my number-one college choice.
I want to apply in the fall. I hope I get in.

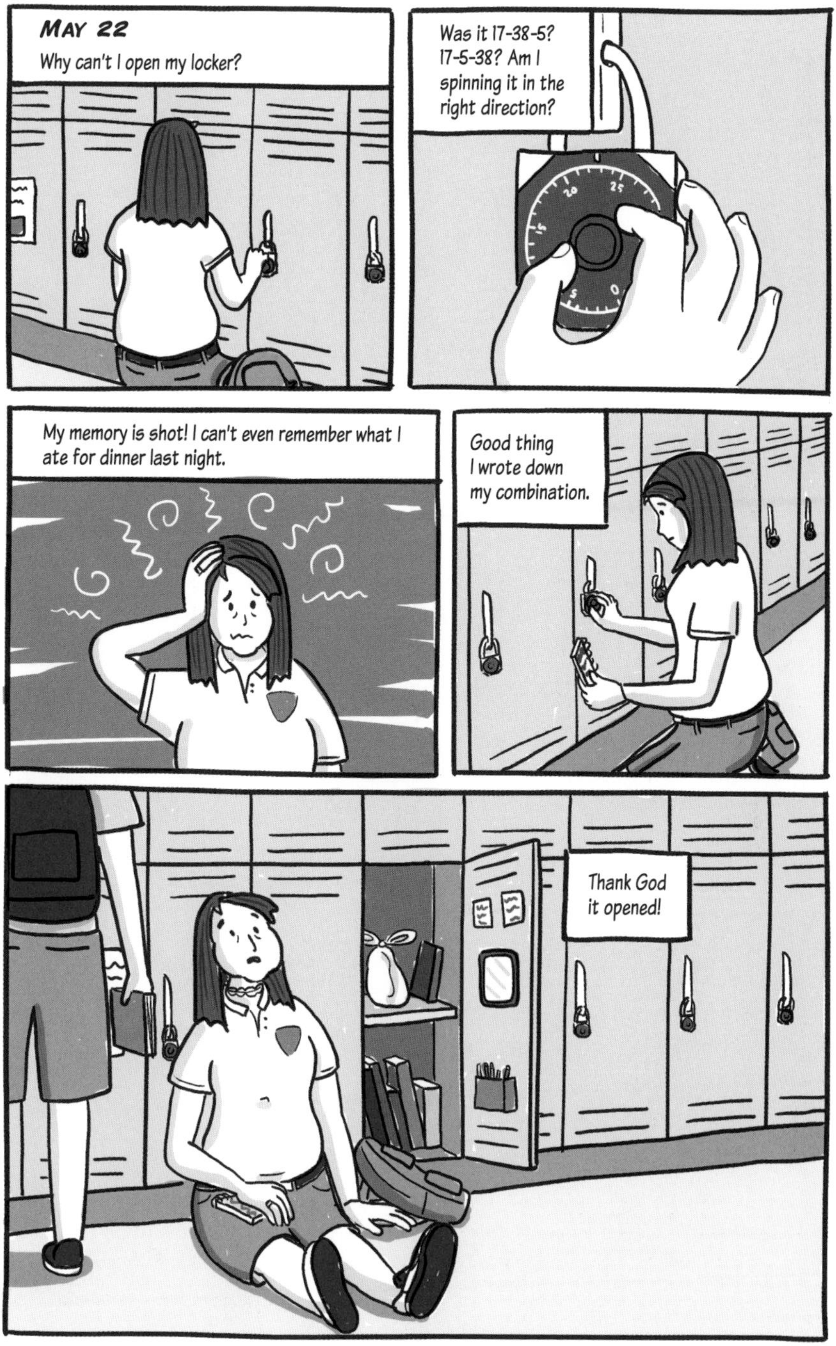
MAY 22
Why can't I open my locker?
Was it 17-38-5? 17-5-38? Am I spinning it in the right direction?
My memory is shot! I can't even remember what I ate for dinner last night.
Good thing I wrote down my combination.
Thank God it opened!

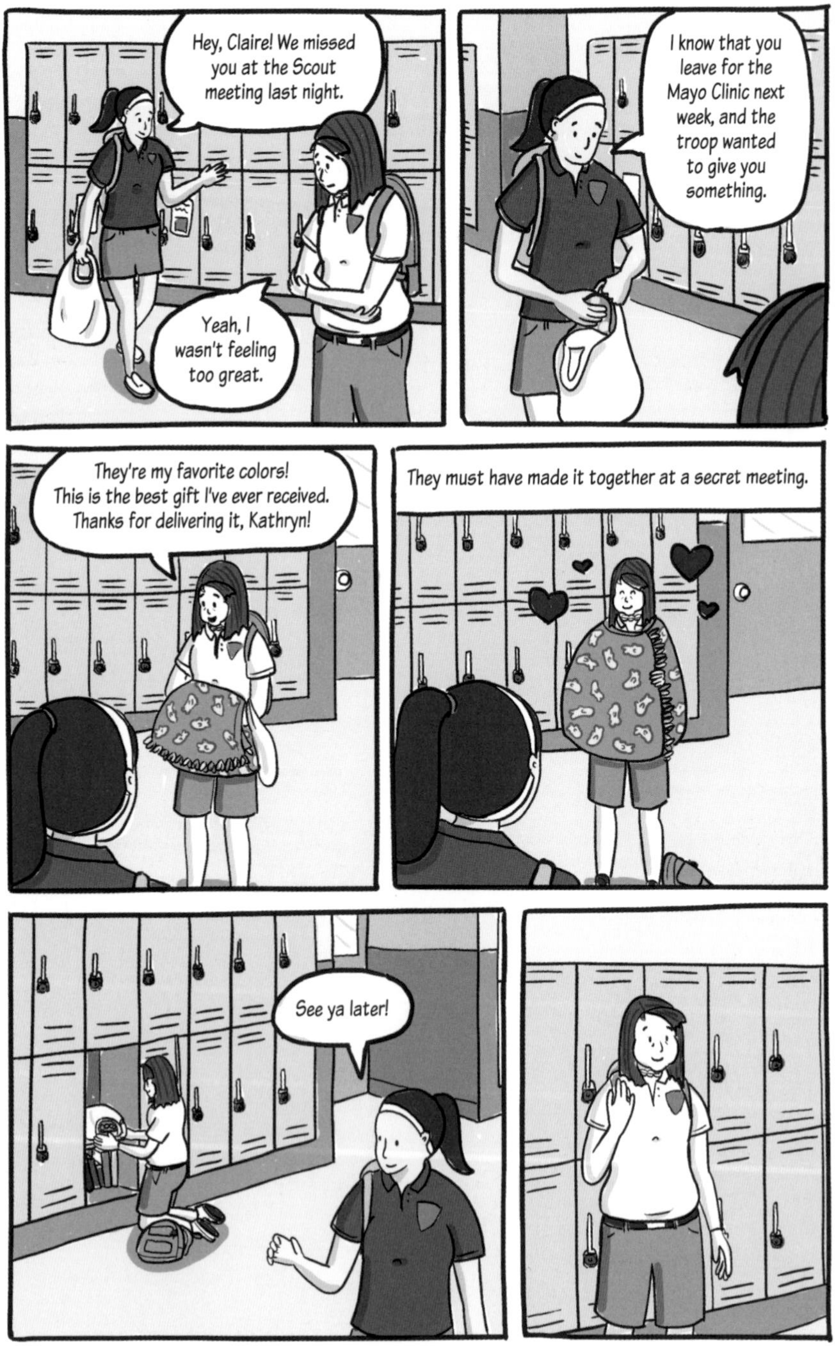
Hey, Claire! We missed you at the Scout meeting last night.
Yeah, I wasn't feeling too great.
I know that you leave for the Mayo Clinic next week, and the troop wanted to give you something.
They're my favorite colors! This is the best gift I've ever received. Thanks for delivering it, Kathryn!
They must have made it together at a secret meeting.
See ya later!

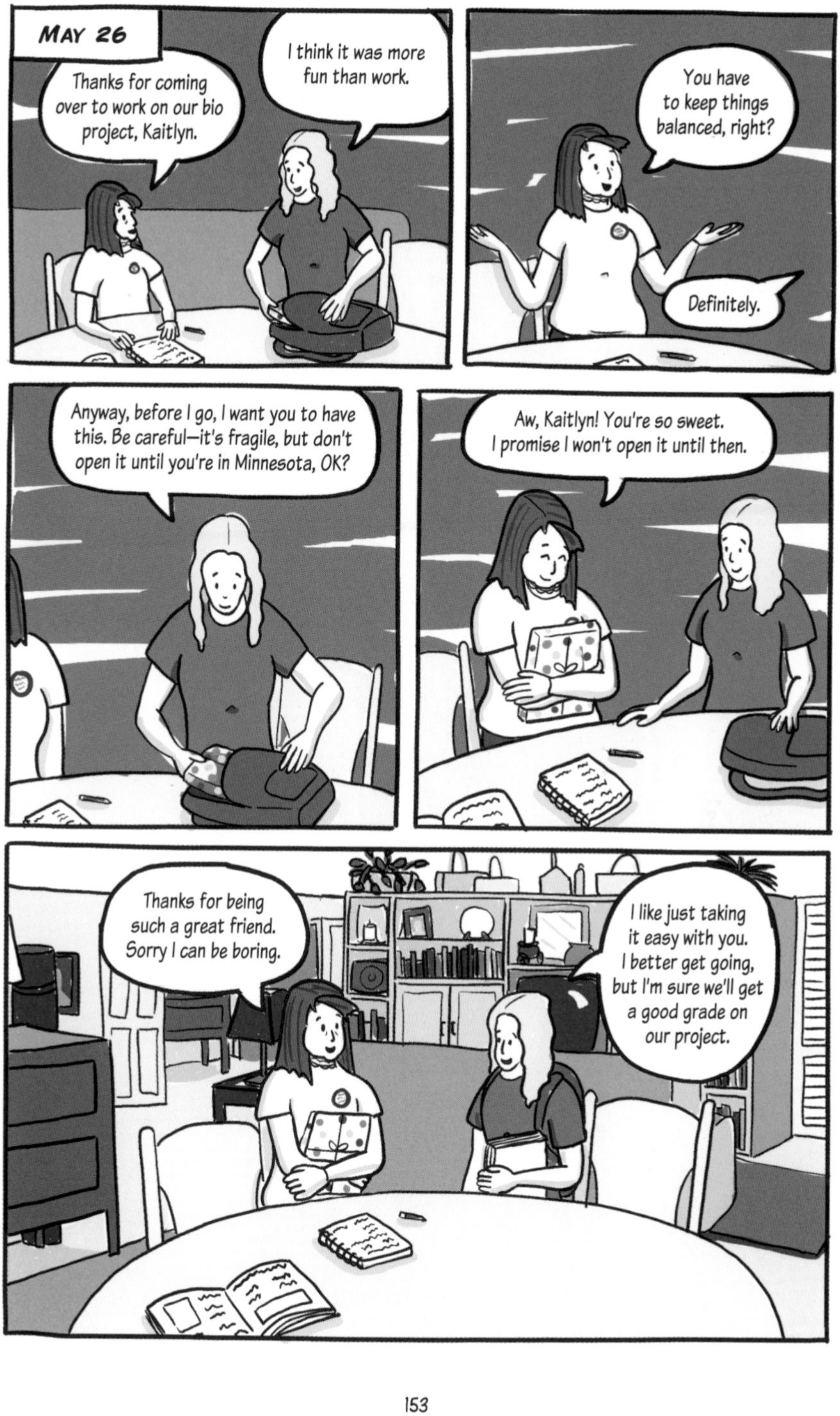
MAY 26
Thanks for coming over to work on our bio project, Kaitlyn.
I think it was more fun than work.
You have to keep things balanced, right?
Definitely.
Anyway, before I go, I want you to have this. Be careful—it's fragile, but don't open it until you're in Minnesota, OK?
Aw, Kaitlyn! You're so sweet. I promise I won't open it until then.
Thanks for being such a great friend. Sorry I can be boring.
I like just taking it easy with you. I better get going, but I'm sure we'll get a good grade on our project.

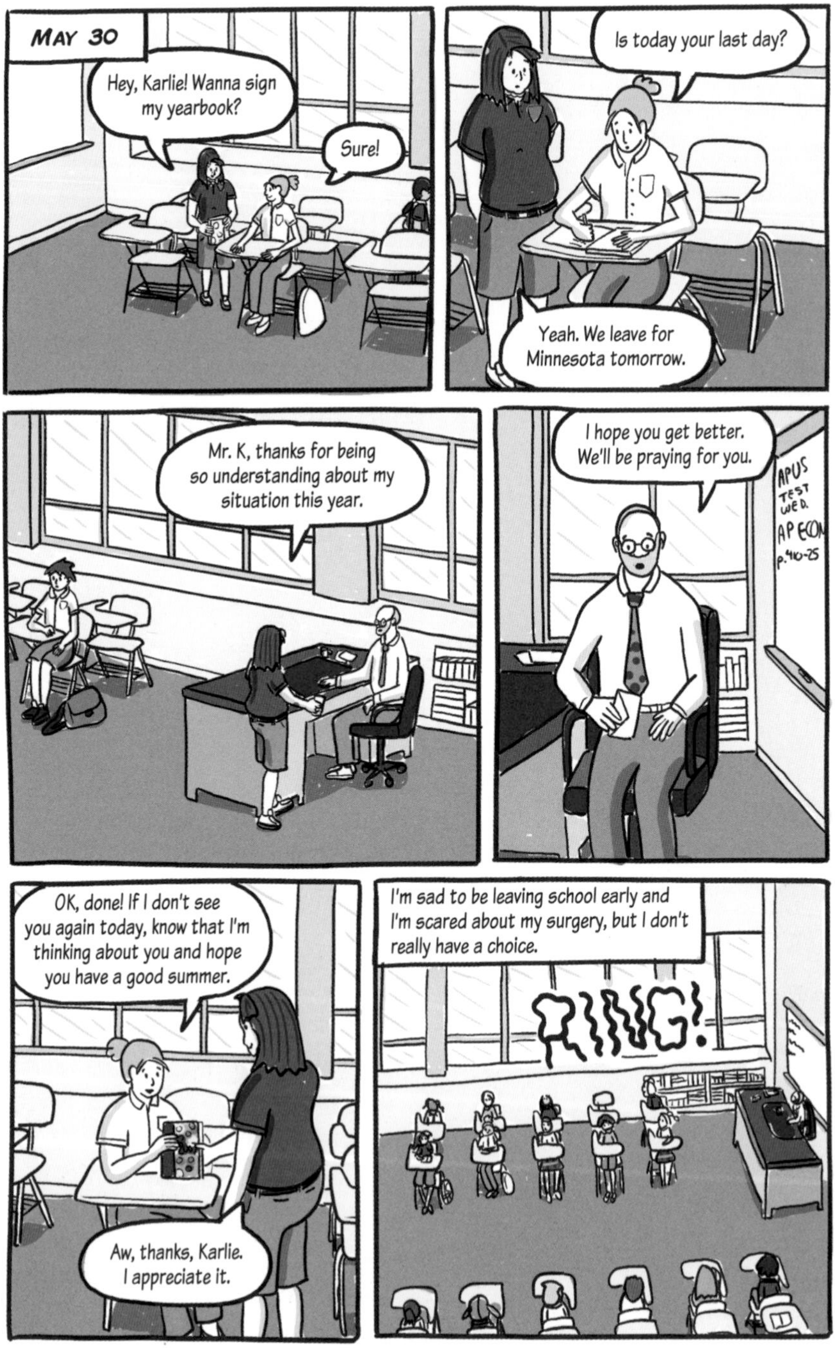
MAY 30
Hey, Karlie! Wanna sign my yearbook?
Sure!
Is today your last day?
Yeah. We leave for Minnesota tomorrow.
Mr. K, thanks for being so understanding about my situation this year.
I hope you get better. We'll be praying for you.
APUS TEST WED.
AP ECON p. 410-25
OK, done! If I don't see you again today, know that I'm thinking about you and hope you have a good summer.
Aw, thanks, Karlie. I appreciate it.
I'm sad to be leaving school early and I'm scared about my surgery, but I don't really have a choice.
RING!

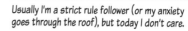
Usually I'm a strict rule follower (or my anxiety goes through the roof), but today I don't care.

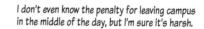
Are you ready?

Yes, we'll be there right when they open.

What we're doing is TOTALLY against the rules.

I don't even know the penalty for leaving campus in the middle of the day, but I'm sure it's harsh.

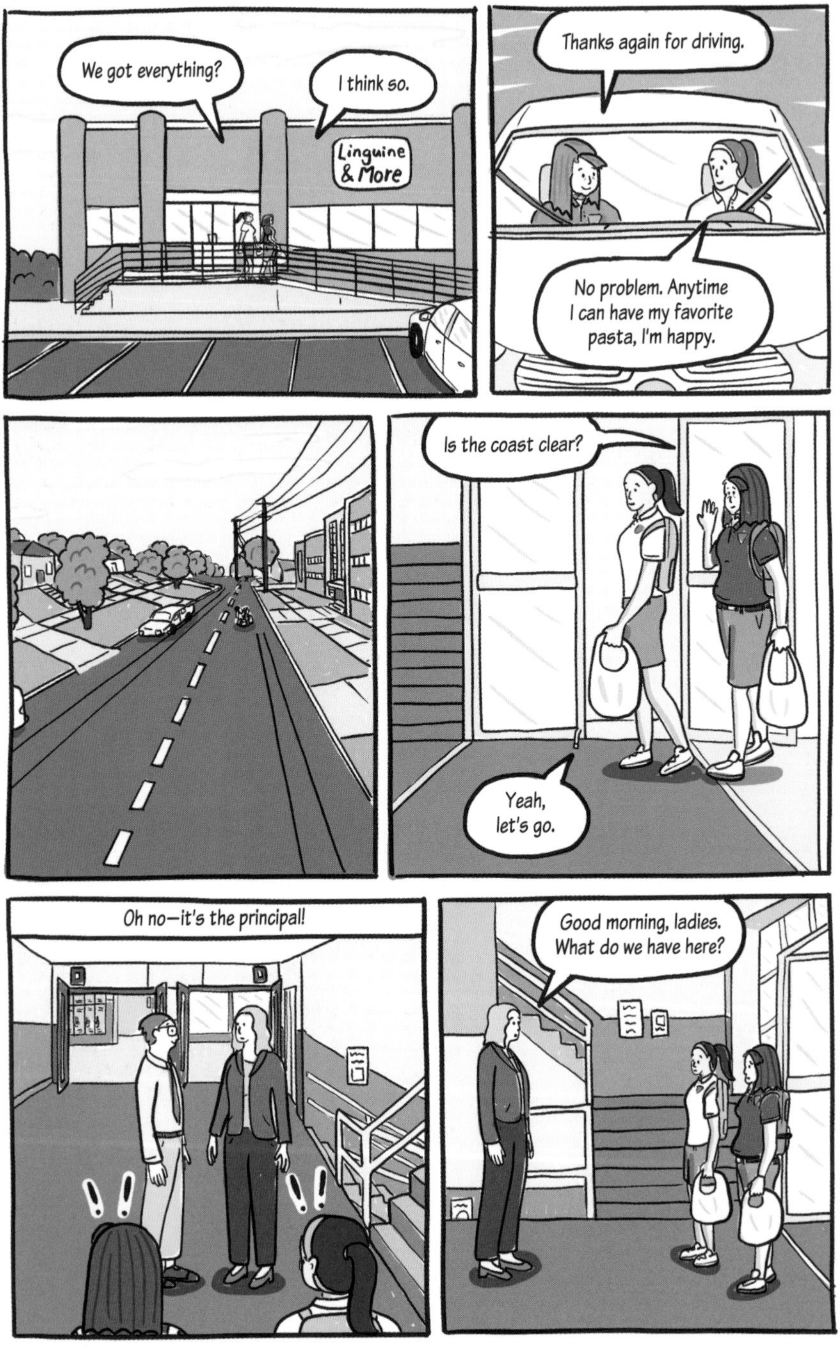
We got everything?
I think so.
Linguine & More
Thanks again for driving.
No problem. Anytime I can have my favorite pasta, I'm happy.
Is the coast clear?
Yeah, let's go.
Oh no—it's the principal!
Good morning, ladies. What do we have here?

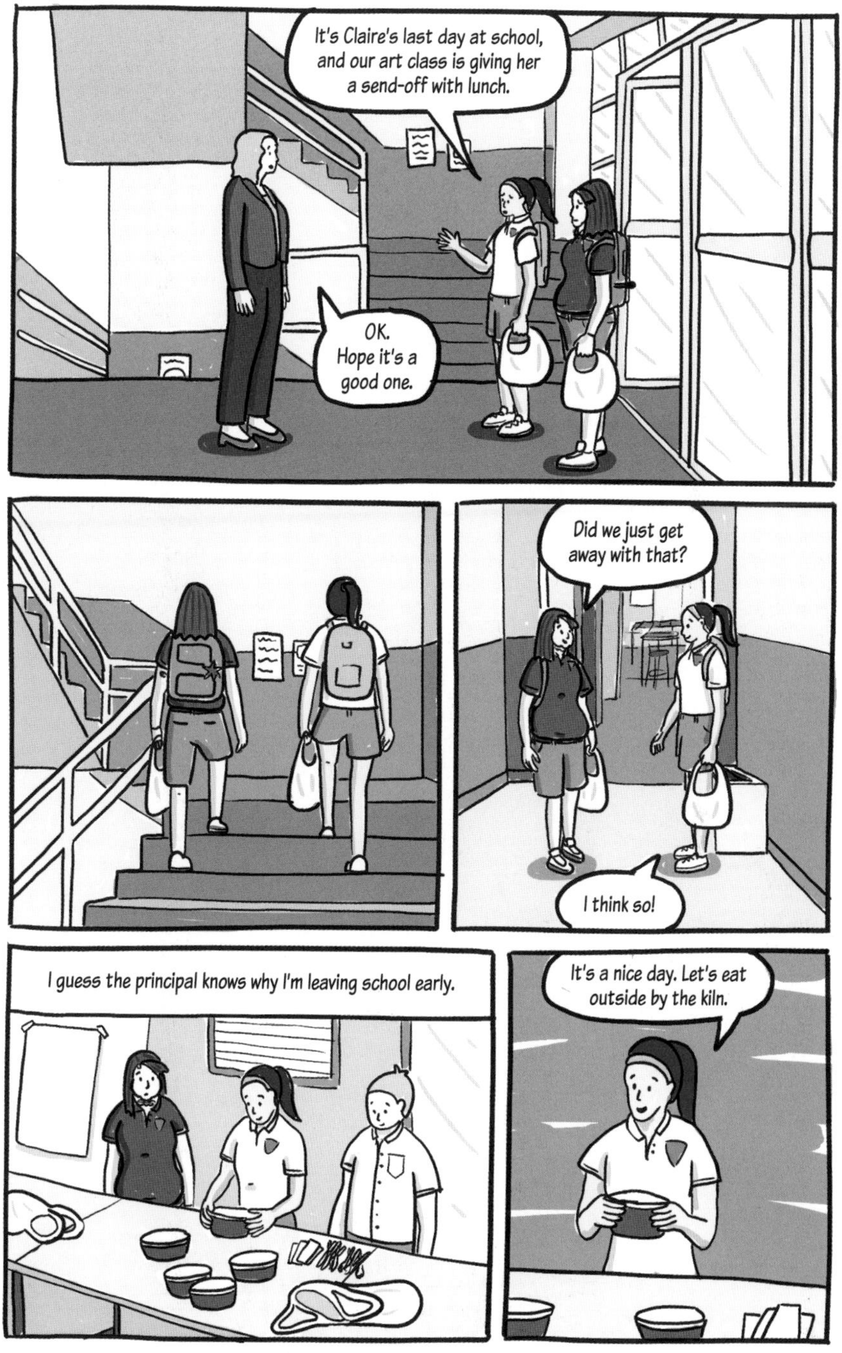
It's Claire's last day at school, and our art class is giving her a send-off with lunch.
OK. Hope it's a good one.
Did we just get away with that?
I think so!
I guess the principal knows why I'm leaving school early.
It's a nice day. Let's eat outside by the kiln.

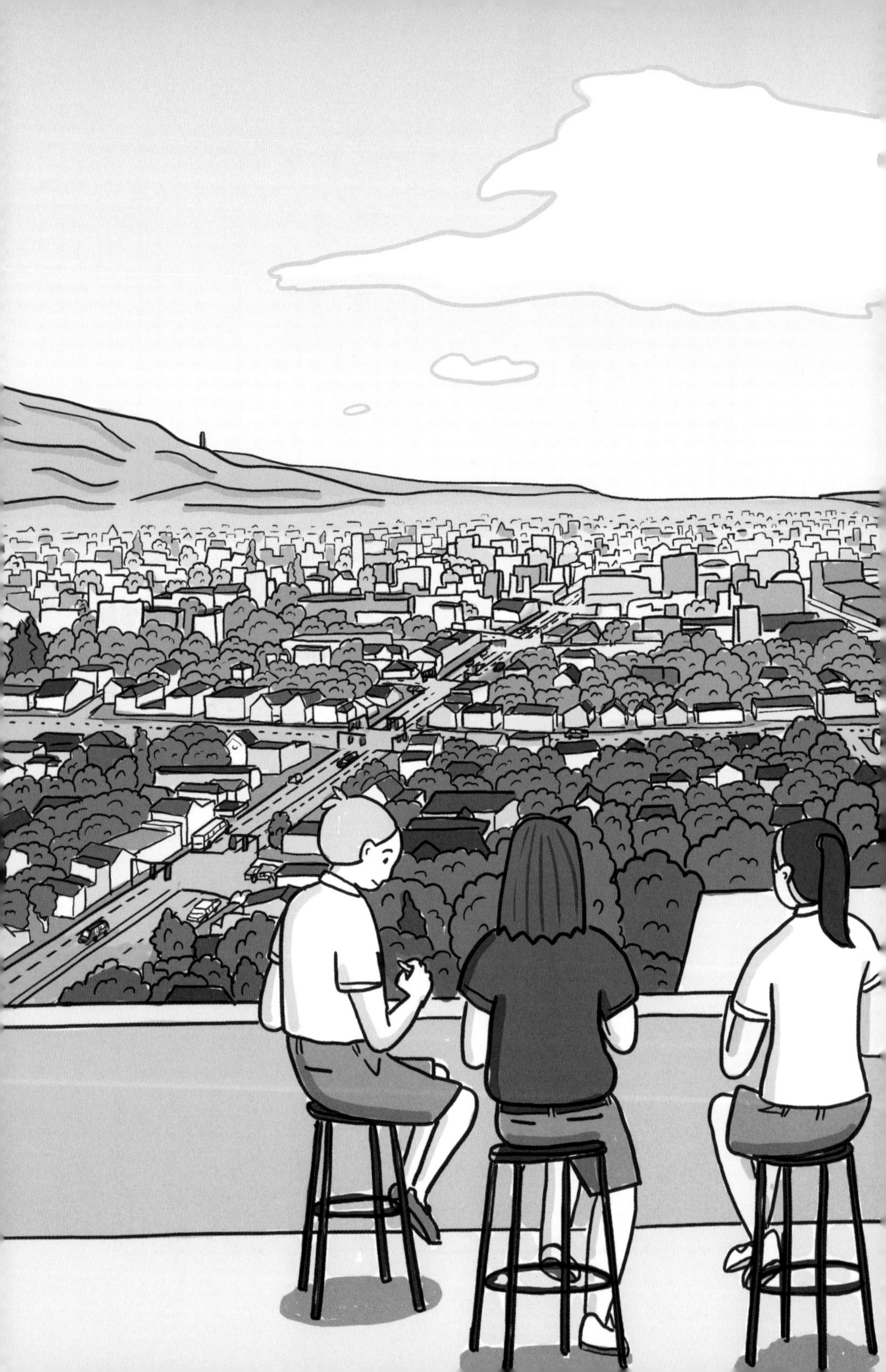

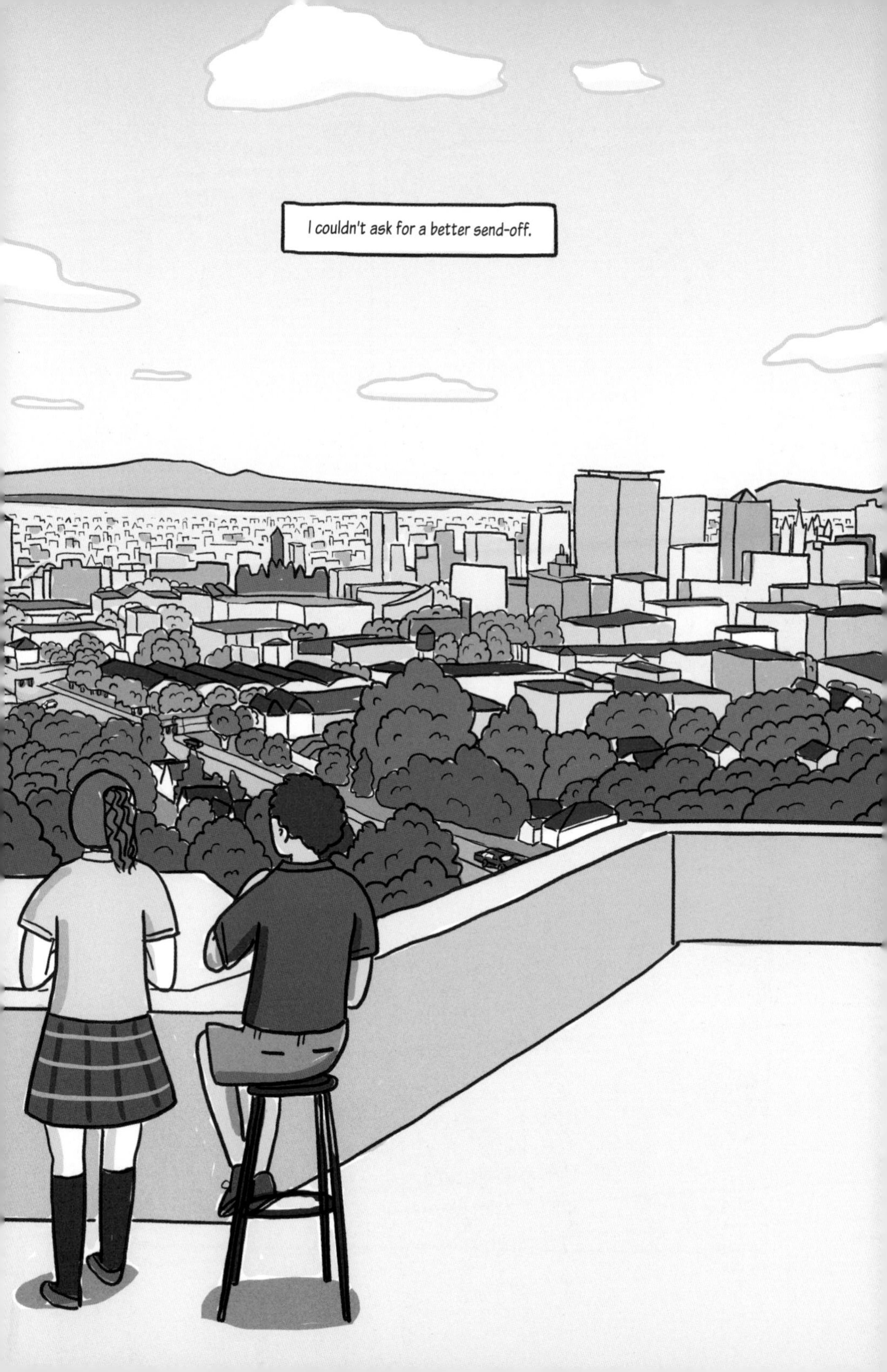
I couldn't ask for a better send-off.

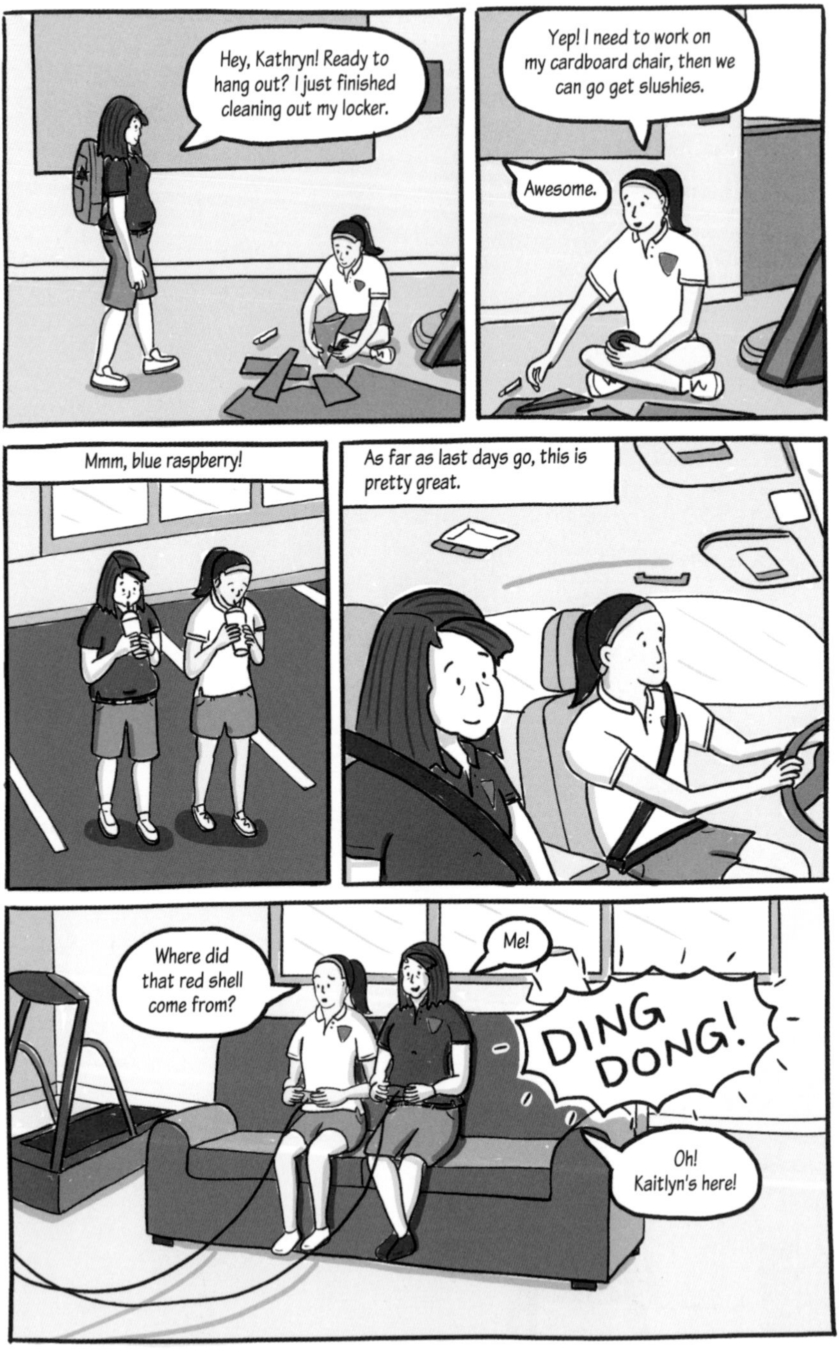
Hey, Kathryn! Ready to hang out? I just finished cleaning out my locker.
Yep! I need to work on my cardboard chair, then we can go get slushies.
Awesome.
Mmm, blue raspberry!
As far as last days go, this is pretty great.
Where did that red shell come from?
Me!
DING DONG!
Oh! Kaitlyn's here!

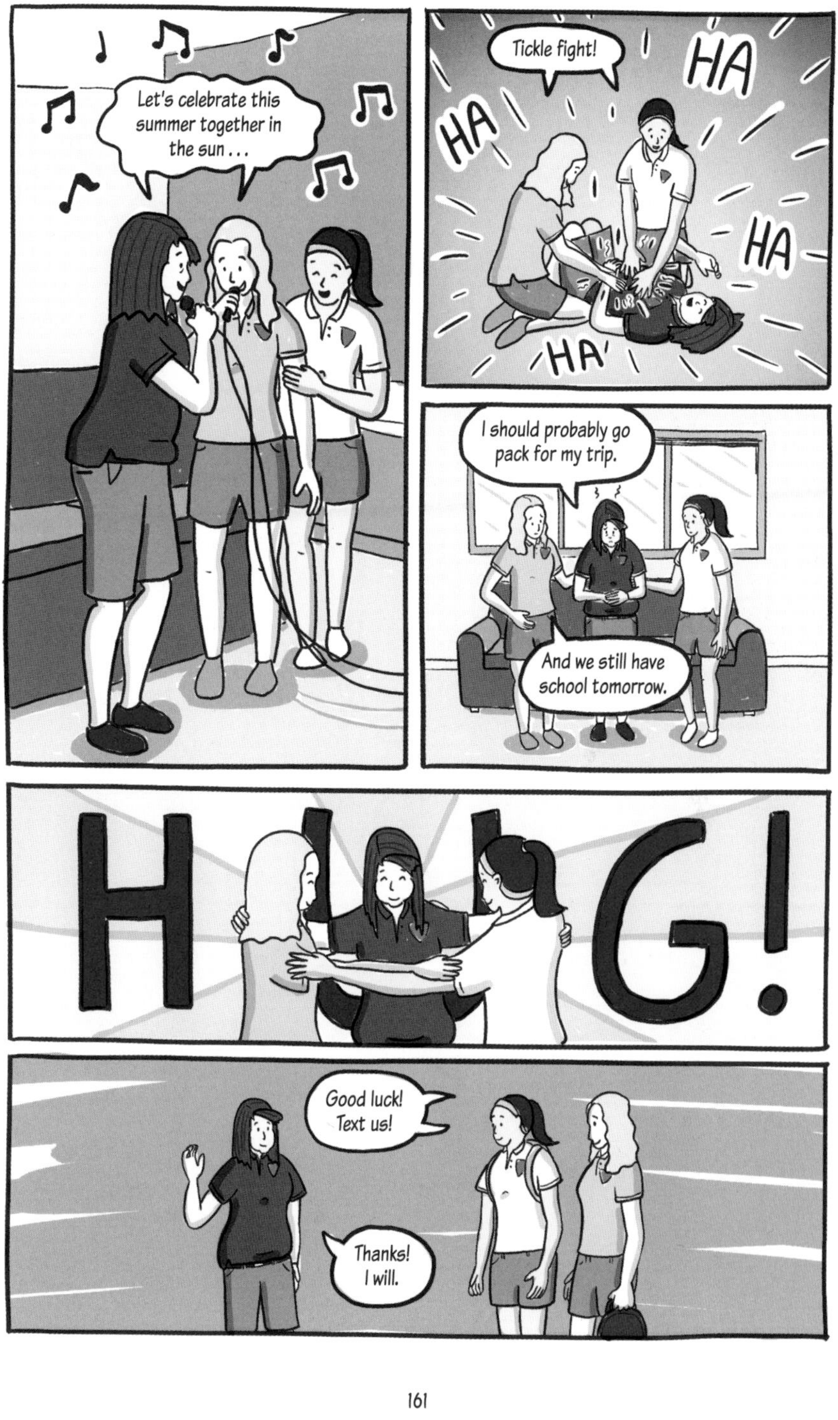
Let's celebrate this summer together in the sun . . .
Tickle fight!
HA
HA
HA
HA
I should probably go pack for my trip.
And we still have school tomorrow.
HUG!
Good luck! Text us!
Thanks! I will.

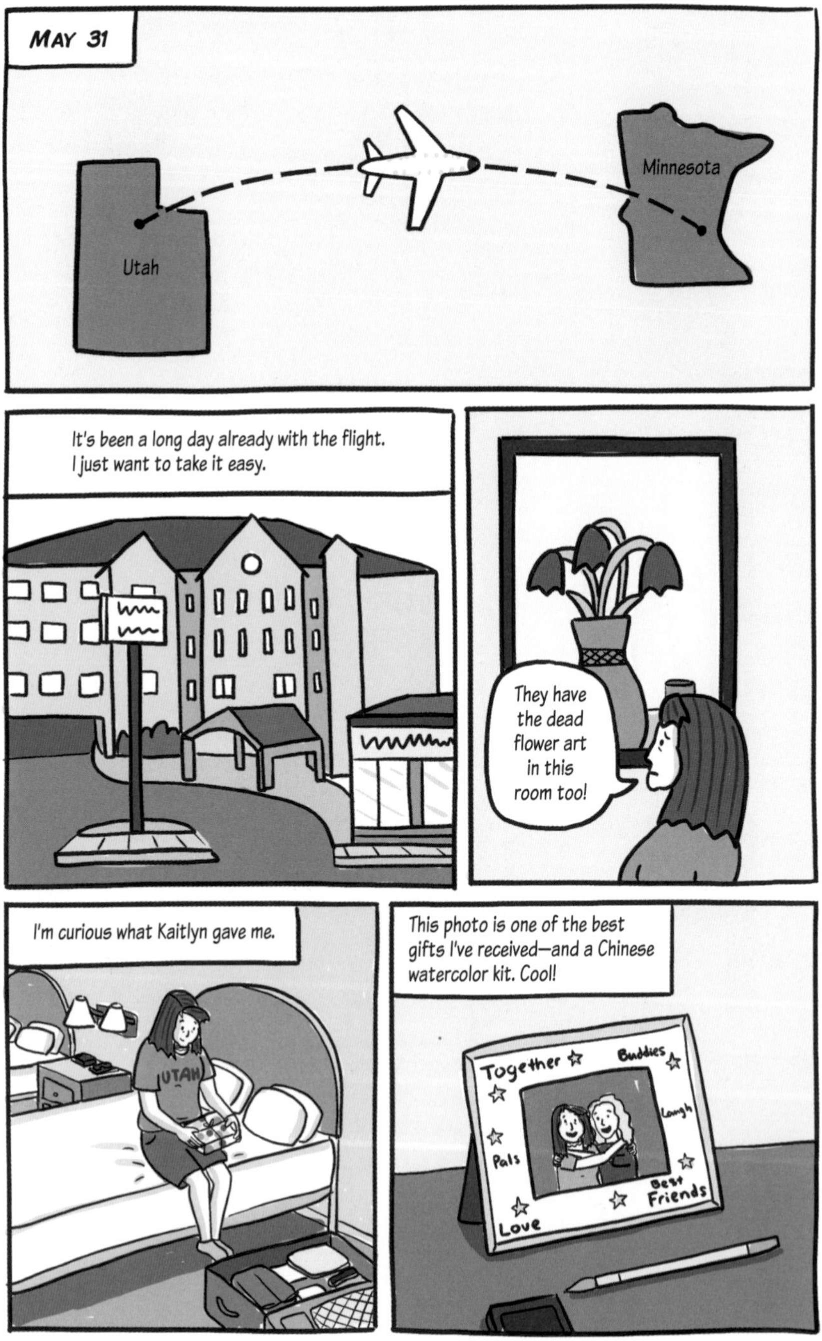
May 31
Utah
Minnesota
It's been a long day already with the flight. I just want to take it easy.
They have the dead flower art in this room too!
I'm curious what Kaitlyn gave me.
UTAH
This photo is one of the best gifts I've received—and a Chinese watercolor kit. Cool!
Together
Buddies
Laugh
Pals
Best Friends
Love

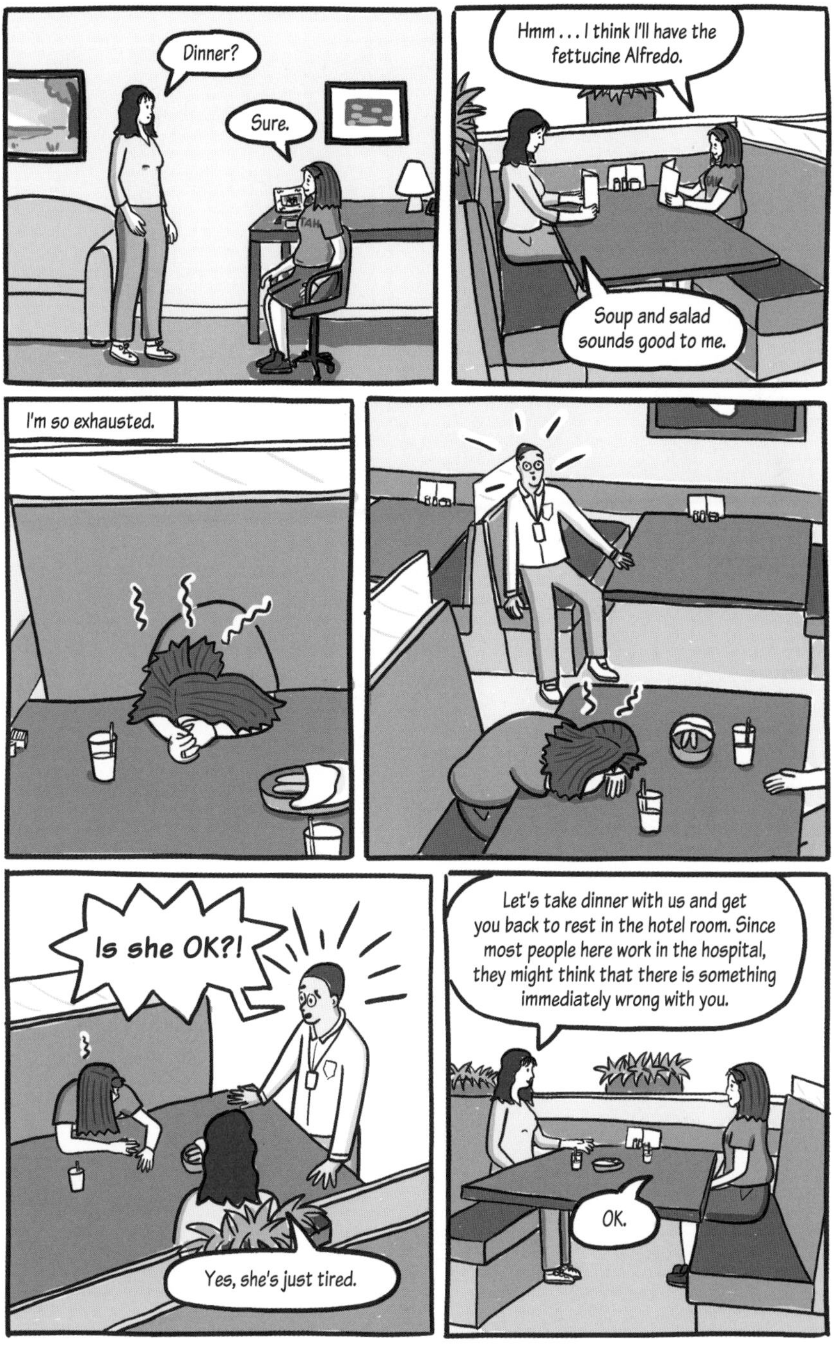
Dinner?
Sure.
Hmm . . . I think I'll have the fettucine Alfredo.
Soup and salad sounds good to me.
I'm so exhausted.
Is she OK?!
Yes, she's just tired.
Let's take dinner with us and get you back to rest in the hotel room. Since most people here work in the hospital, they might think that there is something immediately wrong with you.
OK.

The next few days are filled with doctors' appointments,

another MRI . . .

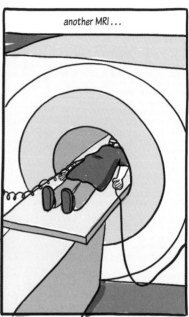

another 24-hour urine collection . . .

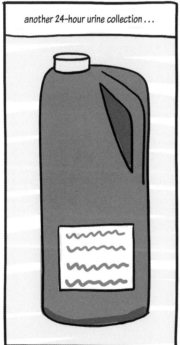

and more blood work.

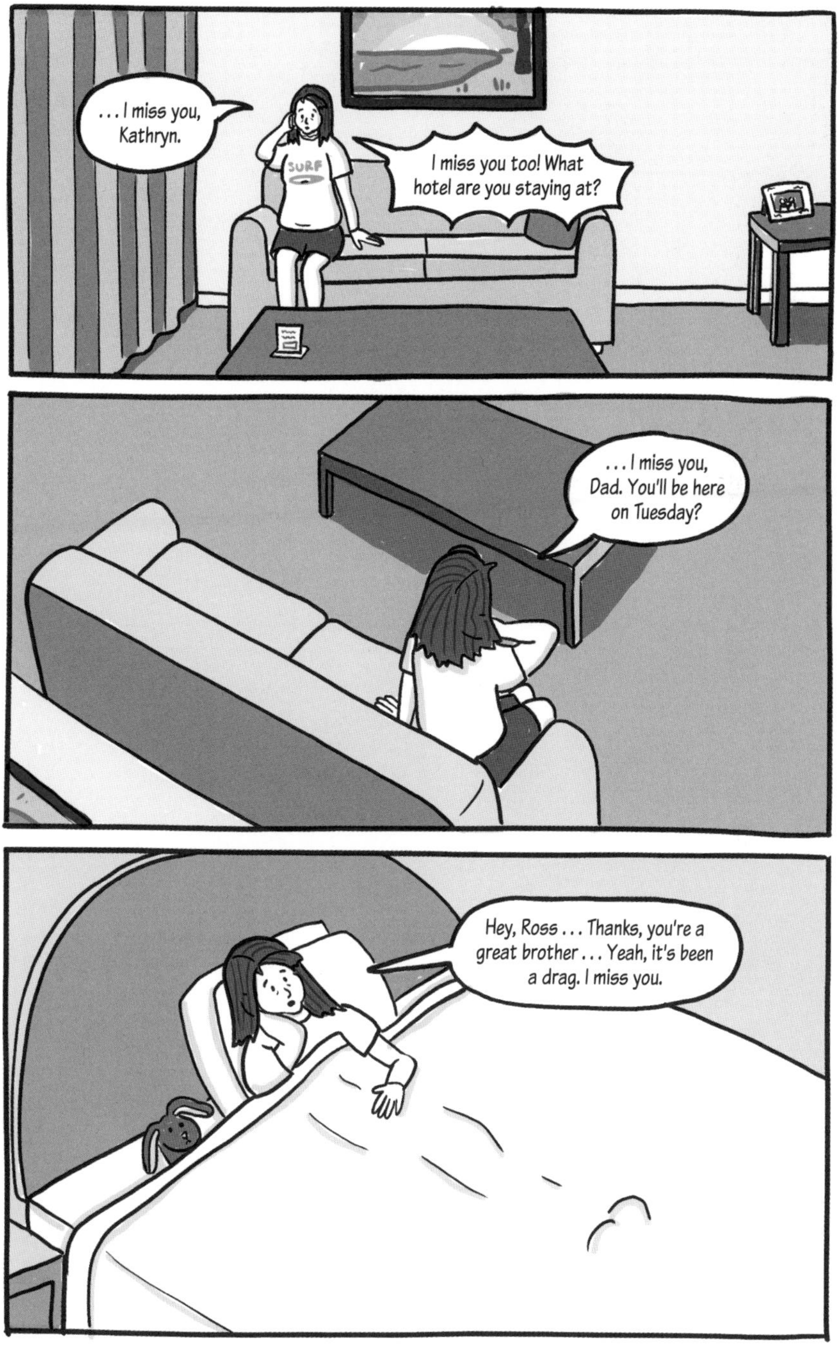

... I miss you, Kathryn.
I miss you too! What hotel are you staying at?
... I miss you, Dad. You'll be here on Tuesday?
Hey, Ross ... Thanks, you're a great brother ... Yeah, it's been a drag. I miss you.

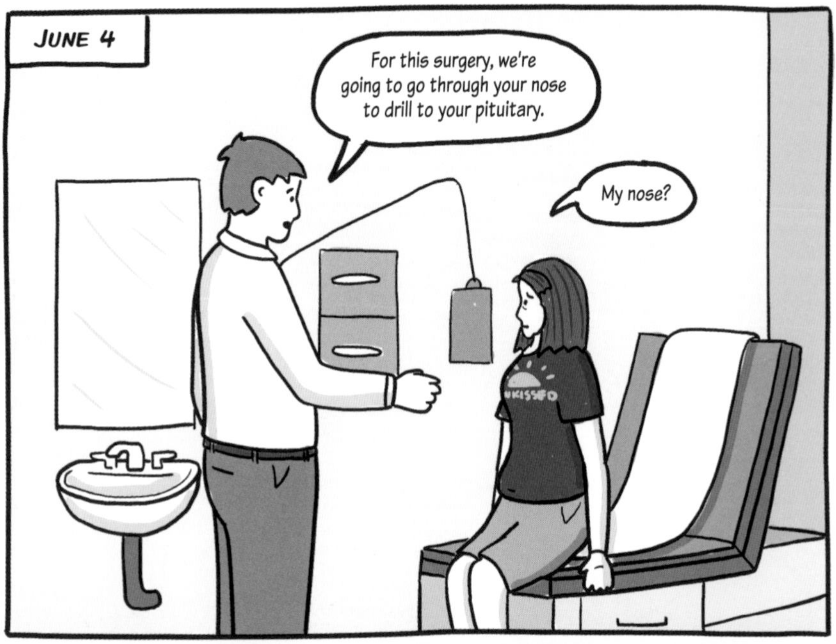
JUNE 4
For this surgery, we're going to go through your nose to drill to your pituitary.
My nose?

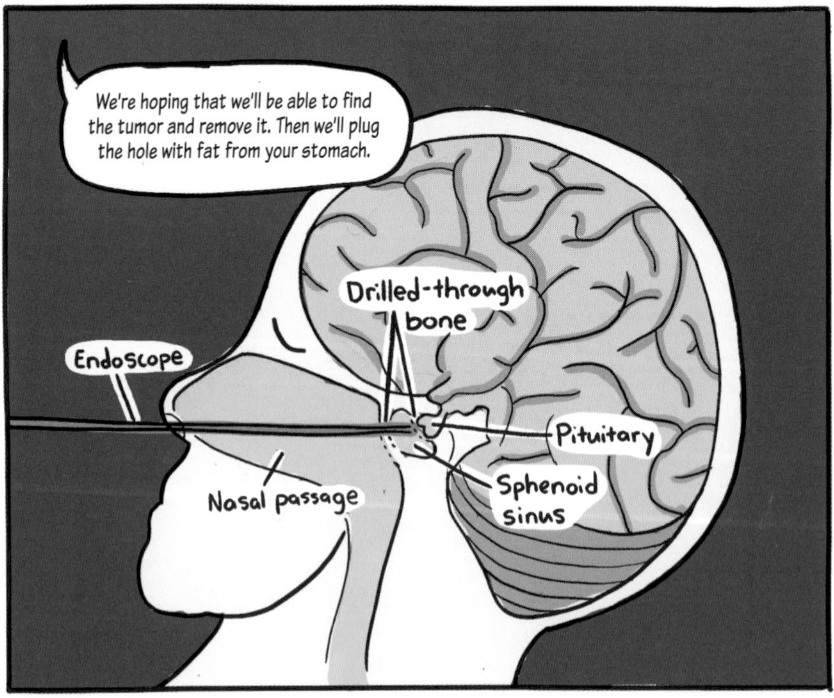
We're hoping that we'll be able to find the tumor and remove it. Then we'll plug the hole with fat from your stomach.
Drilled-through bone
Endoscope
Pituitary
Sphenoid sinus
Nasal passage

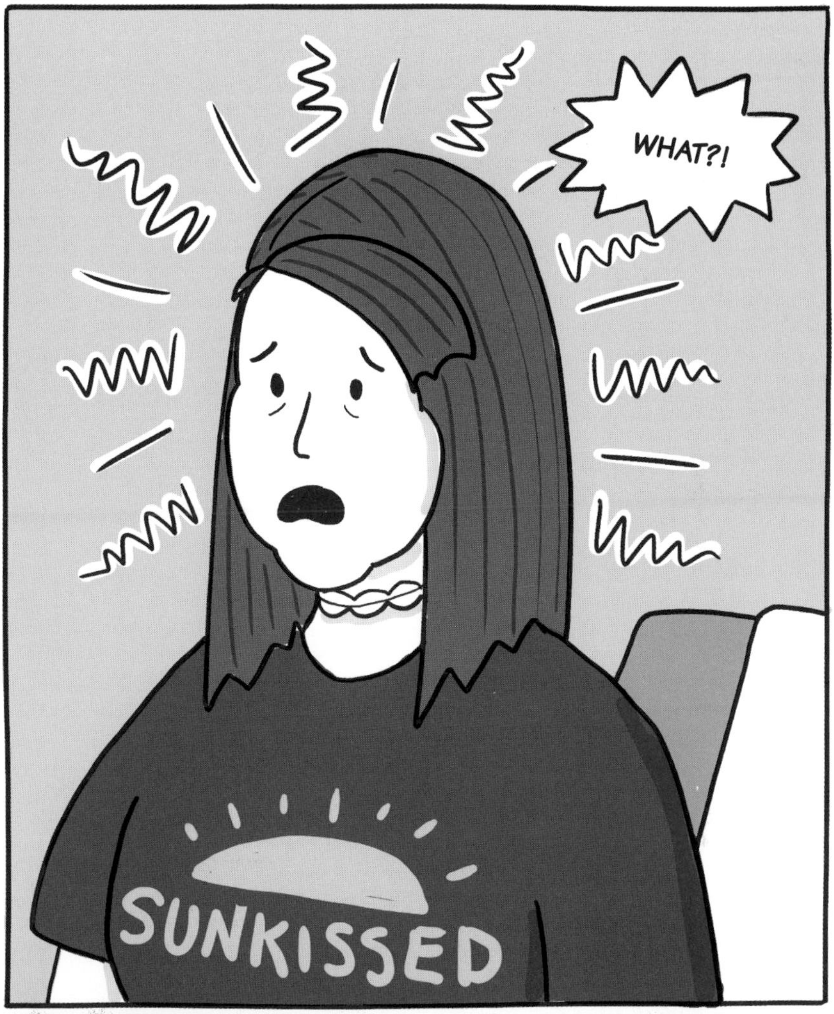
WHAT?!
SUNKISSED

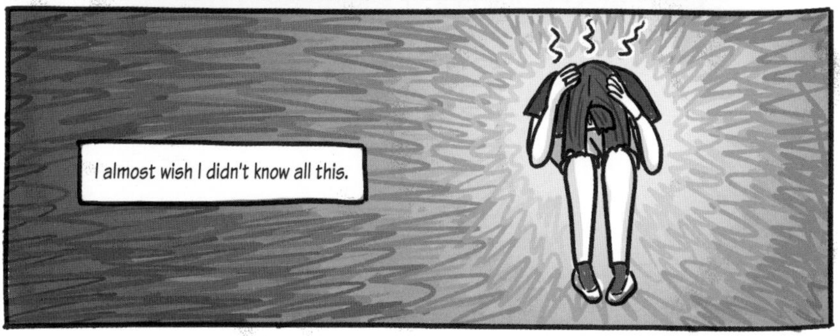
I almost wish I didn't know all this.

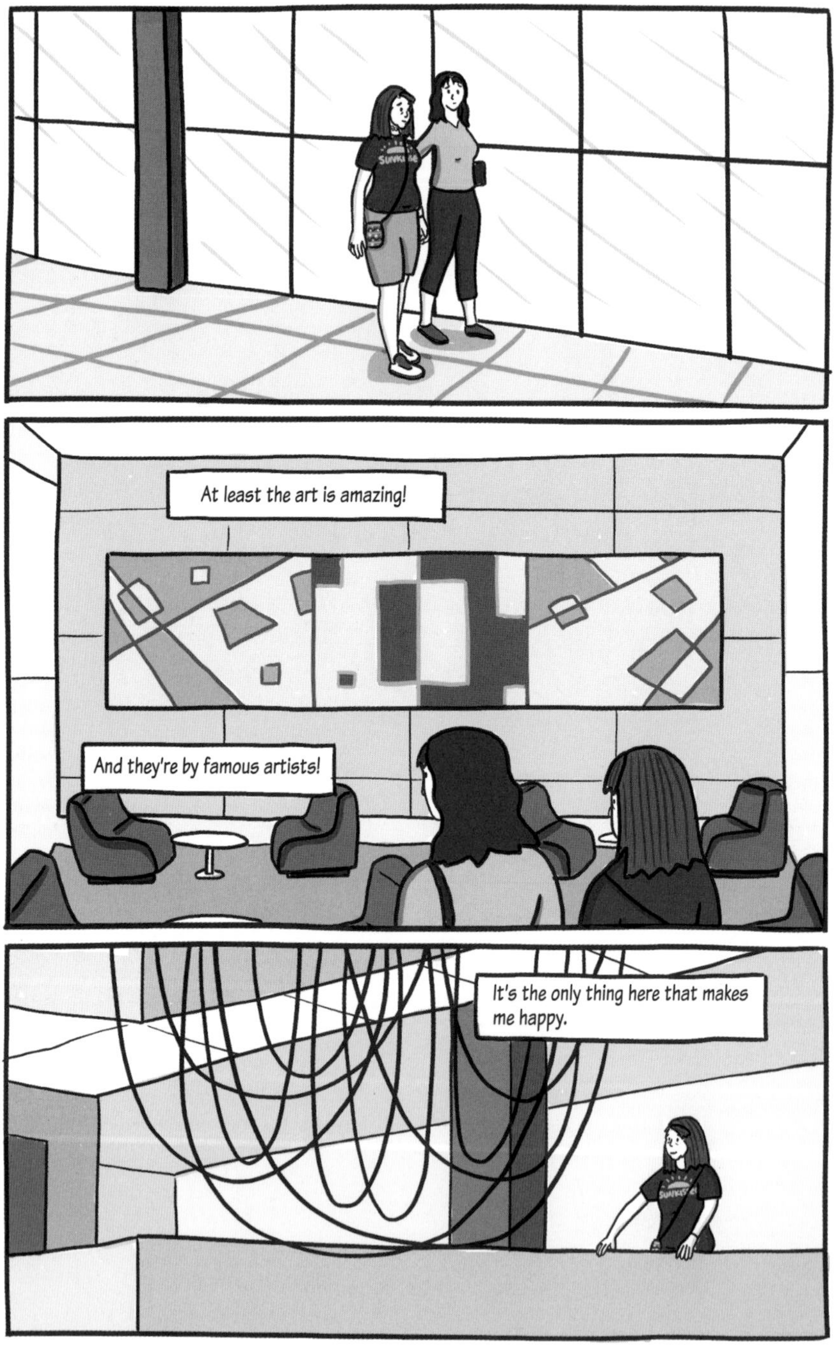
At least the art is amazing!
And they're by famous artists!
It's the only thing here that makes me happy.

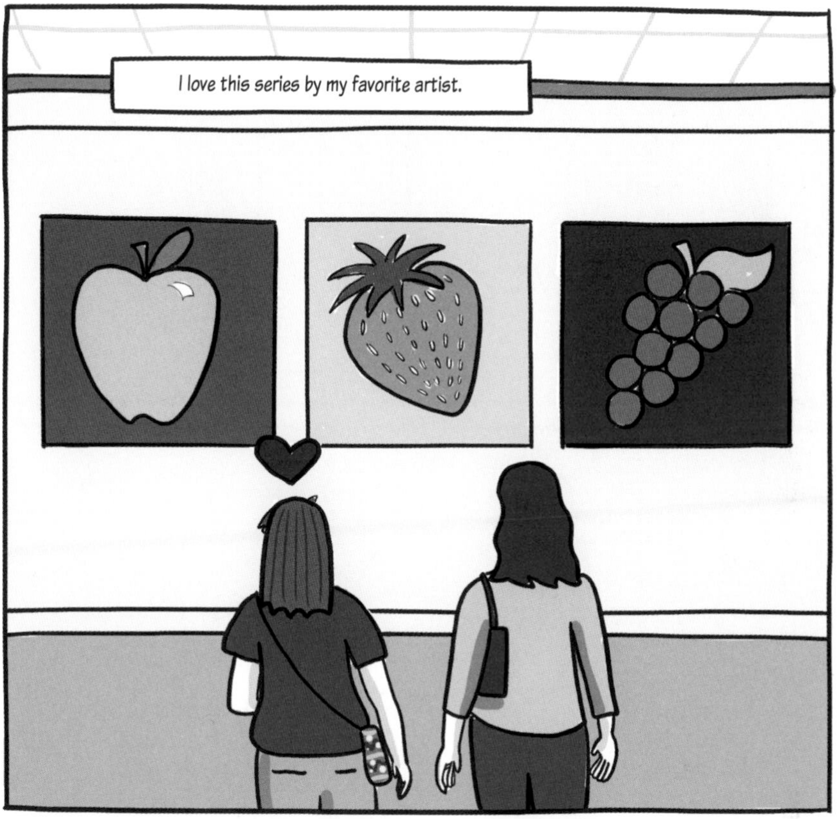
I love this series by my favorite artist.

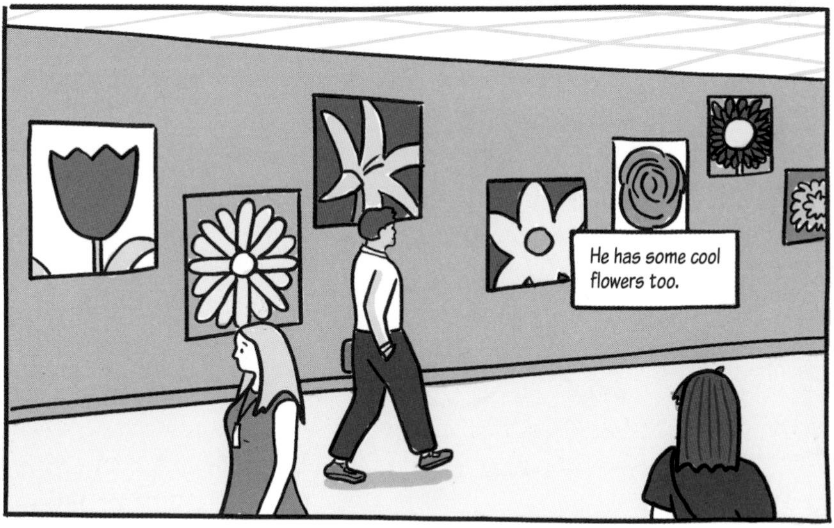
He has some cool flowers too.

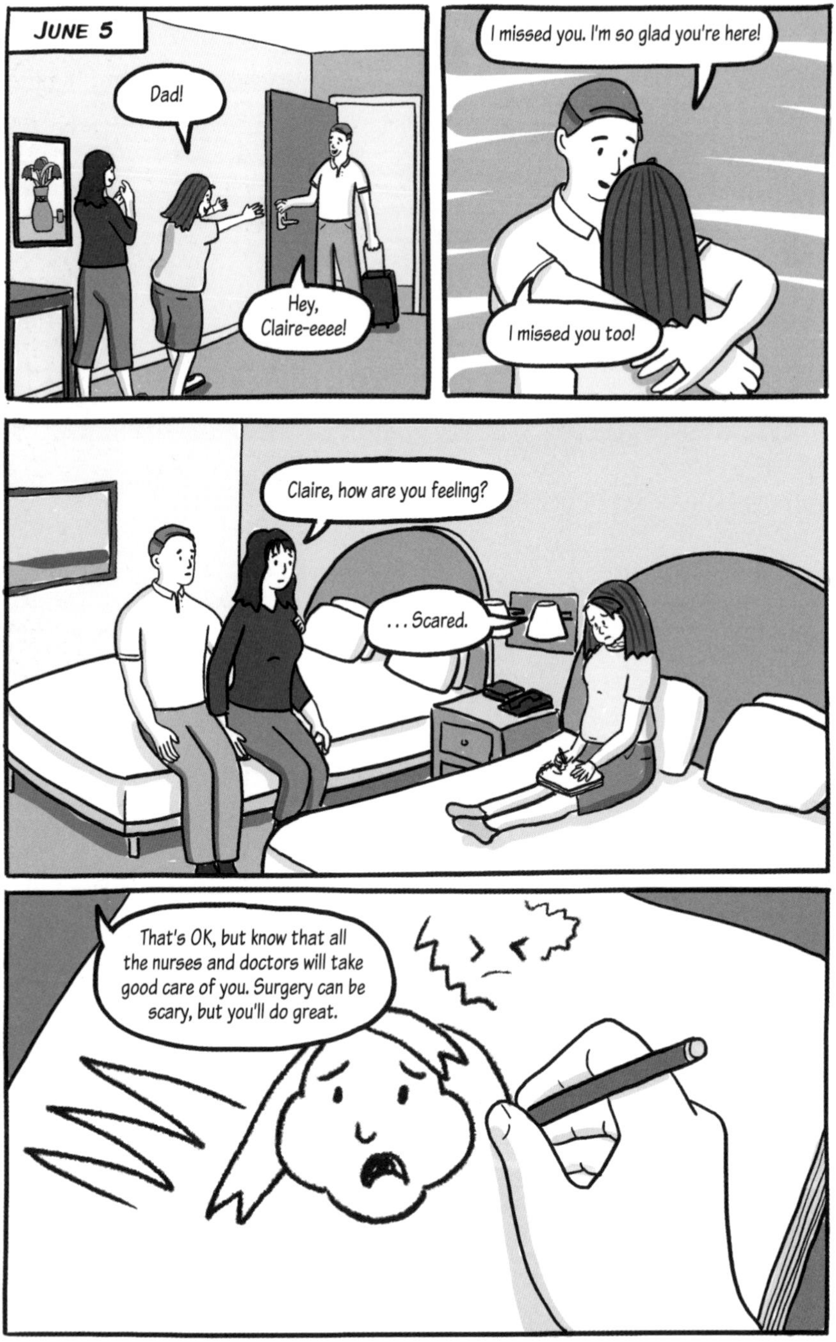
JUNE 5
Dad!
Hey,
Claire-eeee!
I missed you. I'm so glad you're here!
I missed you too!
Claire, how are you feeling?
...Scared.
That's OK, but know that all the nurses and doctors will take good care of you. Surgery can be scary, but you'll do great.

FEAR

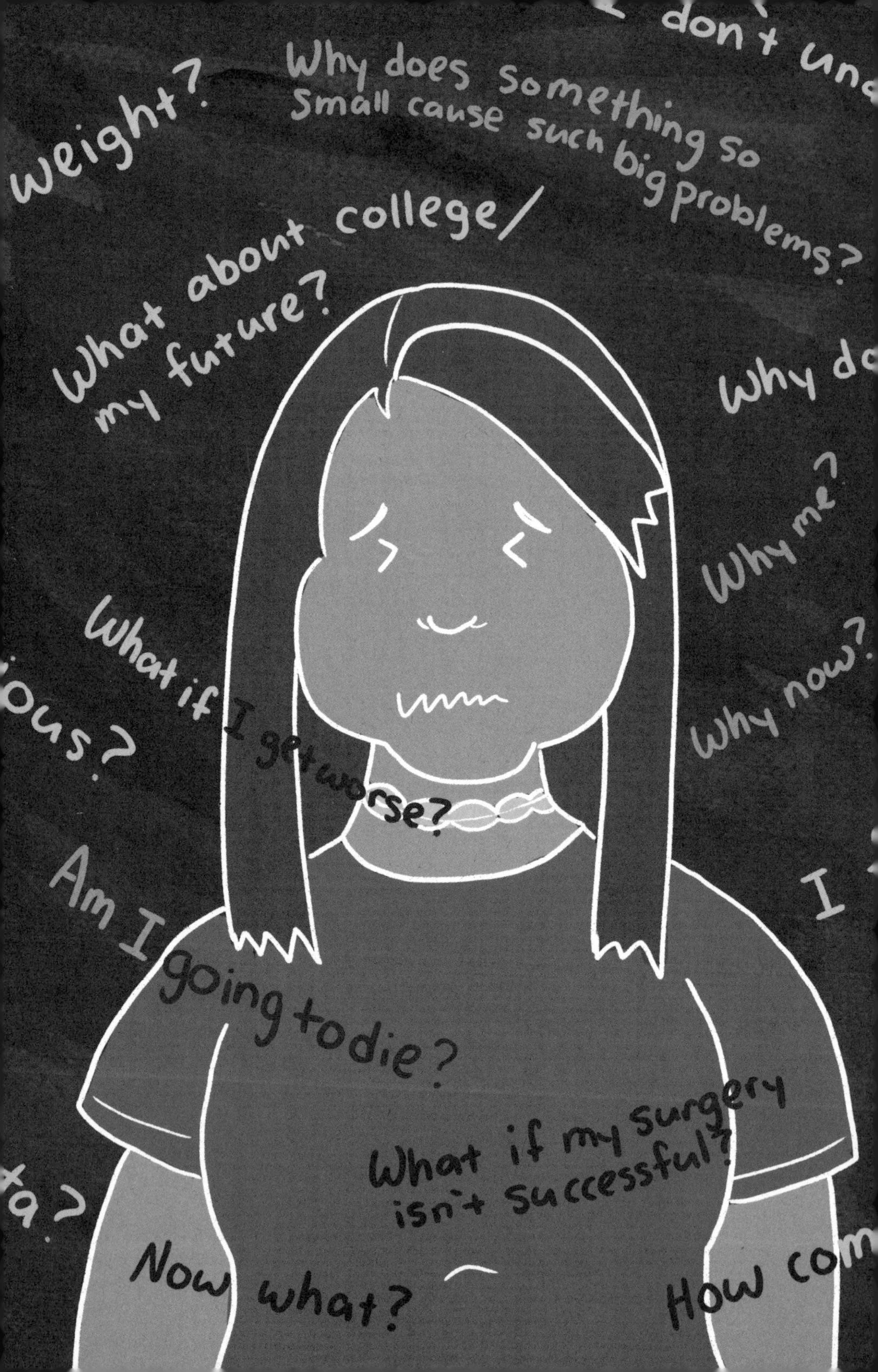
don't un
Weight?
Why does something so small cause such big problems?
What about college/my future?
Why d
Why me?
Why now?
What if I get worse?
ous?
Am I going to die?
I
What if my surgery isn't successful?
ta?
Now what?
How com

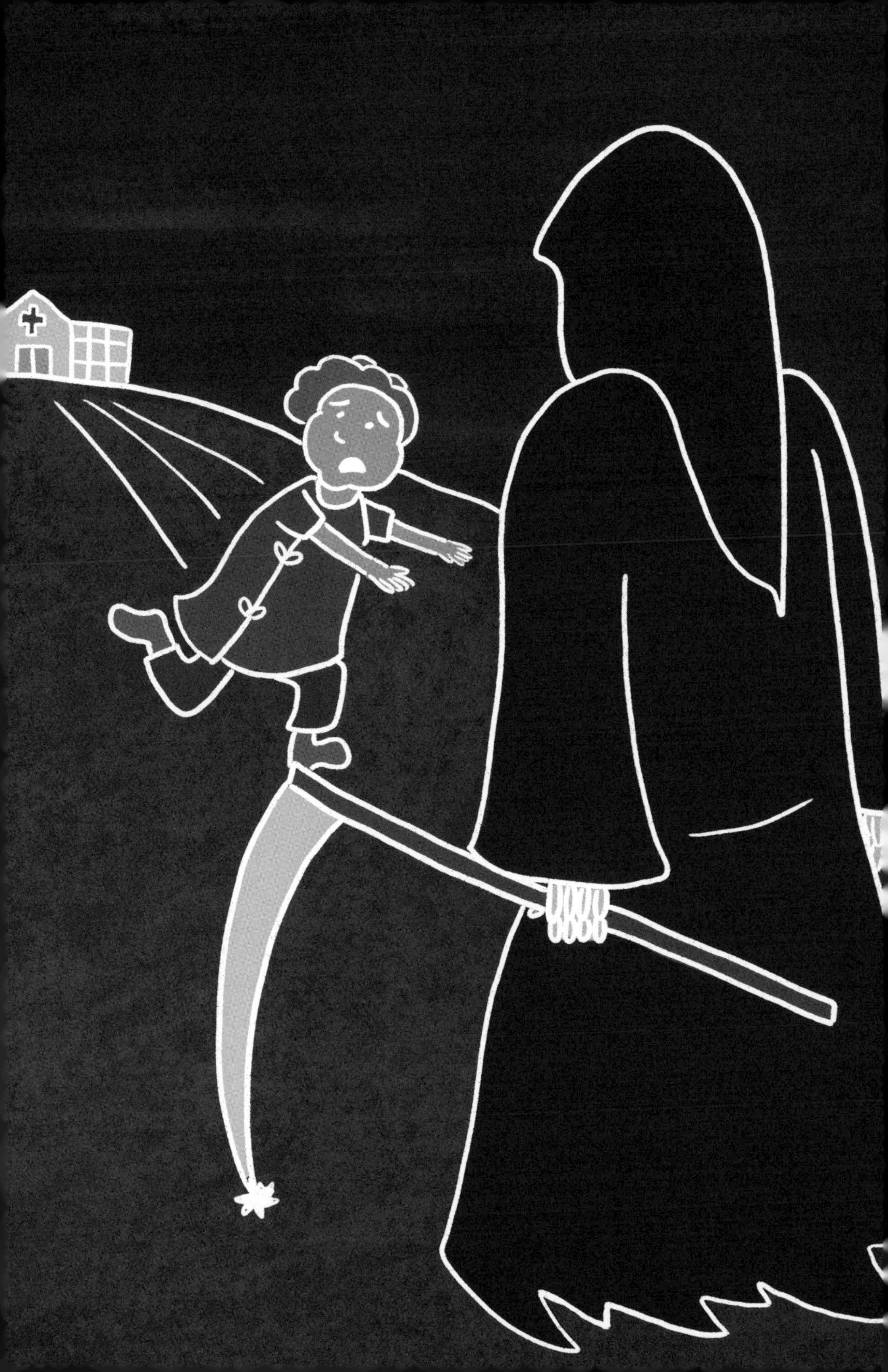

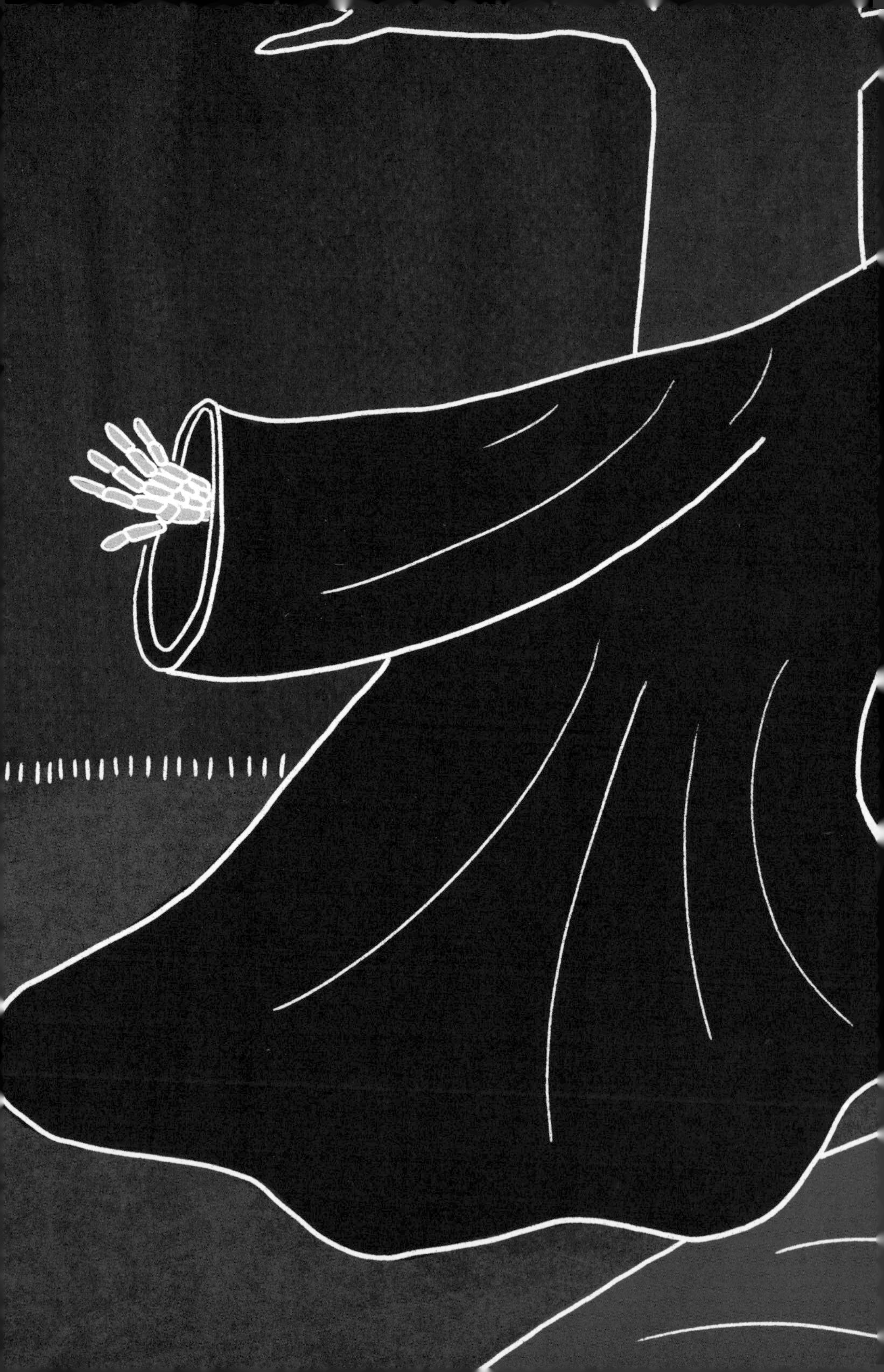

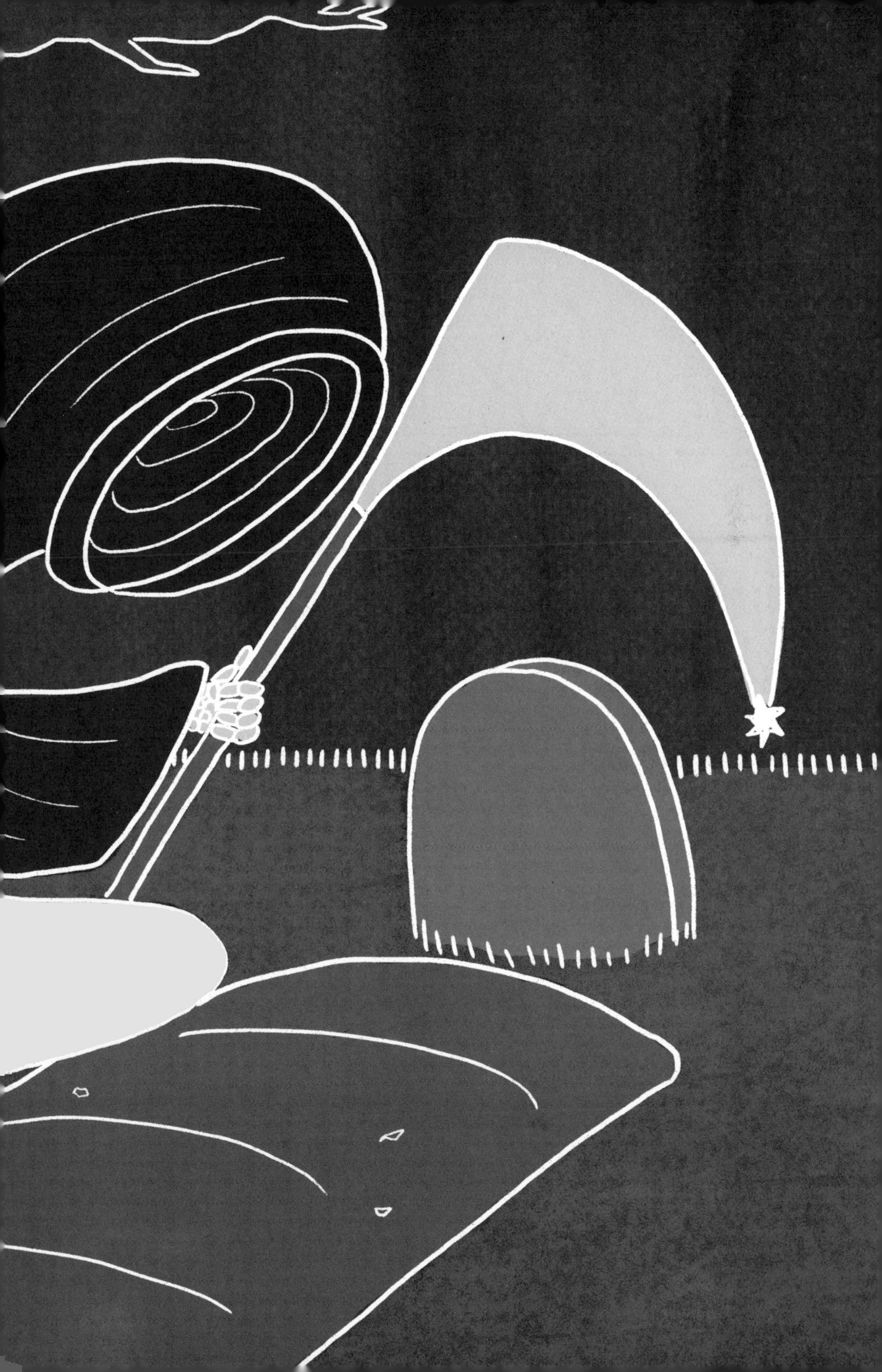

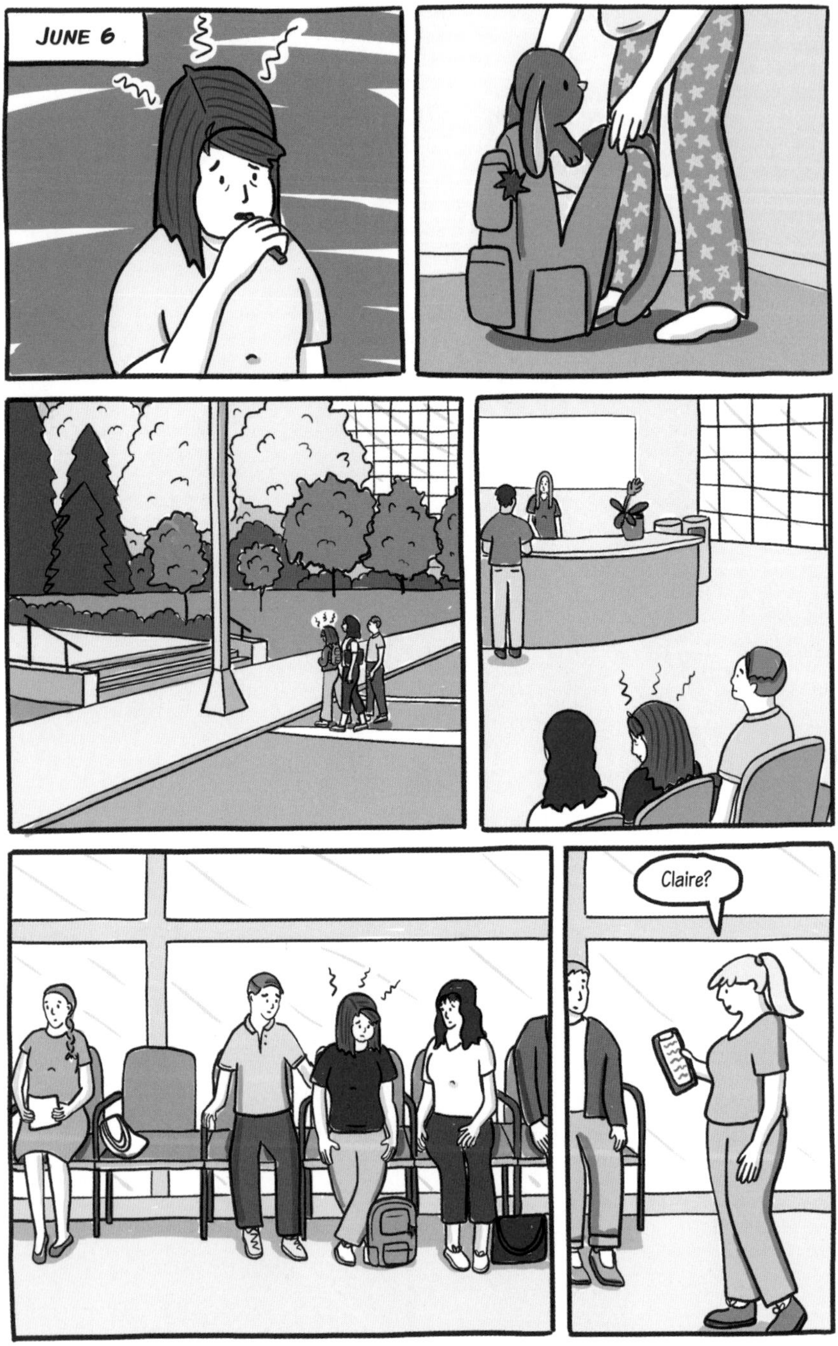
JUNE 6
Claire?

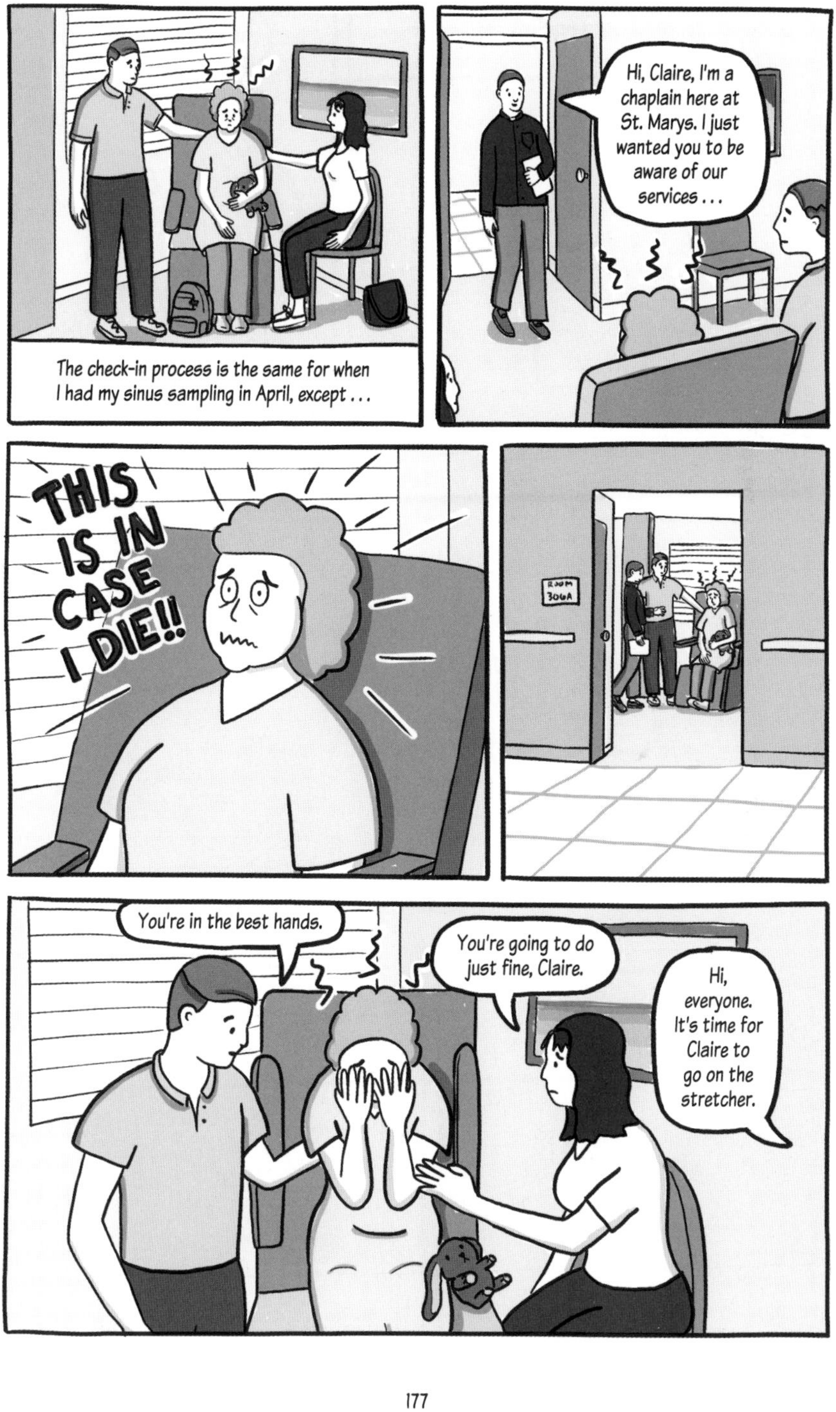
The check-in process is the same for when I had my sinus sampling in April, except . . .
Hi, Claire, I'm a chaplain here at St. Marys. I just wanted you to be aware of our services . . .
THIS IS IN CASE I DIE!!
ROOM 306A
You're in the best hands.
You're going to do just fine, Claire.
Hi, everyone. It's time for Claire to go on the stretcher.

I know I'm seventeen with a stuffed animal, but I'm SO anxious.

OK, say goodbye.

Goodbye.

WAIT!

I'm a minor! I want a parent with me.

Totally milking this while I can.

Erm . . . OK.

I'll come with you.

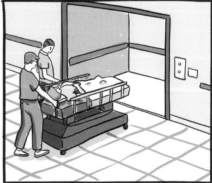

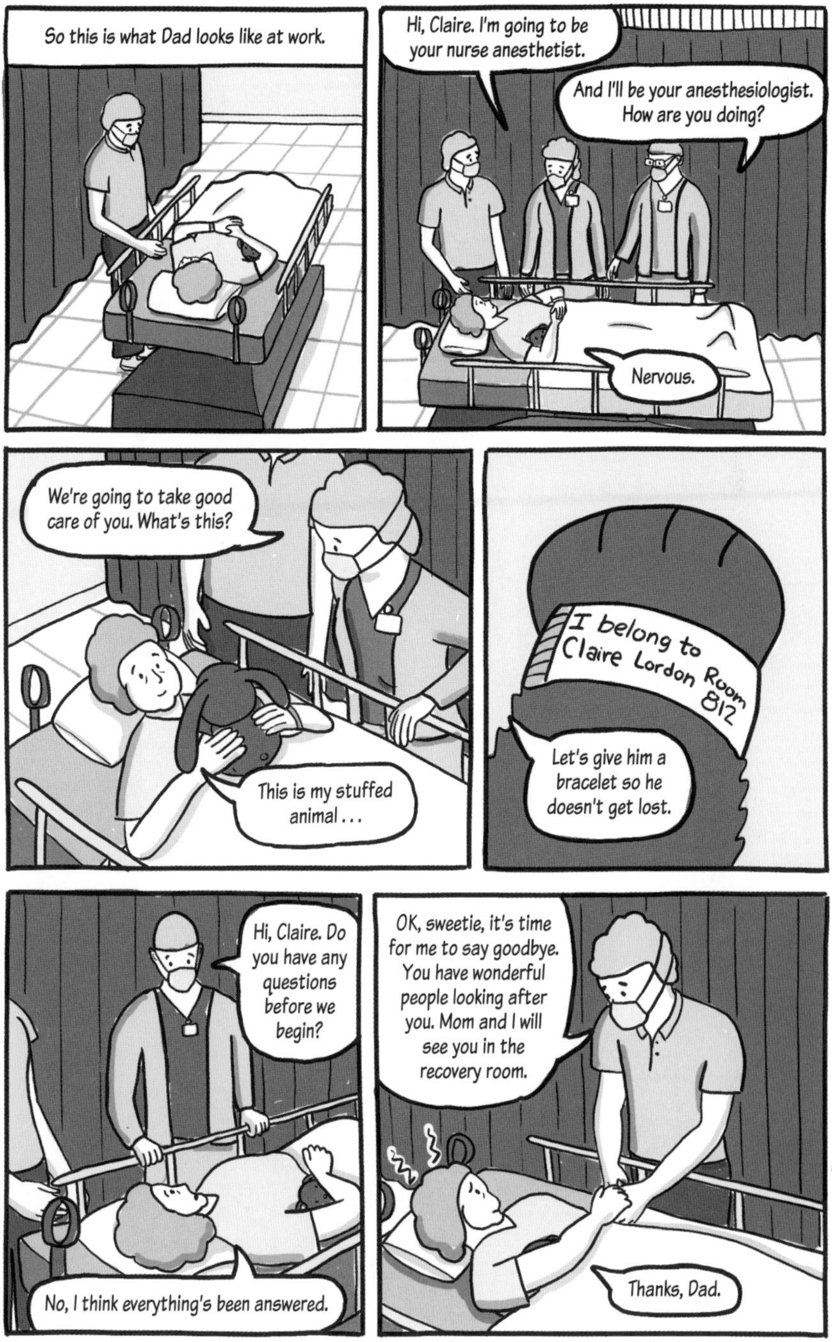
So this is what Dad looks like at work.
Hi, Claire. I'm going to be your nurse anesthetist.
And I'll be your anesthesiologist. How are you doing?
Nervous.
We're going to take good care of you. What's this?
This is my stuffed animal . . .
I belong to Claire Lordon Room 812
Let's give him a bracelet so he doesn't get lost.
Hi, Claire. Do you have any questions before we begin?
No, I think everything's been answered.
OK, sweetie, it's time for me to say goodbye. You have wonderful people looking after you. Mom and I will see you in the recovery room.
Thanks, Dad.

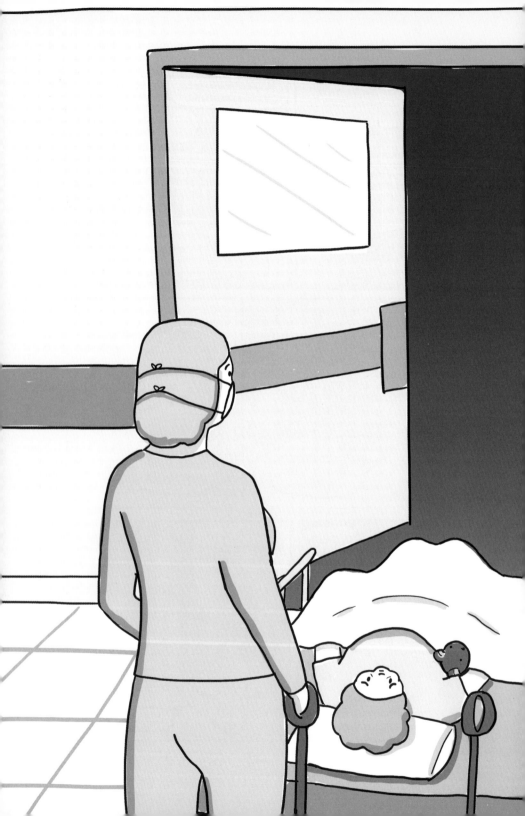

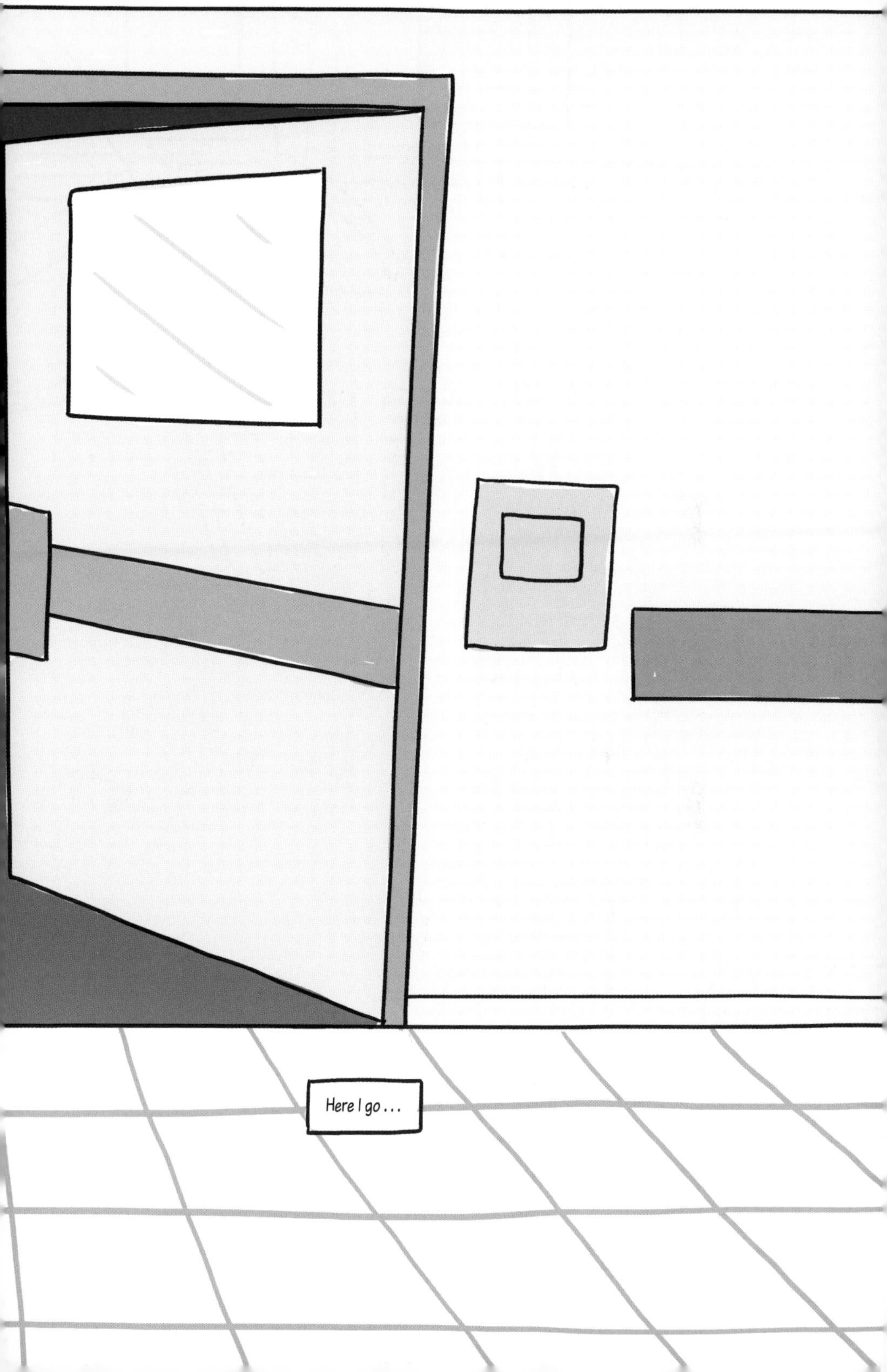
Here I go . . .

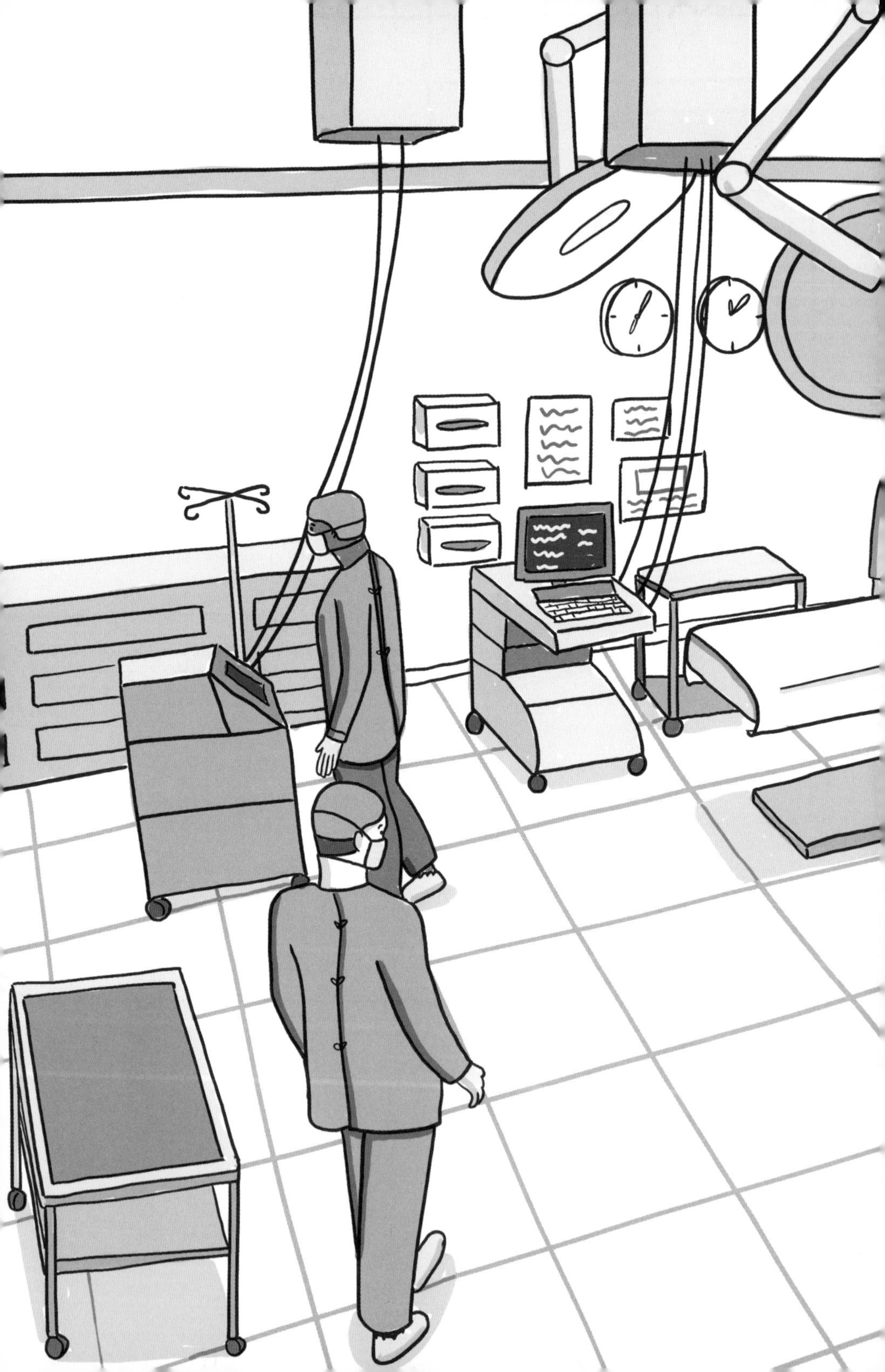

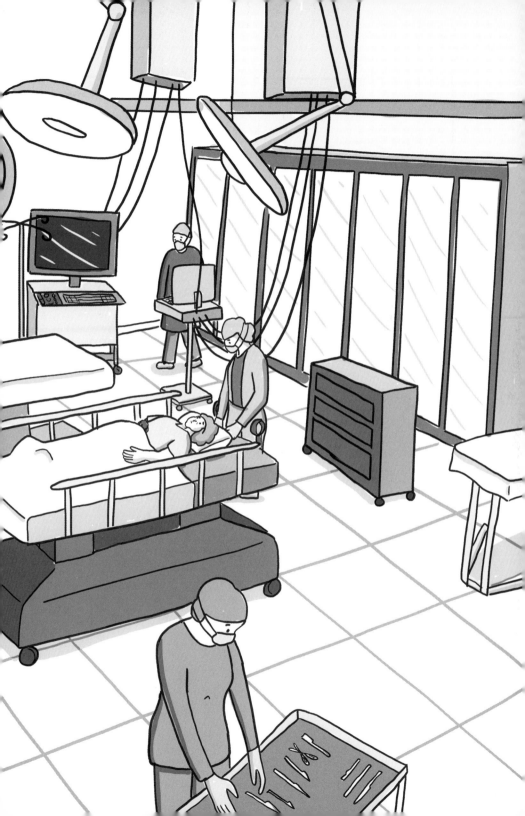

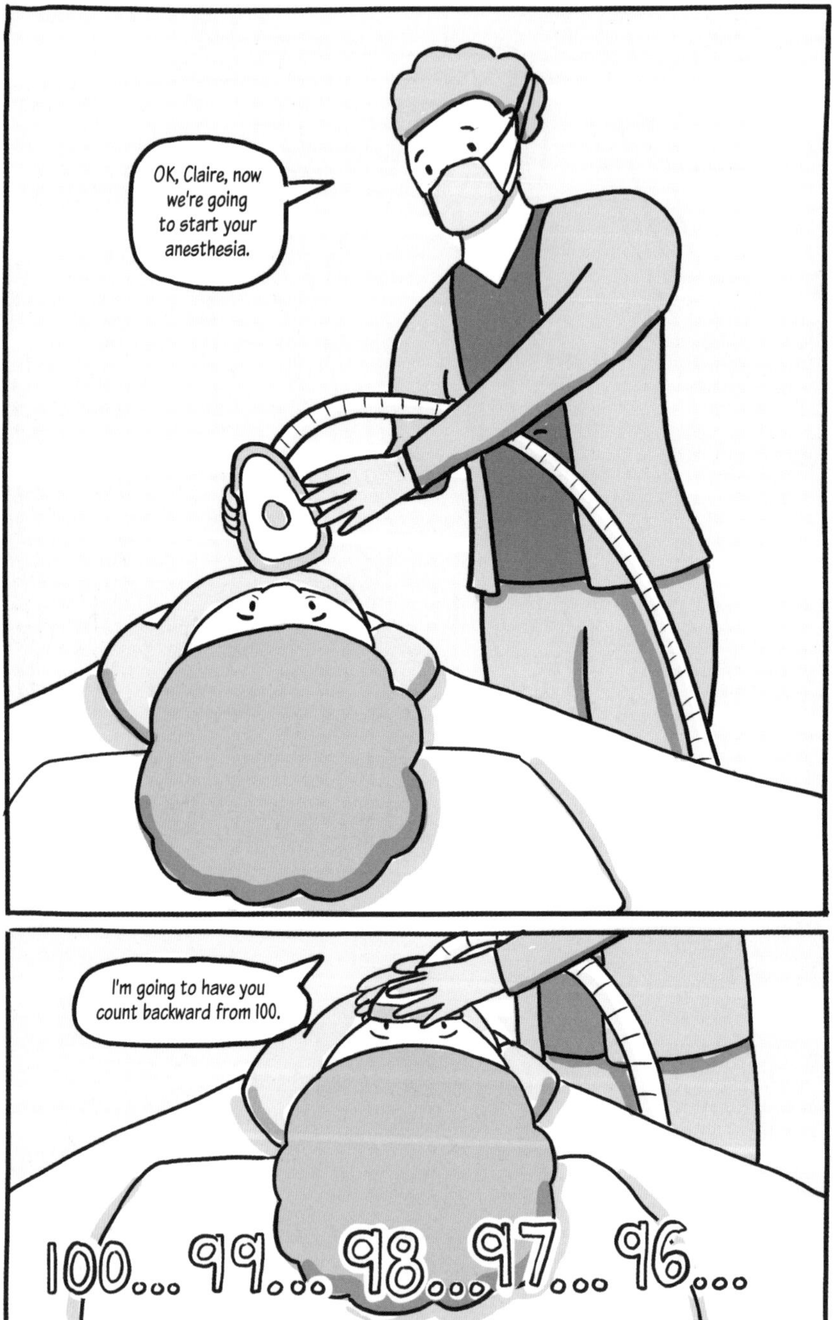
OK, Claire, now we're going to start your anesthesia.
I'm going to have you count backward from 100.
100... 99... 98... 97... 96...

95...
94...
93...
92...
91...
90...
89...
88...
87...
86...

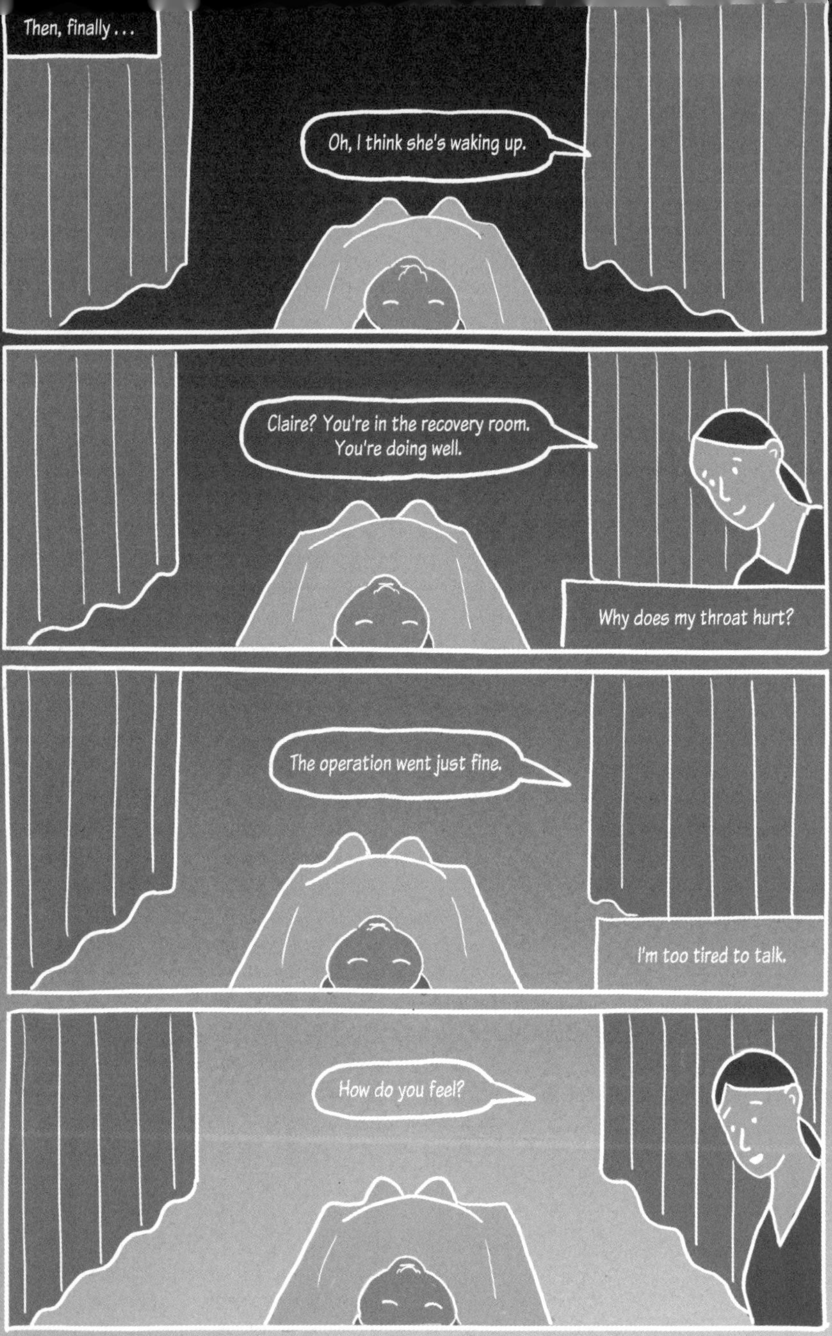

Then, finally . . .
Oh, I think she's waking up.
Claire? You're in the recovery room. You're doing well.
Why does my throat hurt?
The operation went just fine.
I'm too tired to talk.
How do you feel?

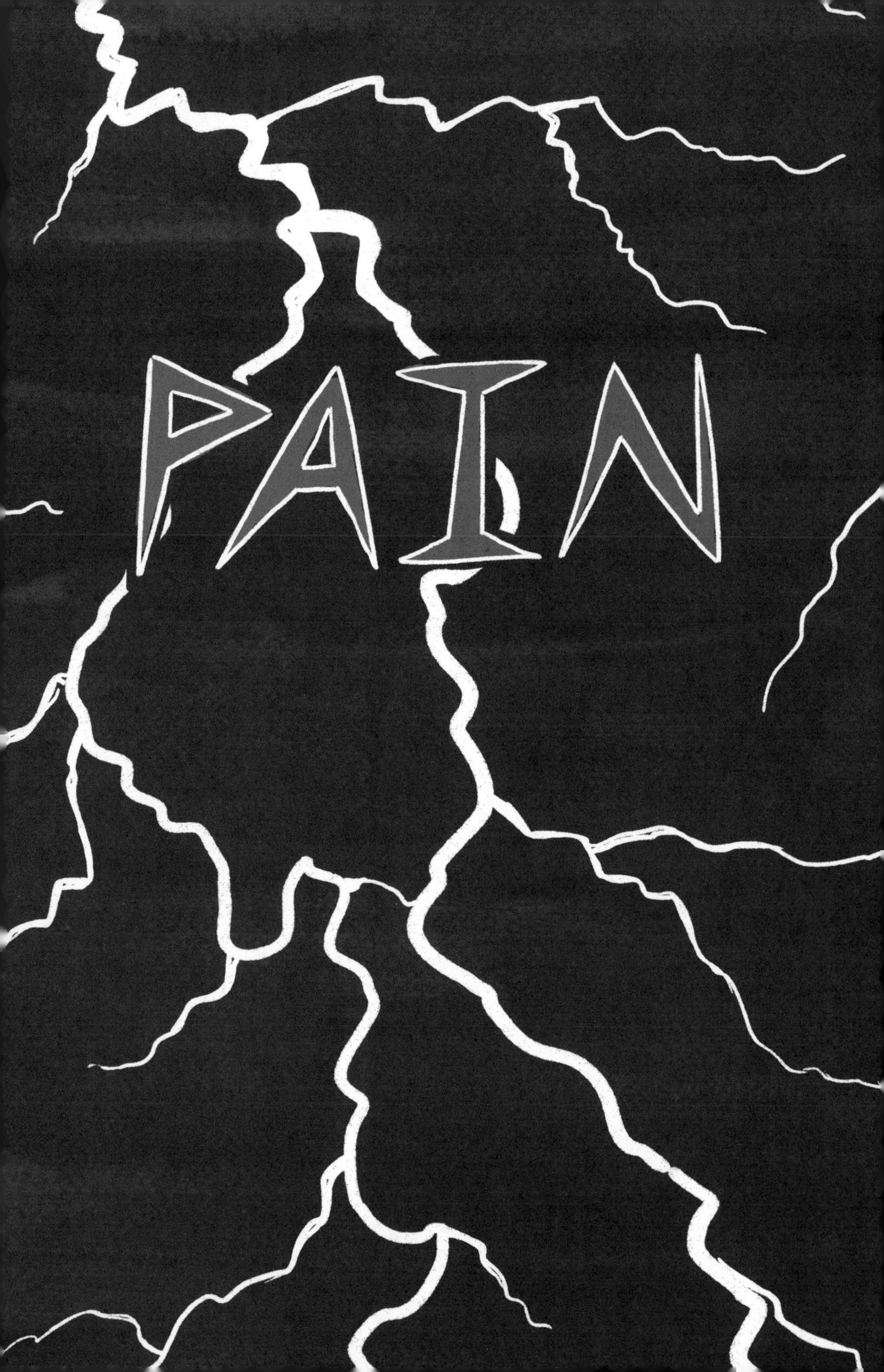
PAIN

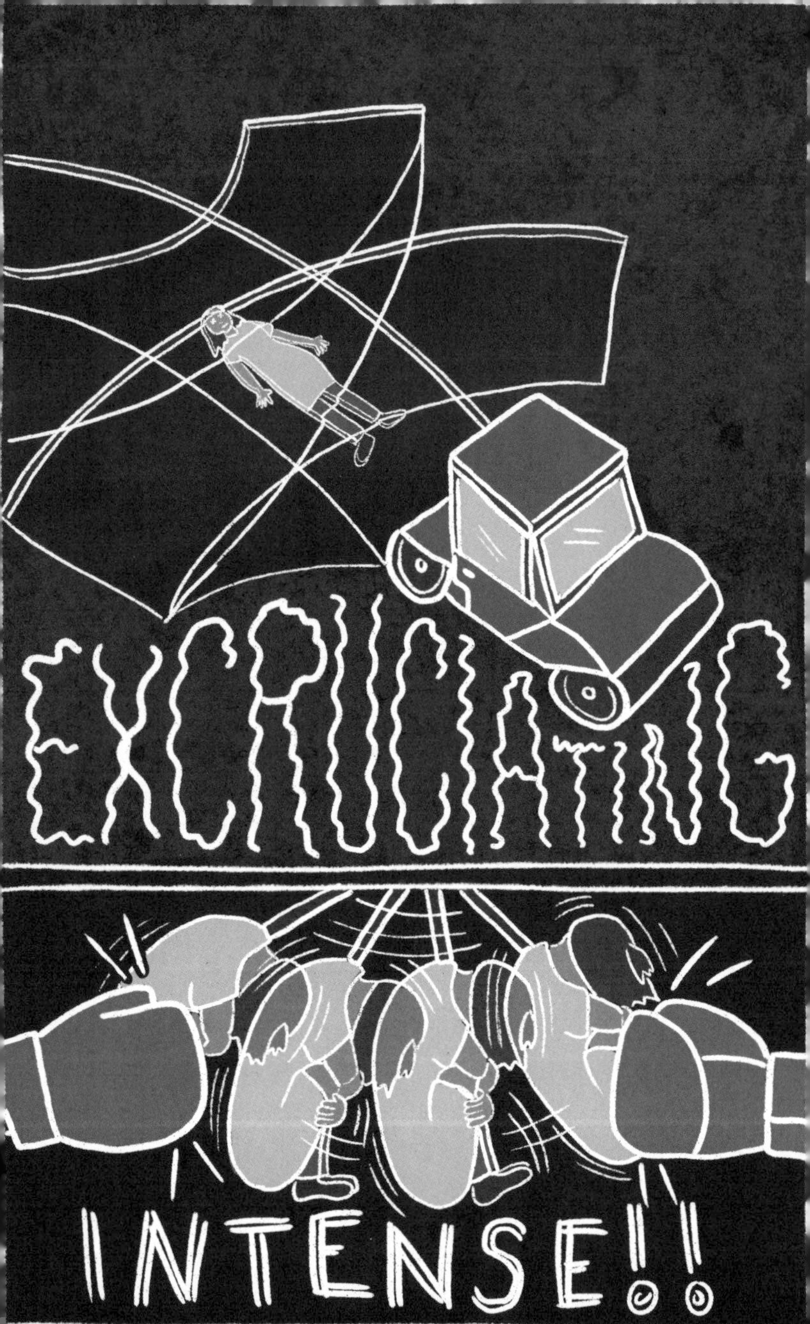
EXCRUCIATING
INTENSE!!

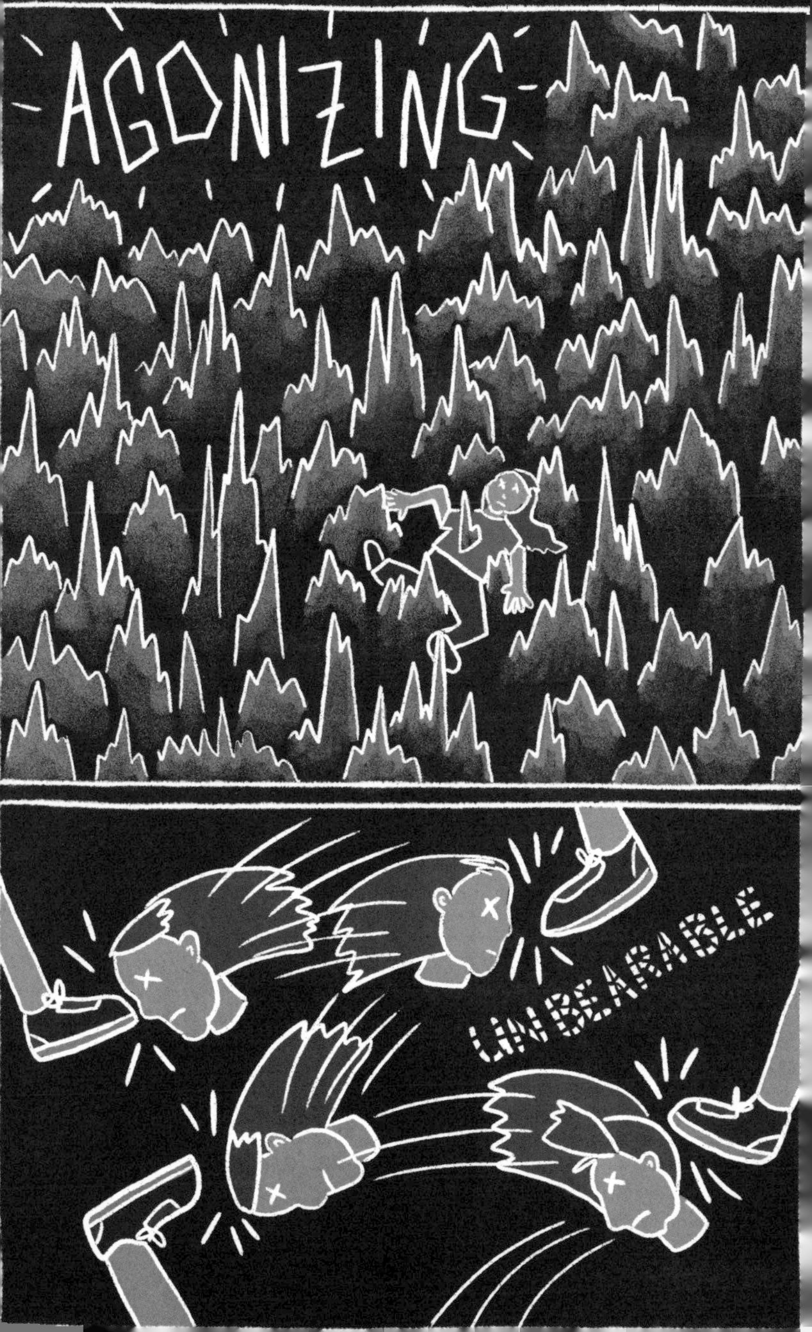
AGONIZING
UNBEARABLE

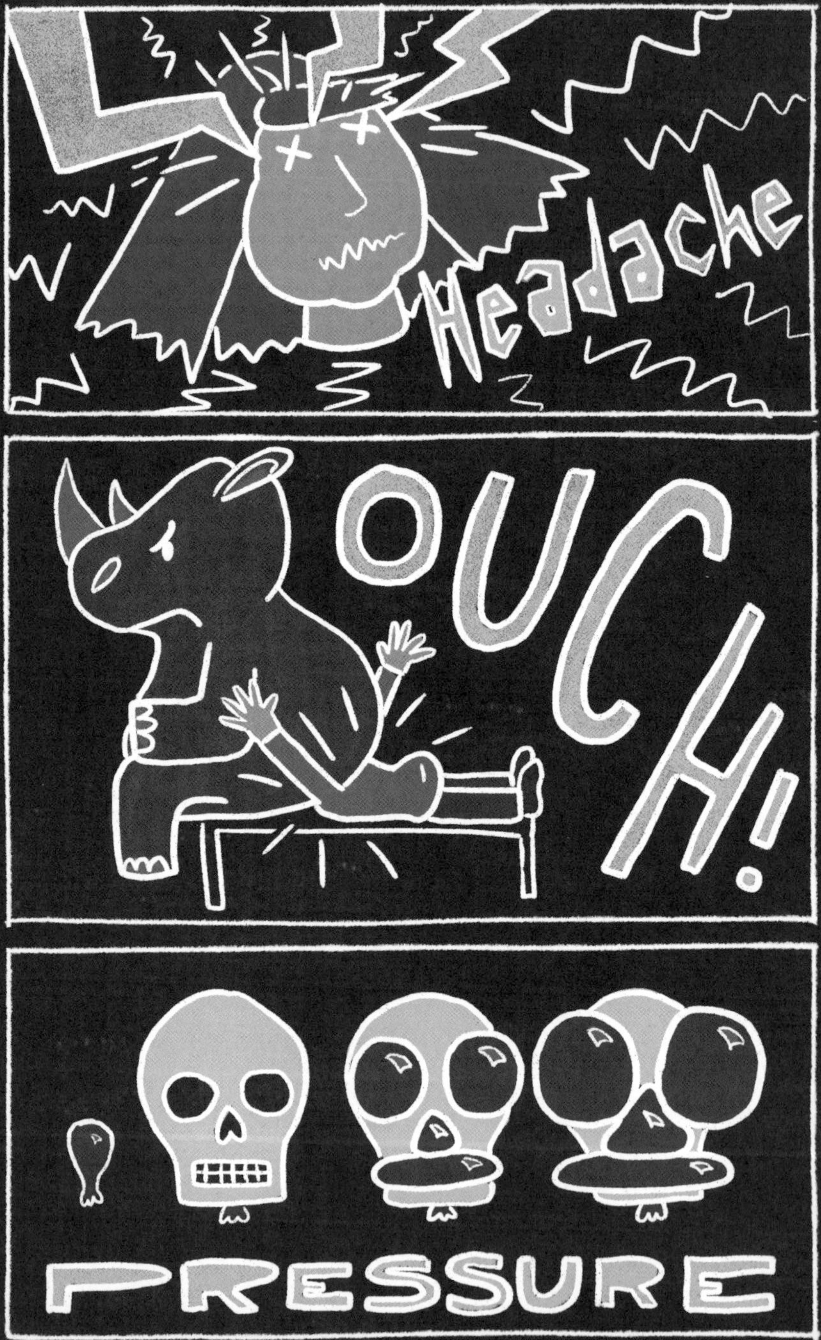
Headache
OUCH!
PRESSURE

I feel like **SHIT.**

I wonder if
dying

feels like

this.

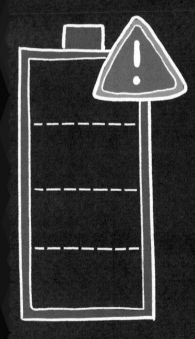

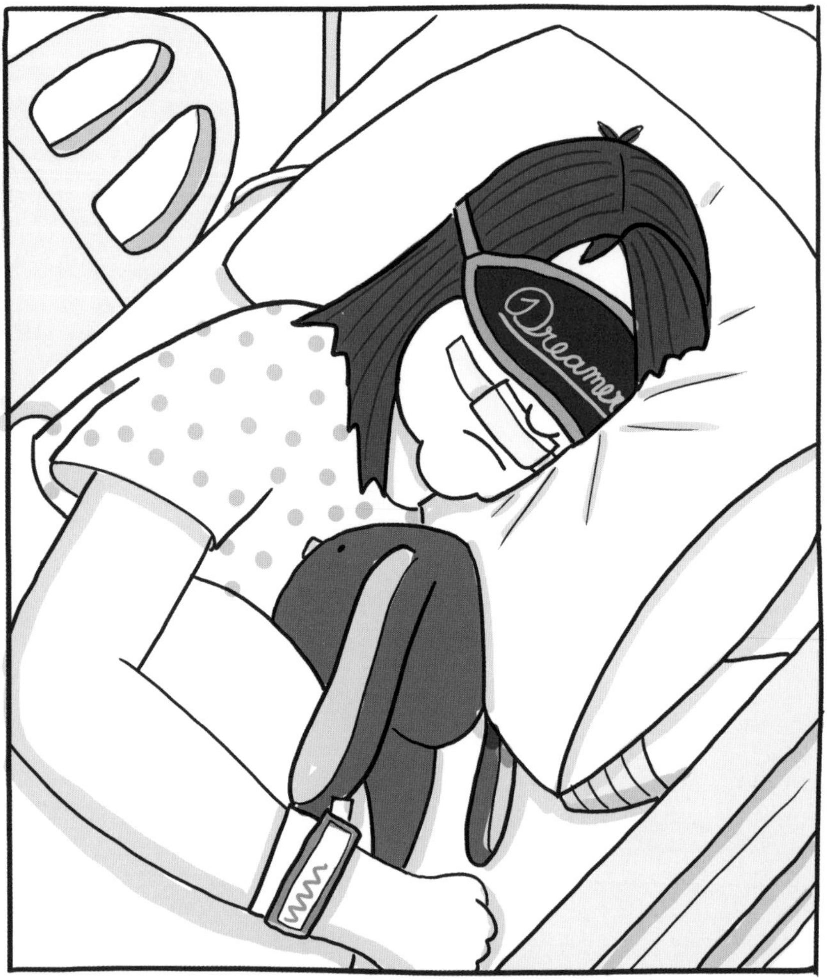
Dreamer

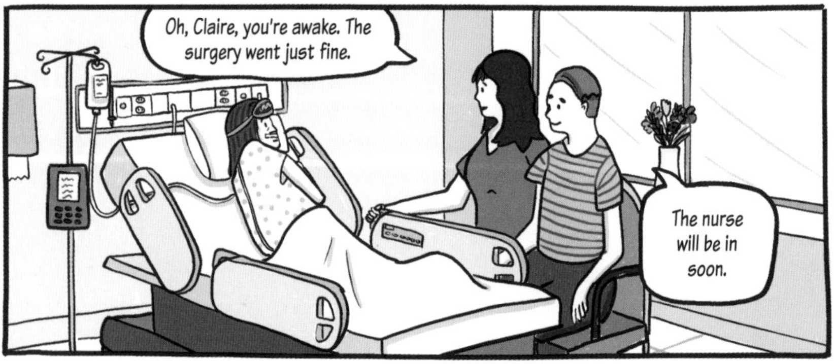
Oh, Claire, you're awake. The surgery went just fine.
The nurse will be in soon.

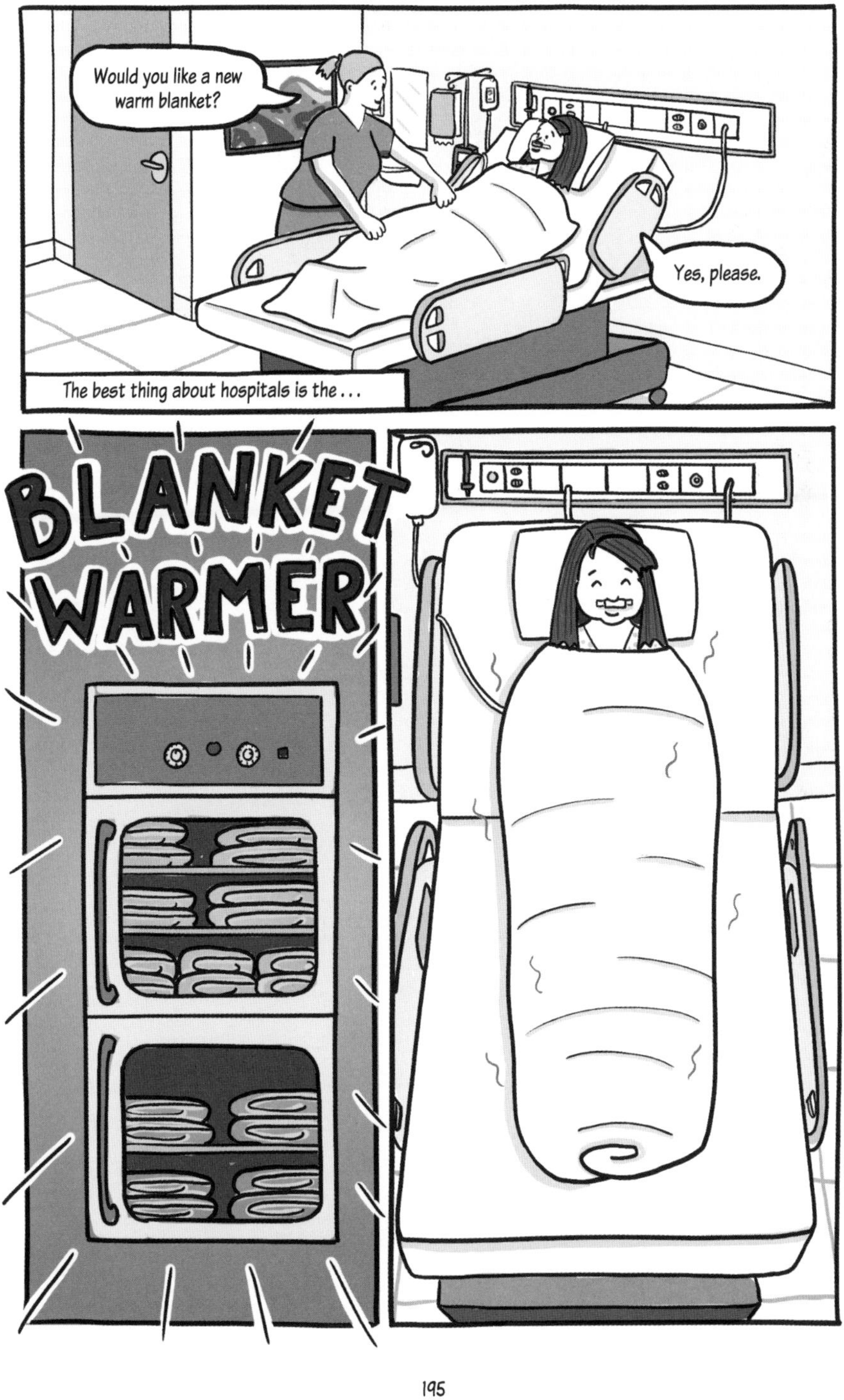
Would you like a new warm blanket?
Yes, please.
The best thing about hospitals is the . . .
BLANKET WARMER

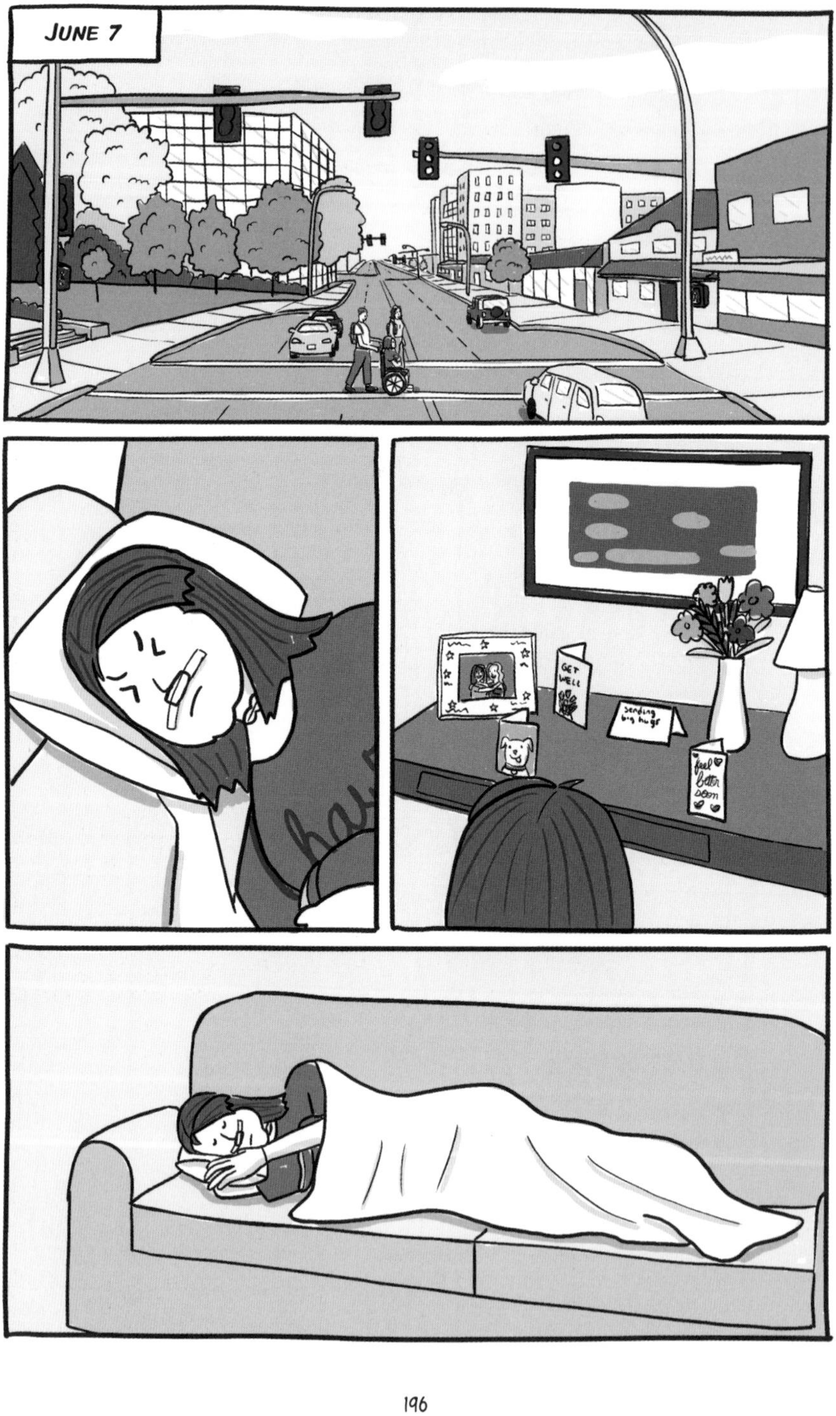
JUNE 7
GET WELL
sending big hugs
feel better soon

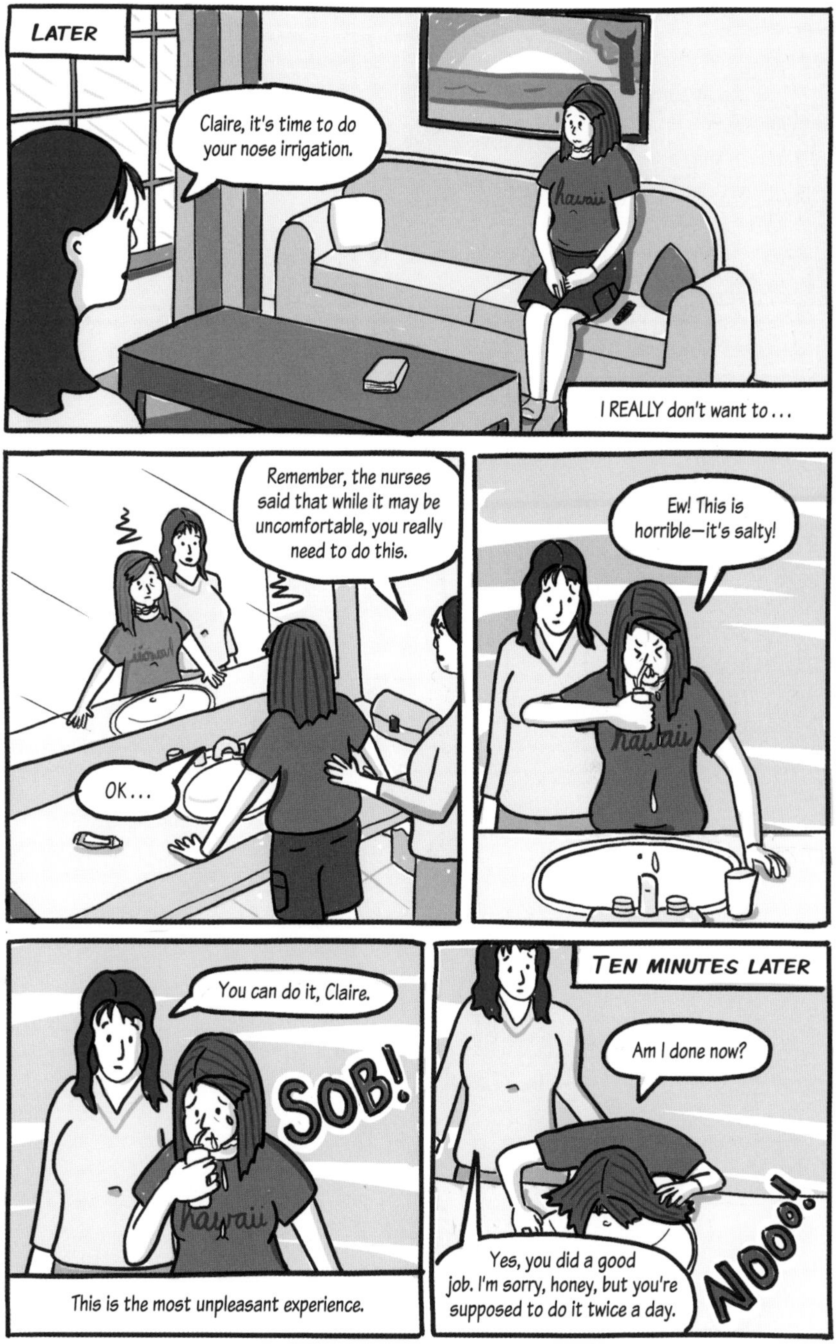
LATER
Claire, it's time to do your nose irrigation.
I REALLY don't want to . . .
Remember, the nurses said that while it may be uncomfortable, you really need to do this.
OK . . .
Ew! This is horrible—it's salty!
You can do it, Claire.
SOB!
This is the most unpleasant experience.
TEN MINUTES LATER
Am I done now?
Yes, you did a good job. I'm sorry, honey, but you're supposed to do it twice a day.
NOOOO!

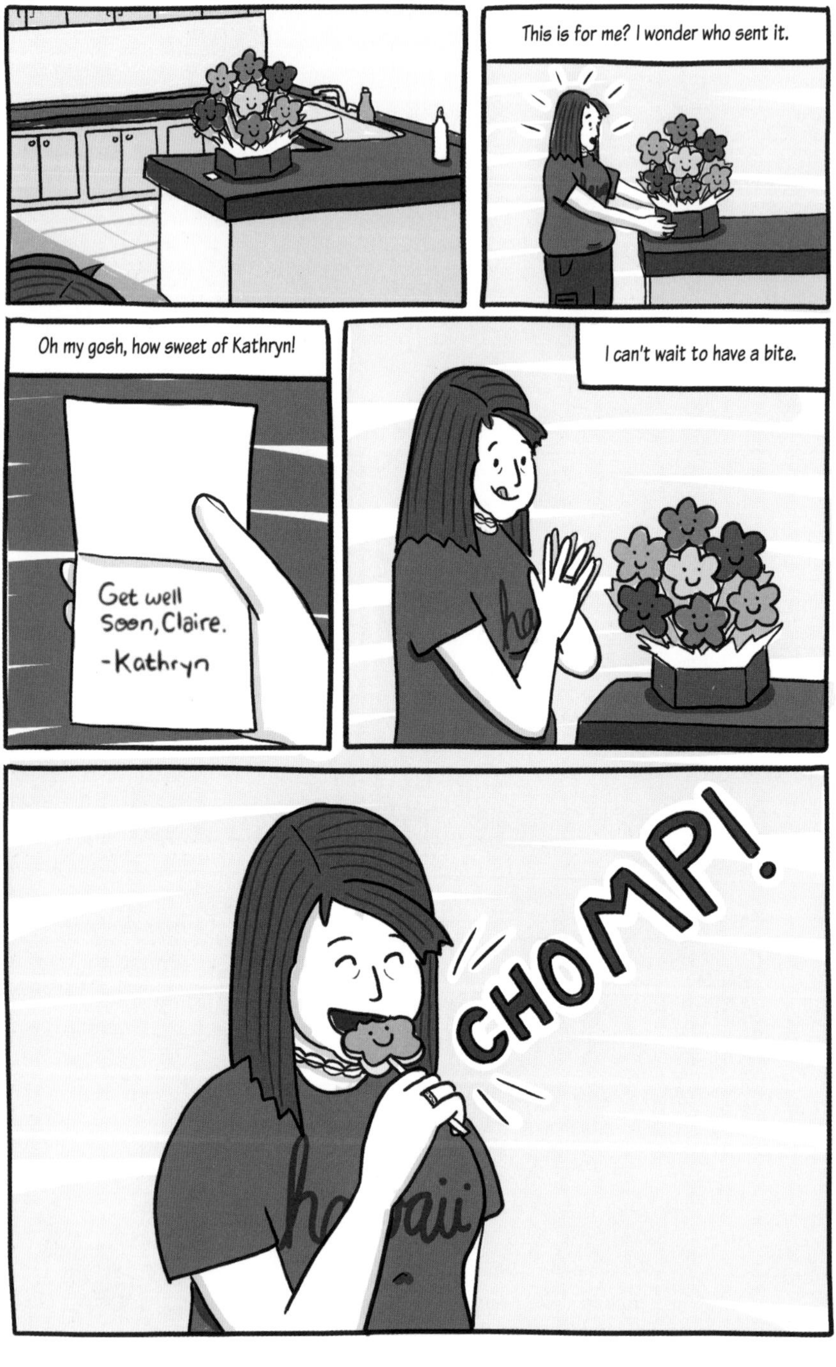
This is for me? I wonder who sent it.
Oh my gosh, how sweet of Kathryn!
Get well soon, Claire.
-Kathryn
I can't wait to have a bite.
CHOMP!

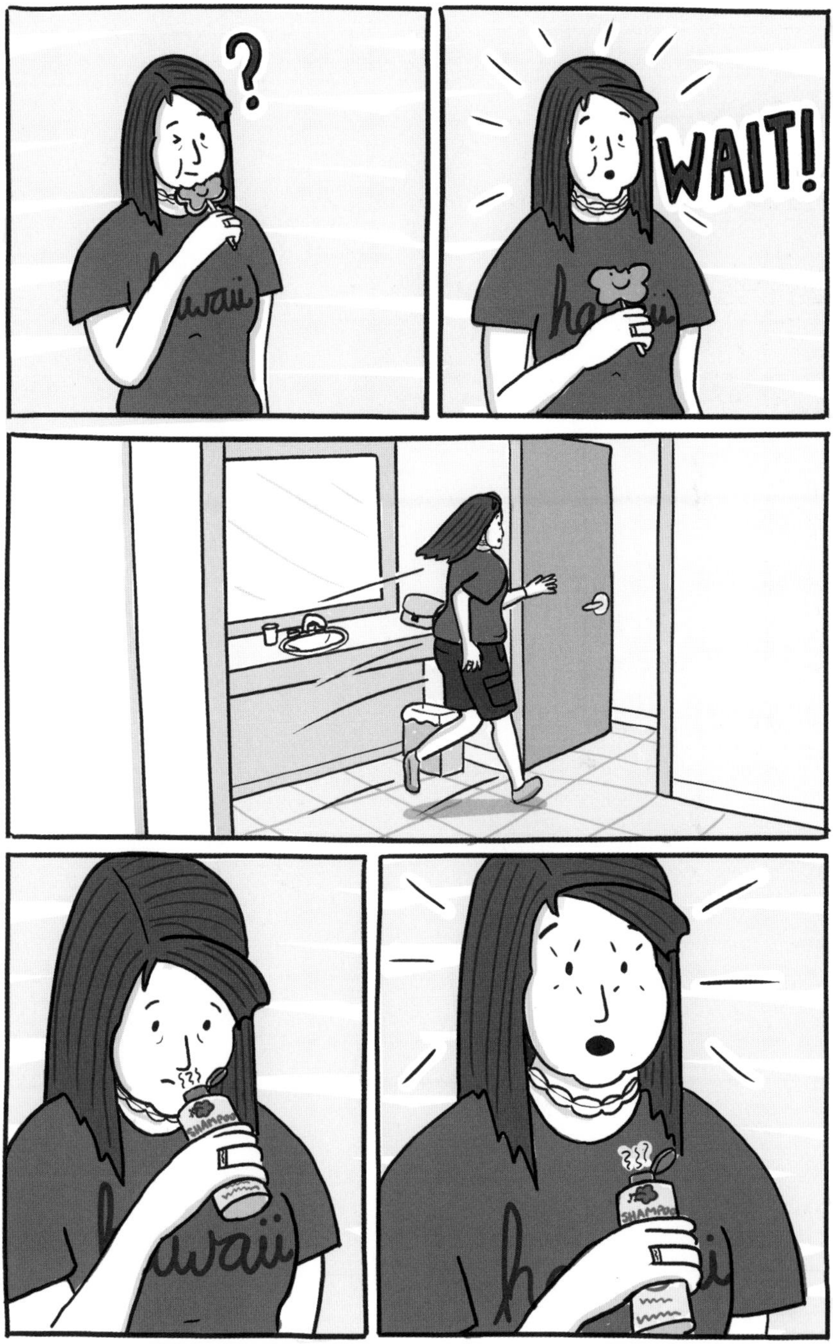
?
WAIT!
hawaii
SHAMPOO

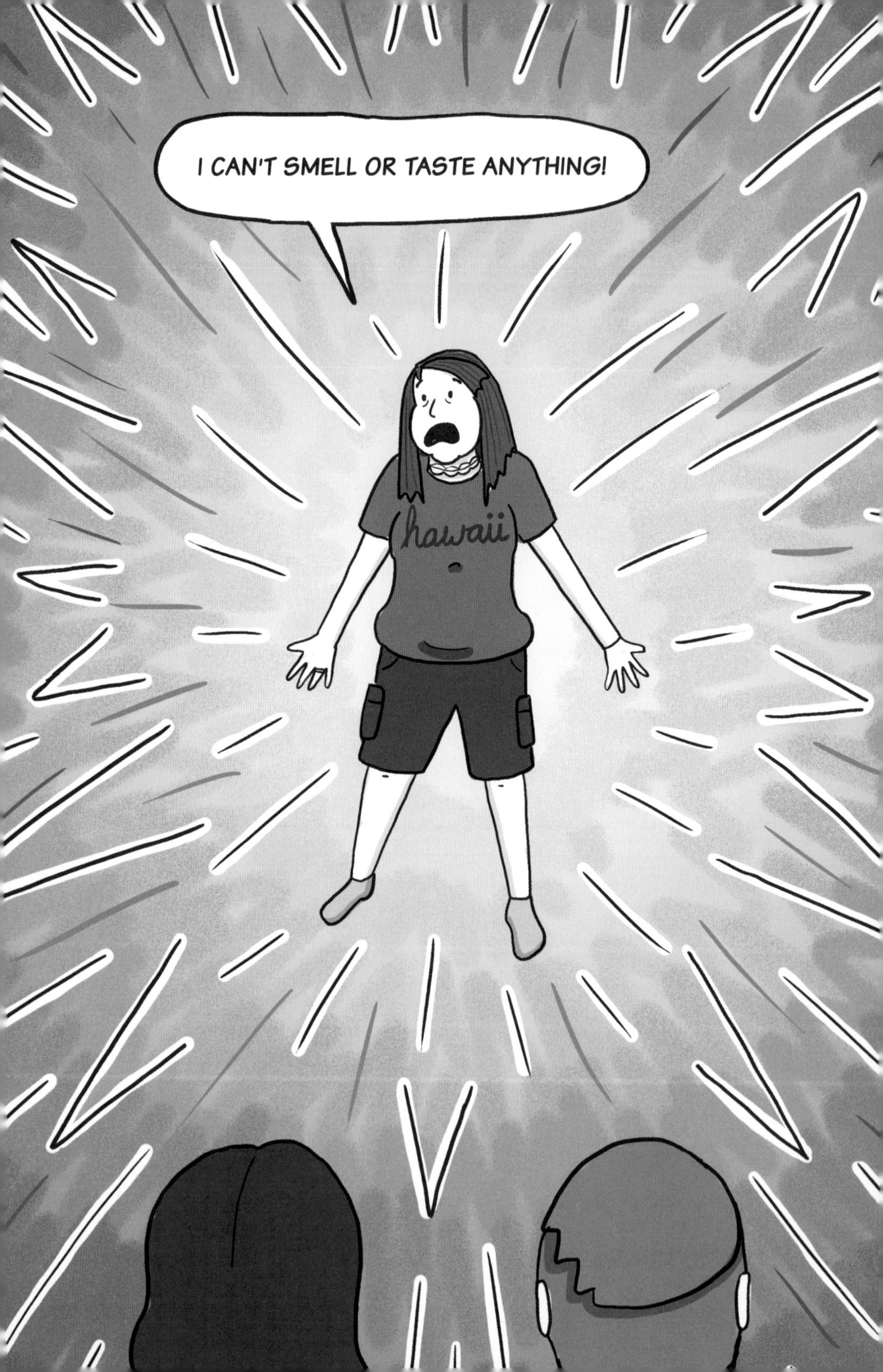
I CAN'T SMELL OR TASTE ANYTHING!
hawaii

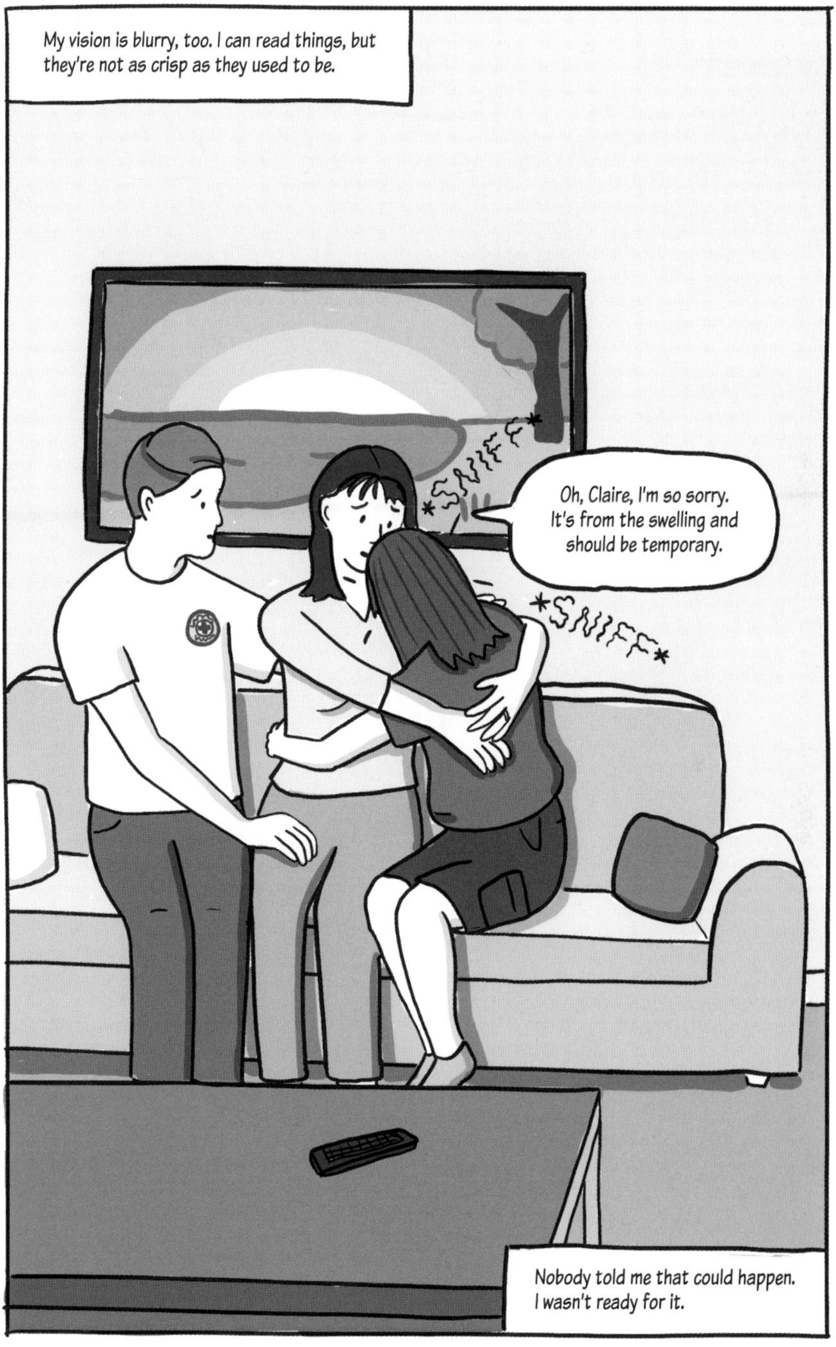
My vision is blurry, too. I can read things, but they're not as crisp as they used to be.
SNIFF
Oh, Claire, I'm so sorry. It's from the swelling and should be temporary.
SNIFF
Nobody told me that could happen. I wasn't ready for it.

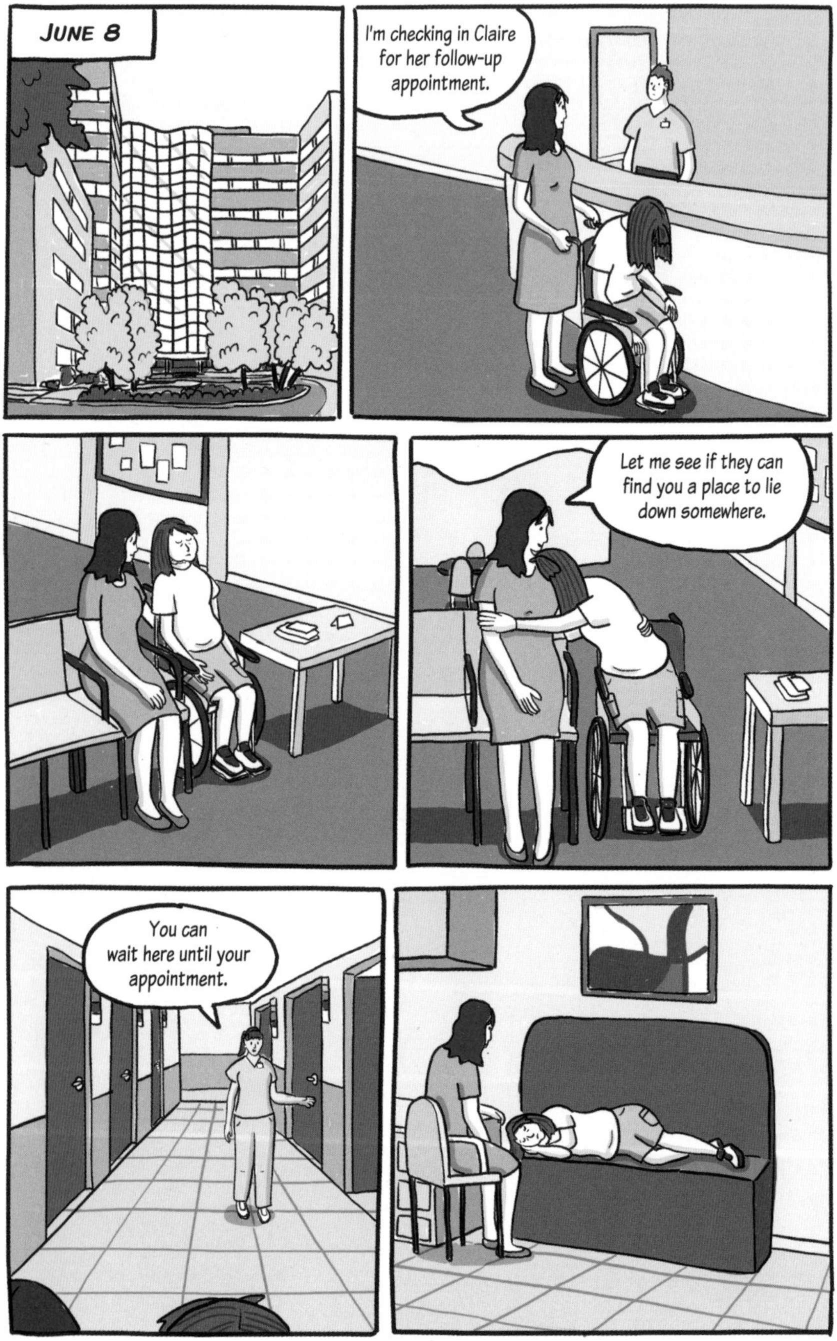
JUNE 8
I'm checking in Claire for her follow-up appointment.
Let me see if they can find you a place to lie down somewhere.
You can wait here until your appointment.

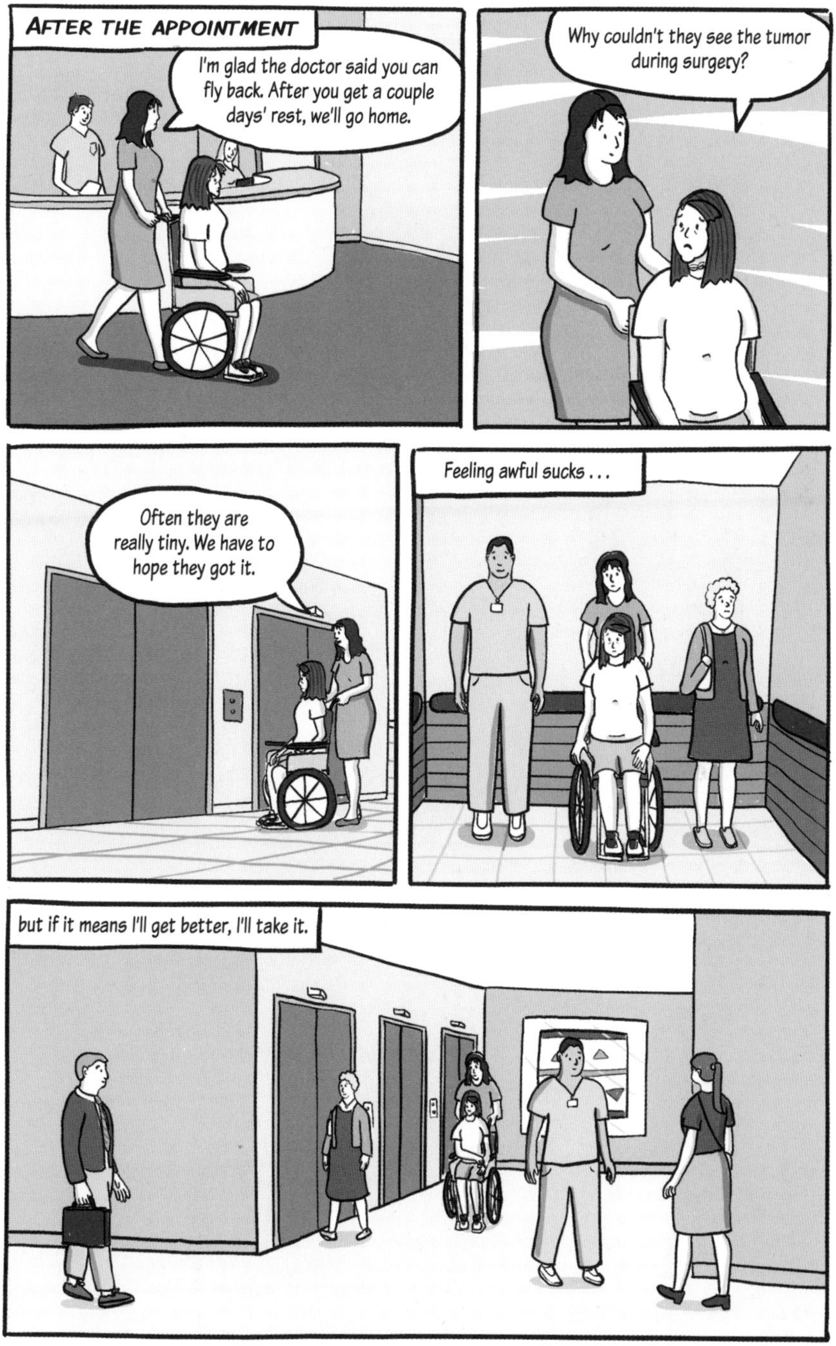
AFTER THE APPOINTMENT
I'm glad the doctor said you can fly back. After you get a couple days' rest, we'll go home.
Why couldn't they see the tumor during surgery?
Often they are really tiny. We have to hope they got it.
Feeling awful sucks . . .
but if it means I'll get better, I'll take it.

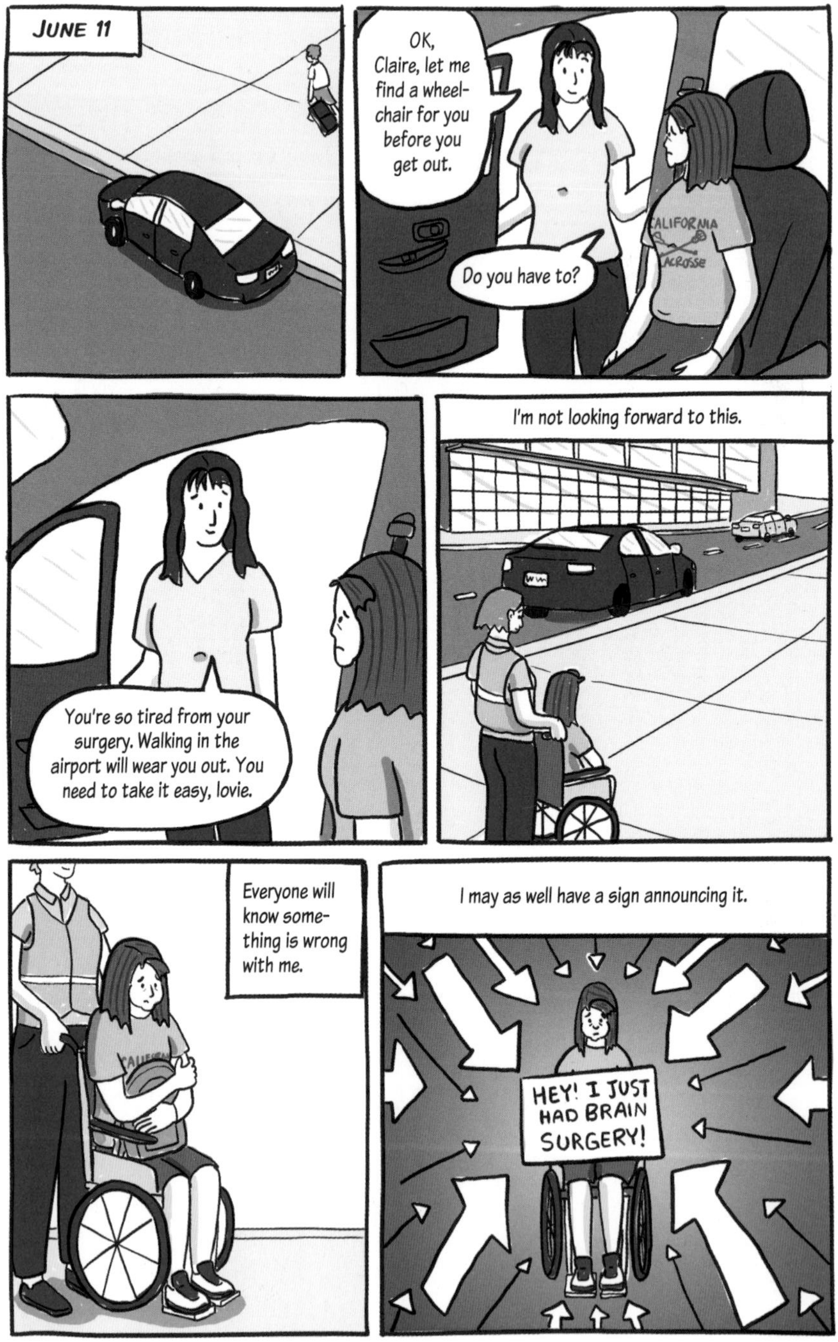
JUNE 11
OK, Claire, let me find a wheel-chair for you before you get out.
Do you have to?
CALIFORNIA LACROSSE
You're so tired from your surgery. Walking in the airport will wear you out. You need to take it easy, lovie.
I'm not looking forward to this.
Everyone will know some-thing is wrong with me.
I may as well have a sign announcing it.
HEY! I JUST HAD BRAIN SURGERY!

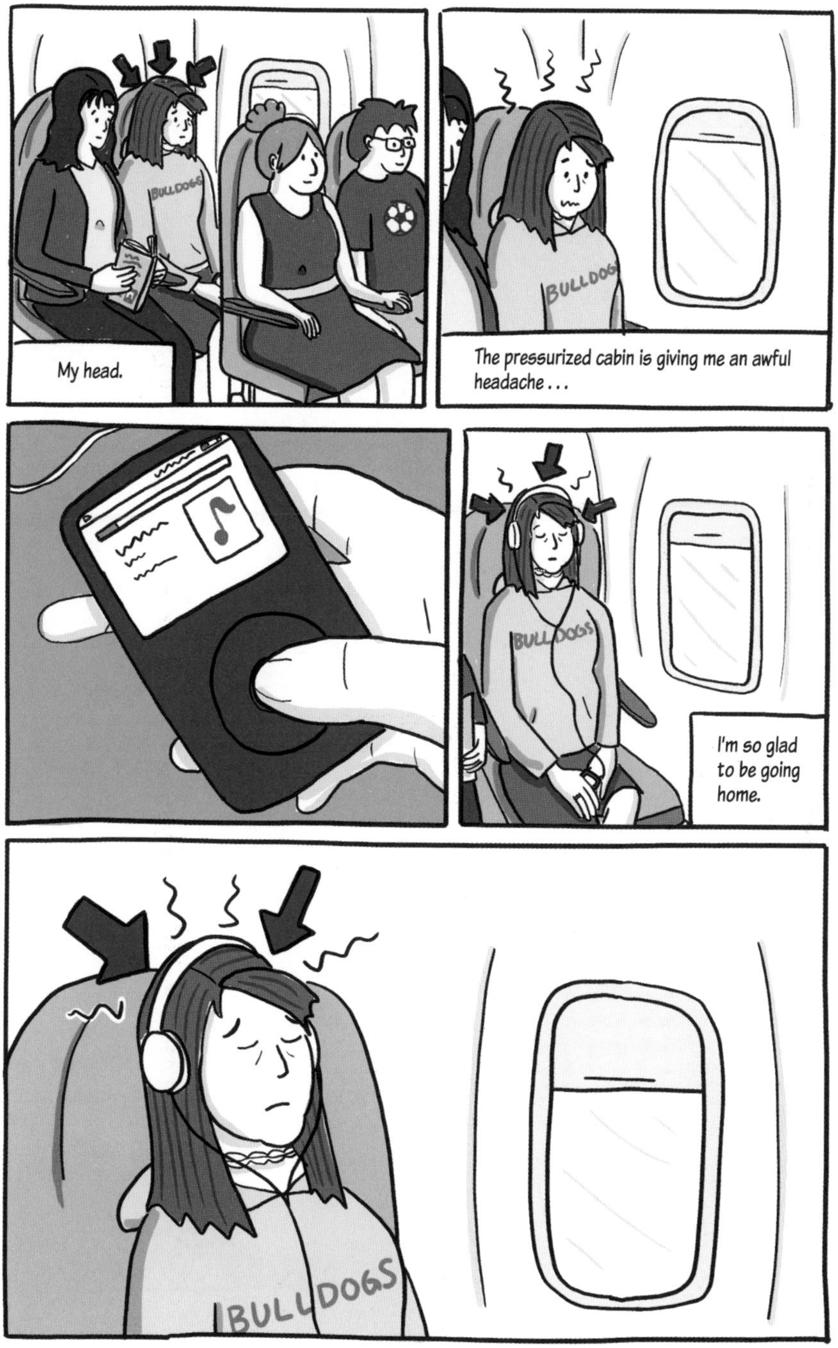
My head.
BULLDOGS
The pressurized cabin is giving me an awful headache . . .
BULLDOGS
BULLDOGS
I'm so glad to be going home.
BULLDOGS

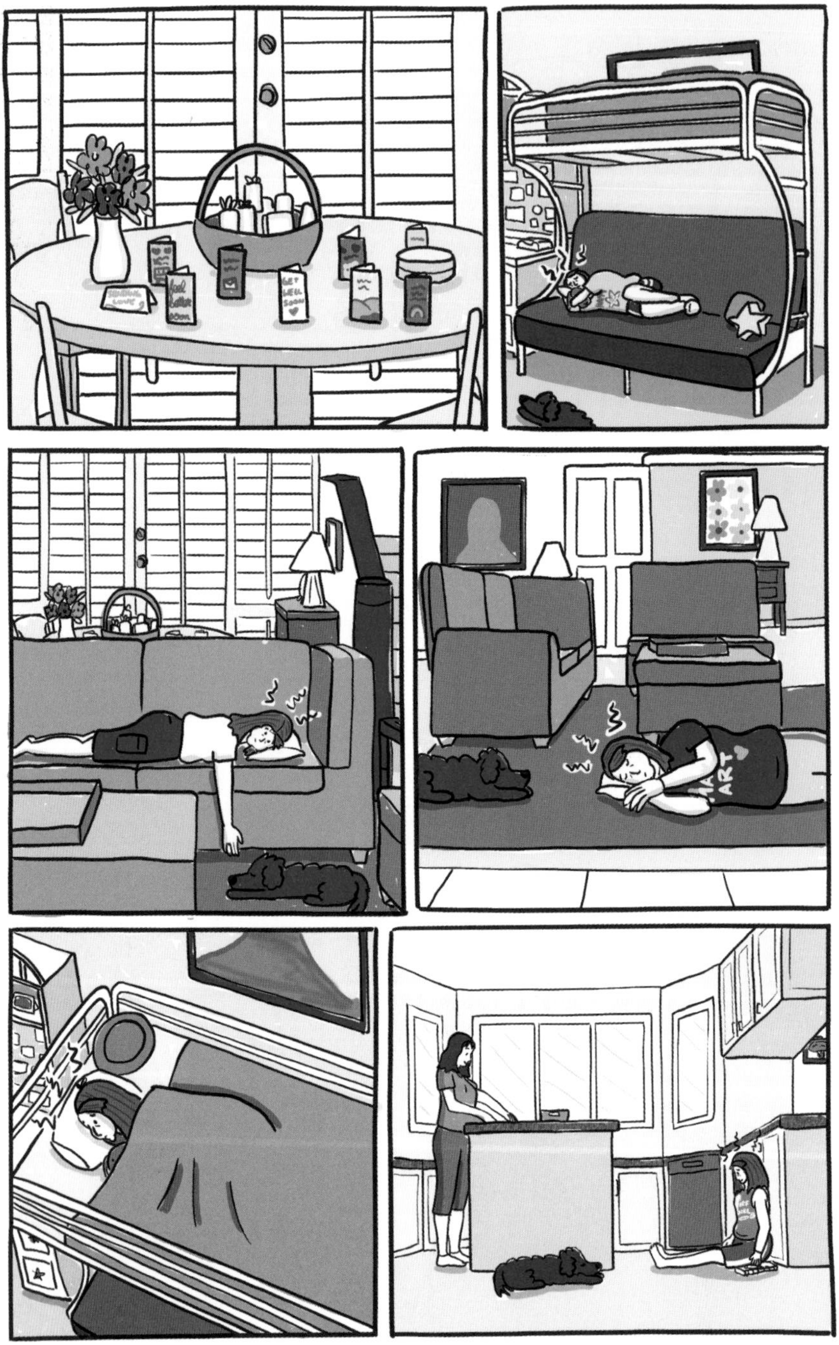
feel better soon
GET WELL SOON

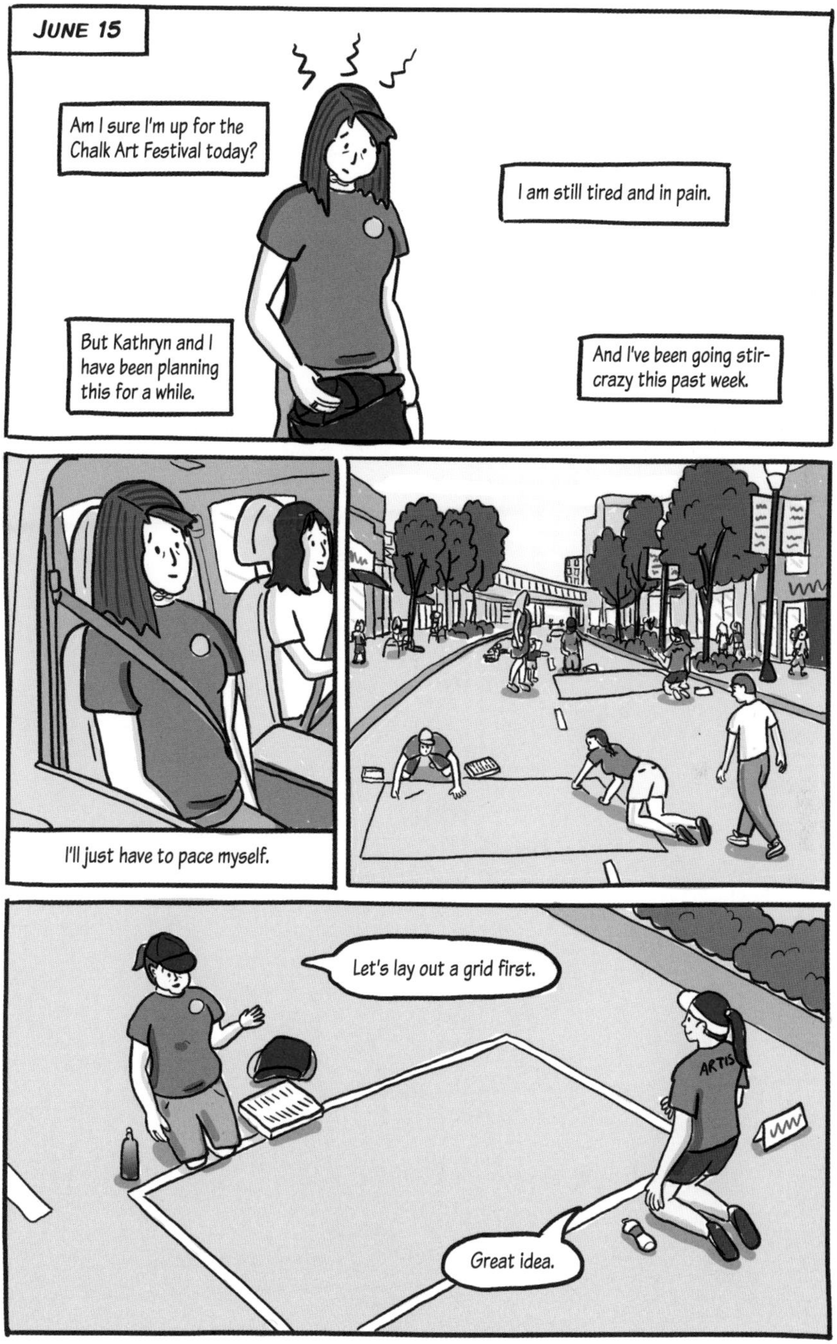
JUNE 15
Am I sure I'm up for the Chalk Art Festival today?
I am still tired and in pain.
But Kathryn and I have been planning this for a while.
And I've been going stir-crazy this past week.
I'll just have to pace myself.
Let's lay out a grid first.
Great idea.

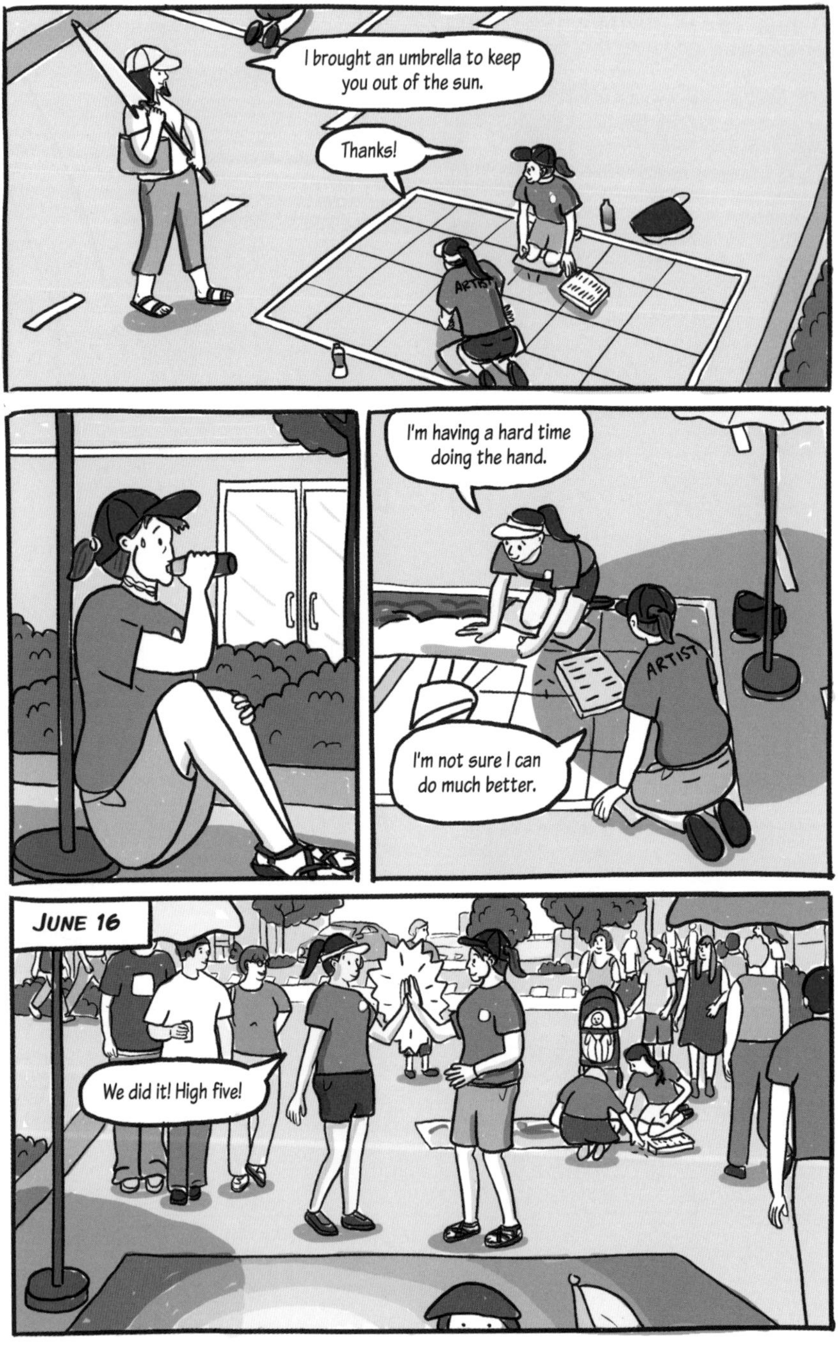
I brought an umbrella to keep you out of the sun.
Thanks!
ARTIST
I'm having a hard time doing the hand.
ARTIST
I'm not sure I can do much better.
JUNE 16
We did it! High five!

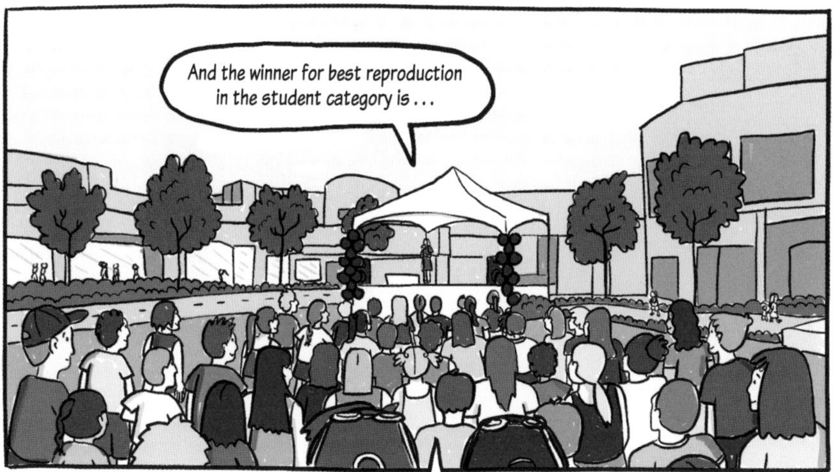
And the winner for best reproduction in the student category is . . .

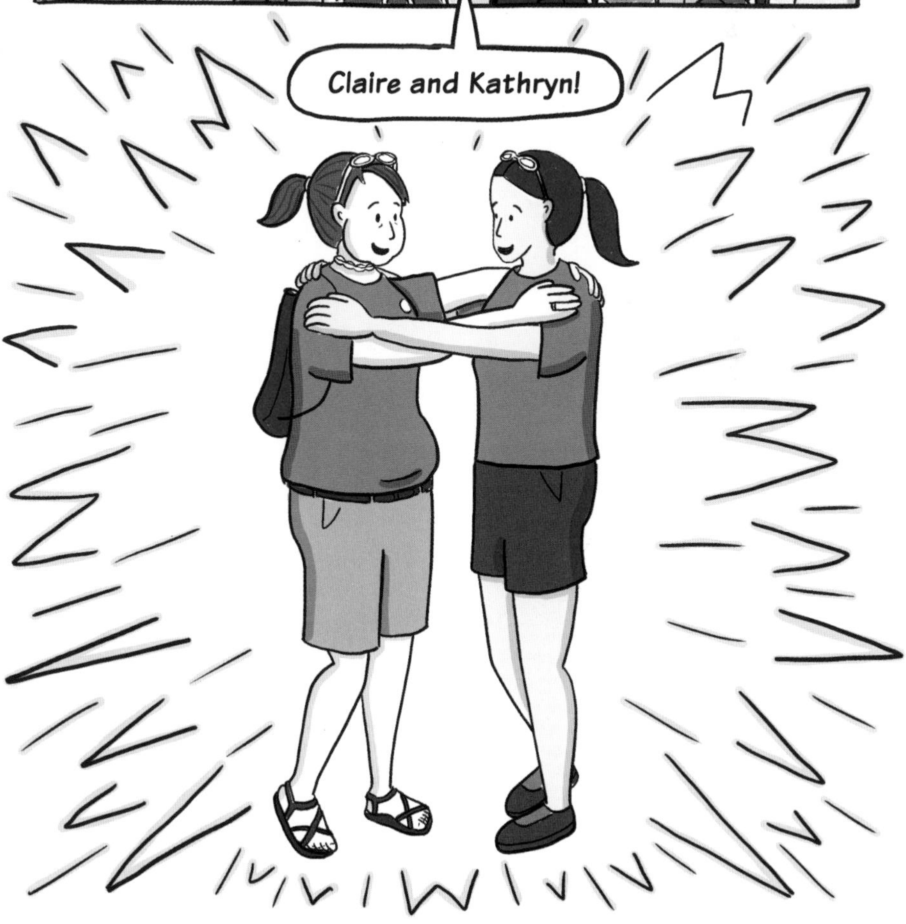
Claire and Kathryn!

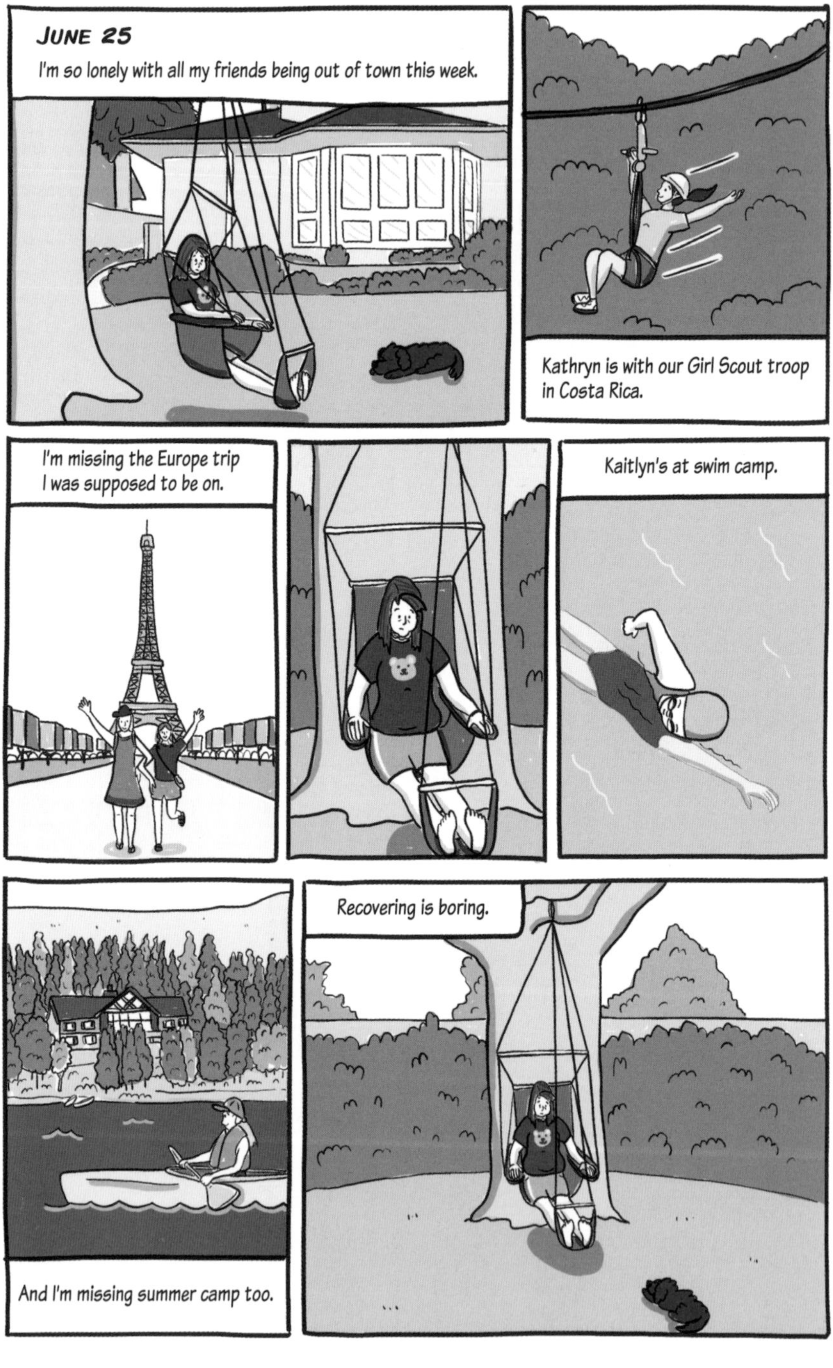
JUNE 25
I'm so lonely with all my friends being out of town this week.
Kathryn is with our Girl Scout troop in Costa Rica.
I'm missing the Europe trip I was supposed to be on.
Kaitlyn's at swim camp.
And I'm missing summer camp too.
Recovering is boring.

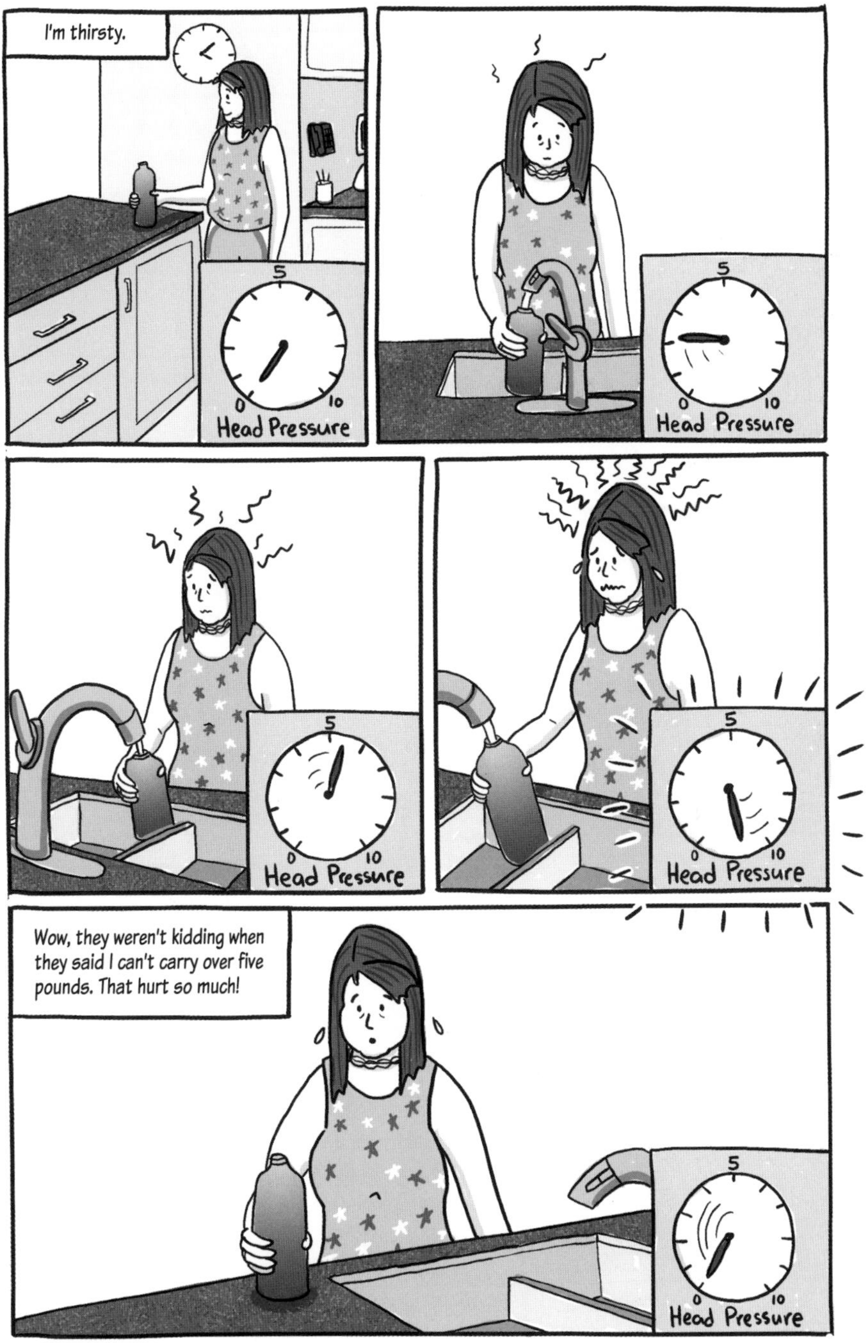
I'm thirsty.
5
0
10
Head Pressure
5
0
10
Head Pressure
5
0
10
Head Pressure
5
0
10
Head Pressure
Wow, they weren't kidding when they said I can't carry over five pounds. That hurt so much!
5
0
10
Head Pressure

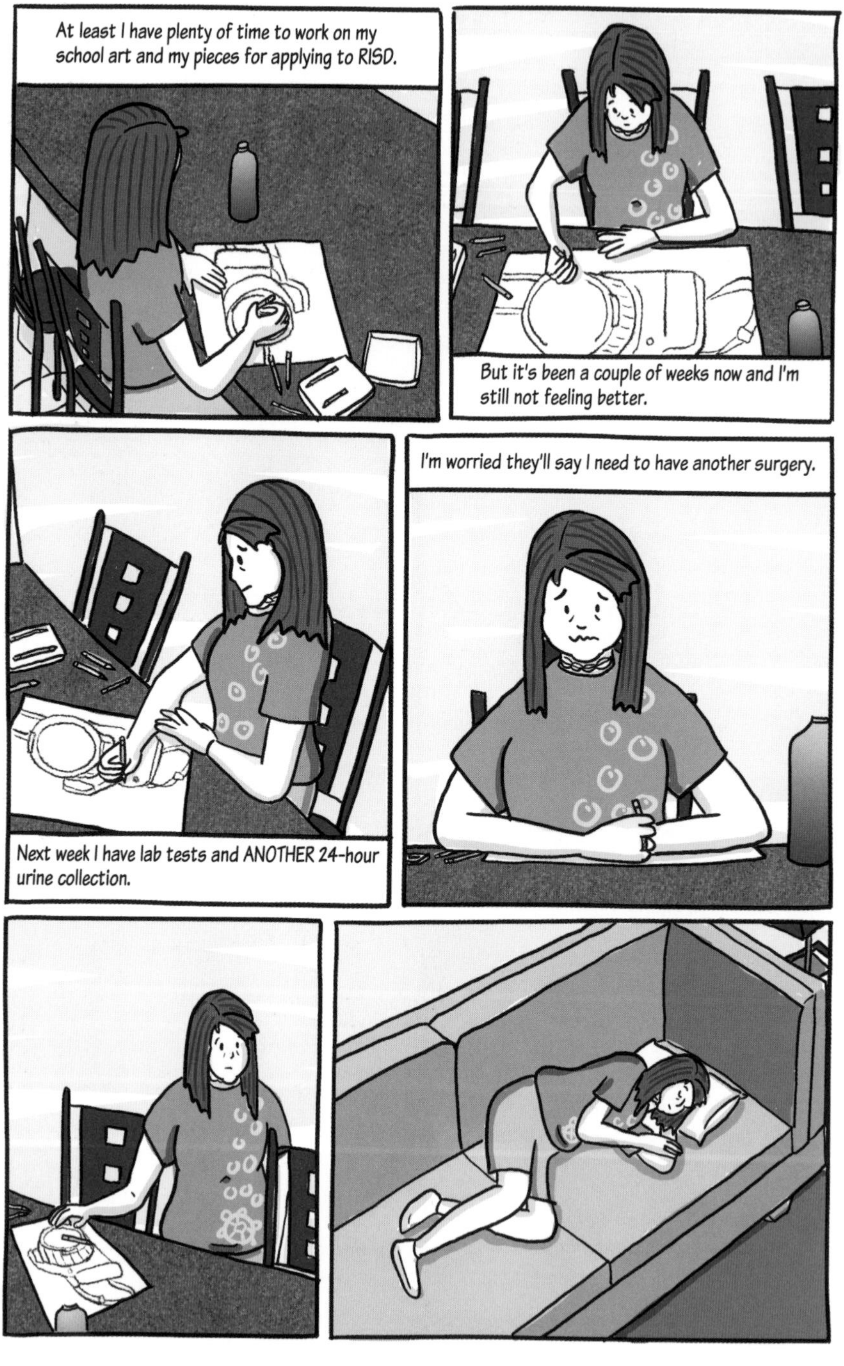
At least I have plenty of time to work on my school art and my pieces for applying to RISD.
But it's been a couple of weeks now and I'm still not feeling better.
Next week I have lab tests and ANOTHER 24-hour urine collection.
I'm worried they'll say I need to have another surgery.

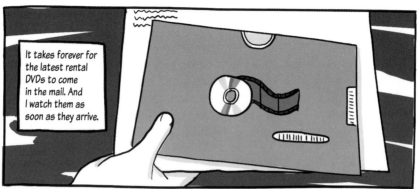

It takes forever for the latest rental DVDs to come in the mail. And I watch them as soon as they arrive.

Nothing's on TV except game shows. I'm learning a lot of random trivia...

What is the largest animal ever known?

The blue whale.

and learning how to cook.

And whip the frosting until it becomes nice and fluffy.

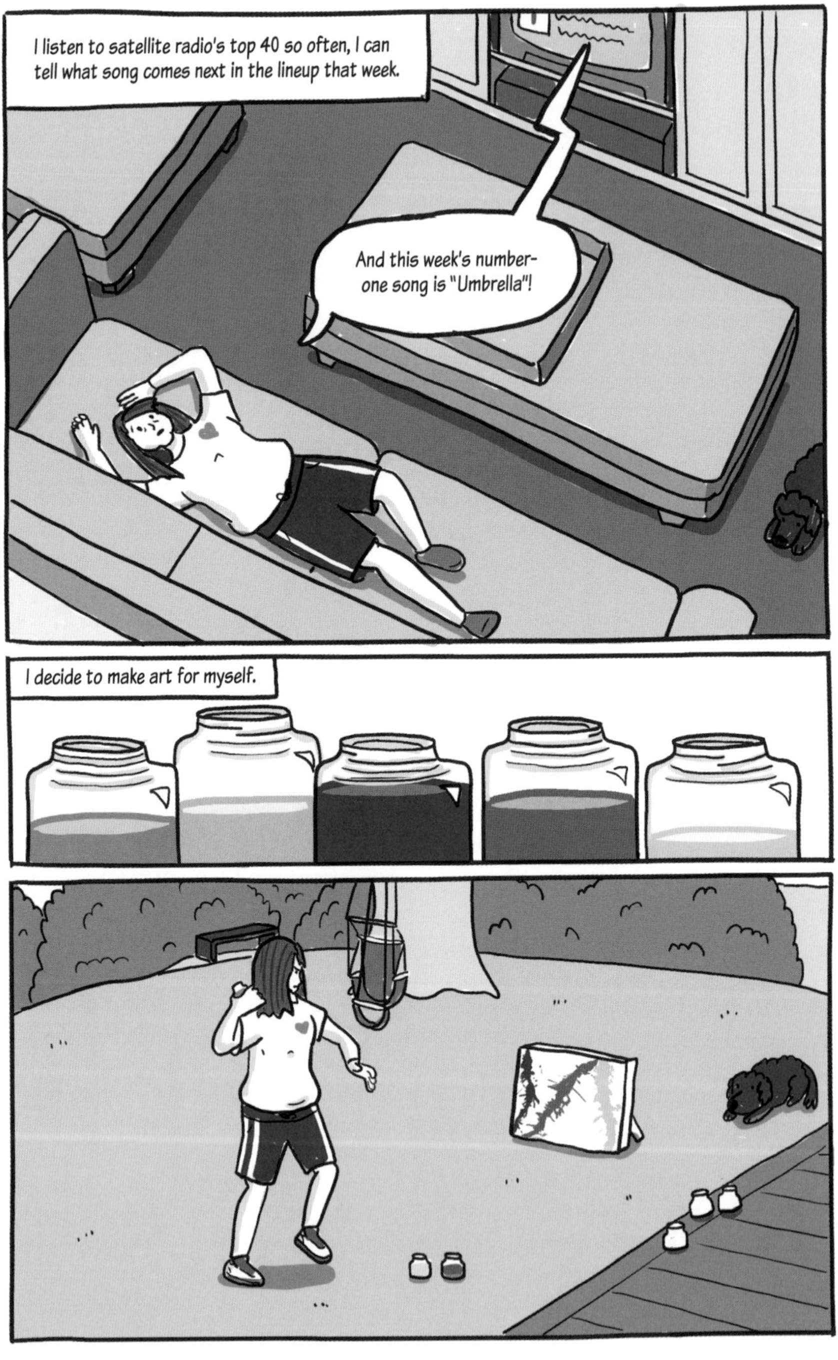
I listen to satellite radio's top 40 so often, I can tell what song comes next in the lineup that week.
And this week's number-one song is "Umbrella"!
I decide to make art for myself.

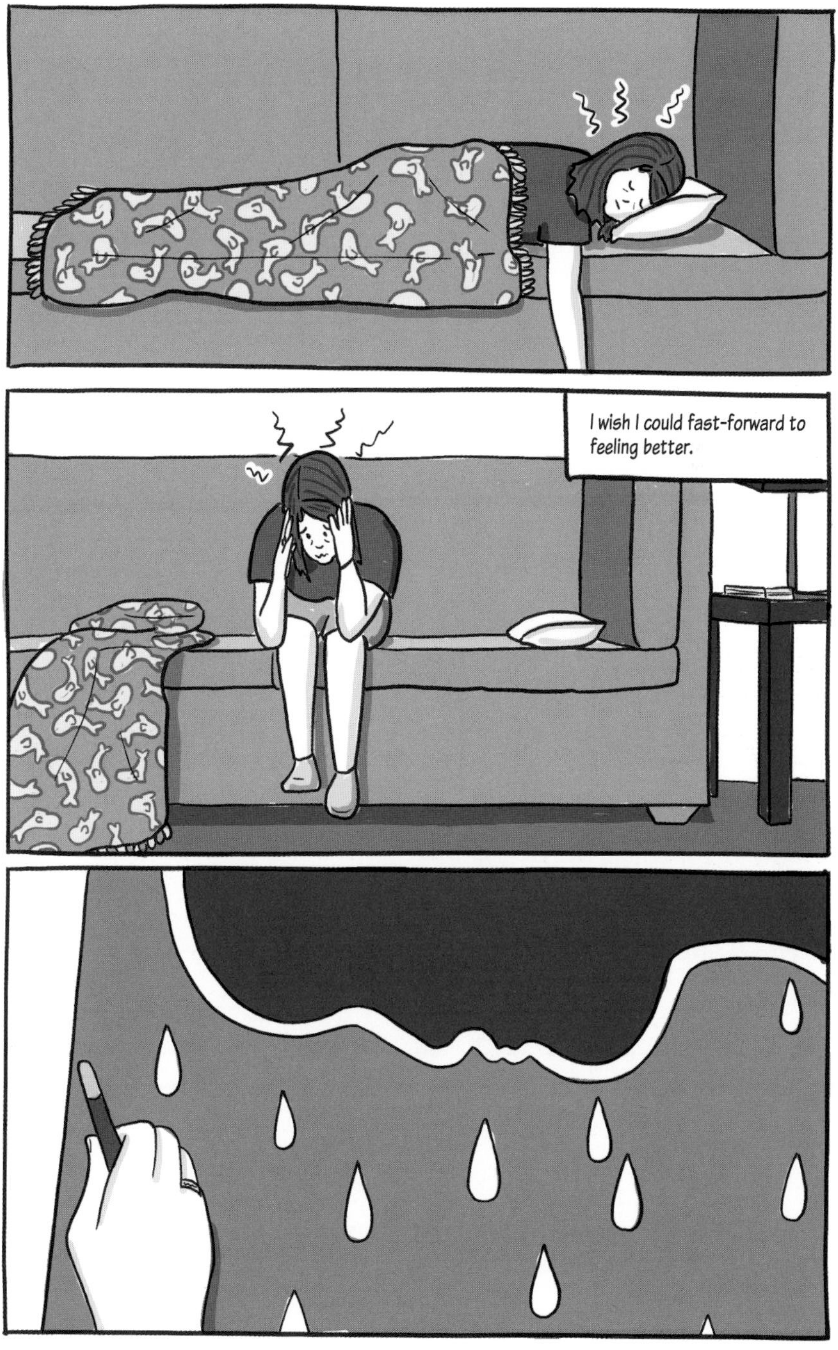
I wish I could fast-forward to feeling better.

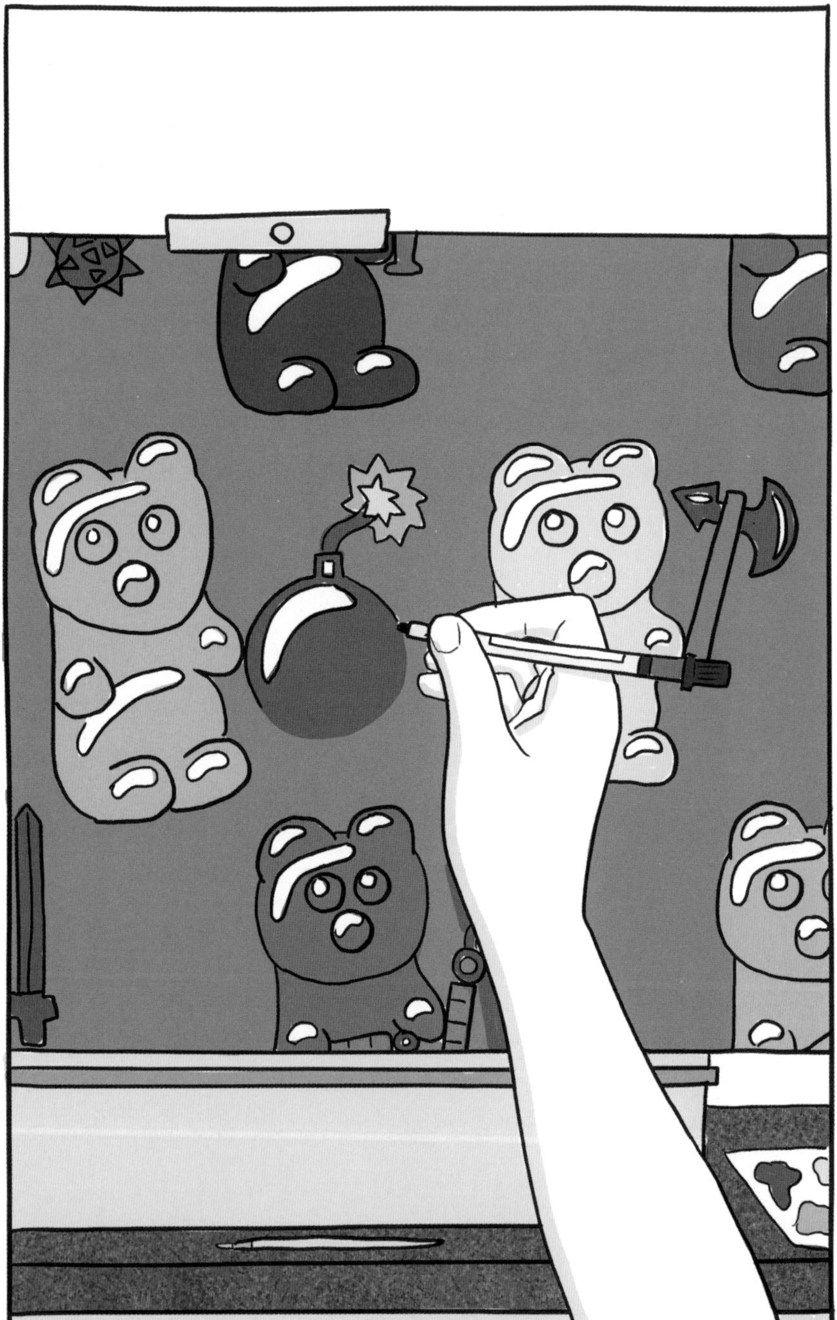

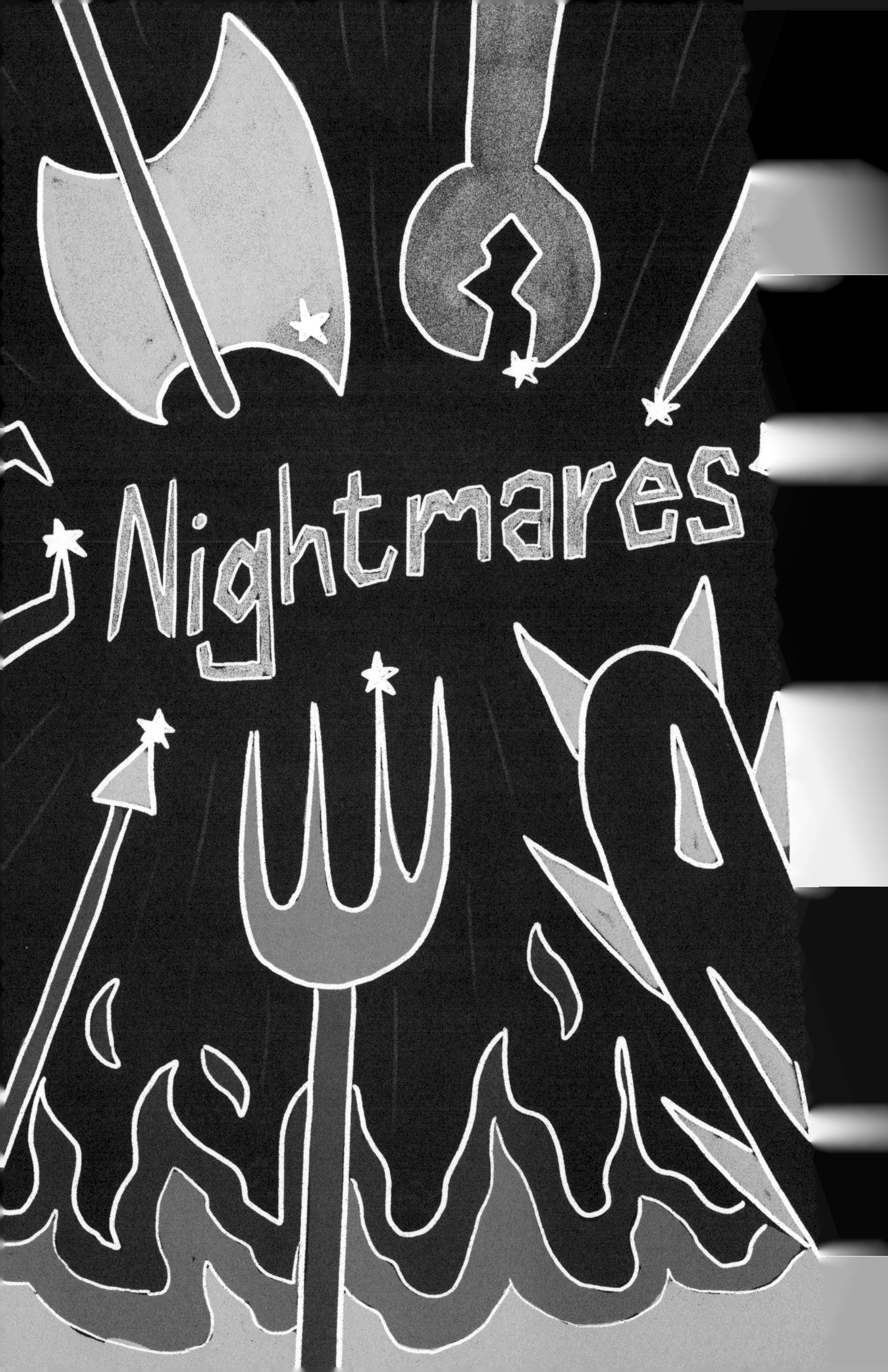
Nightmares

AAH!

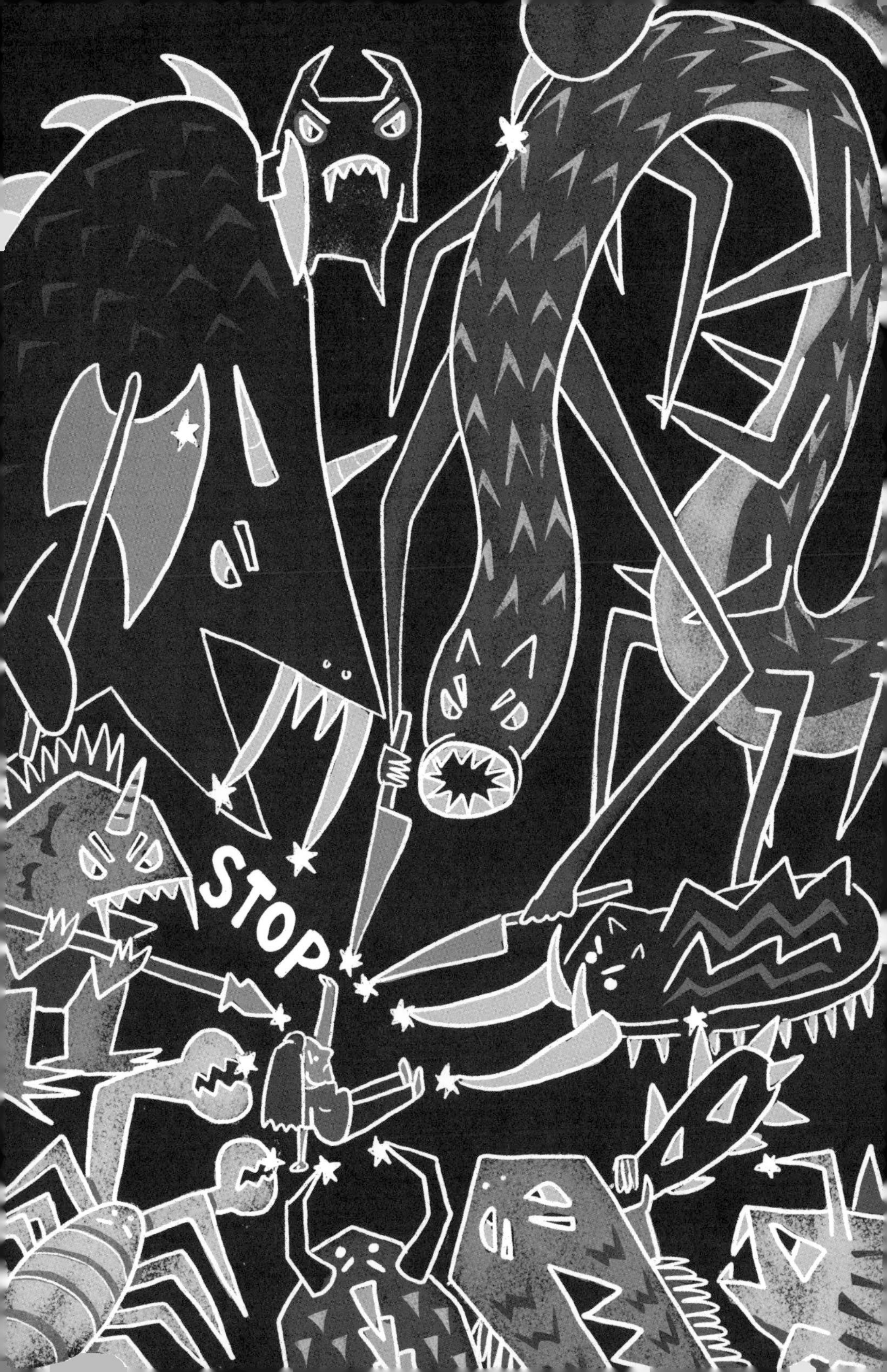
STOP

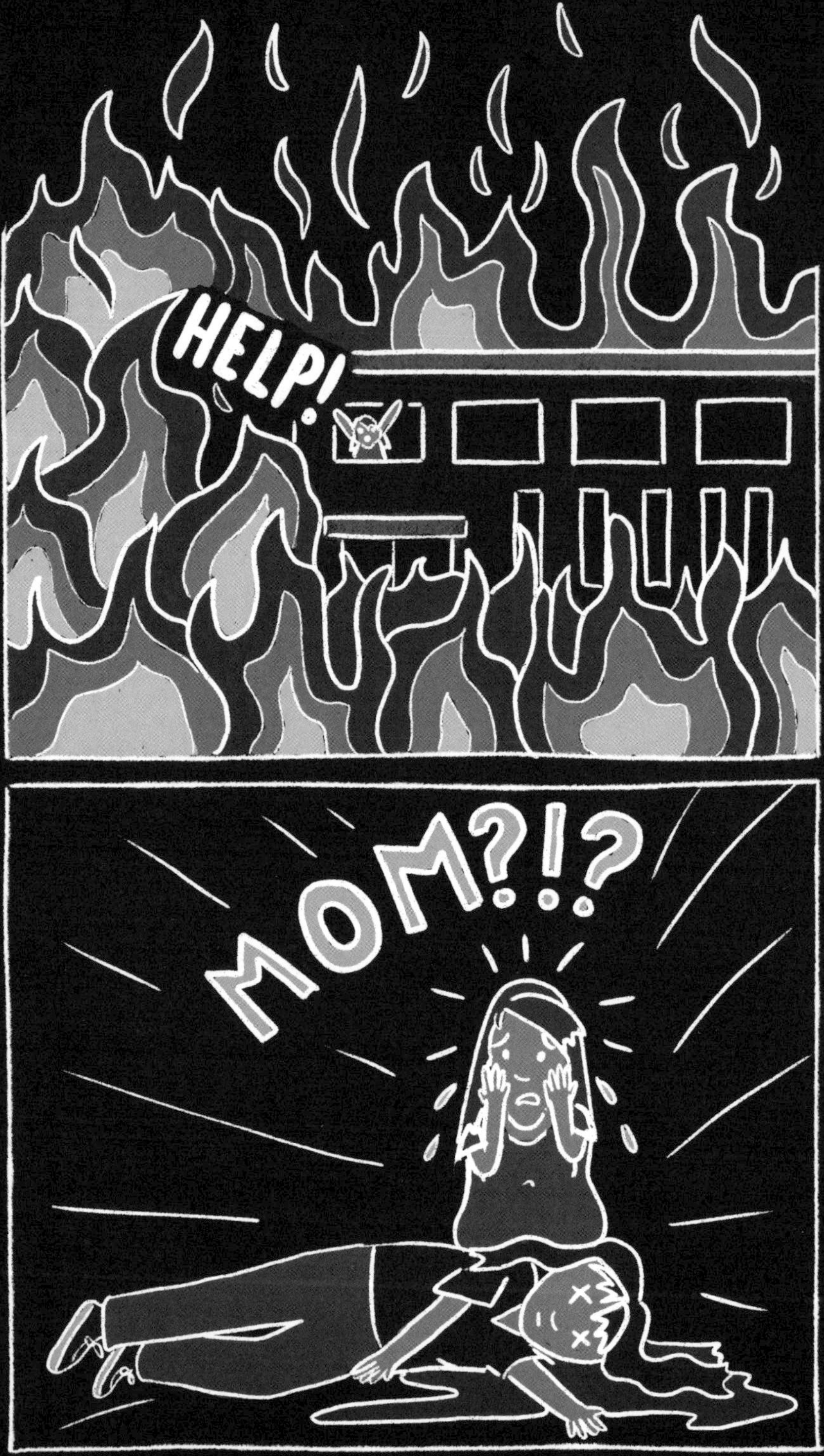
HELP!
MOM?!?

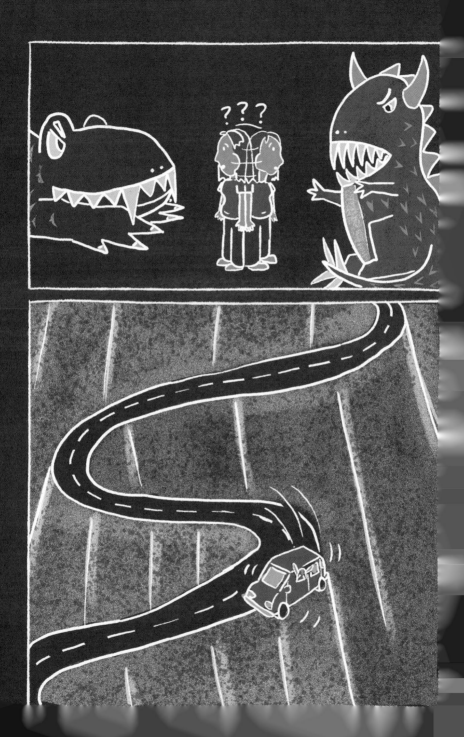

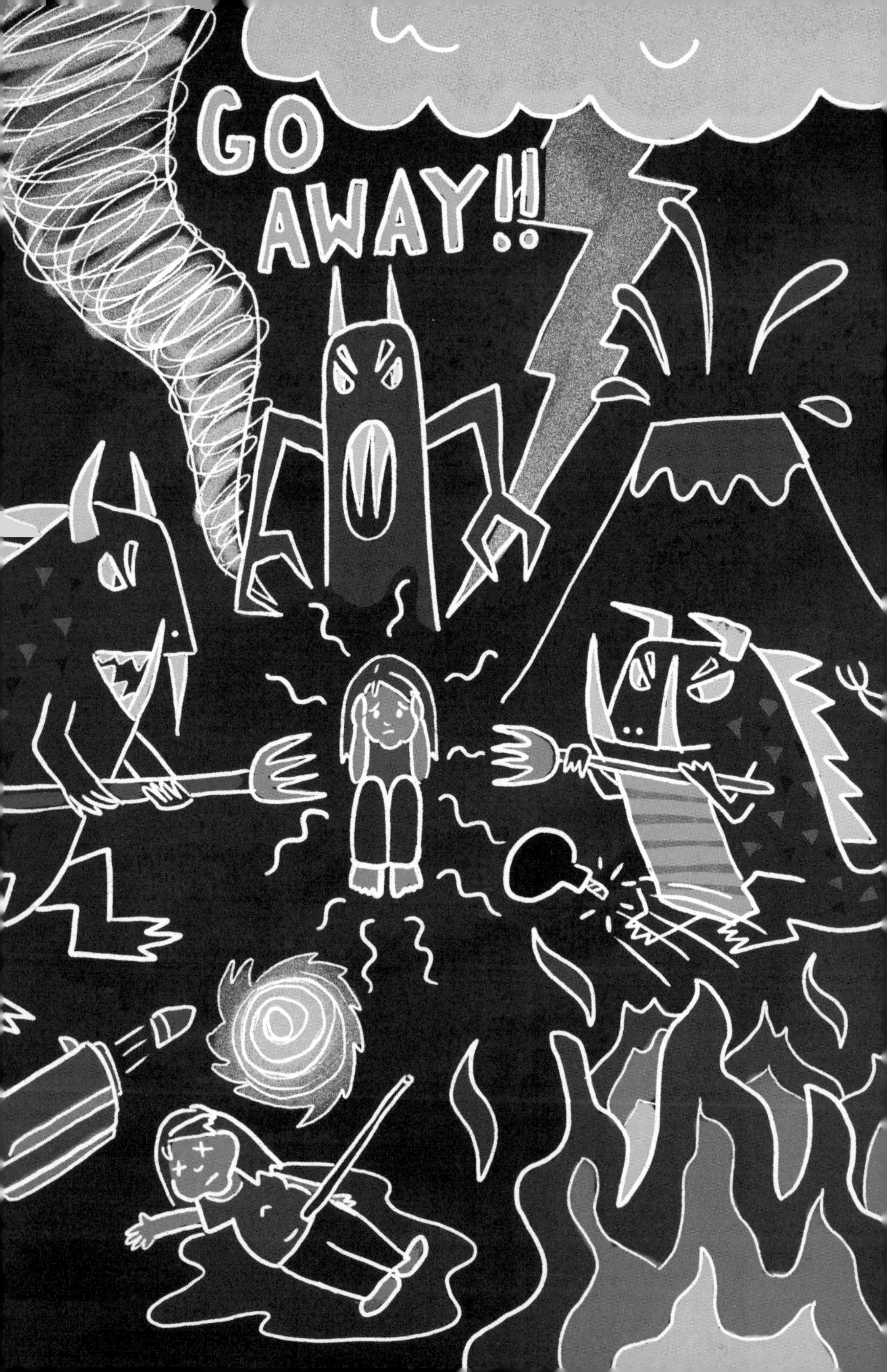
GO AWAY!!

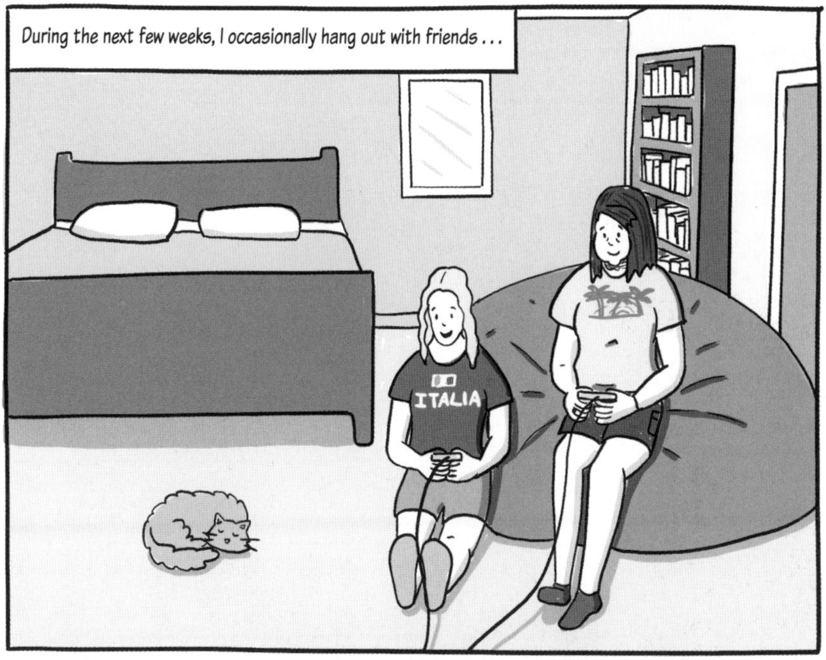
During the next few weeks, I occasionally hang out with friends . . .
ITALIA

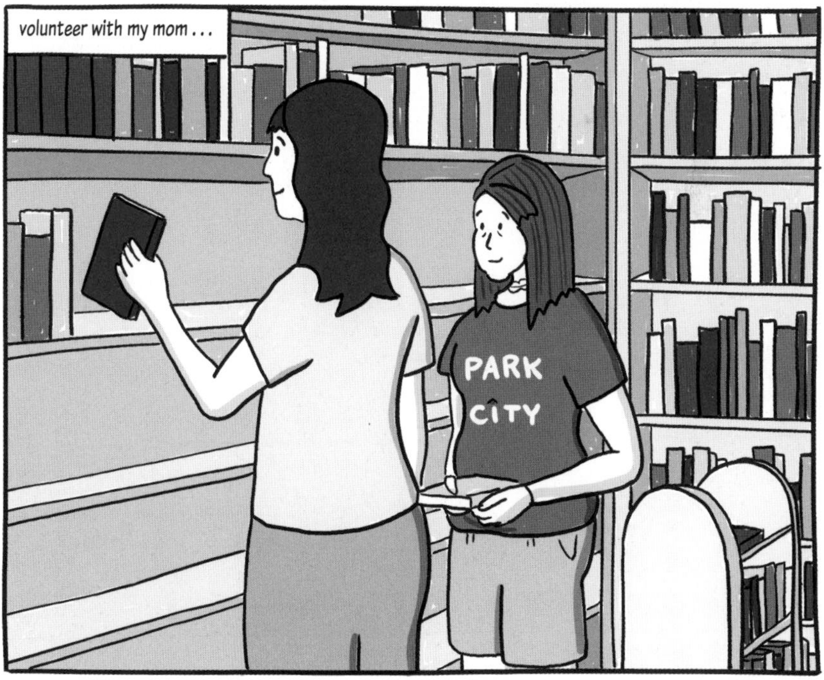
volunteer with my mom . . .
PARK
CITY

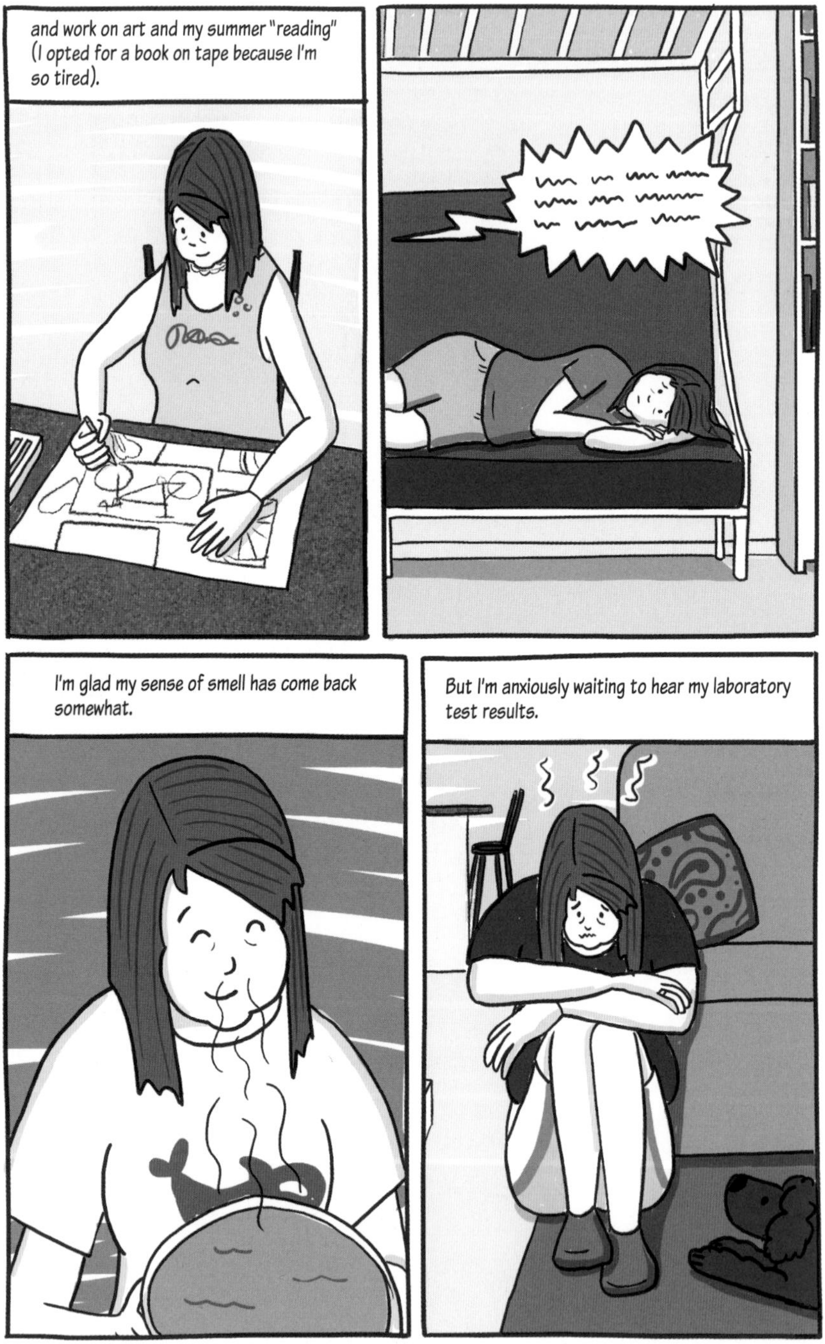
and work on art and my summer "reading" (I opted for a book on tape because I'm so tired).
I'm glad my sense of smell has come back somewhat.
But I'm anxiously waiting to hear my laboratory test results.

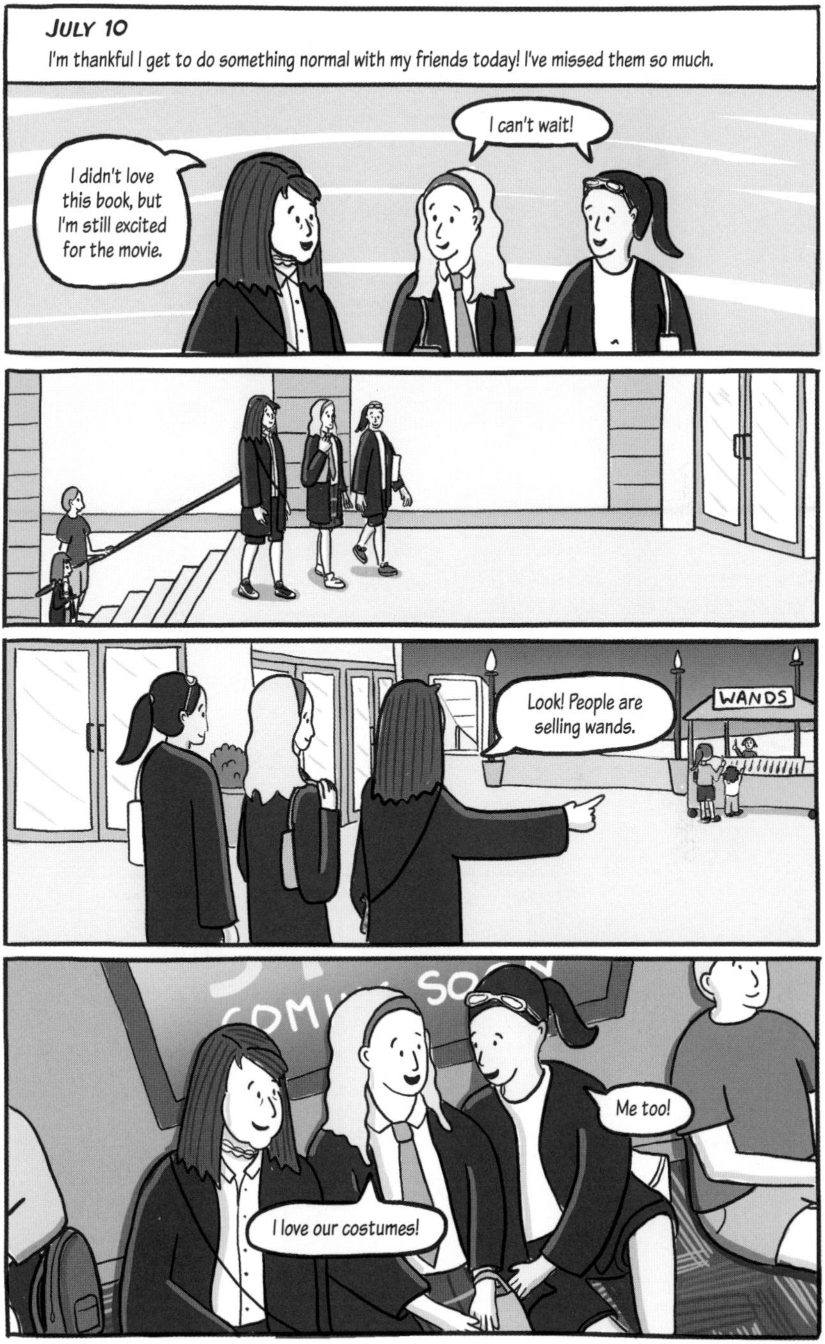
JULY 10
I'm thankful I get to do something normal with my friends today! I've missed them so much.
I didn't love this book, but I'm still excited for the movie.
I can't wait!
Look! People are selling wands.
WANDS
COMING SOON
I love our costumes!
Me too!

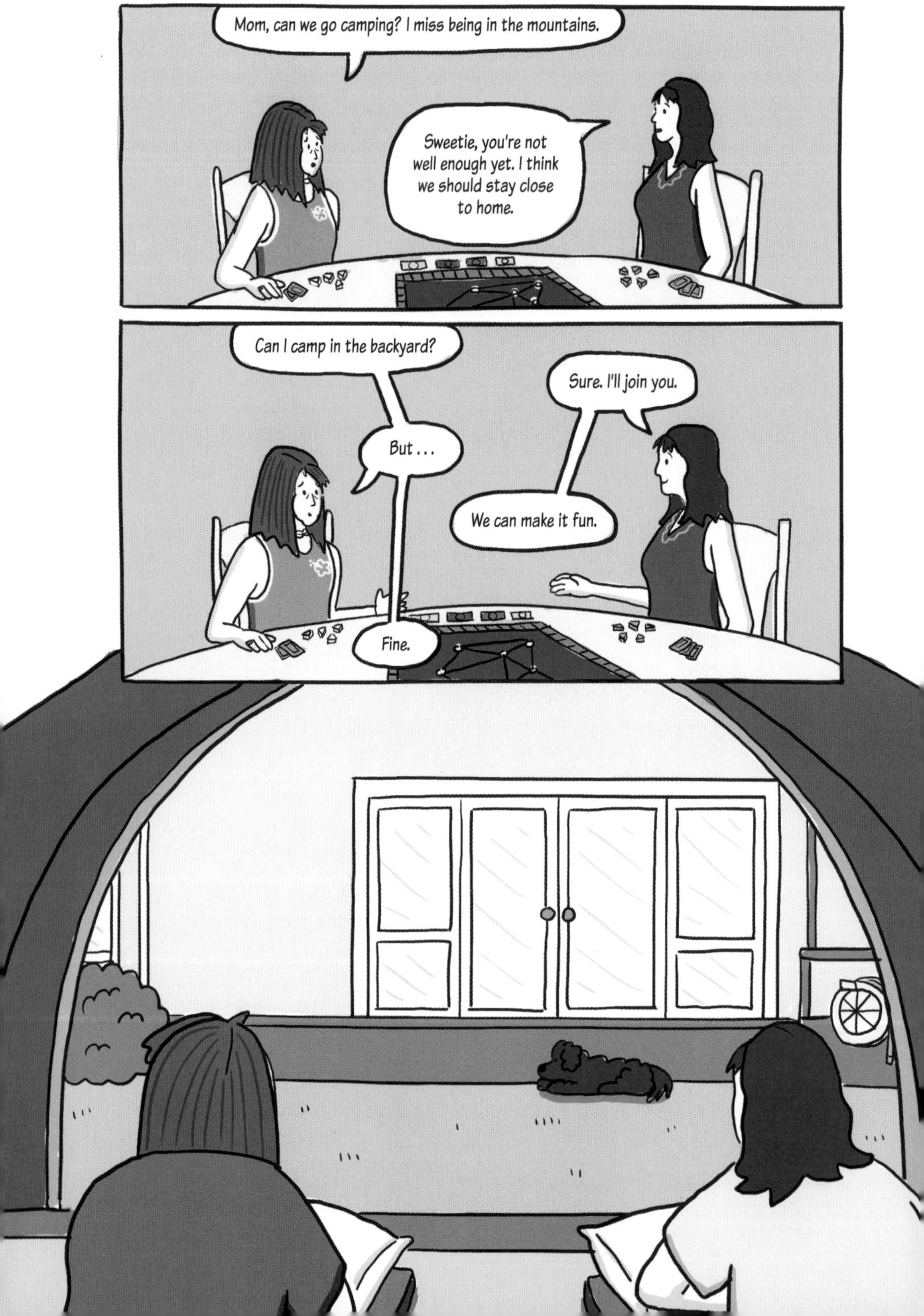
Mom, can we go camping? I miss being in the mountains.
Sweetie, you're not well enough yet. I think we should stay close to home.
Can I camp in the backyard?
Sure. I'll join you.
But . . .
We can make it fun.
Fine.

JULY 23

Unfortunately, your lab work came back and they didn't get the tumor.

I have to have ANOTHER surgery?

What are they going to do? When? What about school?

We've arranged for the surgery as soon as possible, which is next week. This may mean you have to start school late.

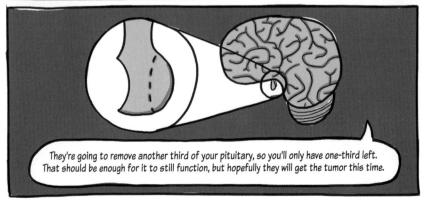

They're going to remove another third of your pituitary, so you'll only have one-third left. That should be enough for it to still function, but hopefully they will get the tumor this time.

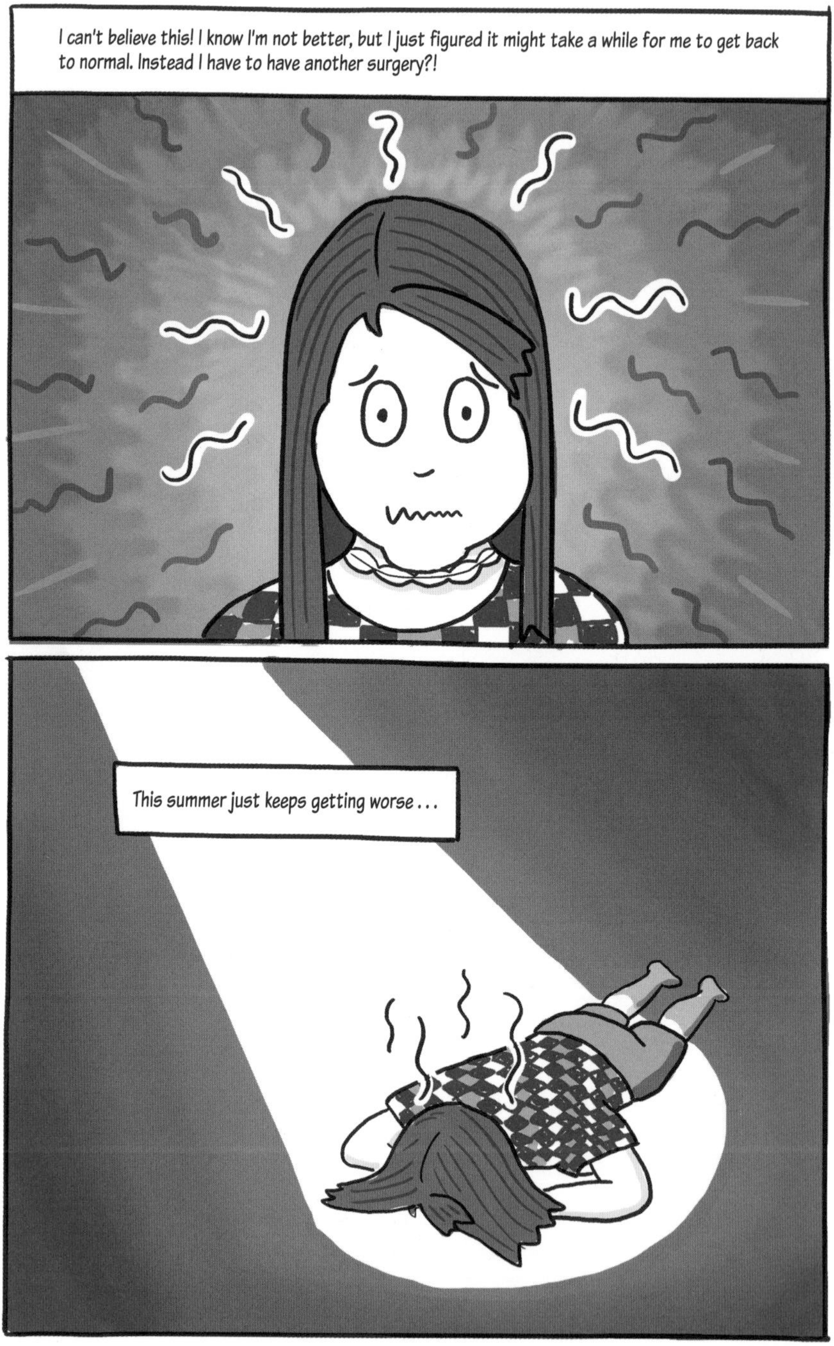
I can't believe this! I know I'm not better, but I just figured it might take a while for me to get back to normal. Instead I have to have another surgery?!
This summer just keeps getting worse . . .

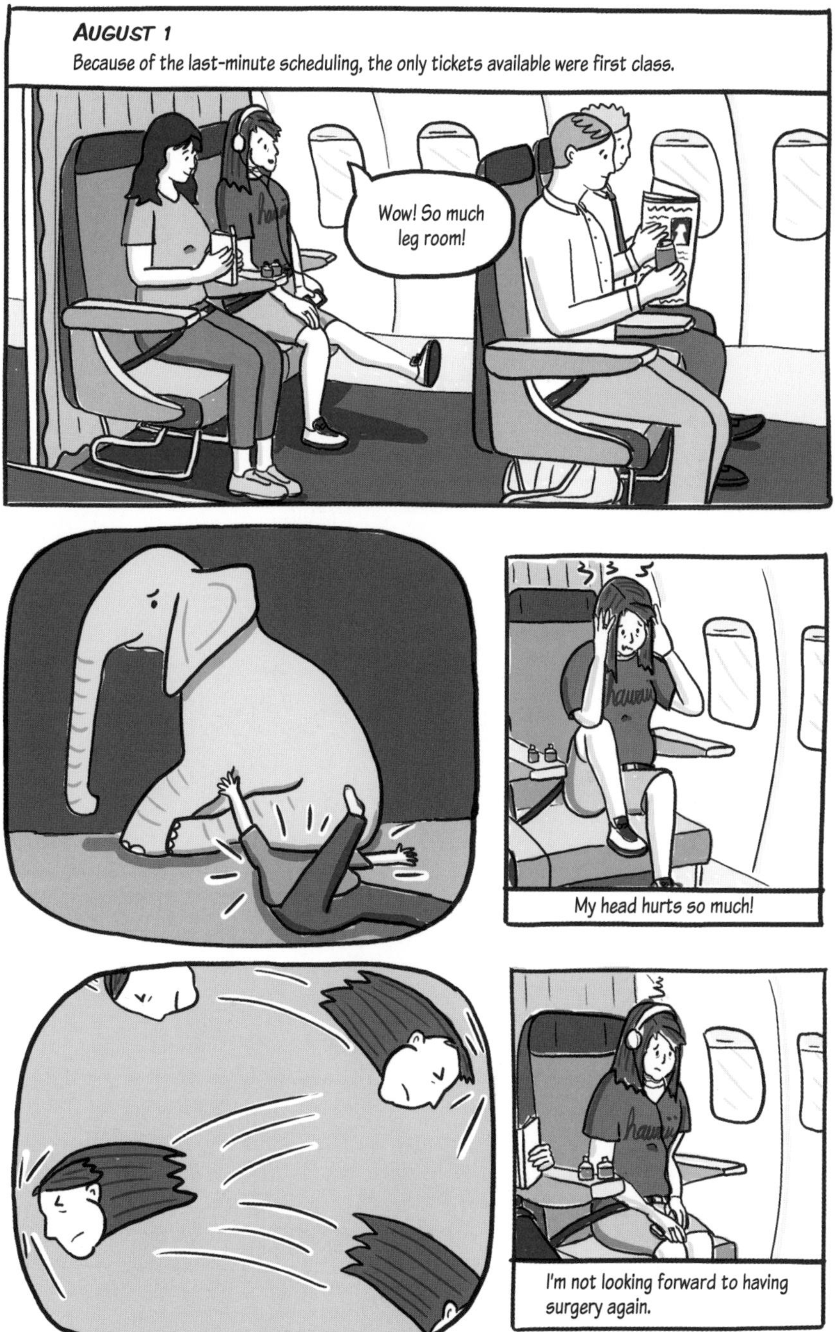
AUGUST 1
Because of the last-minute scheduling, the only tickets available were first class.
Wow! So much leg room!
My head hurts so much!
I'm not looking forward to having surgery again.

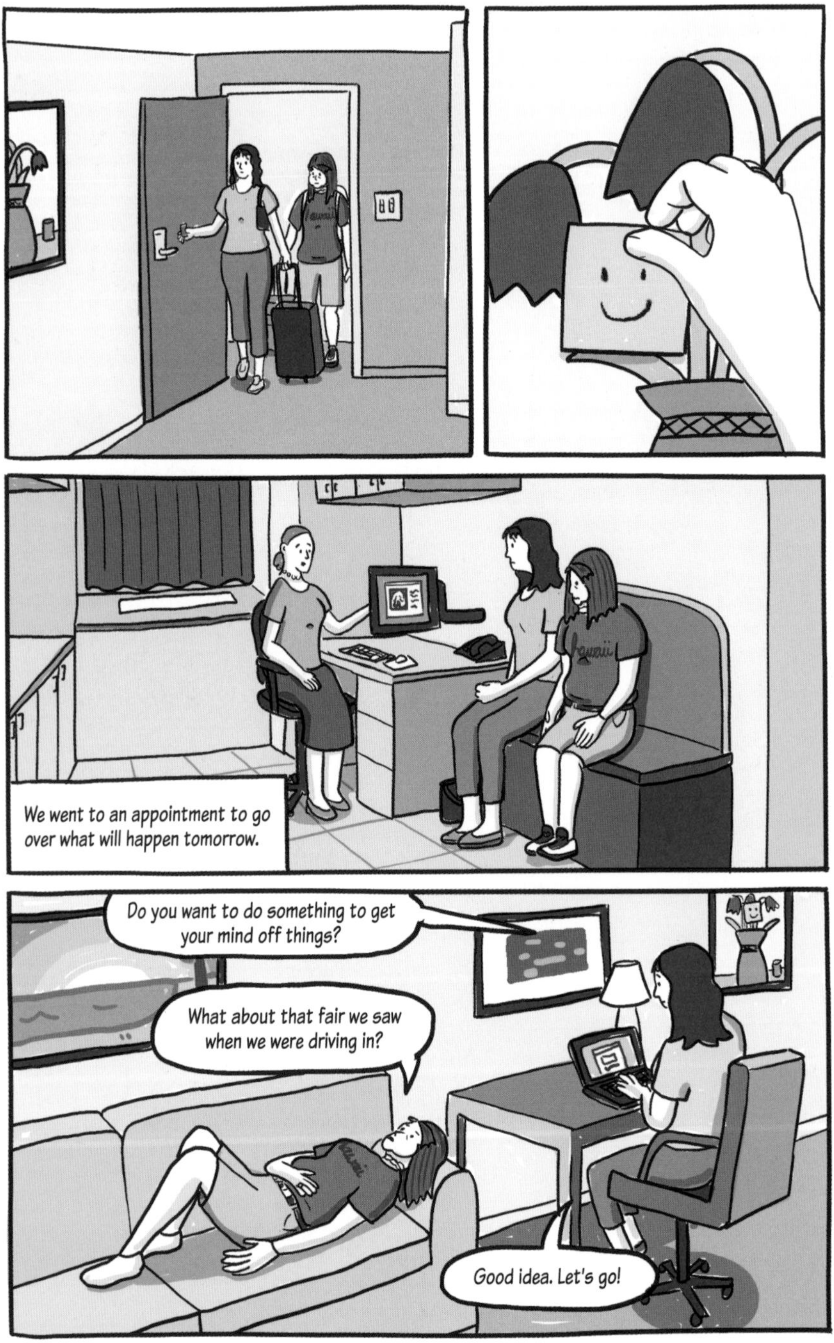
We went to an appointment to go over what will happen tomorrow.
Do you want to do something to get your mind off things?
What about that fair we saw when we were driving in?
Good idea. Let's go!

It was nice to not worry for a couple hours.

But tomorrow they're drilling through my skull again to operate.

I wish I could run away, but I know then I wouldn't get better.

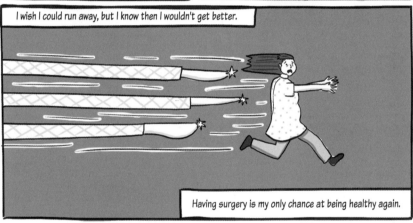

Having surgery is my only chance at being healthy again.

I know we said that last time too, so hopefully this time it will be true.

Hopefully...

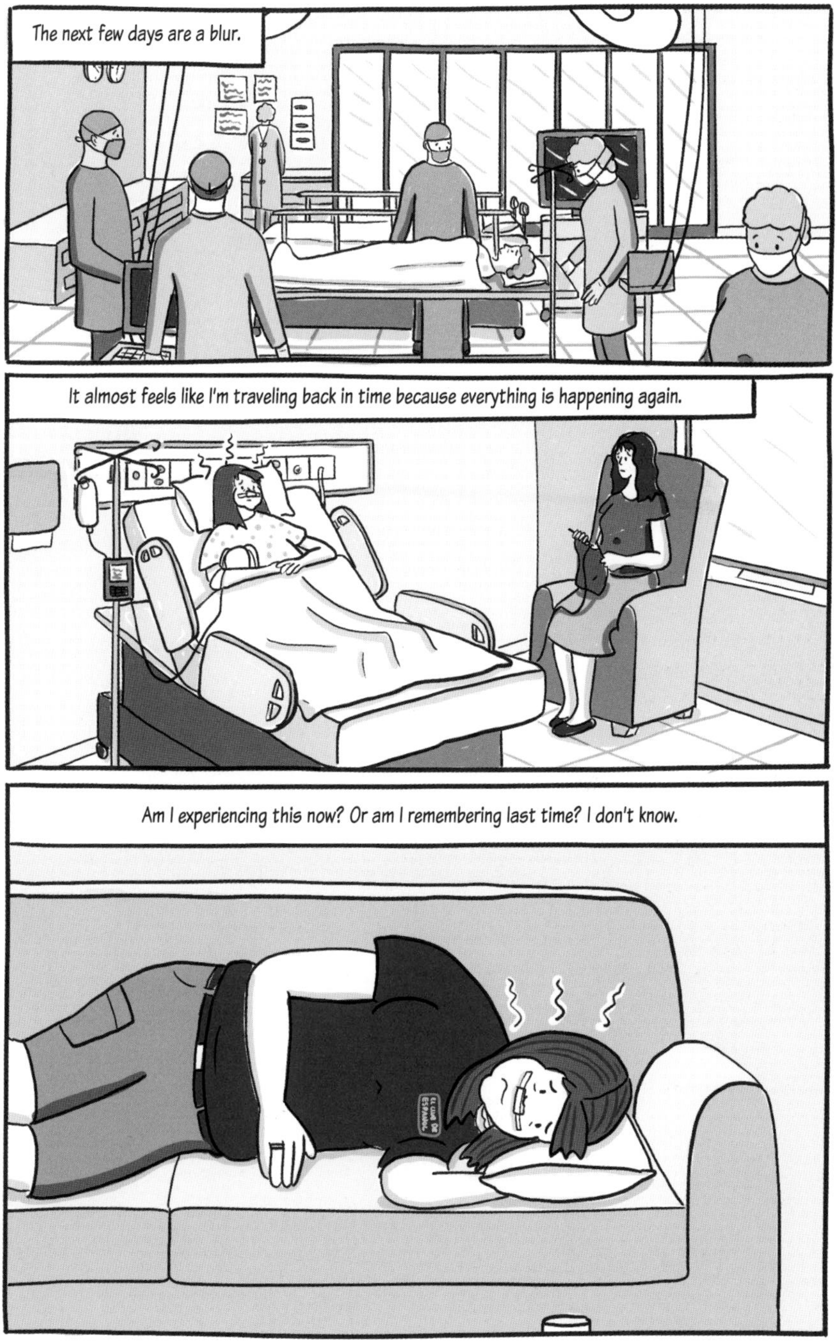
The next few days are a blur.
It almost feels like I'm traveling back in time because everything is happening again.
Am I experiencing this now? Or am I remembering last time? I don't know.

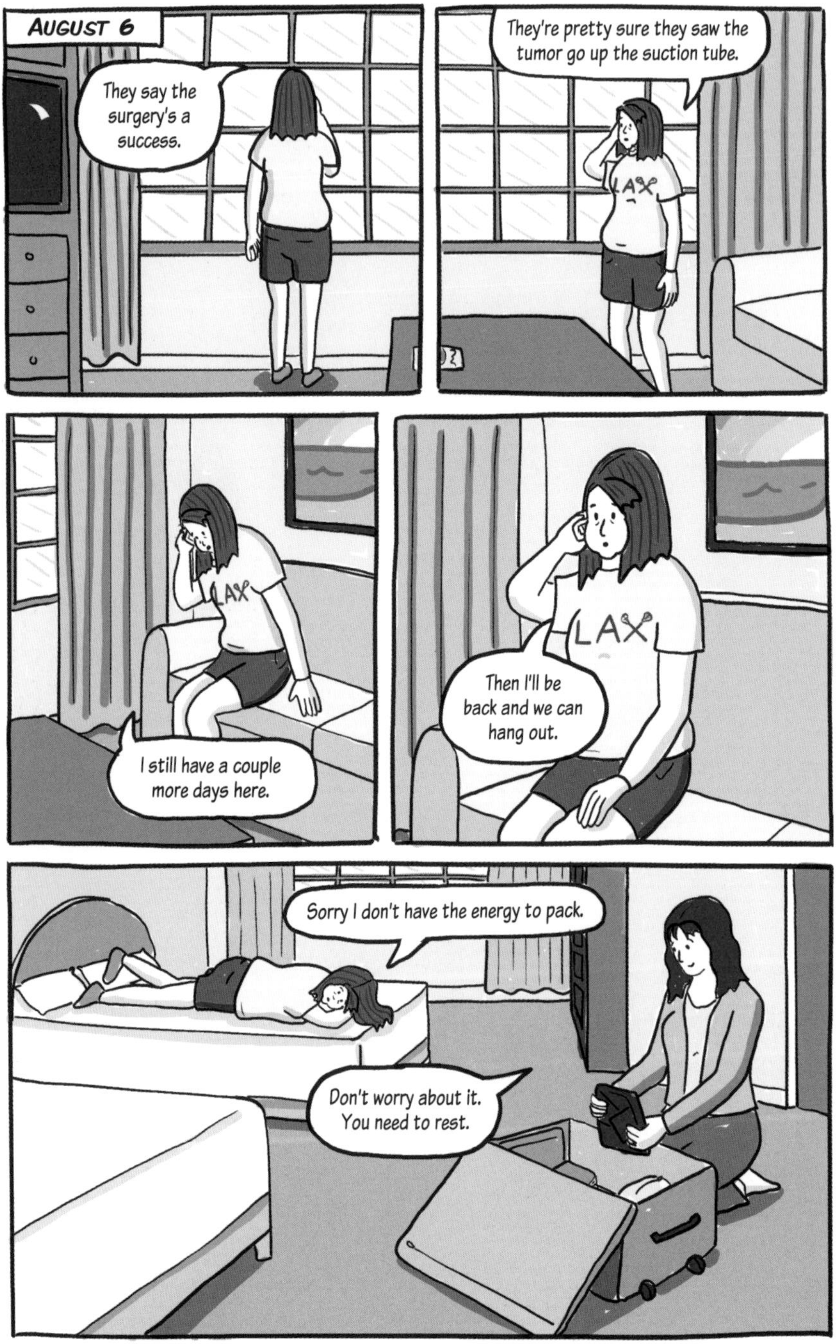
AUGUST 6
They say the surgery's a success.
They're pretty sure they saw the tumor go up the suction tube.
I still have a couple more days here.
Then I'll be back and we can hang out.
Sorry I don't have the energy to pack.
Don't worry about it. You need to rest.

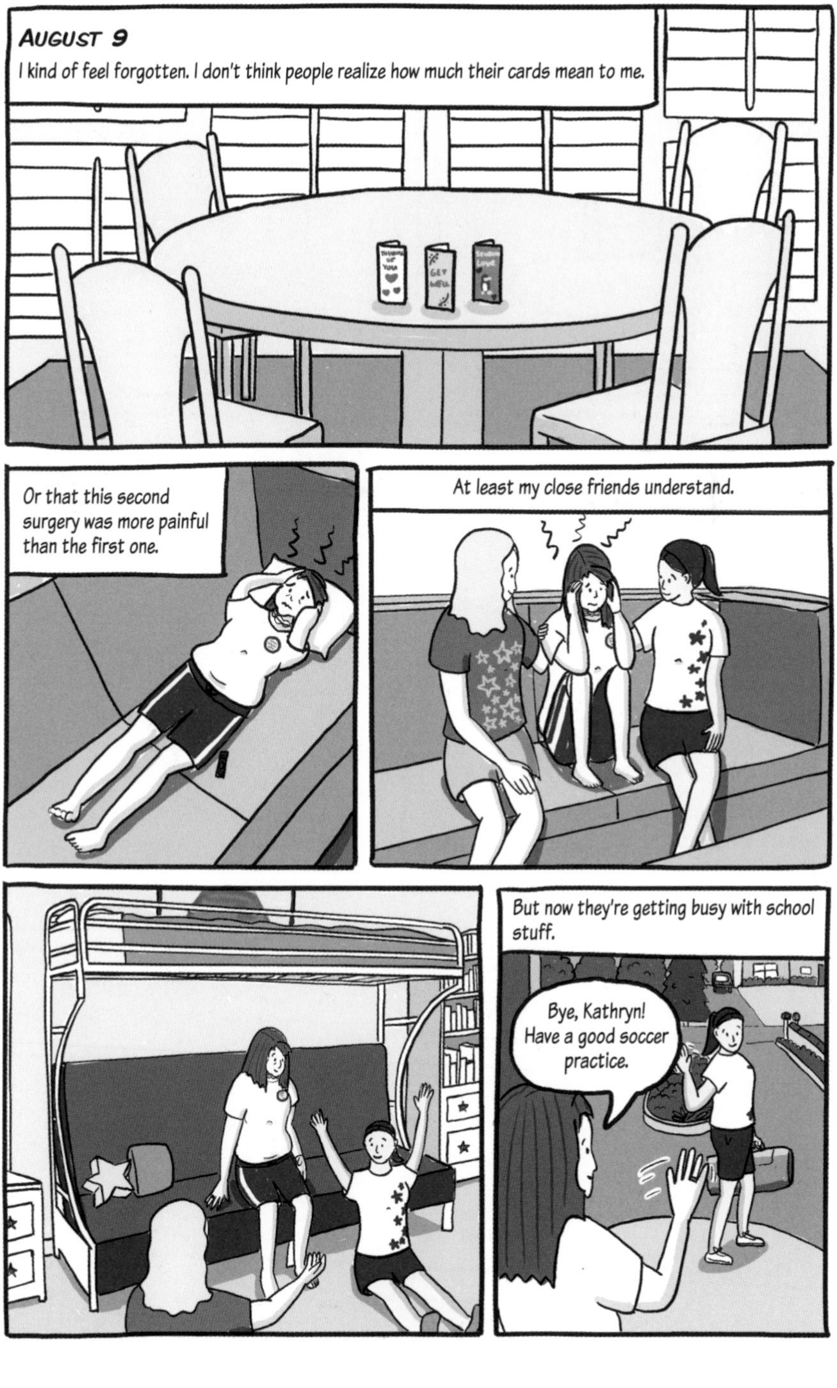
AUGUST 9
I kind of feel forgotten. I don't think people realize how much their cards mean to me.
Or that this second surgery was more painful than the first one.
At least my close friends understand.
But now they're getting busy with school stuff.
Bye, Kathryn! Have a good soccer practice.

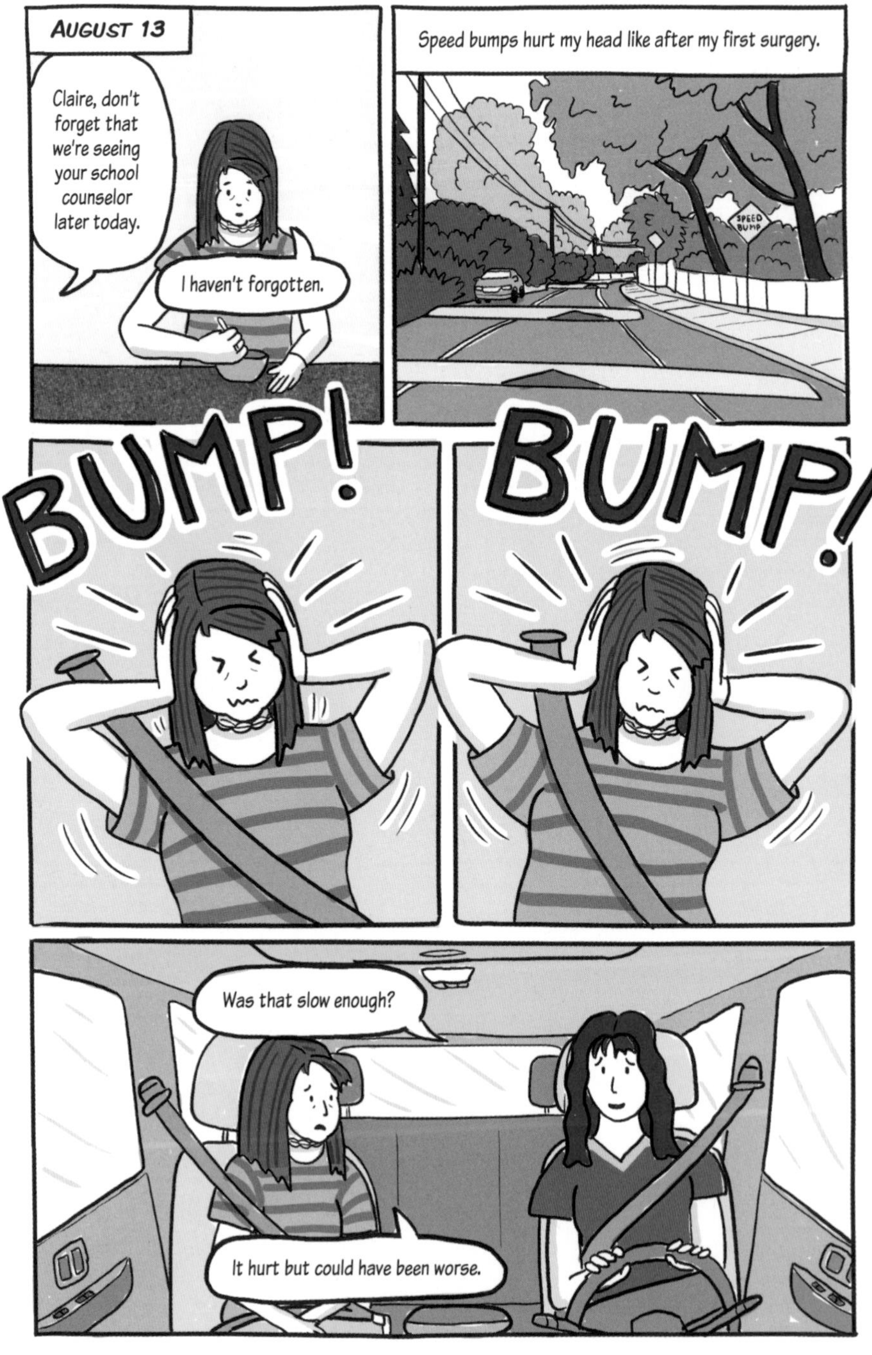
AUGUST 13
Claire, don't forget that we're seeing your school counselor later today.
I haven't forgotten.
Speed bumps hurt my head like after my first surgery.
SPEED BUMP
BUMP!
BUMP!
Was that slow enough?
It hurt but could have been worse.

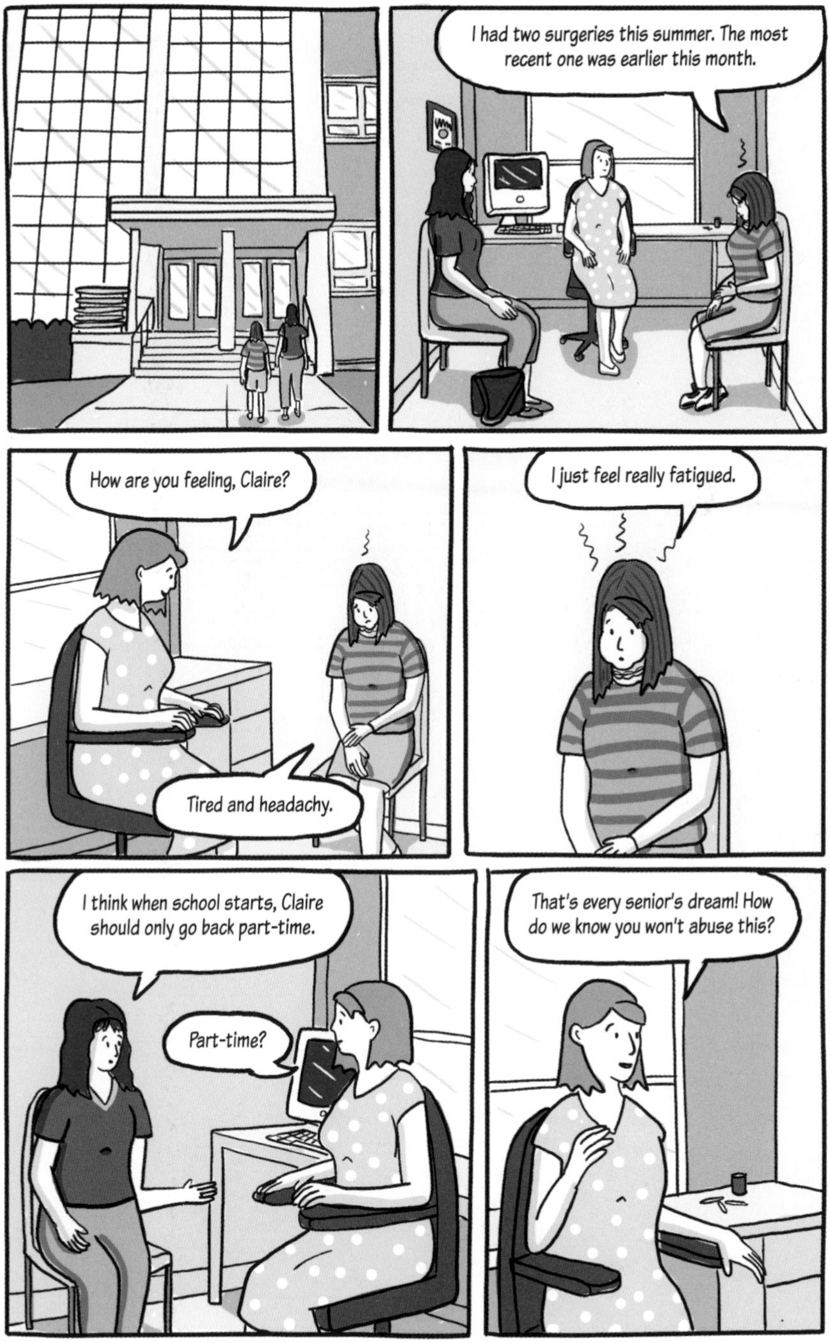
I had two surgeries this summer. The most recent one was earlier this month.
How are you feeling, Claire?
Tired and headachy.
I just feel really fatigued.
I think when school starts, Claire should only go back part-time.
Part-time?
That's every senior's dream! How do we know you won't abuse this?

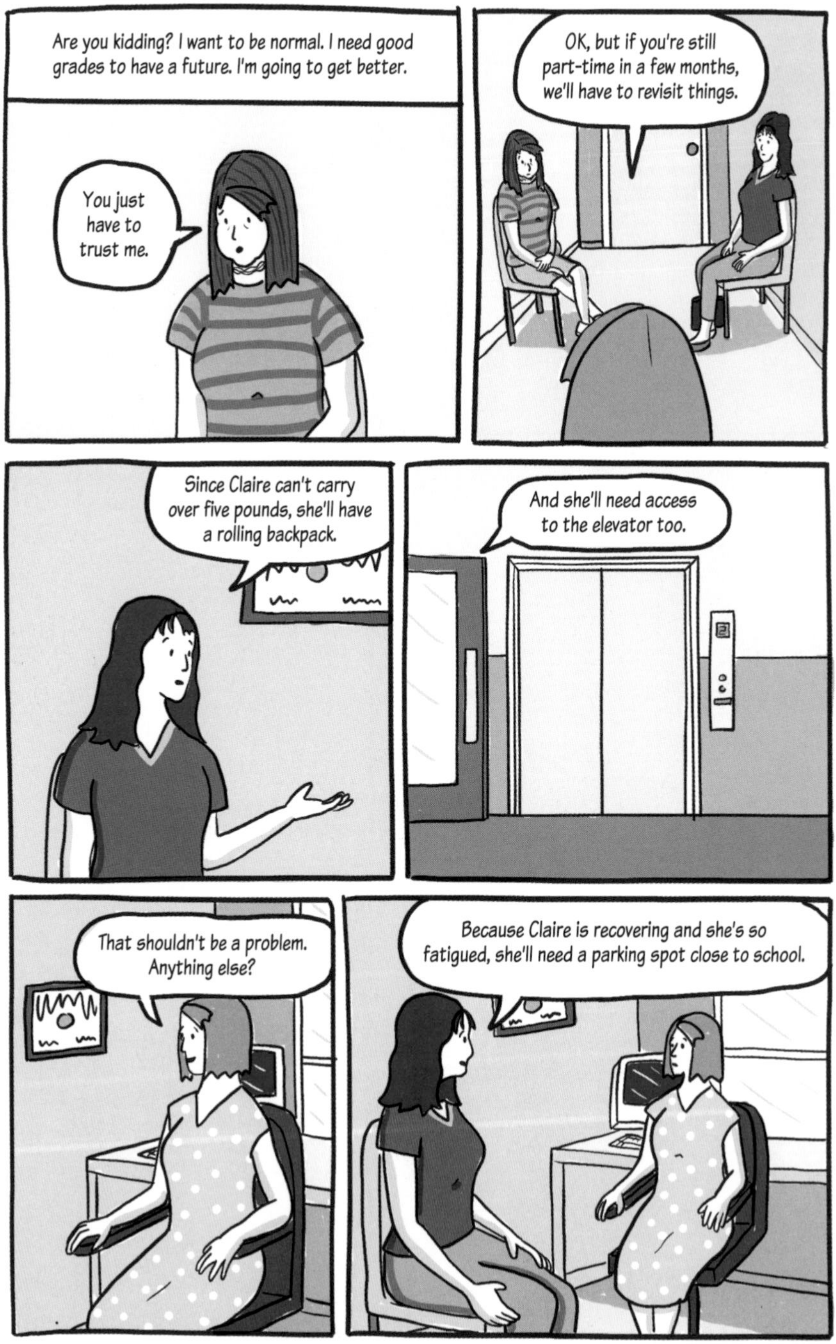
Are you kidding? I want to be normal. I need good grades to have a future. I'm going to get better.
You just have to trust me.
OK, but if you're still part-time in a few months, we'll have to revisit things.
Since Claire can't carry over five pounds, she'll have a rolling backpack.
And she'll need access to the elevator too.
That shouldn't be a problem. Anything else?
Because Claire is recovering and she's so fatigued, she'll need a parking spot close to school.

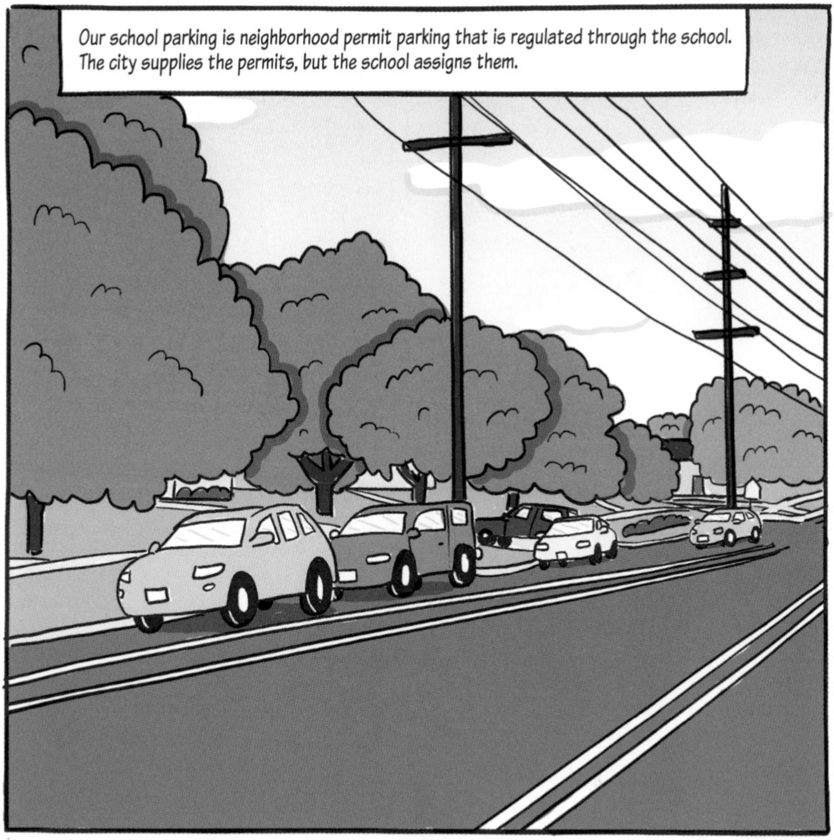
Our school parking is neighborhood permit parking that is regulated through the school.
The city supplies the permits, but the school assigns them.

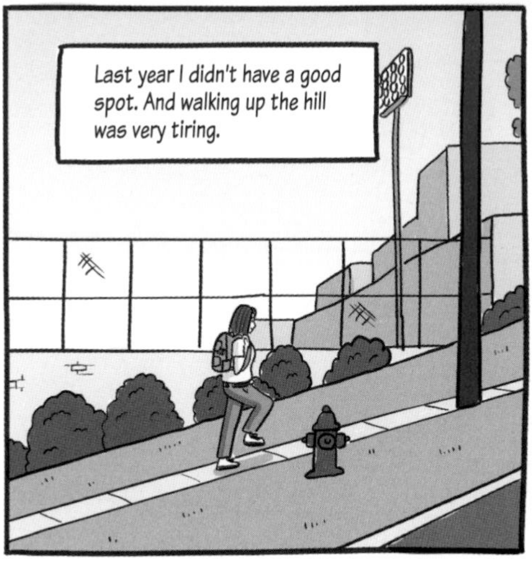
Last year I didn't have a good spot. And walking up the hill was very tiring.

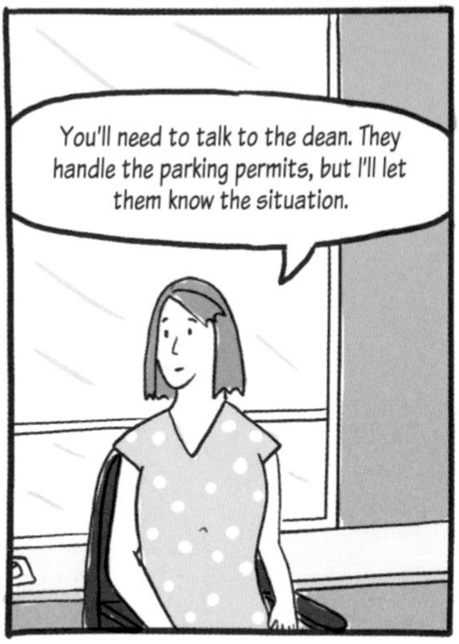
You'll need to talk to the dean. They handle the parking permits, but I'll let them know the situation.

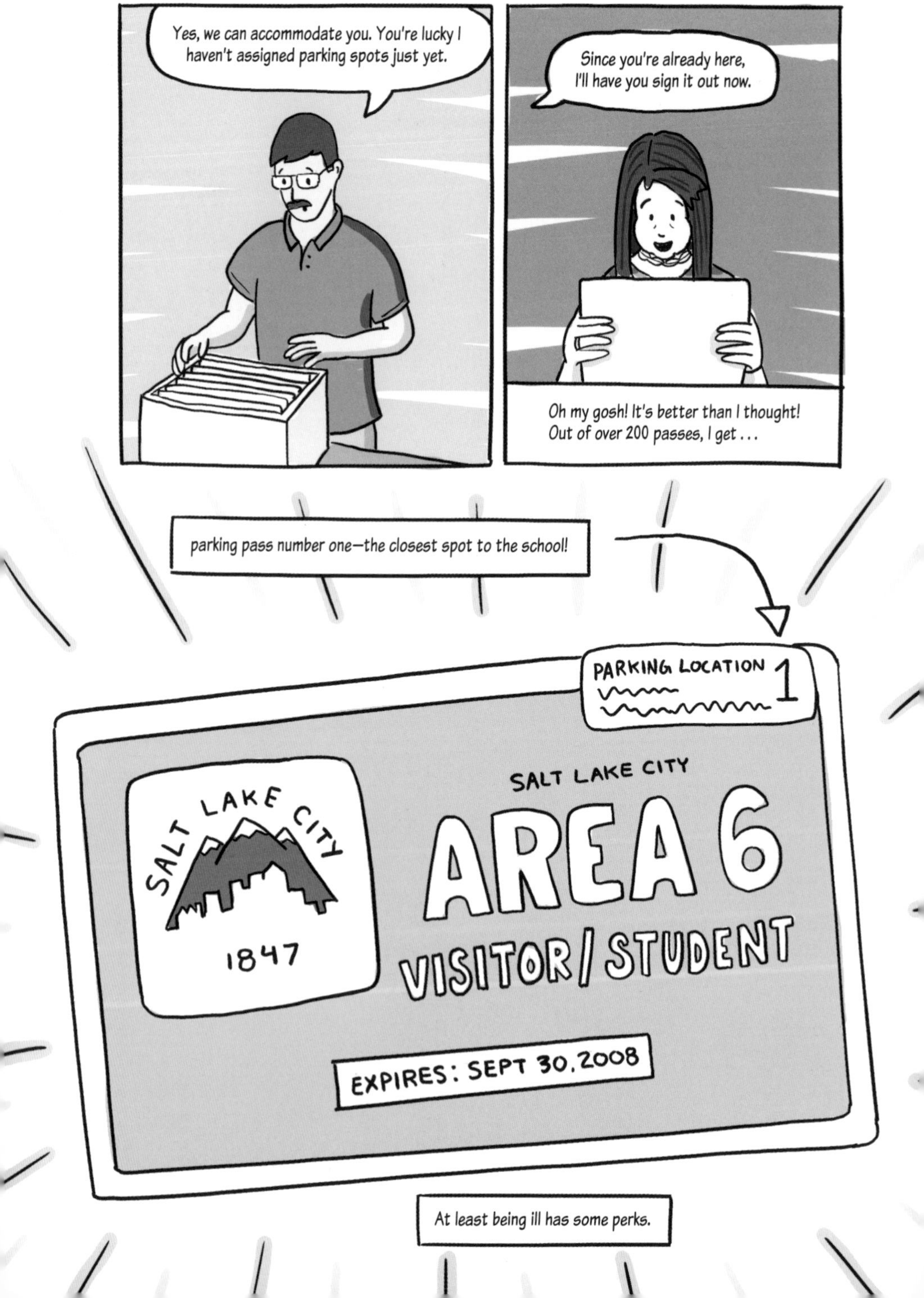
Yes, we can accommodate you. You're lucky I haven't assigned parking spots just yet.
Since you're already here, I'll have you sign it out now.
Oh my gosh! It's better than I thought! Out of over 200 passes, I get . . .
parking pass number one—the closest spot to the school!
PARKING LOCATION 1
SALT LAKE CITY
SALT LAKE CITY
1847
AREA 6
VISITOR/STUDENT
EXPIRES: SEPT 30, 2008
At least being ill has some perks.

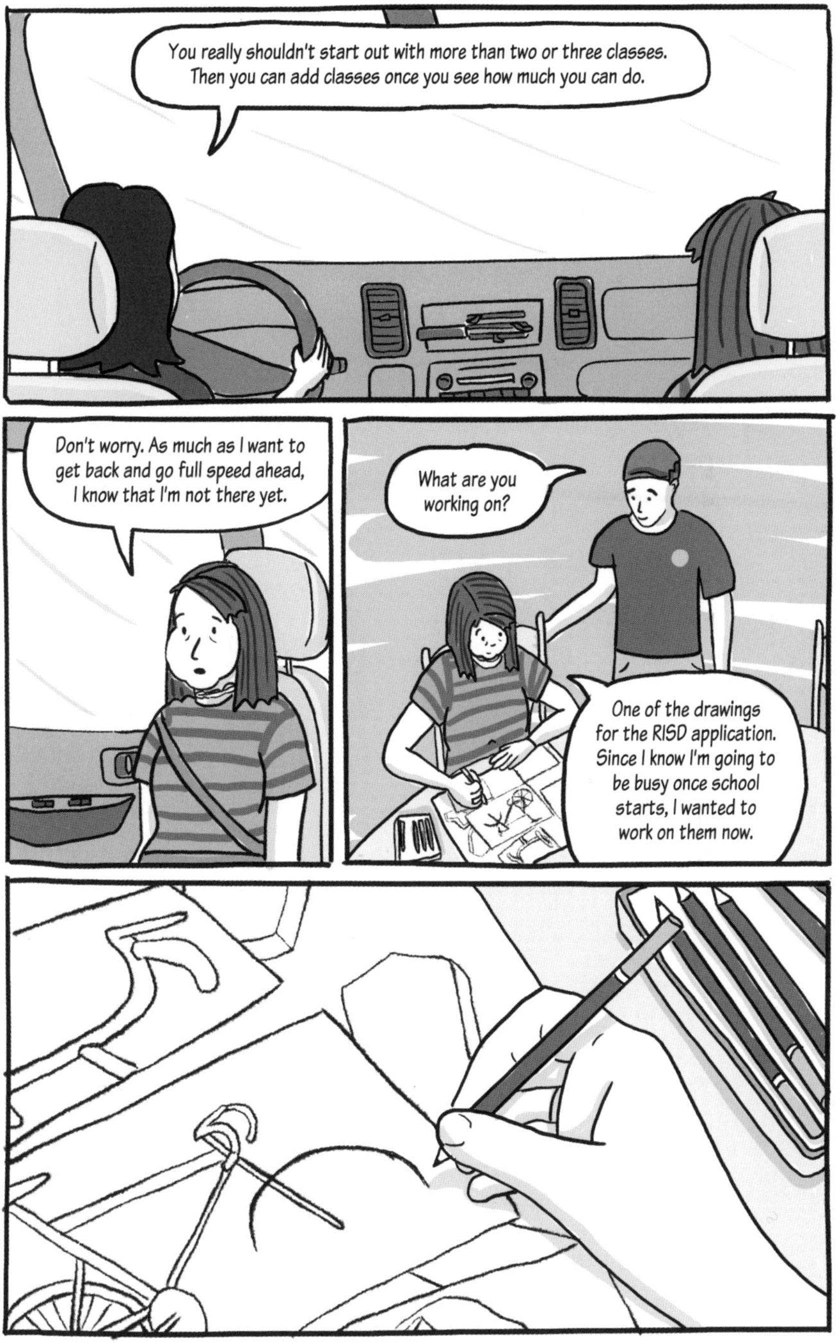
You really shouldn't start out with more than two or three classes. Then you can add classes once you see how much you can do.
Don't worry. As much as I want to get back and go full speed ahead, I know that I'm not there yet.
What are you working on?
One of the drawings for the RISD application. Since I know I'm going to be busy once school starts, I wanted to work on them now.

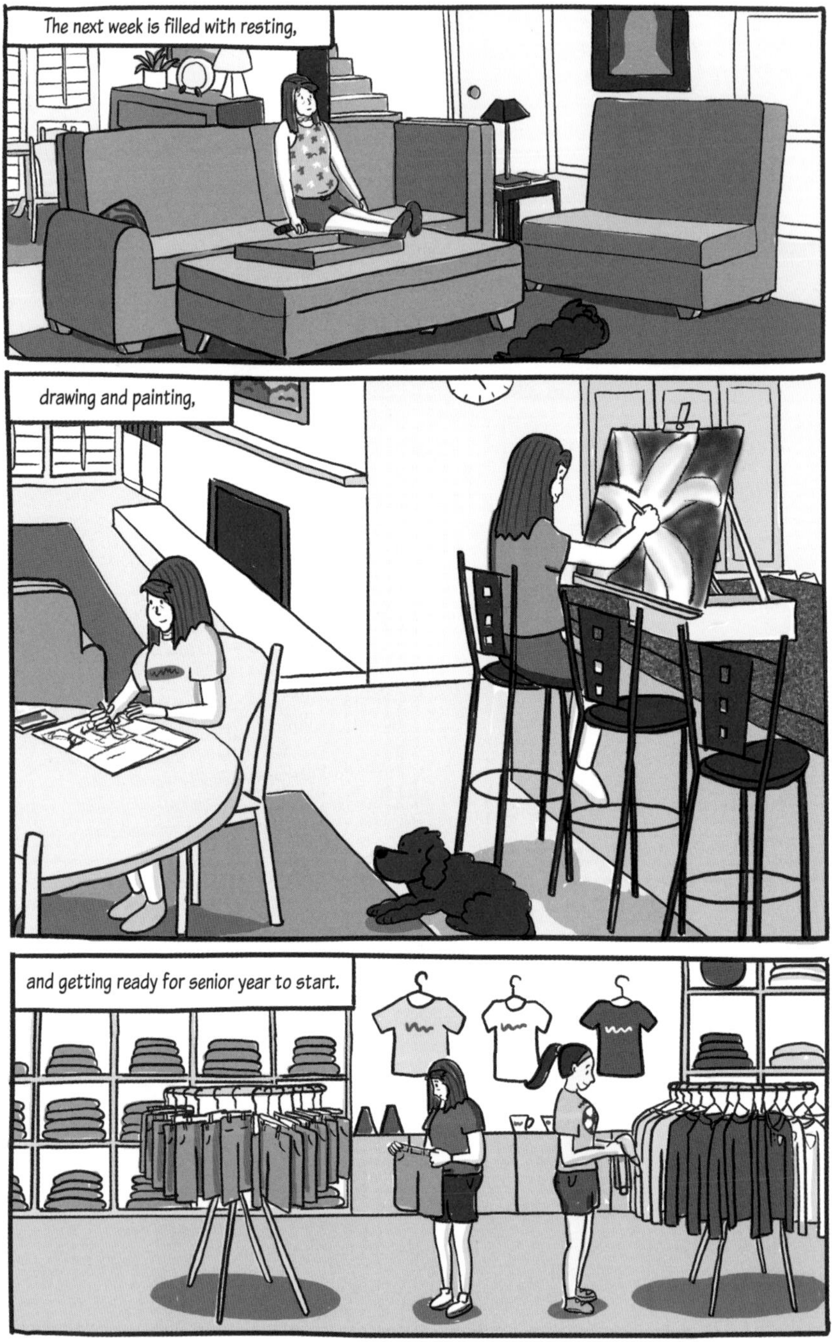

The next week is filled with resting,
drawing and painting,
and getting ready for senior year to start.

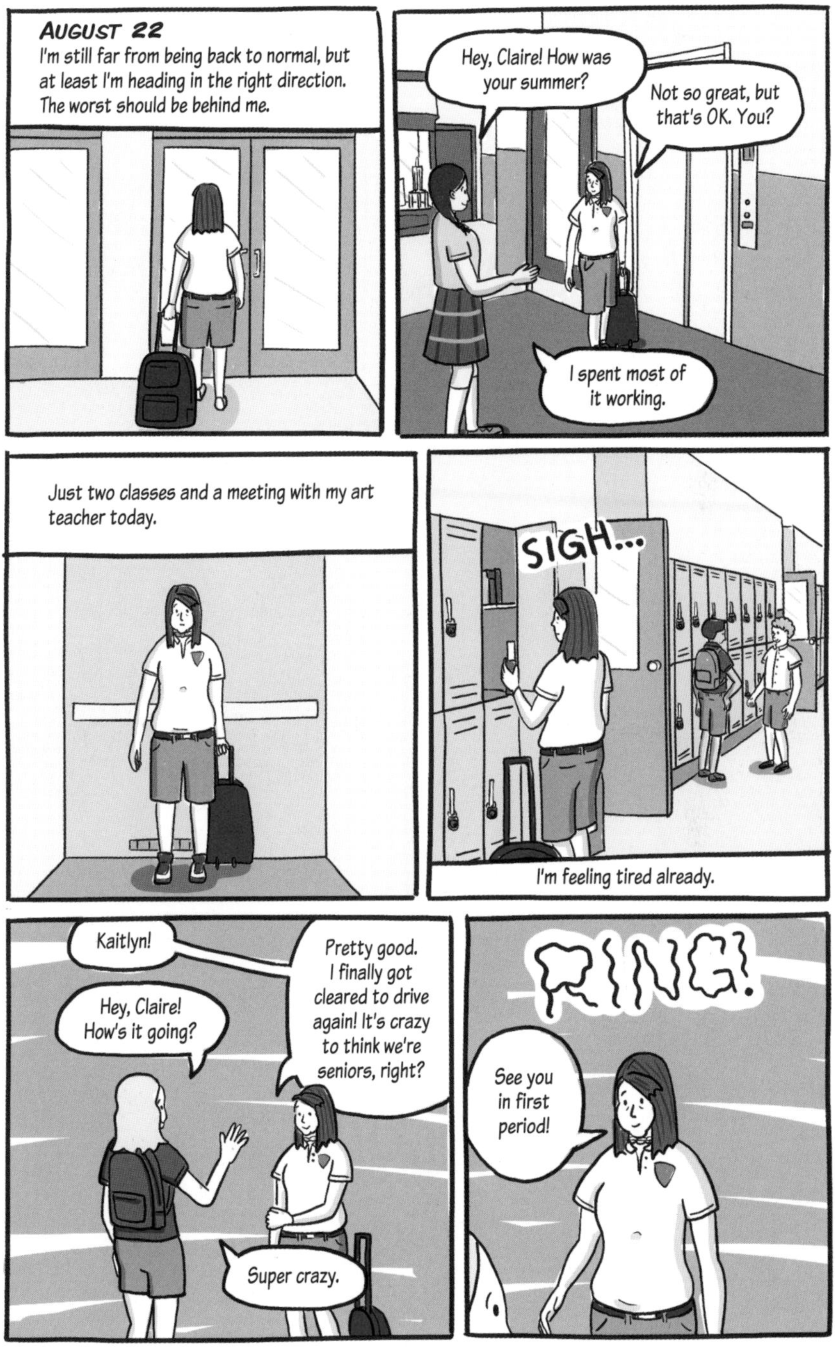
August 22
I'm still far from being back to normal, but at least I'm heading in the right direction. The worst should be behind me.
Hey, Claire! How was your summer?
Not so great, but that's OK. You?
I spent most of it working.
Just two classes and a meeting with my art teacher today.
SIGH...
I'm feeling tired already.
Kaitlyn!
Hey, Claire! How's it going?
Pretty good. I finally got cleared to drive again! It's crazy to think we're seniors, right?
Super crazy.
RING!
See you in first period!

This rolling backpack is SO embarrassing!

welcome to honors physics

welcome to honors physics

Please read the syllabus as I go through it.

Honors physics doesn't seem too bad, but then again, it's only the first day.

Yeah, I think it will be a good class.

I've always enjoyed math, but I think calculus might be a different story.

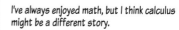

LIMITS DERIVATIVES INTEGRALS

Considering I wasn't fully present for second semester last year, I have some catching up to do.

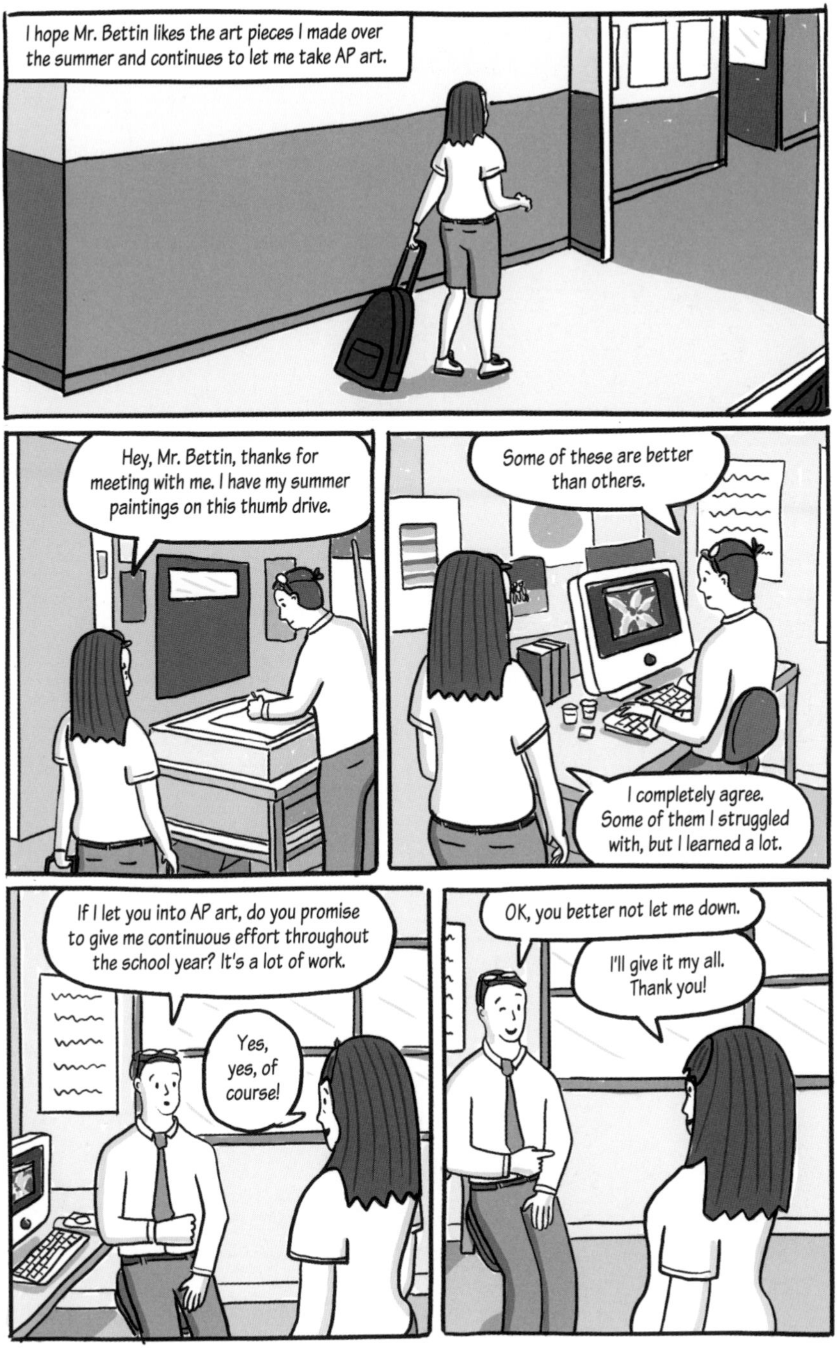
I hope Mr. Bettin likes the art pieces I made over the summer and continues to let me take AP art.
Hey, Mr. Bettin, thanks for meeting with me. I have my summer paintings on this thumb drive.
Some of these are better than others.
I completely agree. Some of them I struggled with, but I learned a lot.
If I let you into AP art, do you promise to give me continuous effort throughout the school year? It's a lot of work.
Yes, yes, of course!
OK, you better not let me down.
I'll give it my all. Thank you!

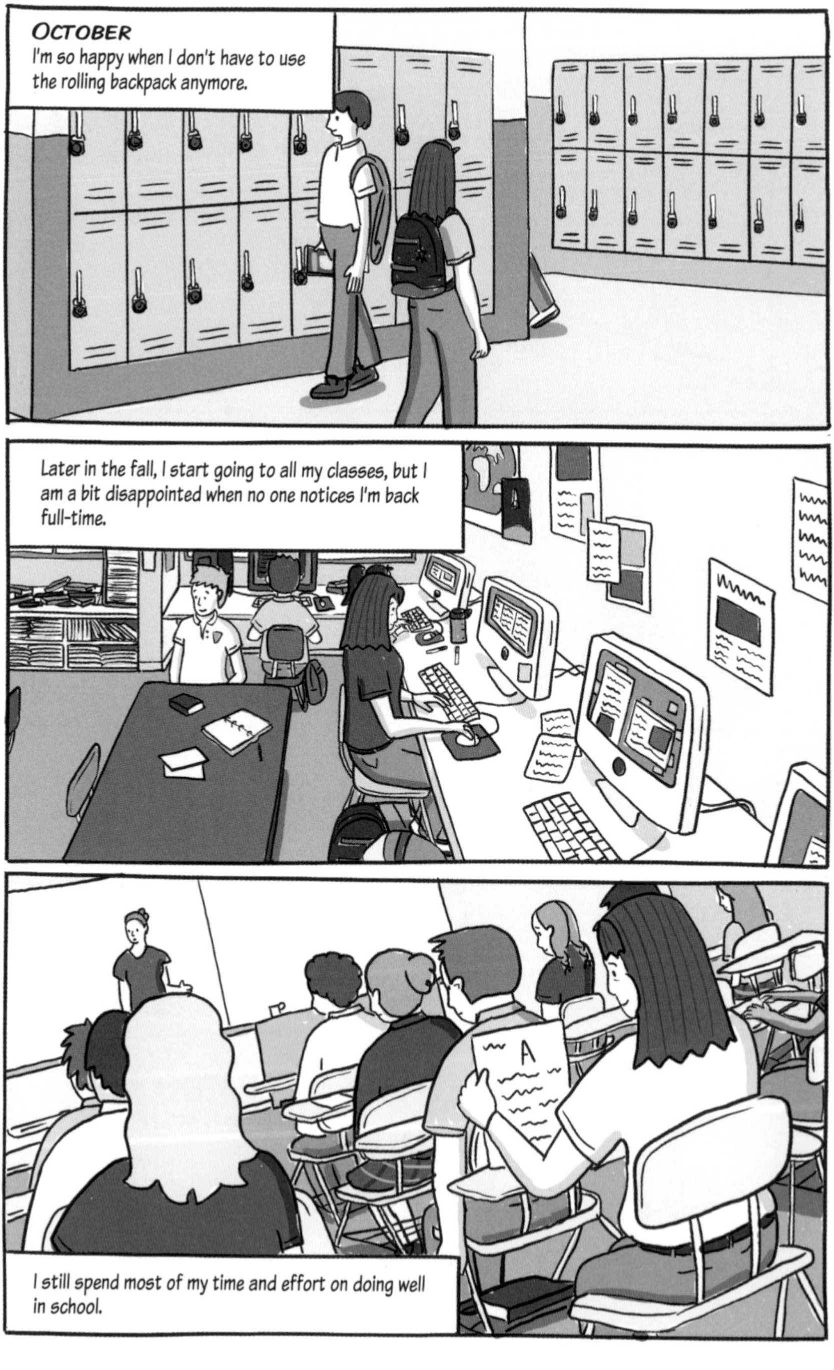
OCTOBER
I'm so happy when I don't have to use the rolling backpack anymore.
Later in the fall, I start going to all my classes, but I am a bit disappointed when no one notices I'm back full-time.
A
I still spend most of my time and effort on doing well in school.

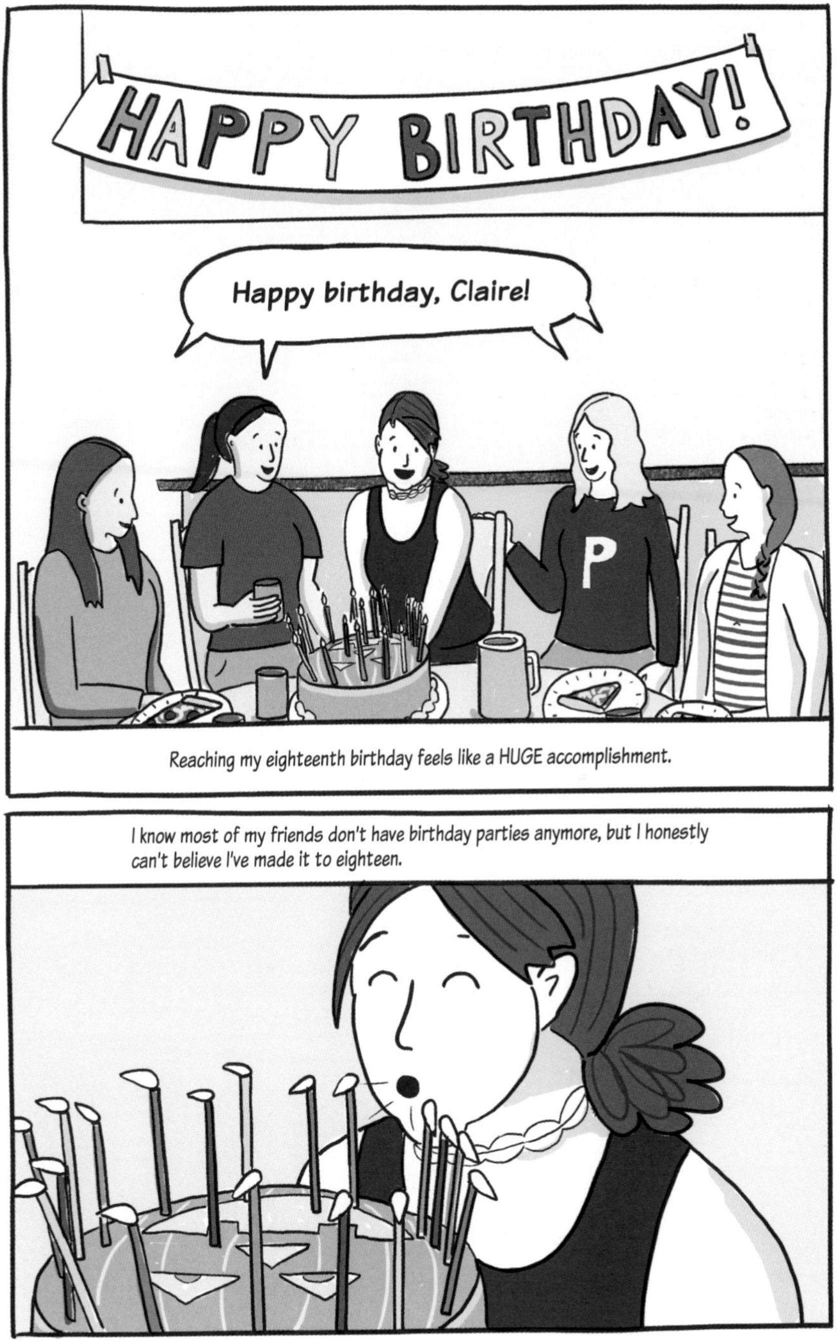
HAPPY BIRTHDAY!
Happy birthday, Claire!
Reaching my eighteenth birthday feels like a HUGE accomplishment.
I know most of my friends don't have birthday parties anymore, but I honestly can't believe I've made it to eighteen.

For AP art, I have to choose a subject to focus on.

I'm stuck on what my subject should be.

What's the best thing you've made so far this year?

My dog piece?

Yes, I think that piece is really your strongest.

I was hoping you might say that. I love that one too, and my dog, Toby, has meant so much to me while I've been sick.

My dog also started my love of drawing. I painted him all the time when I was seven.

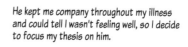

He kept me company throughout my illness and could tell I wasn't feeling well, so I decide to focus my thesis on him.

I continue to go to Scouts. We do volunteer projects, work on badges, and have fun together.
SENIOR
I applied for early admission to RISD and Brown.
BULLDOGS
Brown rejects me and RISD moves my application over to the regular application pool, and then I'm eventually wait-listed.
BULLDOGS

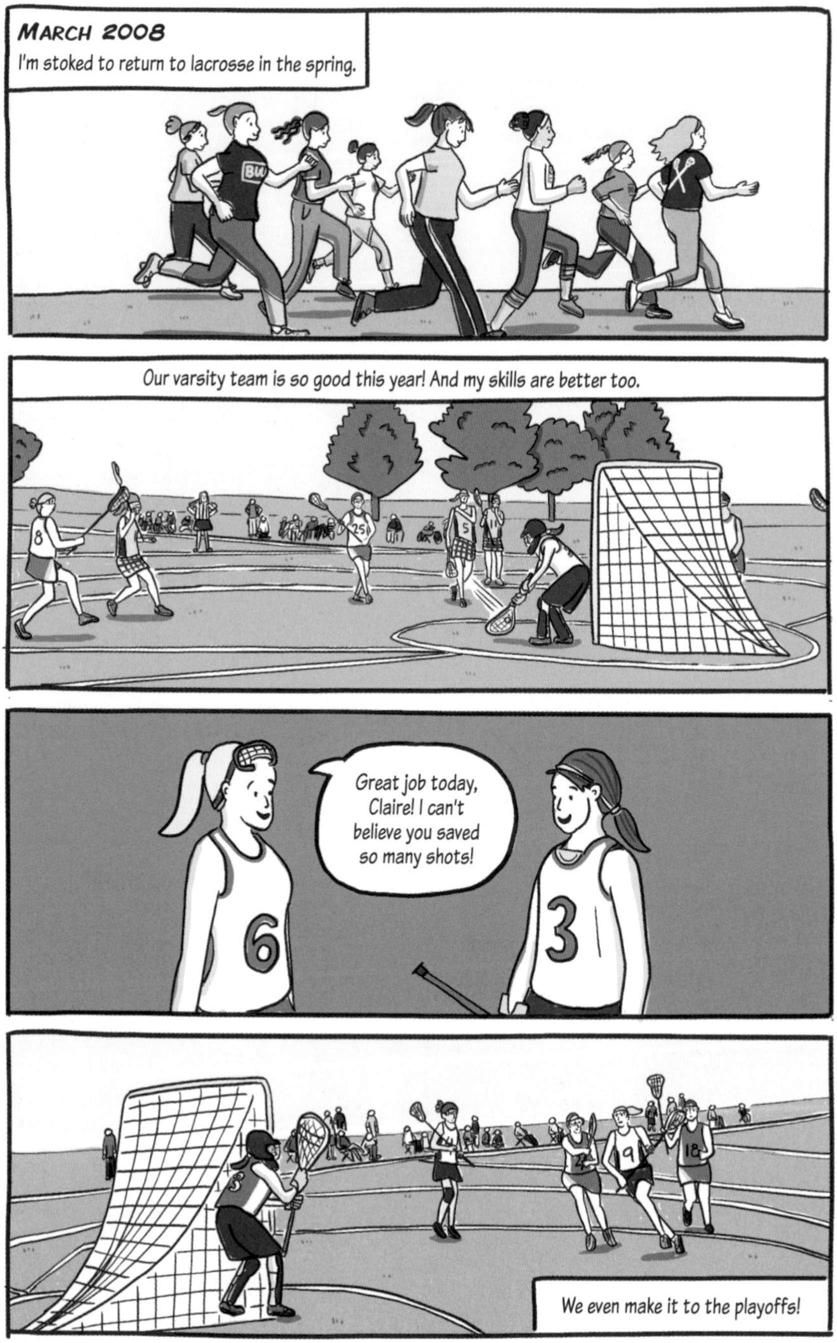
March 2008
I'm stoked to return to lacrosse in the spring.
Our varsity team is so good this year! And my skills are better too.
Great job today, Claire! I can't believe you saved so many shots!
We even make it to the playoffs!

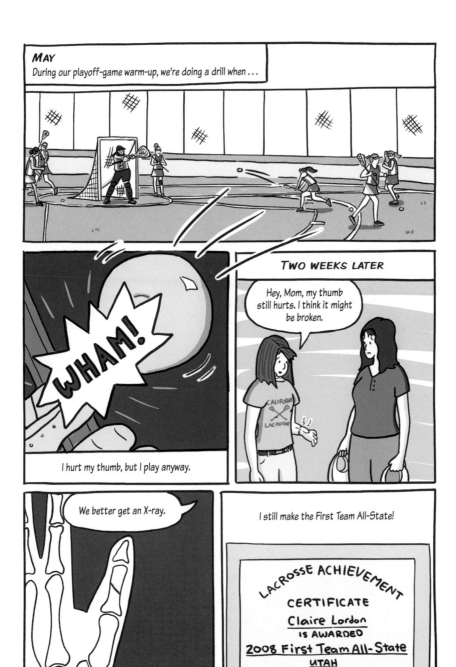

MAY
During our playoff-game warm-up, we're doing a drill when...

WHAM!

I hurt my thumb, but I play anyway.

TWO WEEKS LATER

Hey, Mom, my thumb still hurts. I think it might be broken.

We better get an X-ray.

It's broken.

I still make the First Team All-State!

LACROSSE ACHIEVEMENT
CERTIFICATE
Claire Lordon
IS AWARDED
2008 First Team All-State
UTAH

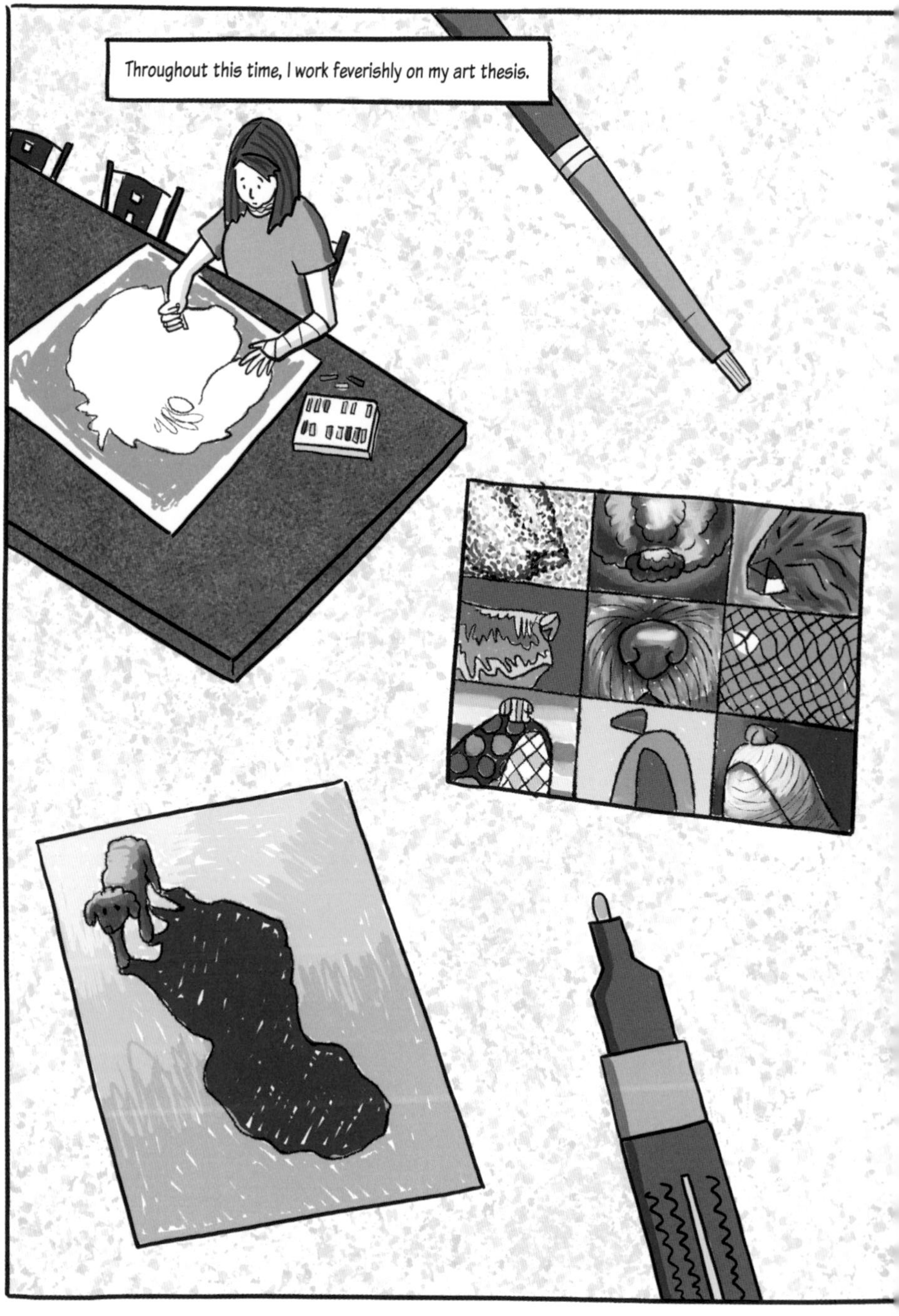
Throughout this time, I work feverishly on my art thesis.

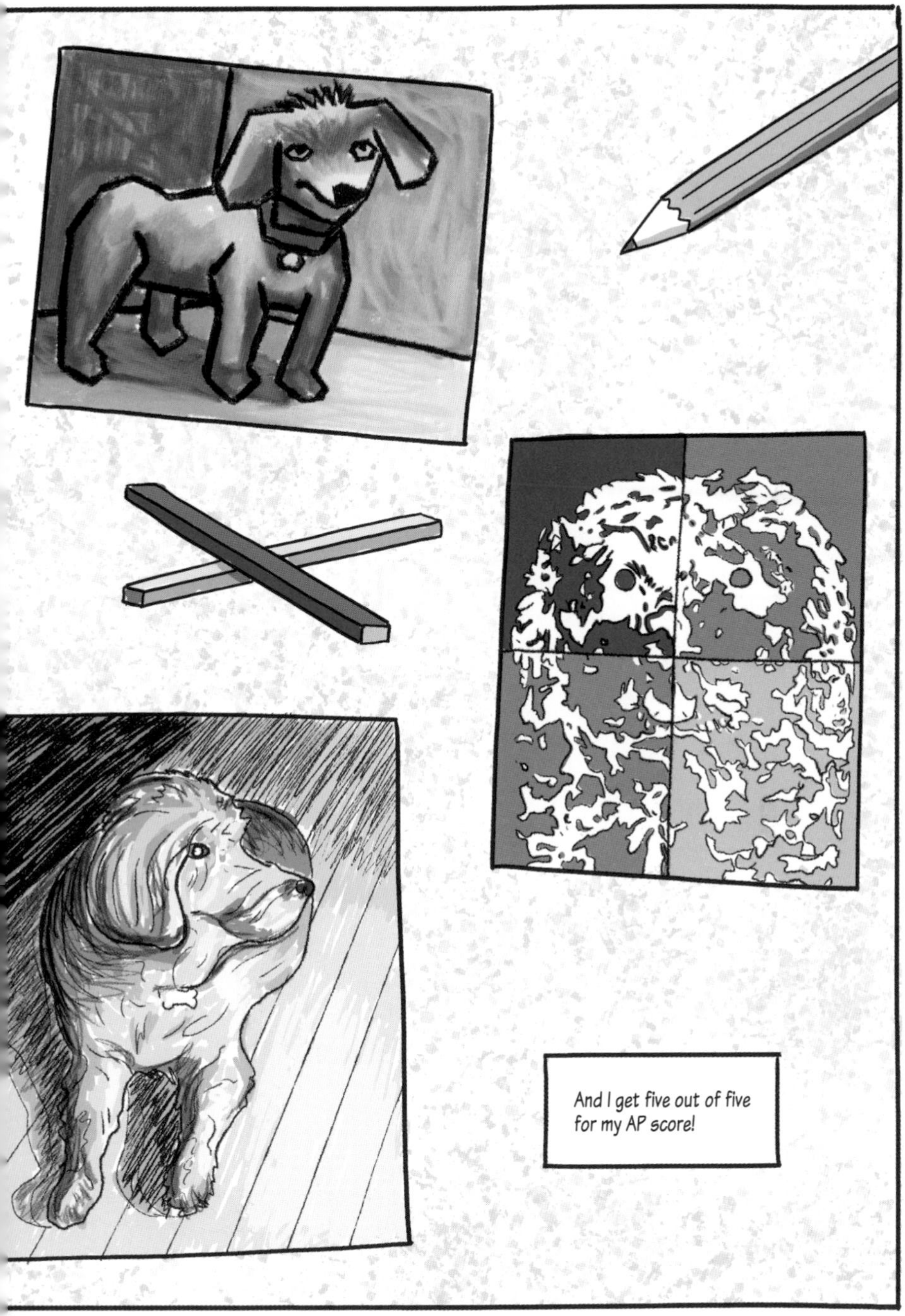
And I get five out of five
for my AP score!

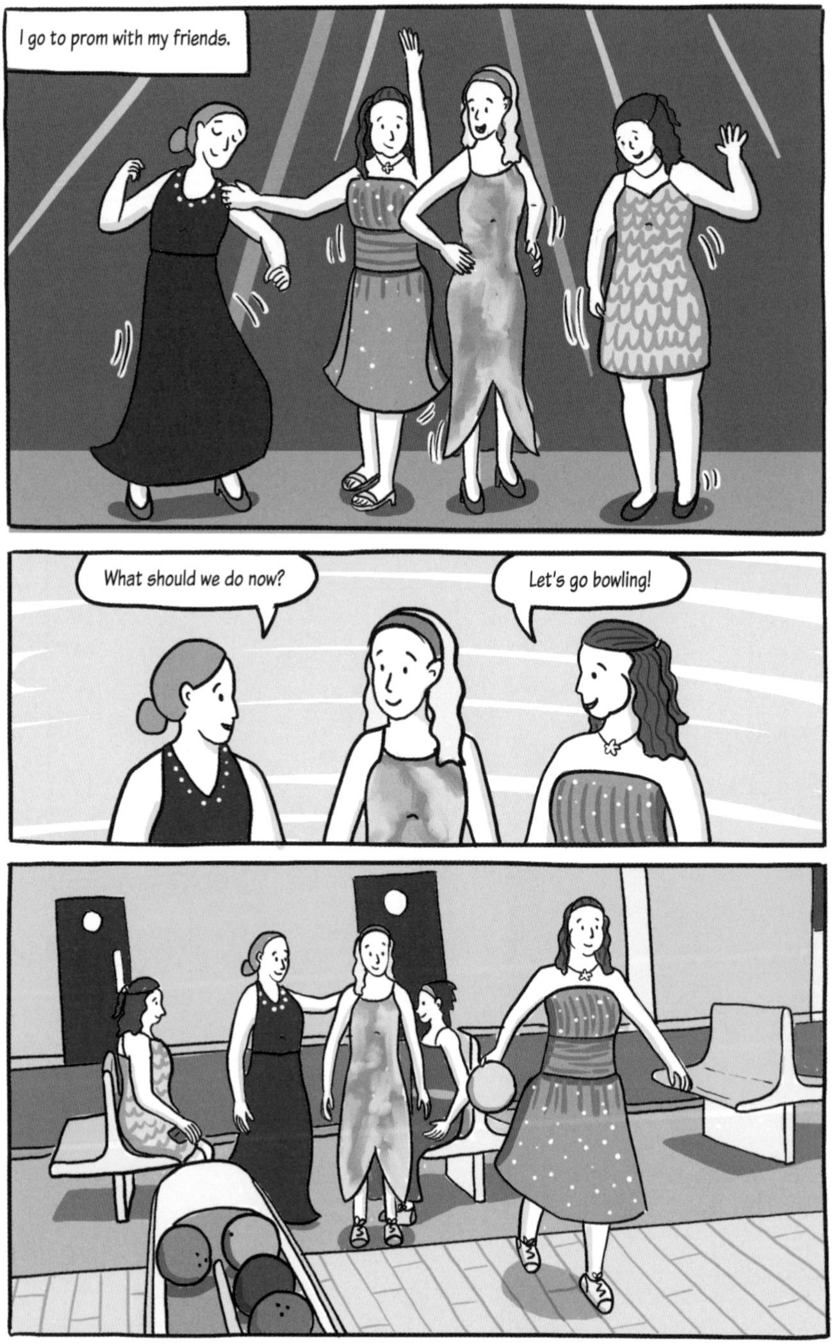
I go to prom with my friends.
What should we do now?
Let's go bowling!

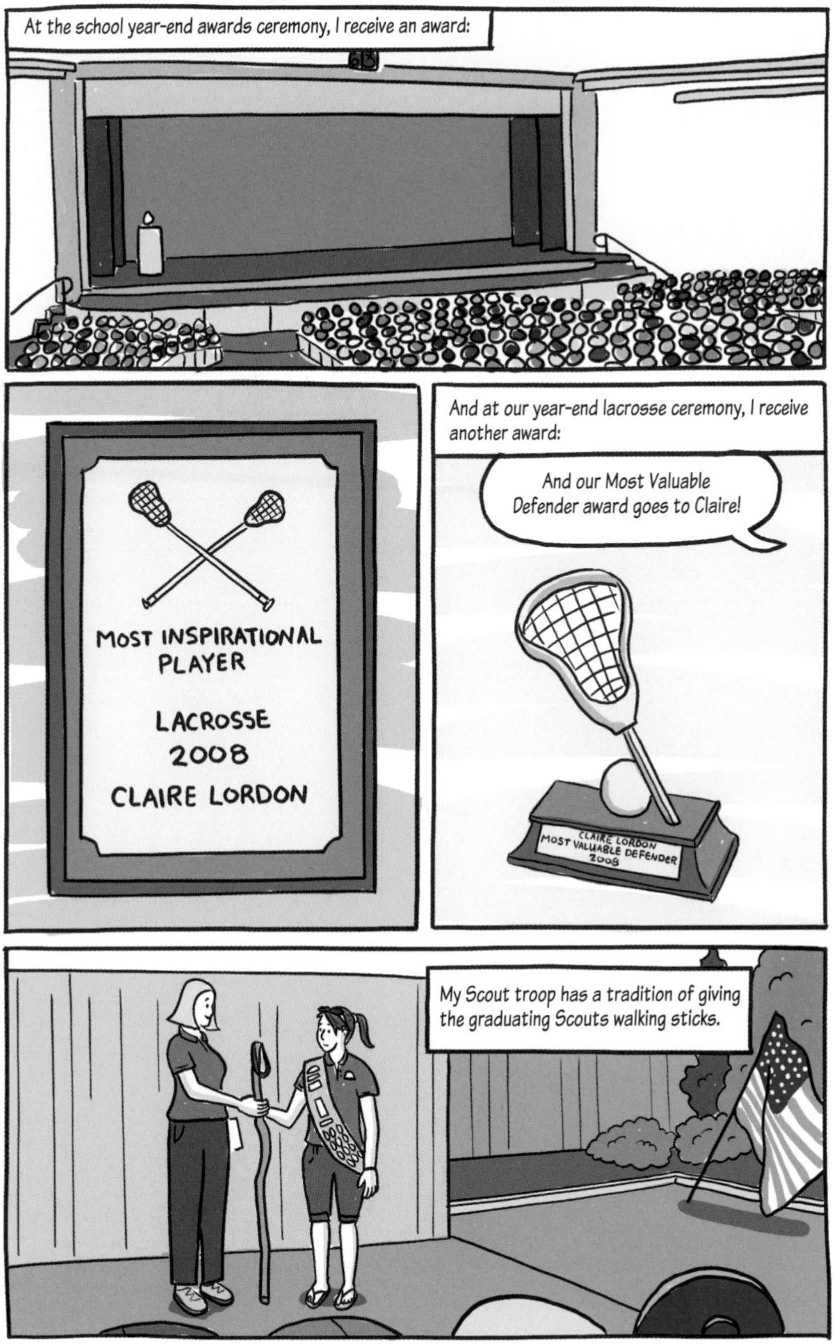

At the school year-end awards ceremony, I receive an award:
MOST INSPIRATIONAL PLAYER
LACROSSE
2008
CLAIRE LORDON
And at our year-end lacrosse ceremony, I receive another award:
And our Most Valuable Defender award goes to Claire!
CLAIRE LORDON
MOST VALUABLE DEFENDER
2008
My Scout troop has a tradition of giving the graduating Scouts walking sticks.

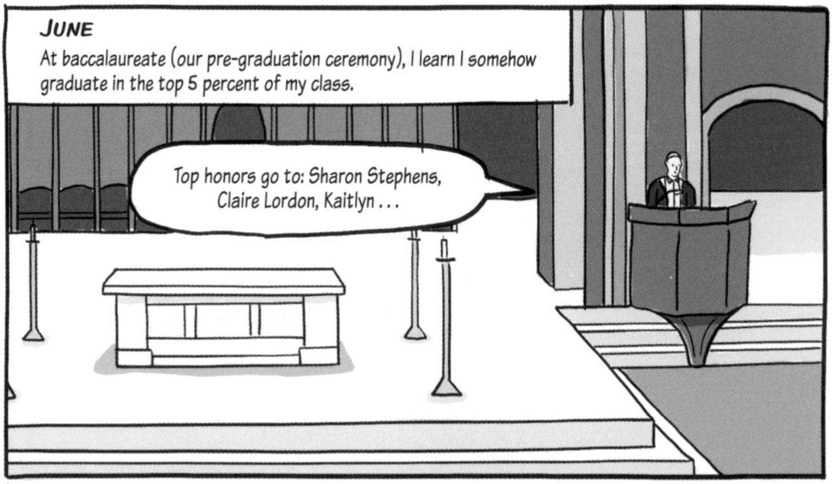
JUNE
At baccalaureate (our pre-graduation ceremony), I learn I somehow graduate in the top 5 percent of my class.
Top honors go to: Sharon Stephens, Claire Lordon, Kaitlyn . . .

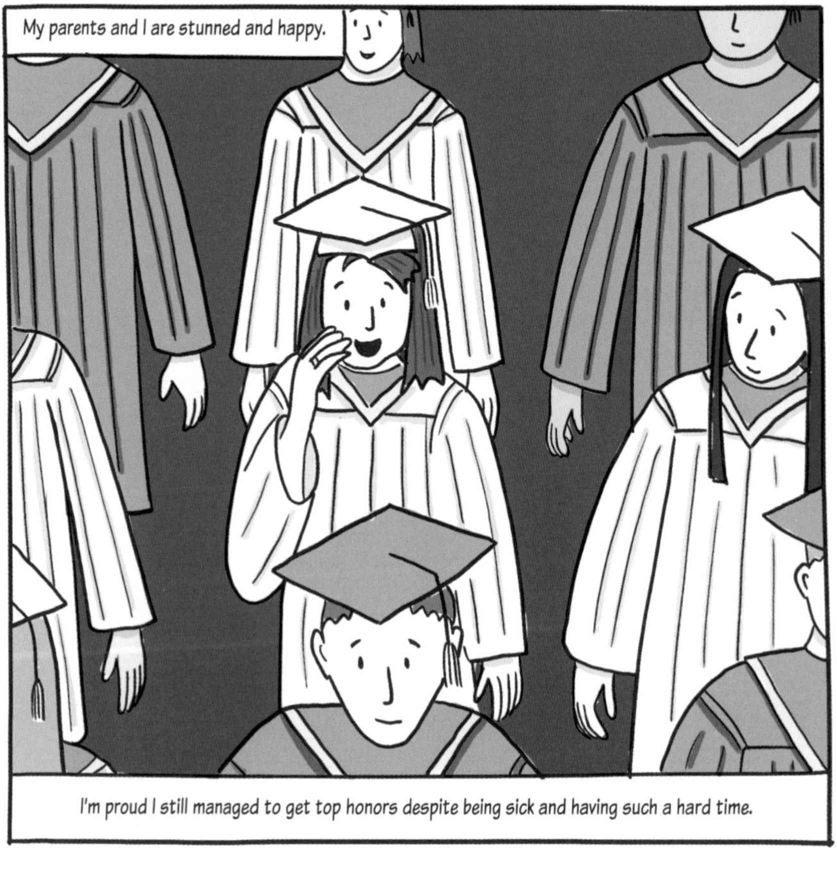
My parents and I are stunned and happy.
I'm proud I still managed to get top honors despite being sick and having such a hard time.

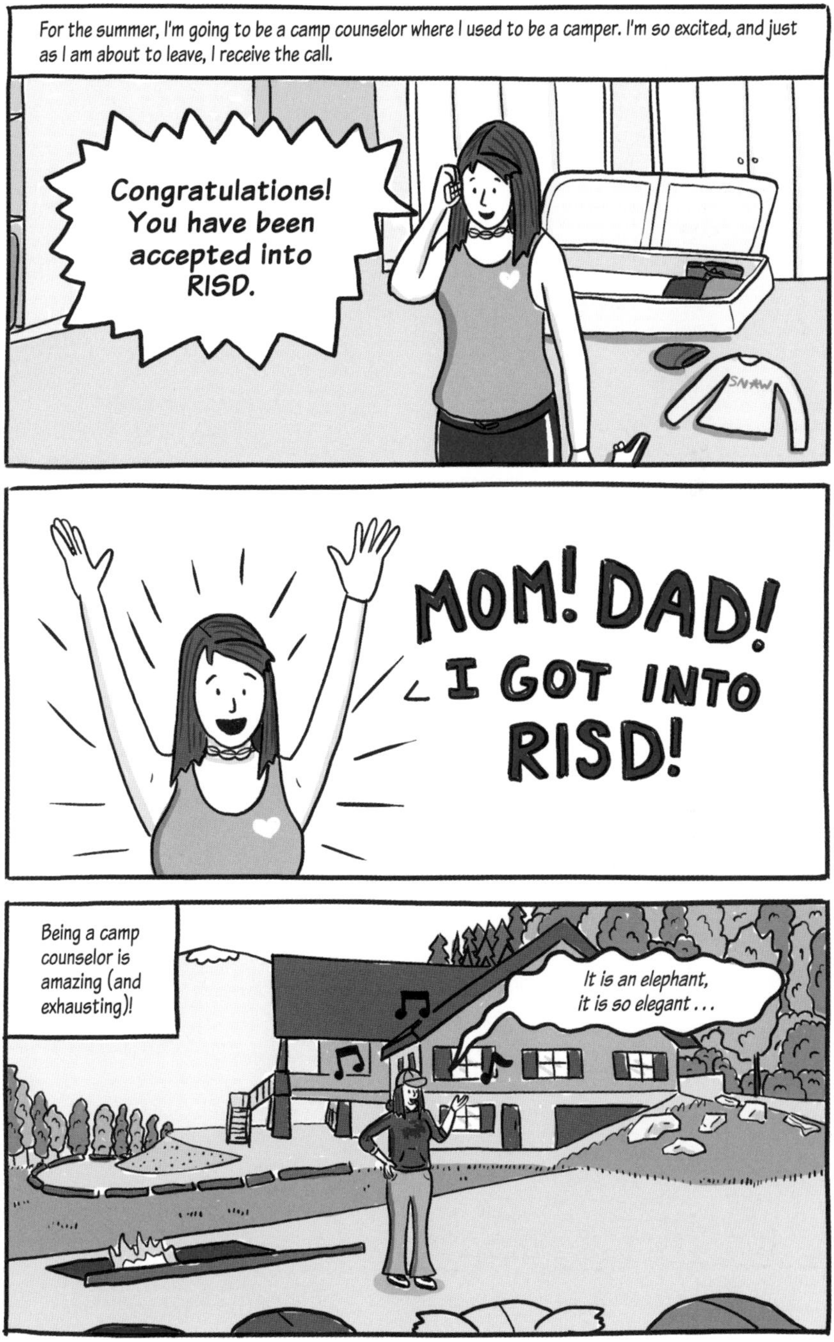
For the summer, I'm going to be a camp counselor where I used to be a camper. I'm so excited, and just as I am about to leave, I receive the call.
Congratulations! You have been accepted into RISD.
MOM! DAD! I GOT INTO RISD!
Being a camp counselor is amazing (and exhausting)!
It is an elephant, it is so elegant . . .

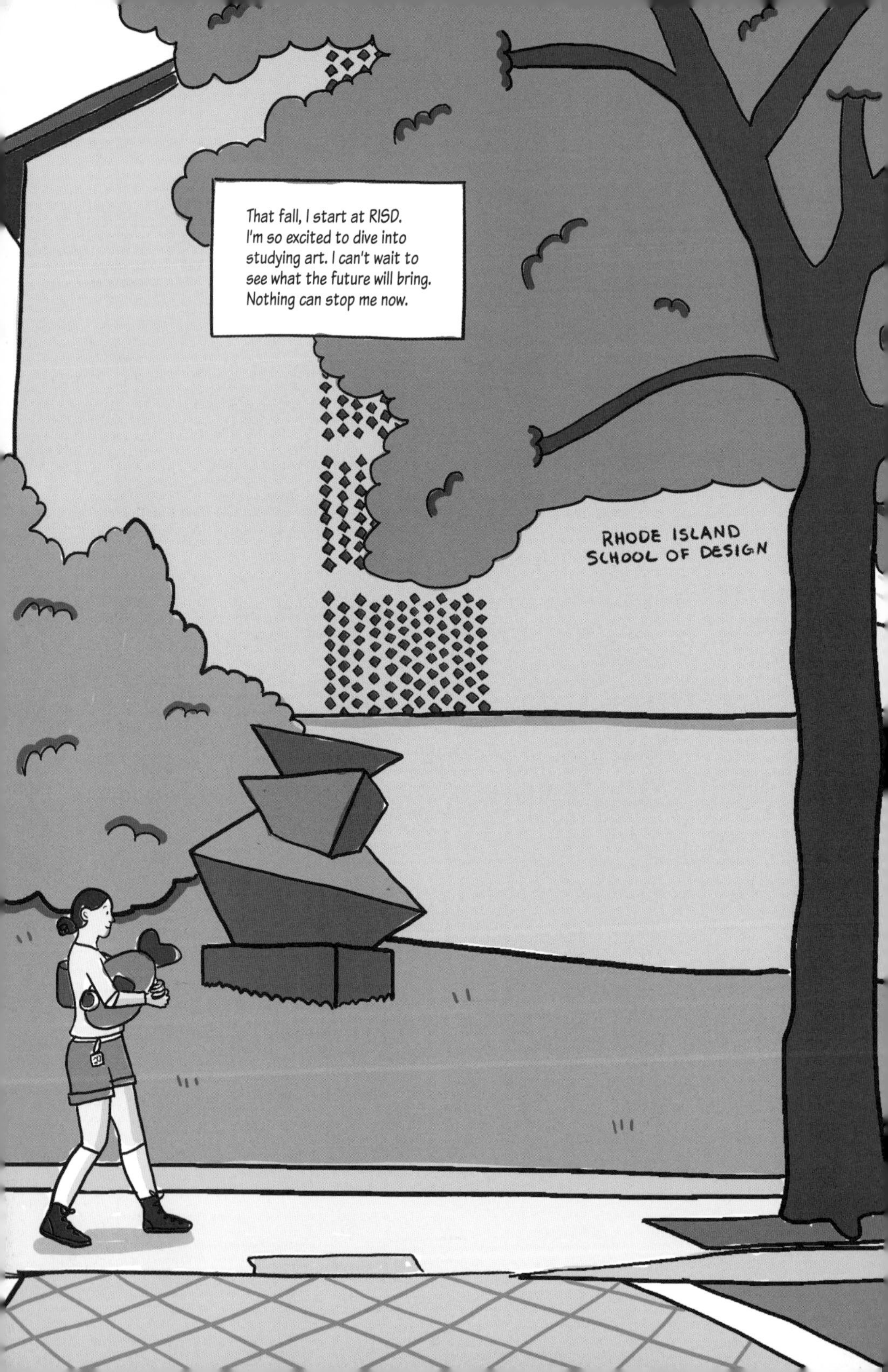
That fall, I start at RISD. I'm so excited to dive into studying art. I can't wait to see what the future will bring. Nothing can stop me now.
RHODE ISLAND SCHOOL OF DESIGN

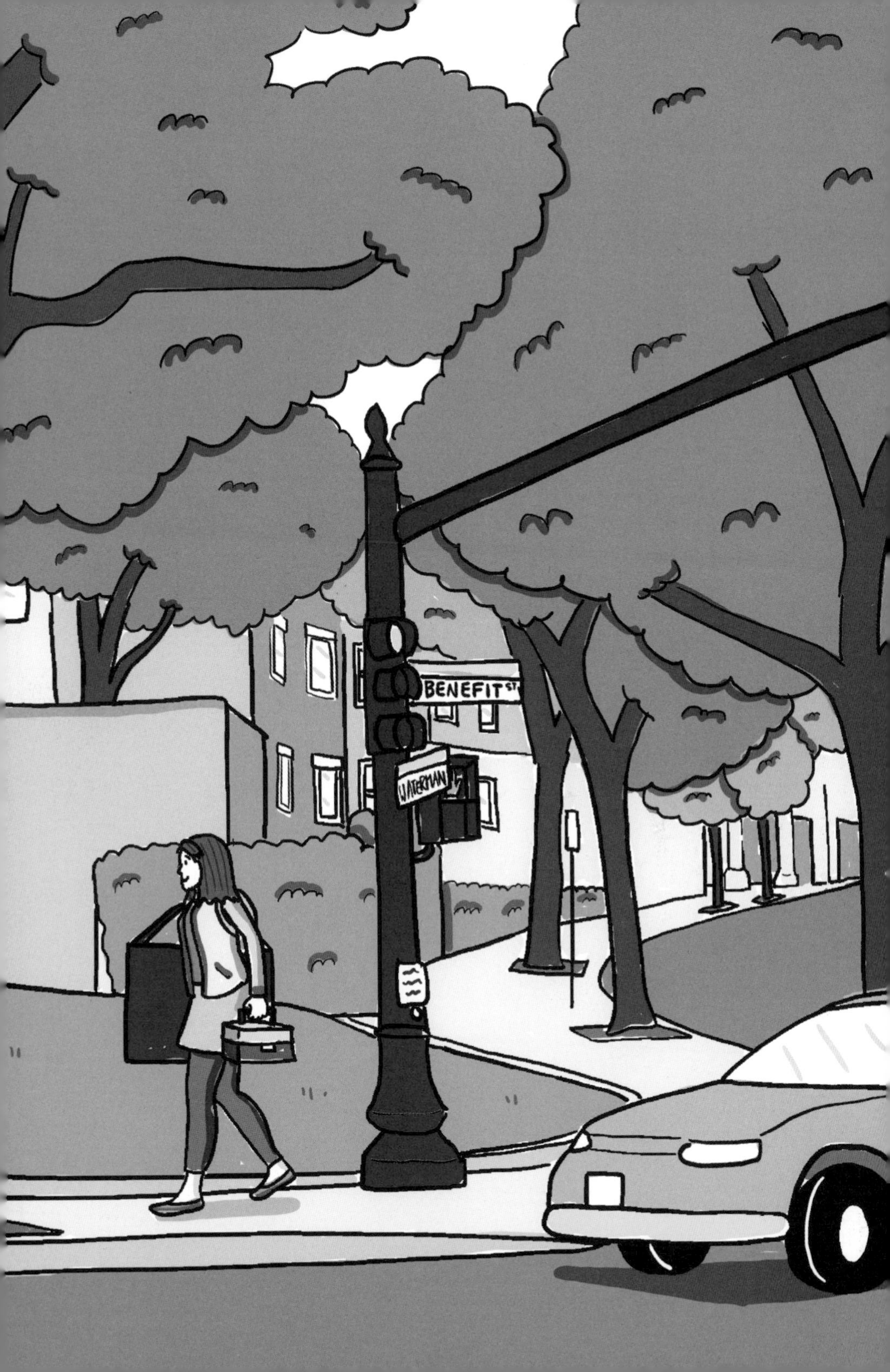
BENEFIT ST
WATERMAN

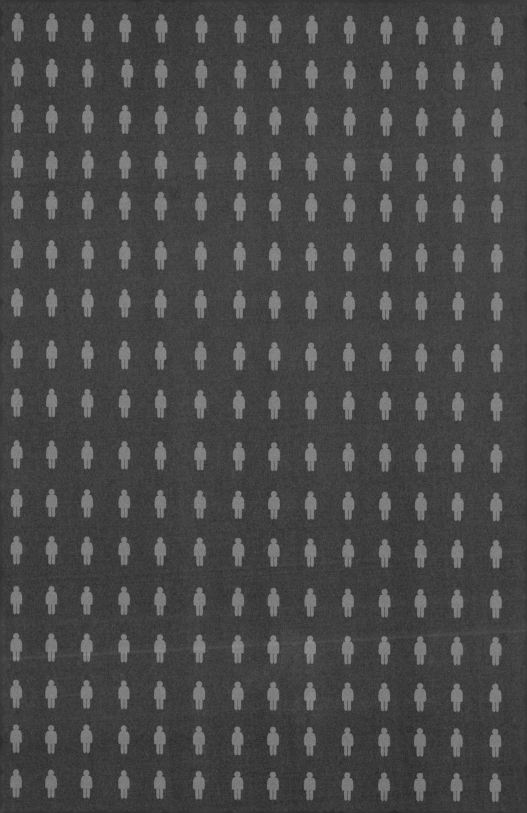

EPILOGUE

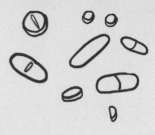

I'd like to say that was the end of all my medical hardships, but it wasn't.

Over my first winter break from college, I came home and visited my doctors. I received news that my hormone levels were still elevated and I needed to go back to the Mayo Clinic for another operation.

Over spring break, my mom and I visited the Mayo Clinic again. Numerous tests confirmed that I wasn't better and was only going to progressively get worse. My pituitary tumor was still telling my adrenal glands to overproduce cortisol. I couldn't have another pituitary surgery, and they couldn't find the tumor with an MRI. My only options were to have my adrenal glands taken out while I was healthy or wait until later, when I could have serious health conditions.

I decided to have my adrenal glands removed that summer. I was in the hospital for quite a few days and felt awful—worse than any previous surgery (which I hadn't thought was possible).

Because of that surgery, I now have to take corticosteroids twice a day for the rest of my life. I won't survive without them.

My doctor told me that other patients who had been through this surgery have been able to run a marathon. That seemed ridiculous and impossible to me, considering I was still struggling with everyday life, but a part of me wanted to run a marathon too.

Though I was happy to think that all my health problems were finally behind me, they weren't. After I graduated from RISD with a degree in illustration, I moved to New York City.

Unfortunately, I felt tired and unwell and had excruciating migraines almost every day. My doctor ordered an MRI, and I was told they saw a tumor—THE tumor. I broke into tears.

I returned to the Mayo Clinic for radiation. The radiation felt like someone tapping on my face between my eyes.

A year later, it was confirmed that my tumor hadn't grown. Over time it's even shrunk.

I joined a local postcollegiate lacrosse team, and we ran a long-distance relay together! Before I knew it, I had run a half-marathon with my teammates.

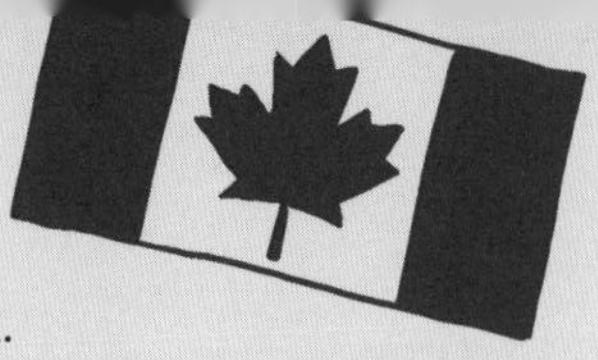

So I decided to do the impossible—run a marathon.

I earned a place in the New York City Marathon and ran it, along with thousands of people. I finished and raised more than $2,000 toward brain tumor research and support.

I also decided that I wanted to be a children's book author-illustrator, and I worked toward this goal. Eventually one publisher took an interest in a story I was working on and offered a contract!

Today, I still struggle with anxiety, depression, and insomnia. But they are all better than they were when I was sick. I now also have PTSD because of my illness, but I'm working with my therapist and doctors on that.

I've done what once seemed impossible. I've survived multiple surgeries and radiation, and I made it through high school and college on schedule.

I've had the encouragement and love of my family and friends; moved to Vancouver, Canada; adopted a dog; traveled; kept playing lacrosse; and started my children's book and art career. I continue to support brain tumor research organizations. I have also run more marathons.

The future is bright.

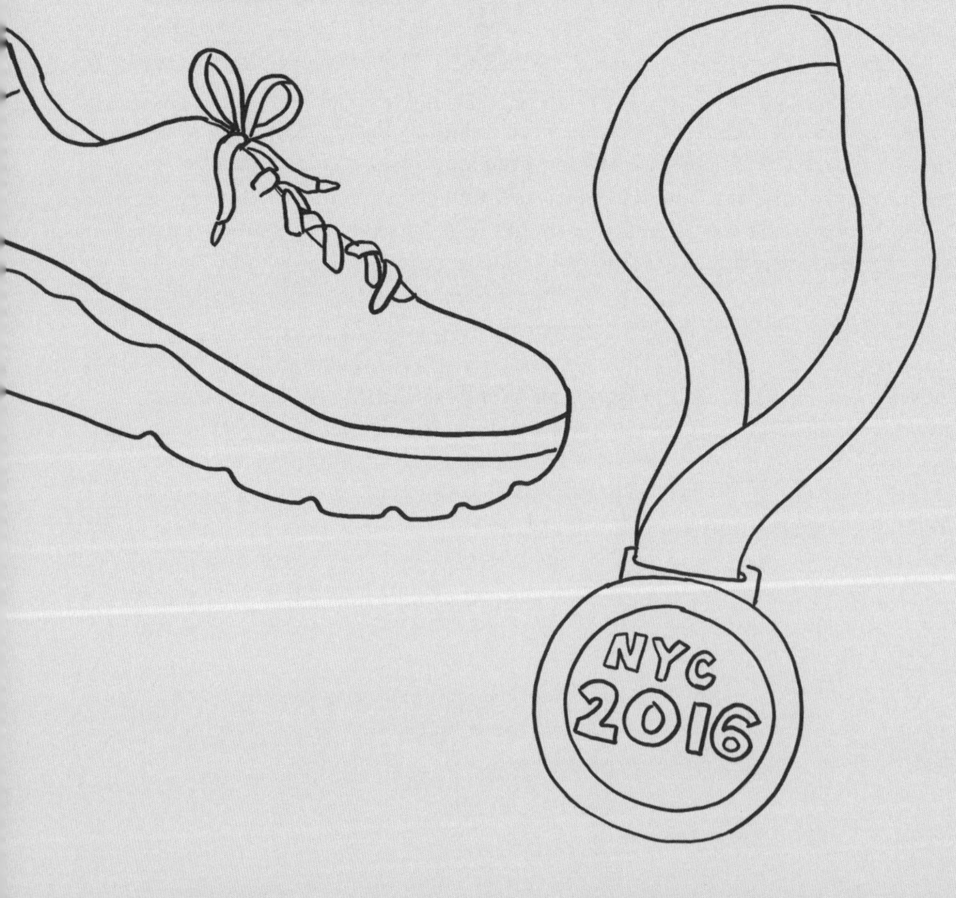
NYC
2016

ACKNOWLEDGMENTS

This book would not have been possible without all the care and support I've received from so many people. I'm overflowing with thanks and appreciation for everyone who believed in me and helped make this book possible, including:

My family for their support. Without their love, guidance, patience, and help, I wouldn't be where I am today. I'd like to thank my parents for being my biggest supporters. Without you, this book wouldn't exist, and I'm forever grateful. Words cannot express the level of my thanks. Thank you for helping me during my darkest times of high school up to today. Thanks for also helping me through the roller coaster of creating this book. I'd also like to thank my brother, Ross, who was a huge ally and supporter throughout the time when I was sick in high school and beyond. I'm sorry I couldn't fit you more into this book (but you had gone off to college). Thanks for still championing me and my work. I'm so glad to have you in my life.

All the medical community I came in contact with through the years. From the receptionists to the brain surgeon, you have all had a huge impact on my life, and I wouldn't be where I am today without all your hard work and care. I wish I could thank you all individually. On the off chance that you read this book, please know how grateful I am. I'd like to send my thanks to the Mayo Clinic especially for all the wonderful care I received there over the years.

My friends, who were an immense support. Big hugs to Kaitlyn and Kathryn for being wonderful friends during a very challenging time for me. I'm sorry I couldn't fit more of my other friends into the book. Please know I am grateful for your compassion, friendship, and care. It meant so much to me to have such amazing people in my life.

All my teachers, who were beyond compassionate to me and my situation. School was stressful, but it was manageable thanks to all the many teachers who were understanding. Shout-out to Mr. Bettin, who was a fantastic art teacher. This book wouldn't be possible without you pushing me to do my best and to keep challenging myself. Dr. Sloan, Mrs. Peterson, and Mrs. Simpson for encouraging my writing.

My Girl Scout troop. Thanks for being so supportive and understanding. Everyone was so nice and treated me with such kindness. Much love to you all. Also, thanks for the goldfish blanket—it really feels like a big hug. I still think it's one of the best gifts I've ever received. It's moved with me many times and I still use it almost daily.

Brian and Janice Ruggles for hosting my family and me multiple times after visits to the Mayo Clinic. Thanks so much for your hospitality and support. It really helped my healing process.

Nicole Paul, Lou Paul, and Samantha Edwards for double-checking some Spanish that I unfortunately ended up cutting from the book. Thanks for your help.

Mr. Cordova, who was the contact for my high school. Thanks for answering my questions and showing me around the campus so I could take some reference photos.

My critique groups. This book wouldn't be what it is today without you. The Critters—Anna Raff and Lori Richmond—thanks for your feedback. The Critique Boutique—Meridth McKean Gimbel, Zara González Hoang, Lorian Tu, Jesse Sima, and Miranda Ireland—thanks for helping me shape this book in its early stages.

Sour Patch Kids for existing. Nothing else could quite power me through creating this book when it got tough (somehow that sour-and-sweet combination really works).

Sean McCarthy, for being an incredible agent and supporting this book from the very beginning. Thank you for finding it a wonderful home with Candlewick.

Everyone at Candlewick, thank you for making this book as incredible as it is. To my editor, Kate Fletcher, who championed this story when it was very rough. Thanks for pushing me to make it even better. I'd also like to thank Lisa Rudden for your wonderful book design work. To everyone else at Candlewick, including Alex Robertson and Gregg Hammerquist, thank you from the bottom of my heart.

Rob, thank you for believing in me. I'd like to thank you especially for looking over my sketches to fix my glaring perspective mistakes. Also, thanks for supporting me when I was reliving every tough moment. I appreciate everything you did for me.

RESOURCES

American Brain Tumor Association
www.abta.org

Brain Tumour Foundation of Canada
www.braintumour.ca

Cushing's Disease News
www.cushingsdiseasenews.com

National Institute of Mental Health
www.nimh.nih.gov

National Suicide Prevention Lifeline
www.suicidepreventionlifeline.org
1-800-273-8255 or call 988

Pituitary Network Association
www.pituitary.org

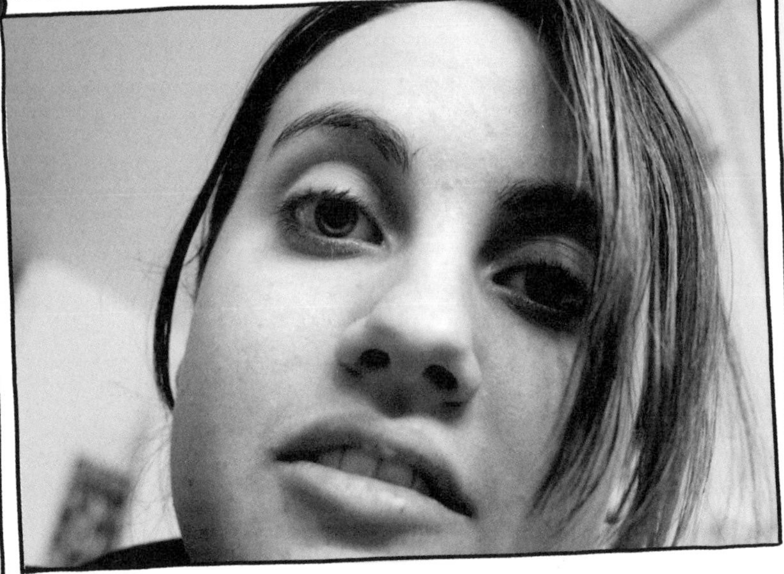

Selfie
May 2007

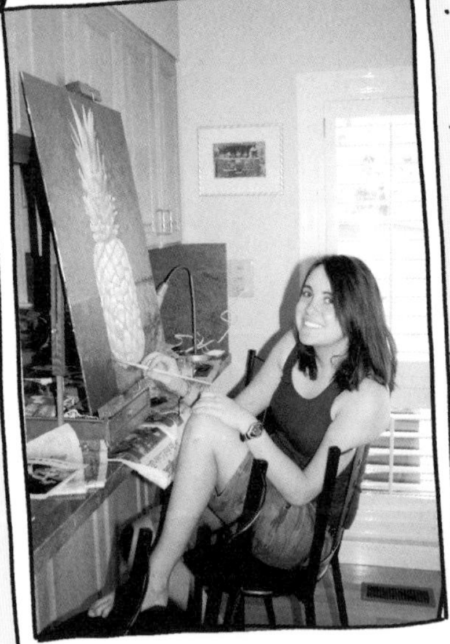

Painting
July 2007

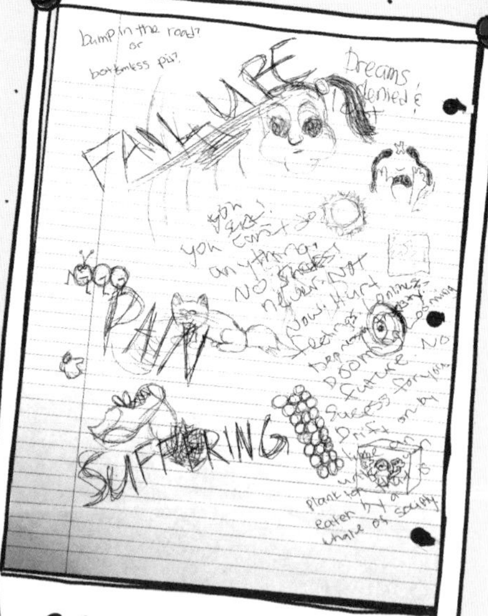
bump in the road?
or
bottomless pit?
Dreams denied
FAILURE
PAIN
SUFFERING

School notebook page
2007

Recovering after
ankle surgery
February 2007

The night before my
first pituitary surgery
June 2007

Resting with my cat,
Marshmellow
July 2007

Saying goodbye to
my dog Toby before
leaving for college
August 2008

OCT 1 1 2023

For anyone feeling lost, misunderstood,
or like a medical mystery. And for my
seventeen-year-old self.

3 1398 00537 8105

Copyright © 2023 by Claire Lordon

This is a work of nonfiction. The events and experiences detailed herein
have been described from the author's memory. Some names, identities,
and circumstances have been changed to protect the privacy and/or
anonymity of the various individuals involved.

All rights reserved. No part of this book may be reproduced,
transmitted, or stored in an information retrieval system
in any form or by any means, graphic, electronic, or
mechanical, including photocopying, taping, and recording,
without prior written permission from the publisher.

First edition 2023

Library of Congress Catalog Card Number 2022951401
ISBN 978-1-5362-1367-6

23 24 25 26 27 28 APS 10 9 8 7 6 5 4 3 2 1

Printed in Humen, Dongguan, China

This book was typeset in Komika.
The illustrations were created digitally.

Candlewick Press
99 Dover Street
Somerville, Massachusetts 02144

www.candlewick.com